The Illustrated Directory of
MODERN AMERICAN
WEAPONS

The Illustrated Directory of
MODERN AMERICAN
WEAPONS

Edited by David Miller

ZENITH PRESS

A Salamander Book

First published in 2002 by Zenith Press, an imprint of MBI Publishing Company LLC, Galtier Plaza, Suite 200, 380 Jackson Street, St. Paul, MN 55101 USA

© Salamander Books, 2002

An imprint of Anova Books Company Limited
www.anovabooks.com

MBI Publishing Company titles are also available at discounts in bulk quantity for industrial or sales-promotional use. For details write to Special Sales Manager at MBI Publishing Company, Galtier Plaza, Suite 200, 380 Jackson Street, St. Paul, MN 55101 USA.

To find out more about our books, join us online at www.zenithpress.com.

ISBN 978-0-7603-1346-6

Credits

Project Manager: Ray Bonds
Designers: Interprep Ltd

Reproduction: Anorax Imaging Ltd
Printed and bound in: Italy

The Editor

David Miller is a former officer in the British armed forces, who spent his service in England, the Falkland Islands, Germany, Malaysia, the Netherlands, Scotland, and Singapore. He subsequently worked as a freelance author and for three years as a journalist for Jane's Information Group, including as a staffer on the authoritative *International Defense Review*. He was Editor of the two-volume Jane's *Major Warships*, and has written more than forty other works, many of them related to modern weapons and warfare.

Acknowledgments

The publishers wish to thank the various branches of the U.S. Department of Defense for making available both information and photographs for this book, and in addition the many weapons manufacturers who kindly provided material, in particular Boeing, General Dynamics Land Systems, Lockheed Martin, Raytheon, and United Defense. The publishers are also grateful to E. Nevill and TRH Pictures, whose photographs appear on pages 125, 140-141, 144-145, 176-177, 199, 252-253, 370-373, 448-449.

Contents

Introduction	8
Strategic Weapons Systems	16
Combat Aircraft	50
Support Aircraft	124
Special Electronic and Reconnaissance Aircraft	158
Unmanned Aerial Vehicles (UAVs)	196
Air-to-Air Missiles	210
Air-to-Surface Weapons	226
Surface Warships	264
Submarines	310
Naval Weapons Systems	324
Tanks and Fighting Vehicles	350
Land Warfare – Indirect Fire Weapons	380
Land Warfare – Direct Fire Weapons	404
Air Defense Systems	420
Small Arms	438

Introduction

When the Cold War ended ten years ago, it seemed to usher in a new era of global tranquillity and harmony, instead of which the United States now finds itself facing threats and dealing with military situations of a totally novel kind. Despite earlier terrorist attack, who would have dared to predict that the World Trade Center would have been utterly destroyed with terrible loss of life, that fighter aircraft would now routinely patrol the skies above the country's major cities, or that U.S. ground troops would be fighting a ground war in Afghanistan? But all those events are a matter of record, and the U.S. armed forces are now gearing themselves up for a long and inevitably bitter war against terrorism and the roots of terrorism. It is, therefore, an appropriate time to look at the equipment with which the nation's armed forces are going to fight that war.

LAND FORCES

The forces which take part in the land campaigns and which come to the closest grips with the enemy are the Army and the Marine Corps. These provide a diverse and complementary mixture of capabilities which present military commanders with a wide range of options for conducting ground missions. The Army mission is to undertake sustained combat operations on land, but this also includes power projection and, wherever necessary, forcible-entry operations. The Marine Corps, which is an integral part of the United States naval forces, provides expeditionary forces, capable of projecting combat power ashore and conducting forcible-entry operations in support of naval campaigns or as part of joint task forces. It should, however, always be borne in mind that land forces very rarely operate independently and will always work in close coordination with aviation and naval forces.

U.S. ARMY

The Army maintains four active corps headquarters, six heavy divisions, four light divisions, and two armored cavalry regiments. Heavy forces, which comprise armored and mechanized divisions equipped with M1 Abrams tanks, M2 Bradley fighting vehicles, AH-64 Apache attack helicopters, and the M109 Paladin field artillery system, are trained and equipped for operations against enemy armies equipped with modern tanks and armored fighting vehicles. The light forces, which comprise airborne, air assault, and light infantry divisions, are designed to undertake forcible-entry operations and for operations in special terrain, such as mountains, jungles, and urban areas. These light and heavy forces can operate either independently or in combination to provide the mix of combat power needed for specific contingencies.

Since 1999 the Army has been undertaking the force transformation initiative, which is a major modernization of both its structure and its equipment, the goal being to field forces which are both highly mobile and more lethal; this initiative has already resulted in the fielding of new and more responsive brigades. The long-term goal is to remove the present distinction between heavy and light forces, in order to create a standard force (termed the Objective Force) for the entire Army. This new force structure will be more responsive and more capable, and procurement of "off-the-shelf" medium armored vehicles to achieve this has already started.

The implementation has already resulted in changes such as the reduction of one company in each combat battalion and the addition of a reconnaissance troop to each brigade, while the responsibility for combat service support has been moved from combat battalions to forward support battalions. There is also

Right: Army infantryman positions an M252 81mm mortar.

a much greater emphasis on command, control, and information support structures. The reorientation also extends to the Army National Guard and the Army Reserves. The National Guard is some 350,000 strong, and is organized into fifteen enhanced separate brigades, eight combat divisions, three separate brigades, and various support units for divisions, corps, and theaters. The Army Reserve is some 205,300 strong, assigned primarily to combat support and combat service support units.

NAVAL FORCES

The overall size and structure of the U.S. naval forces are determined by the diverse roles they are required to perform in support of the national defense strategy, major determinants for naval strategic planners being the need for forward presence and rapid response to peacetime crises. The main components of the naval forces are aircraft carriers, amphibious ships, attack submarines, surface combatants, mine warfare ships, and ballistic-missile submarines, but further vital components include maritime patrol aircraft and sea-based helicopters, as well as the ships that perform support and logistics functions. The maritime force numbers well over 300 vessels, the most important elements of which are twelve aircraft carrier battle groups (CVBGs) and twelve amphibious ready groups (ARGs). Together, these forces provide a diverse mix of sea-based capabilities for conducting peacetime, crisis-response, and major contingency operations.

CVBGs typically consist of a nuclear-powered carrier (CVN), its air wing, surface combatants, attack submarines, and combat logistics support ships. Each ARG nominally comprises a large-deck amphibious assault ship, a transport dock ship, a dock landing ship, and an embarked Marine Expeditionary Unit (Special Operations Capable) [MEU(SOC)]. Since 1999, a CVBG has been deployed in the Southwest Asian region on a nearly continuous basis to support

Below: U.S. forces regularly participate in nuclear, biological, and chemical warfare exercises.

Above: Aboard USS Peleliu a Marine AV-8B is ready for a night strike on Afghanistan, late 2001.

contingency operations; this has been accomplished by adjusting CVBG deployments in other regions. Plans call for a CVBG to remain on continuous deployment in Southwest Asia in the near term, thus obviating the need for the Air Force to provide Aerospace Expeditionary Forces (AEFs) to fill any gaps in CVBG presence. In the other two theaters, the Indian Ocean and the Mediterranean, where a CVBG or ARG may not be constantly on patrol, one of those forces is located within a few days transit time of the region and can be dispatched promptly if circumstances require.

MARINE CORPS
Marine units are employed as part of Marine Air-Ground Task Forces (MAGTFs) consisting of four elements: command, ground combat, aviation combat, and combat service support. A Marine Expeditionary Force (MEF) is the largest MAGTF organized for combat, comprising one or more divisions, aircraft wings, and force service support groups. The Marine Corps maintains three MEFs in the active force, headquartered in California (I MEF), North Carolina (II MEF), and Okinawa (III MEF). Embarked on amphibious ships, MEU(SOC)s each consisting of about 2,200 Marines and sailors are task-organized and deployed continuously in or near regions of vital U.S. interest. These forces provide a swift and effective means of responding to fast-breaking crises and can remain on station for extended periods of time, ready to intervene or take action if needed. Over the past several years, the Marine Corps has closely integrated its reserve force with the active component, providing specific units to augment and reinforce active capabilities. In addition to these general-purpose forces, the Marine Corps has formed and employed a significant special capability in its Chemical/Biological Incident Response Force (CBIRF), which as its title suggests is designed to provide a rapid initial response to chemical/biological incidents.

AIR FORCE
The Air Force completed its transition to its new expeditionary deployment concept in FY 2001, under which fighter/attack aircraft and selected additional force elements are grouped into ten Aerospace Expeditionary Force (AEF)

packages, the goal being to enhance the predictability of deployments and to improve the quality of life for Air Force personnel by minimizing unexpected contingency deployments. Each AEF unit is prepared to deploy for a 90-day period on a fixed, 15-month cycle. Although a given unit may not actually be called on to deploy during its designated period of availability, it must remain ready to move at short notice throughout that time. Individual AEFs may differ in composition, but each is designed to provide comparable combat power to theater commanders, and all will provide air superiority, ground attack, command, control, intelligence, surveillance, and reconnaissance capabilities for sustained operations. In the event that a contingency escalated into a major theater war, additional AEFs would be deployed.

The changes necessary to implement this new structure have not required the formation of a new command structure, while unit identities, basing locations, and readiness levels have remained unchanged. While there may be some adaptations in training sequences, such adjustments are being identified and refined as experience is gained in operating the new concept. Airlift, tanker,

*Above: Sailors aboard today's American submarines, such as the latest
Seawolf-class SNN, face increasing technological sophistication; they
need to be highly trained specialists.*

and low-density/high-demand forces (such as command-and-control aircraft)
have not been designated as AEF components, but evaluation continues of
possible future options to limit deployment pressures on these forces as well,
particularly in the improved management of E-3 Airborne Warning and Control
System (AWACS) deployments.

SPECIAL OPERATIONS FORCES
There has been a rapid increase in Special Operations Forces (SOF) over the
past thirty years; their task has been and is to conduct operations, both
offensive and defensive, against new enemies of the United States. These SOF
are found from the Army, Navy, Air Force and Marine Corps, but their ethos is
unique. Much of their equipment is standard to their parent services, but other
items have been developed to help them conduct their unique operations.

Much of this SOF equipment is described in this book, but some inevitably, remains classified.

CONCLUSION

The equipment which is described in the following pages is in the great majority of cases the finest available to any armed force in any country in the world, and certainly in the breadth of capability, availability, and standard of maintenance it is without comparison. The vast majority has been designed and developed in the United States, but the nation's military has not been too proud to adopt equipment developed in friendly countries, where appropriate, such as the British Harrier jet fighter, the Norwegian Penguin missile, and the German 120mm tank gun.

It must never be forgotten, however, that not one item in this panoply of hardware is of any value at all without the men and women who operate and control it, who interpret its output, or who coordinate its operation with other pieces of equipment. Nor can wars be fought and won by remote control. In the campaign in Afghanistan, for example, the B-52s carried out their bombing

campaign and both manned and unmanned aircraft carried out reconnaissances, but in the end it was ground troops, both soldiers and Marines, who had to go in on vehicles and foot to defeat and round-up the Taliban and the Al-Qaida terrorists in the mountains and caves.

Finally, it must always be remembered that security depends upon the readiness of the defenses, which is partially a result of the functionality, maintenance standards, and availability of the equipment. More than that, however, it also depends upon the mental and physical preparedness of the people in the system, who, as the events of 11 September 2001 showed, must be ready for new dangers from new enemies, carrying out unexpected types of attack on targets which had previously seemed secure. The war may be long, sometimes bloody, and frequently frustrating, but there is no doubt that the United States will prevail.

Below: Readying the deadly F-117 stealth aircraft for a mission requires a large team; maintaining it is as important as flying it.

Strategic Weapons Systems

The United States is the world's only military superpower and the bedrock upon which this power is based is its strategic arsenal, which consists of three elements, known as the "strategic triad." The air-based element is its three types of bomber, the B-52 Superfortress, B-1B Lancer, and B-2 Spirit, all of which are capable of carrying nuclear-weapons, either free-fall (gravity) bombs or air-launched cruise missiles. Their bases are vulnerable to missile strikes but all can take-off at short notice and can then remain airborne for days at a time, being refueled by airborne tankers, and can then land at one of dozens of air bases around the world. All are equipped with a comprehensive range of electronic countermeasure devices to enable them to overcome enemy electronic and missile defenses, giving them a high probability of getting through to their targets. Unlike missiles, these bombers can be turned back at any time prior to the release of the weapons and they have the huge advantage that, again unlike the strategic missiles, they can also be used to drop conventional (ie, non-nuclear) bombs. The latter has enabled them to participate with great effectiveness in conflicts such as Vietnam, the Gulf War, Kosovo, and most recently in Afghanistan.

The land-based intercontinental ballistic missile (ICBM) force currently consists of Minuteman III and Peacekeeper missiles, although the latter are due to be withdrawn in the near future. These missiles are maintained at a high degree of readiness and are capable of being launched within a very few

minutes of warning being given. Their nuclear warheads are extremely powerful and precise, and once launched the probability of them reaching the right target is extremely high.

The sea-based deterrent consists of 18 (soon to be 14) Ohio-class submarines armed with Trident missiles, with five on patrol at any one time, sheltering in the depths of the world's oceans. The chances of any hostile nation finding one such SSBN are very small and of finding more than one infinitesimally so. They thus provide assured survival not only against any current threat but also any new threat in the foreseeable future.

Each leg of the triad has its own unique advantages and none is without some disadvantage, and it would be folly for the United States to follow the British and French lead and concentrate their entire strategic resources in one leg only. The end of the Cold War was widely expected to usher in an era of global harmony and understanding, in which strategic weapons systems might well become superfluous. Instead, as events have so clearly demonstrated in the Gulf, former Yugoslavia, and now Afghanistan, the world is a very unsafe and uncertain place – more so, in many ways, than during the Cold War – and all three elements of the strategic triad remain as vital and as necessary to U.S. defense as ever.

Below: B-2 first prototype on its fourth flight, showing its unique shape.

Boeing LGM-30G Minuteman III

Type: land-based ICBM system.
Manufacturer: Boeing Company.
Weight: (missile) 79,432lb (36,030kg).
Dimensions: length 59.9ft (18.3m); diameter 5.5ft (1.7m).
Guidance: inertial system (Rockwell International).
Propulsion: three solid-propellant rocket motors; first stage, Thiokol; second stage, Aerojet-General; third stage, United Technologies.
Performance: speed approx. 15,000mph (24,000kph, Mach 23); range 6,000 miles+ (9,600km+); ceiling 700 miles (1,120km).
Warheads: one W62 170 kiloton (kT) nuclear warhead in General Electric Mk 12 re-entry vehicle; or one W78 335 kT nuclear warhead in General Electric Mk 12A re-entry vehicle.

The Minuteman strategic weapon system has had an extraordinary life, as one system after another has been proposed to replace it. Even the Peacekeeper, the only successor system to enter service, will be phased out by the end of 2003, leaving the 40-year-old Minuteman as the only land-based element of America's strategic triad. The Minuteman III system consists of an intercontinental range ballistic missile (ICBM) and a single nuclear warhead mounted in a maneuverable re-entry vehicle. The missiles are located in individually hardened silos which are connected to an underground launch control center through a network of hardened cables. Launch crews, each of two officers, work in shifts to provide around-the-clock alert in the launch control center. A variety of communication systems provide the National Command Authorities (NCA) with highly reliable, virtually instantaneous direct contact with each launch crew. Should communications be lost between the

Left: Boeing Minuteman III is successfully launched, Vandenburg AFB.

Right: Technicians perform electrical checks on Minuteman III in its silo.

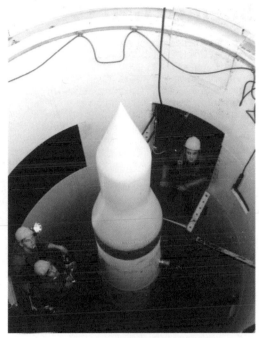

launch control center and its remote missile launch facilities, specially configured EC-135 airborne launch control center (ABLCC) aircraft automatically assume command and control of the isolated missile or missiles. Fully qualified airborne missile combat crews aboard these aircraft would then execute the NCA orders.

The Minuteman weapon system was conceived in the late 1950s and deployed in the early 1960s. At that time Minuteman was a revolutionary concept and bringing it successfully into service was an extraordinary technical achieve-ment. The previous generation, such as Atlas and Titan, had comprised relatively slow-reacting, liquid-fueled ICBMs, but the Minuteman system, consisting of missiles, basing components, and a command system, incorporated significant advances. From the beginning, Minuteman missiles have provided a quick-reacting, inertially guided, highly survivable component to America's nuclear triad. Minuteman's maintenance concept capitalizes on high reliability and a "remove-and-replace" approach to achieve a near 100 percent alert rate.

The Minuteman system has evolved through state-of-the-art improvements to meet new challenges and assume new missions. Modernization programs have resulted in new versions of the missile, expanded targeting options, significantly improved accuracy, and greatly enhanced survivability. Today's Minuteman weapon system is the product of forty years of unceasing enhancement, a process which still has not ended.

The current force consists of 530 Minuteman IIIs split between four locations: Grand Forks Air Force Base (AFB), North Dakota; Minot AFB, North Dakota; Malmstrom AFB, Montana; and F. E. Warren AFB, Wyoming. Up to now, these missiles have been carrying three MIRVed warheads, but in order to comply with the internationally agreed warhead totals these are being "downloaded" to carry just one warhead each. Coupled with this is the cancellation of development programs for new ICBMs and the decision to retire the Peacekeeper ICBM by 2004, which means that from that time Minuteman will become the only land-based ICBM in the U.S. national deterrent triad. Thus, the Department of Defense is conducting an extensive life extension program to keep Minuteman fully serviceable and effective for at least the next twenty years. This program includes replacement of the guidance system, remanufacture of the solid-propellant rocket motors, replacement of standby power systems, repair and upgrading the launch facilities, installation of updated, survivable communications equipment, and new command and control consoles.

Boeing LGM-118 Peacekeeper

Type: land-based ICBM system.
Manufacturer: Boeing Company.
Weight: (missile) 195,000lb (88,452kg).
Dimensions: length 71ft (21.6m); diameter: 7.7ft (2.4m).
Guidance: inertial system (Autonetics Division of Rockwell International).
Propulsion: first three stages, solid-propellant; fourth stage, storable liquid (by Thiokol, Aerojet, Hercules and Rocketdyne).
Performance: speed approx. 15,000mph (24,000kph, Mach 23); range 6,000 miles+ (9,600km+); ceiling 700 miles (1,120km).
Warheads: Ten W87 300kT nuclear warheads in Avco Mk21 re-entry vehicles.

After many attempts to find a successor to the Minuteman, the Peacekeeper was eventually selected in order to fullfil one of the key goals of the strategic modernization program by providing increased numbers and credibility to the land-based leg of the U.S. strategic triad. However, after initial plans to procure several hundreds, the order was eventually cut back to just fifty missiles. The Peacekeeper is capable of delivering ten multiple independently targeted re-entry vehicles (MIRVs) with greater accuracy than any other ballistic missile.

The ICBM system consists of three major elements: the boost system, the post-boost vehicle system, and the re-entry system. The boost system launches the missile into space and consists of three rocket stages, mounted atop one another and which fire in succession, each stage exhausting its solid propellant materials through a single movable nozzle that guides the missile along its flight path. Following the burnout and separation of the boost system's final (third) rocket stage, the post-boost vehicle cruises through space and maneuvers in order to deploy the re-entry vehicles in sequence towards their pre-determined targets. This post-boost vehicle system is made up of a maneuvering rocket, and a guidance and control system. It is 4 feet (1.21m) long and weighs about 3,000lb (1,363kg).

The top section of the Peacekeeper is the re-entry system, which consists of the deployment module, up to ten cone-shaped Mk21 re-entry vehicles (RVs), and a shroud. This shroud, which protects the re-entry vehicles during the ascent into space, is topped with a nose cap, which contains a rocket motor to separate it from the deployment module. The deployment module provides structural support for the RVs and carries the electronics needed to activate and deploy them. Each RV is mechanically attached to the deployment module and is covered with ablative material which protects it during re-entry through the atmosphere. Each RV is launched in turn, being unlatched by gas pressure from an explosive cartridge broken by small, exploding bolts, a procedure which allows it to separate from the deployment module with minimum disturbance. Each deployed RV then follows a ballistic path to its target.

The Air Force achieved initial operational capability (IOC) of ten deployed Peacekeepers at F. E. Warren AFB, Wyoming, in December 1986, and full operational capability (FOC) was achieved in December 1988 with the establishment of a squadron of fifty missiles. With the end of the Cold War, the U.S. has revised its strategic policy and has agreed to eliminate the multiple re-entry vehicle Peacekeeper ICBMs by the end of the year 2003 as part of the Strategic Arms Reduction Treaty II (SALT II). With the demise of the Peacekeeper system, the Minuteman III will be left as the sole American ICBM system (see previous entry).

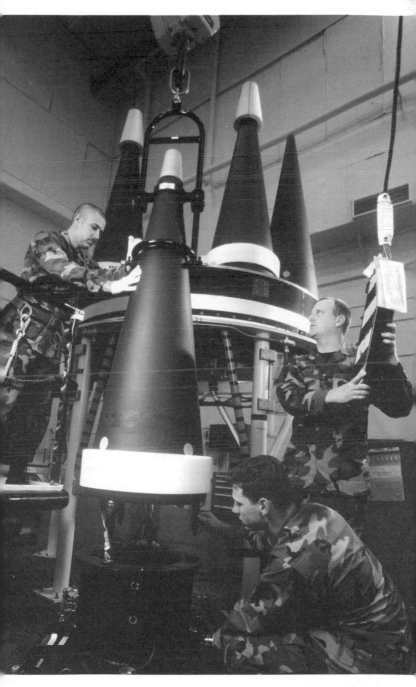

Above: Each black re-entry vehicle houses a 300kT nuclear warhead.

Lockheed Martin UGM-96A Trident I (C-4)/UGM-133A Trident II (D-5)

System	Trident I (C-4)	Trident II (D-5)
Type	Submarine-launched ballistic missile system (SLBM)	
Manufacturer	Lockheed Martin	Lockheed Martin
Weight (missile)	72,420lb (32,850kg)	130,270lb (59,090kg)
Dimensions length diameter	34.1ft (10.4m) 6.16ft (1.9 m)	44.0ft (13.4m) 6.9ft (2.1m)
Guidance	Inertial with stellar reference update	Inertial with stellar reference update
Propulsion	3-stage solid propellant	3 stage solid propellant
Performance speed range ceiling throw weight	15,000mph (24,000kph) 4,000nm (7,400km) 700 miles (1,120km) 3,307lb (1,500kg)	15,000mph (24,000kph) 6,500nm (12,000km) 700 miles (1,120km) 6,172lb (2,800kg)
Warheads	8 x Mk4 RVs in MIRV formation; W76 warheads, each 100kT	Maximum 16 x RVs; 8 x RVs (START I); 4 x RVs (START II); W76 warhead at 100kT or W88 warhead at 475kT

The Trident submarine-launched ballistic missile (SLBM) system is currently in service in two versions – Trident I (C-4) and Trident II (D-5) – both of them aboard Ohio-class nuclear-powered ballistic missile submarines (SSBN). Each of the first eight Ohio-class SSBNs from USS *Ohio* (SSBN-726) to USS *Nevada* (SSBN-733) is armed with 24 Trident I (C-4) submarine-launched ballistic missiles, while the remaining 10 boats are armed with 24 Trident II (D-5) missiles, but this is in the process of change.

The Trident I (C-4) missile was conceived as a successor to the Poseidon SLBM and was designed to attain 60 percent greater range in order to give the SSBNs much greater searoom, thus making it very much more difficult for them to be found and thus increasing their survivability. This increased range was achieved by using higher energy propellants, the addition of a third stage rocket motor, and by using micro-electronics and lighter materials. These Trident I (C-4) SLBMs entered service in 1979 aboard converted Lafayette-class SSBNs which had previously embarked Poseidon missiles, twelve of these ships being eventually armed with the new missile, sixteen in each ship. Of those converted SSBNs, six were deactivated in 1994, followed by the

Above: Trident I (C-4) is launched off the Florida coast.

remaining six in 1996, leaving the Ohio-class as the sole type of SSBN in the U.S. Navy.

Meanwhile, the Trident I (C-4) went to sea aboard the first of the Ohio-class, USS *Ohio* (SSBN-726), in 1981; there were twenty-four aboard each ship and eventually eight of these ships were so equipped. The guidance system for the Trident I (C-4) is both smaller and lighter than in Poseidon and utilises a stellar sensing unit to update the missile's position and thus improve its accuracy. The fire control system is the Mk 98 with a digital fire-control computer. The C-4 carries the Mk 4 re-entry vehicle (RV) and has an optional MaRV (Manoeuvrable Re-entry Vehicle) package (Mk 500 Evader) to enable it to penetrate ABM (Anti-Ballistic Missile) defenses in keeping with its second strike, retaliatory role. One of the features of the design is the "aerospike," a telescopic rod which automatically extends from the missile nose on launch. Using a phenomenon known as "supercavitation" it reduces drag to give the same aerodynamic effect as a much longer, pointed nose. This enables the designers to extend the maximum diameter of the missile forwards (ie, employing a much blunter nose), thus increasing the internal volume. Missiles can be launched from the submarine whether on the surface or submerged, being ejected from the launch tube using a gas generator, which is analogous to the cold-launch technique of the Peacekeeper missile. The first stage motor ignites once the missile is clear of the surface.

A decision was taken early in the Trident I program to upgrade the entire missile, which led to the Trident II (D-5), which now equips the last ten Ohio-class SSBNs – from USS *Tennessee* (SSBN-734) to the final ship to be built, USS *Louisiana* (SSBN-743), both inclusive. The D-5 development program started in 1975. It was primarily intended to improve the accuracy of the warheads but, as shown in the specifications table, it is a much larger missile, being both longer and with greater diameter, and with a very considerable increase in launch weight from 72,420lb (32,850kg) in Trident I to 130,270lb (59,090kg) in Trident II. The result is an increase in throw- weight (ie, the weight of RVs that can be carried) and range. The advantages of the new missile were clearly shown when the British, who had just started the design of their new Vanguard-class SSBNs to take sixteen Trident I (C-4), abandoned this work and restarted, designing their new boats around sixteen of the much improved Trident II (D-5).

The resulting system has, for the first time, given the U.S. Navy's SSBN force a combination of accuracy and warhead yield which results in a "hard target kill" capability against a target anywhere on earth. The practical payload limit, depending upon the range required, is twelve MIRVs, but implementation of the START I limits (START = Strategic Arms Reduction Treaty) reduced this to eight, while START II has reduced it yet further to four. Reentry vehicles can be Mk 4 with W76 warheads (100kT each), or Mk 5 RVs with W88 warheads (475kT each). A total of 400 W88 warheads has been produced and the remainder of the force is expected to be fitted with the W76 warheads..

As of 2002 the position was that the number of Ohio-class SSBNs was being reduced to fourteen, all of which would be armed with the Trident II (D-5). This means that of the eight boats originally armed with Trident I (C-4), four will be re-roled to other tasks, their missiles being removed for the last time in FY 2003. The other four will be modified to embark Trident II (D-5) missiles, giving a homogenous fleet of fourteen Ohio-class SSBNs, all armed with the same Trident II (D-5) SLBMs.

Below: Trident II (D-5) blasts-off from Cape Canaveral, 30 June 1988.

Above: Trident II (D-5) is lowered into its tube aboard USS Ohio (SSBN-726).

Boeing B-1B Lancer

Type: strategic bomber.
Manufacturer: Boeing Company (formerly Rockwell International).
Weight: empty approx. 190,000lb (86,183kg); max takeoff 477,000lb (216,367kg).
Dimensions: wingspan, wings forward 136.7ft (41.7m), wings swept 78.2ft (23.8m); length 146.0ft (44.5m); height 34.0ft (10.4m).
Powerplant: four General Electric F-101-GE-102 turbofans, each of 30,000lb (13,600kg)+ thrust with afterburner.
Performance: speed 900mph (1,440kph, Mach 1.25) at sea level; range approx. 6,475nm (12,000km), unrefueled; ceiling 30,000ft (9,144m)+.
Armament: three internal weapons bays accommodating up to 84 Mk 82 general purpose bombs or Mk 62 naval mines, 30 CBU-87/89 cluster munitions or CBU-97 Sensor Fused Weapons and up to 24 GBU-31 JDAM GPS guided bombs or Mk 84 general purpose bombs.
Crew: four (aircraft commander, co-pilot, offensive systems officer, and defensive systems officer).

With the B-2 and B-52, the B-1B forms America's long-range bomber force providing massive and rapid delivery of precision and non-precision weapons against any potential adversary anywhere around the globe on short notice. The original version was the B-1A, of which the USAF acquired four prototype flight test models in the 1970s, which continued tests through 1981, even though the program had been canceled in 1977 and the type never went into production. The B-1B is a very considerably improved version, which was initiated by the Reagan administration in 1981, with the first production model flying in October 1984; the first production aircraft was delivered to Dyess Air Force Base, Texas in June 1985 and initial operational capability (IOC) was achieved on 1 October 1986. The last of 72 B-1Bs was delivered 2 May 1988.

The B-1B has a blended wing/body configuration, which combines with the variable-geometry design and turbofan engines to provide long range and high cruising speed with great survivability. The variable-geometry (swing-wing) is set forward for takeoff, landing and high-altitude maximum cruise and is swept to the rear for high subsonic and supersonic flight. The B-1B's speed, superior handling characteristics, and large payload make it a key element of any joint/composite strike force.

President Carter ordered development of the B-2 stealth bomber (see entry), but the prototype was not due to fly until the late 1980s when President Reagan entered office in 1981. Reagan was determined to improve America's defenses and he ordered a batch of 100 improved B-1B production models, giving the USAF and the manufacturer Rockwell (now part of Boeing) the problem of getting it into production, then into service early enough to make a useful contribution to Strategic Air Command's strength before the B-2 arrived. That very ambitious timescale called for a five-year program, rather than the seven to ten years normally needed to field a major weapons system.

The B-1A had already been designed to have a much lower radar cross-section (RCS) than the B-52 it would replace, but by the early 1980s the Soviet Union was developing improved air defense systems intended to cope with U.S. ALCM and Tomahawk cruise missiles, using weapons such as the SA-10 and SA-N-6. Such developments made the Rockwell bomber seem increasingly vulnerable, so steps were taken to lower its RCS even further, with the inlets being redesigned and the variable ramps needed for Mach 2 flight eliminated. The revised design had inlet sides and splitter plates swept slightly backwards from the vertical, and incorporated curved ducts and streamwise radar absorbing baffles. Radar absorbing material (RAM) was also added as a liner for the inside of the intakes. The original aircraft had a prominent fuselage dorsal spine, which had been fitted to house the electrical cabling associated with the

Left: B-1B is bombed-up for an operational mission over former Yugoslavia, using conventional weapons. This picture shows how smoothly the various surfaces are blended into each other, a major feature in reducing the radar cross-section.

aircraft's Westinghouse ALQ-153 tail-warning system, but the USAF opted t[o] integrate the tail-warning task directly into the ALQ-161, thus enabling the spin[e] to be removed, and reducing the RCS yet further.

Other measures to reduce the RCS included modifications to the nos[e] radome cavity and to cavities in the fuselage side fairings. A special adhesiv[e] tape was also applied to all seams in the skin once system testing had bee[n] completed, and prior to painting. This tape was electrically conductive, and thu[s] linked all the skin panels together into a common conducting surface, thu[s]

eliminating surface discontinuities which would re-radiate energy. As a result of all these measures, the RCS of the B-1B is one-hundredth that of the B-52, and one-seventh that of the FB-111.

The B-1B's ability to deliver conventional weapons is being improved under a multi-stage Conventional Mission Upgrade Program (CMUP). CMUP Block C, fielded in August 1997, gave B-1Bs the capability to drop cluster bombs, while

Below: Flying high, B-1B's afterburners blast it toward Afghanistan, 2002.

the Block D changes (due to be completed in 2003) allow the aircraft to carry up to twenty-four JDAM guided bombs (eight in each of its three weapon bays), accommodate an Integrated Defensive Electronic CounterMeasures (IDECM) towed decoy intended to enhance the survivability of the aircraft, and add a new communication/navigation system. A planned Block E modification will allow the B-1B to carry Wind-Compensated Munitions, the Joint Standoff Weapon (JSOW), and the Joint Air-To-Surface Standoff Missile (JASSM), while Block F will make further improvements to the bomber's defensive system.

Other upgrades being projected for the B-1B include the addition of a satcoms terminal and a Link 16 datalink, a cockpit upgrade, and modifications to the aircraft's radar. The current defensive avionics system consists of the ALQ-161A radio frequency surveillance/electronic countermeasures system, the tail warning function, and the expendable countermeasures system, and is supplemented by the ALE-50 Towed Decoy System.

The first B-1B squadron was declared operational at Dyess AFB, Texas, in October 1986, well ahead of the Congressional 1987 deadline. The 100th and final

B-1B was delivered on 2 May 1988, since when the type has equipped three squadrons of Air Combat Command, and two of the Air National Guard. There are currently 51 primary mission aircraft in the active inventory (72 actual), and 18 with the ANG (20 actual), and a further two aircraft are used in test programs.

The B-1B was designed to fly low-level, high-speed missions which impose greater strain on the airframe than the high-altitude missions of the B-52. Each airframe is expected to have a 10,000 hour service life, allowing it to remain in service until around 2020, when, like the B-2, it will retire long before the much older B-52.

The B-1B holds several world records for speed, payload and distance. The aircraft was first used in combat in support of operations against Iraq during Operation Desert Fox in December 1998 and has subsequently been used in Operation Allied Force in the former Yugoslavia and in Afghanistan in 2001/2002.

Below: B-1B gets airborne on another mission against the Taliban/Al-Qaida.

Boeing B-52 Stratofortress

Type: strategic bomber.
Manufacturer: Boeing Military Airplane Co.
Weight: empty, approx. 185,000lb (83,250kg); max takeoff 488,000lb (219,600kg).
Dimensions: wingspan 185.0ft (56.4m); length 159.1ft (48.5m); height 40.7ft (12.4m).
Powerplant: eight Pratt & Whitney TF33-P-3/103 turbofans, each with up to 17,000 pounds (7,711kg) thrust.
Performance: speed 650mph (1,040kph, Mach 0.86); ceiling 49,712ft (15,151.5m); unrefueled range, 8,800 miles (7,652nm, 14,080km).
Armament: approx. 70,000lb (31,500kg) mixed ordnance, bombs, mines, air-launched cruise missiles, Harpoon anti-ship and Have Nap missiles.
Crew: five (aircraft commander, co-pilot, radar navigator, navigator, and electronic warfare officer), with six ejection seats.

The Boeing B-52 Stratofortress is a long-range, heavy bomber, with an unparalleled history, having been been at the forefront of U.S. military operations for forty-eight years, most recently in the attack on Afghanistan, with many years of service still to go. It can undertake a wide variety of missions and is capable of flying at high subsonic speeds at altitudes up to 50,000ft (15,166.6m), carrying payloads ranging from nuclear weapons, through cruise

missiles and mines, to precision-guided conventional ordnance, all of which can be delivered anywhere in the world with absolute navigational accuracy.

There are currently eighty-five B-52s in the active force and nine in the reserve force. The B-52A first flew in 1954, and the B model entered service in 1955, and a variety of models were then produced; total production was 744 aircraft, with the last, a B-52H, delivered in October 1962. The first of 102 B-52Hs was delivered to Strategic Air Command in May 1961. The H model can carry up to twenty air-launched, nuclear-armed cruise missiles, six on a rotary launcher in the bomb-bay, the remainder under the wings on pylons.

In addition, it can carry the conventional-armed cruise missiles of the types that were launched in several contingencies during the 1990s, starting with Operation Desert Storm and culminating with Operation Allied Force. Only the H model is still in the Air Force inventory and all are assigned to either Air Combat Command and the Air Force Reserves.

In a conventional conflict, the B-52 can perform strategic attack, air interdiction, offensive counter-air and maritime operations. During Desert Storm, B-52s delivered 40 percent of all the weapons dropped by Coalition forces. It is also highly effective when used for ocean surveillance, and can assist the U.S. Navy in anti-ship and mine-laying operations; for example, two B-52s, in two hours, can monitor 140,000 square miles (364,000 square kilometers) of ocean surface.

There is a five-strong crew, seated on two levels. On the flight deck are the pilot and co-pilot, with the electronic warfare officer just behind them, facing to the rear and beside the seat once occupied by the gunner. On the lower deck are the radar navigator/bombardier and the en route navigator.

All B-52s are equipped with numerous electronic systems, including a comprehensive electronic countermeasures (ECM) suite. One of the most recent additions is the electro-optical viewing system that uses platinum silicide forward-looking infrared (FLIR) and high resolution low-light-level television (LLTV) sensors to augment targeting, battle assessment, and flight safety, thus further improving the bomber's combat ability and low-level flight capability. Pilots wear night vision goggles (NVGs) to enhance their vision during night operations; these goggles provide greater safety during night operations by increasing the pilot's ability to visually clear terrain, avoid enemy radar, and see other aircraft in a covert/lights-out environment. Starting in 1989, on-going modifications incorporated the global positioning system (GPS), heavy stores adapter beams for carrying 2,000 pound munitions. As currently configured,

Left: B-52 ready to take-off for a bombing attack on Afghanistan.

Above: Classic view of a great airplane – B-52 en route to Afghanistan.

Above: Eight Pratt &Whitney turbofans lift a B-52 aloft on another mission.

the aircraft has an unrefueled combat range in excess of 8,800 miles (14,080km), but with aerial refueling its range is limited only by crew endurance.

All B-52s were built with self-defense armament in the tail, which were aimed and fired by a gunner located on the flight-deck. Originally, there were four 0.5in (12.7mm) machine guns, but these were replaced in later models by a single M61A1 Vulcan 20mm cannon. However, no such weapons are now carried. A major improvement, currently under consideration, is a Boeing proposal to re-engine the entire fleet with Rolls-Royce/Allison RB-211 engines, which would be leased rather than sold to the Air Force.

The aircraft has demonstrated its flexibility in every conflict in which it has participated, which in recent years has included the Gulf War (Operation Desert Storm), the conflict in the Balkans (Operation Allied Force) and most recently the operations against the Taliban and Osama bin Laden's al Qa'ida terrorists in Afghanistan. In Iraq B-52s struck targets ranging from wide-area troop concentrations, through fixed installations to leadership bunkers, and the sheer power of its attacks totally destroyed the morale of Iraq's much-vaunted Republican Guard. During the Gulf War one group of B-52s took off from Barksdale Air Force Base, Loiusiana, launched conventional air-launched cruise missiles and returned safely to Barksdale in a 35-hour, non-stop combat mission, the longest strike mission in the history of aerial warfare. During Operation Allied Force, B-52s opened the conflict with conventional cruise missile attacks and then transitioned to delivering general purpose bombs and cluster bomb units on Serbian army positions and staging areas. Again, in Afghanistan, B-52s were at the forefront of operations, dropping conventional bombs with devastating accuracy on Taliban forces, the bombs being "talked" onto their targets by U.S. forward air controllers (FACs) located on the ground among Afghanistan's Northern Alliance forces.

The Stratofortress has been the backbone of the manned strategic bomber force for the United States for almost 50 years and is capable of dropping or launching the widest array of weapons in the U.S. inventory. This includes gravity bombs, cluster bombs, precision guided missiles, and joint direct attack munitions. Updated with modern technology, the B-52 will continue to be capable of delivering the full complement of joint developed weapons and will continue into the middle of the 21st century as a vital component of the U.S. defense system. Current engineering analyses show the B-52's life span to extend beyond the year 2045, suggesting that it could well be possible for this mighty weapons system to achieve an unrivaled record of one hundred years in operational service.

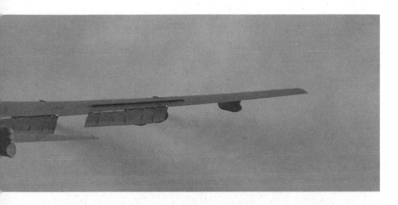

Below: Cockpit of a B-52H, with throttles and controls for eight engines.

Northrop Grumman B-2A Spirit

Type: Strategic bomber.
Manufacturer: Northrop Grumman.
Weight: empty, 153,700 lb (69,717kg); normal takeoff, 336,500lb (152,600kg); max takeoff, 376,000lb (170,550kg).
Dimensions: wingspan 172ft (52.4m); length 69ft (20.9m); height 17ft (5.2m).
Powerplant: four General Electric F118-GE-100 turbofans, each of 17,300lb (7,850kg) thrust.
Performance: max. speed high subsonic (approx Mach 0.85); ceiling: 50,000ft (15,000m); range (typical, hi-hi-hi) 6,300nm (11,667km).
Armament: 40,000lb (18,000kg) of ordnance in internal bays.
Crew: two (pilot, co-pilot/mission commander).

The B-2 was originally intended to be a high-altitude bomber, but in 1984 a redesign of the wing carry-through structure, carried out at a cost of around $1,000 million and which added eight months to the design process, achieved two major goals. First, the increased structural efficiency gave greater strength for less weight, curing an identified weight-growth problem, but also provided enough strength for the aircraft to undertake low-altitude, terrain-following flights. Second, the redesign significantly reduced the radar cross-section (RCS) and, while actual figures remain a closely guarded secret, the design goal was probably a reduction to at least an order of magnitude less than that of the B-1B. The B-1B is known to have an RCS of less than 10.76sq ft (1sq m), suggesting that the likely figure for the Northrop aircraft is less than 1.07sq ft (0.1sq m) and possibly half that.

The first B-2 was shown to the public on 22 November 1988, when it was rolled out of its hangar at Air Force Plant #42, located at Palmdale, California. First flight took place on 17 July 1989 and the 509th Bomb Wing was formed at Whiteman AFB, Missouri on 1 April 1993 to operate the new bomber, with the first actual unit, 393rd Bomb Squadron, forming on 27 August 1993 and receiving its first aircraft, named *Spirit of Missouri,* on 3

December of that year. The B-2 was granted limited operational status on 1 January 1997, and Initial Operational Capability (IOC) followed on 1 April 1997. Whiteman AFB remains the B-2's only operational base, with depot maintenance being performed by Air Force contractors and managed at the Oklahoma City Air Logistics Center at Tinker AFB, Oklahoma.

Like the Lockheed F-117A stealth fighter, the B-2 has the simplest possible front profile, with two straight, moderately swept leading edges meeting at the nose to ensure that the main RCS sidelobes in the forward sector are well away from the direction of flight. The massive sawtooth trailing edge is made up from fourteen straight edges, aligned at one of two fixed angles, a layout which will direct radar energy reflected from the trailing edges into two directions well away from the immediate rear of the aircraft. Each wing side has a drag rudder and elevon on the outboard trailing edge, plus two more elevons on the next-inboard section. The central "beaver tail" forms another moving surface. The aircraft has no vertical stabilizer, a feature that helps reduce RCS. There is a quadruplex digital flight control system developed by General Electric, which incorporates fly-by-wire controls, plus a sophisticated stability-augmentation system.

Segmented inlets on the upper wing feed air to the engines buried within the fuselage. A secondary inlet mounted just ahead of the main inlet, and offset slightly outboard, also draws in air, perhaps for engine bay and efflux cooling. The inlets make a significant contribution to total RCS. A redesign was needed to get these right, and to solve manufacturing problems associated with their complex shape. The engine efflux is discharged via recessed cut-outs in the wing upper surface. Lined with heat-resistant carbon-carbon material, these open-topped ducts are probably intended to spread the exhaust laterally to reduce IR signature. Two doors on the upper surface of each nacelle are opened when the aircraft is taxying and flying at low speed. These are auxiliary inlets used to supply extra air to the engines.

Left: The first prototype B-2 takes off on its first flight on 17 July 1989. It flew to Edwards from Palmdale.

All B-2s were built on production tooling, so using the term "prototype" is slightly misleading; however, Air Vehicle #1 was rolled out on 22 November 1988, and made its first flight on 17 July 1989, followed by a further five, all of which were assigned to development testing. At the end of its trials program, totaling 81 sorties, the first aircraft was placed in storage in 1993, but the others were reassigned as operational aircraft.

The USAF originally planned to procure 133 B-2s, but the planned force was steadily reduced, until in October 1991 the U.S. Congress set the number at only 16, The Air Force managed to fund one more in FY92 and another four in FY93, but that was it and production ended in the mid-1990s, with the tooling being placed in storage. Subsequent attempts by Congress to authorize a follow-on batch of twenty aircraft were overruled by the Clinton administration, although the first aircraft was brought out of storage and rebuilt as an operational aircraft, making twenty-one in total.

The first sixteen aircraft were delivered to the Block 1 standard and were armed with B83 or Mk 84 nuclear weapons. The next three aircraft

Right: B-2 has a range of 6,300nm on internal fuel alone, and considerably more if it receives air-to-air refueling, as here.

(#17-19) were built to Block 2 standard, following which #12-#16 were retrofitted to the same standard. Block 2 equipped the aircraft with partial terrain-following capability, the GPS-Aided Targeting System (GATS), and allowed it to operate from forward bases. A minor modification, Block 20, enabled aircraft to deliver sixteen Joint Direct Attack Munitions (JDAMS) and also gave them a limited capability to handle the new AGM-137 missile. The final aircraft, #20 and #21 (the rebuilt #1), were completed to Block 30 standard, to which the other nineteen will be upgraded. Block 30 has full low-observability performance, full JDAM launch capability, and can carry up to eighty Mk 82, thirty-six M117 or eighty Mk 62 bombs.

When the aircraft first entered service, caulk and pressure-sensitive tape were used to shield the gaps around panels and doors. In flight, the tape tended to peel away from the skin, allowing the exposed gaps to reflect radar energy. During regular depot maintenance, the B-2 is being given an improved anti-radar coating based on magnetic radar-absorbing materials (MagRAM), while high-access areas of the airframe are being retrofitted with 119 easily removable panels. MagRAM is an iron-filled

elastomer which stores radar energy rather than conducting it. The radar reflection from the gaps around a MagRAM-coated panel will be absorbed before it can escape, removing the need to caulk and tape the gap. These modifications will increase the aircraft's weight by 3,666lb (1,660kg), but should reduce the time needed for low-observable maintenance from 20.8 maintenance hours per flying hour to less than ten.

In the original design it was intended that the B-2 would have a contrail-suppressing system, which would have been located in two bays immediately outboard of the main wheel wells and would have sprayed highly corrosive chemicals into the exhaust. However, this scheme was

Above: The unique shape of the B-2 makes it virtually "invisible" to radar.

abandoned in favor of using a rearward-facing laser radar to detect contrails, allowing the pilot to move to an altitude where the contrails cease, and the spaces intended for the contrail-suppressing system are now available for other uses.

The B-2 was designed for a service life of 40,000 hours, so in theory could out-last the B-52 (with a service life of more than 30,000 hours) or the B-1B (10,000 hours). In practice, the retirement date of the B-2 will probably be determined by attrition of the small number built.

AGM-129A Advanced Cruise Missile

Type: air-launched cruise missile.
Manufacturer: Raytheon (General Dynamics).
Weight: <3,500lb (1,588kg).
Dimensions: length 20.9ft (6.4m); diameter 2.4ft (0.7m); wingspan 10.3ft (3.1m).
Propulsion: Williams International F-112-WR-100 turbofan, 732lb (332kg) static thrust.
Performance: cruise speed 434kt (500mph/805kmh).
Guidance: GPS/INS.
Warhead: W-80-1 nuclear.
Platforms: B-52H.

The AGM-129A ACM entered development in 1983 with the aim of providing significant improvements over the AGM-86 ALCM, particularly with increased range, improved accuracy and reductions in both the radar cross-section (RCS) and IR signature. Unlike AGM-86, AGM-129 exists only in a nuclear-armed form, carrying a single W-80 Mod 1 warhead, which has two yields, either 5kT or

Right: The AGM-129A was intended to replace the ALCM; in the event only 460 were built.

150kT, weighs 290lb (131kg), and is 2.6ft (0.8m) long and 11.8in (300mm) in diameter. It was originally planned to produce 1,460 AGM-149s but as a result of the end of the Cold War and the various subsequent nuclear limitation treaties, production was halted after 460 had been built. There are sixty-six nuclear-capable B-52Hs in the USAF inventory, each of which can carry a maximum of twelve ACMs.

The AGM-129 is intended to evade air- and ground-based defenses in order to strike heavily defended, hardened targets at any location within any potential enemy's territory. To achieve this it is essential that the design should minimize the possibility of detection by hostile sensors and numerous measures have been taken to achieve this. The fuselage has a sharp, four-planar nose, straight-sided circular fuselage, forward-angled wings, and a beaver tail, and the entire exterior is coated in radar-absorbent material (RAM) and painted with low-reflective paint. The air intake is flush, with a hidden lip, and the exhausts are designed to minimize the IR, radar, and acoustic signatures. The wings, fin, and elevators are all folded while the missile is being carried by the aircraft and extend on release, at which point the Williams F-111 turbojet is also powered-up.

Ohio-class

Type: SSBN.
Displacement: surfaced 16,764 tons; submerged 18,750 tons.
Dimensions: length 560.0ft (170.7m); beam 42.0in (12.8m); draught 33.0ft (11.3m).
Propulsion: 1 x General Electric S8G natural-circulation, pressurized-water nuclear reactor; turbo-reduction drive; ca. 35,000shp; one shaft.
Performance: submerged 25kt; maximum operational diving depth 984ft (300m).
Armament: 24 tubes for Trident II (D-5) SLBMs (see notes); four 21in (533mm) torpedo tubes.
Complement: 163 (two crews).

The U.S. Navy's first submarine-launched ballistic missile (SLBM) was the UGM-27 Polaris (A-3) which became operational in George Washington-class SSBNs in 1960. This was succeeded by the much improved UGM-73 Poseidon, which first went to sea in 1973 at the height of the Cold War, and eventually equipped the entire fleet. All of these SSBNs of the Washington-, Ethan Allen-, and Lafayette-classes carried sixteen missiles in vertical launch tubes in two rows of eight abaft the sail. These missiles were, however, characterized by relatively short range, the two major consequences being that the SSBNs had to carry out their patrols sufficiently close to Soviet territory to ensure that they would reach their targets, and as a consequence forward bases were established at Holy Loch, Scotland, Rota, Spain, and on Guam in the Pacific. This was not an ideal arrangement, since it meant that Soviet land-, air-, and sea-based intelligence assets could monitor U.S. SSBNs as they entered and left these bases, and that the areas where they patrolled were fairly limited. This did not mean that individual SSBNs were easy to find, but only that the Soviets knew roughly where to start their searches.

As a result of these considerations development of an entirely new missile was started in the 1970s, whose essential characteristic was to be much greater range, which required a larger missile. This, in its turn, required a larger submarine to take full advantage of its capabilities. At first, Congress balked at the immense cost of the new missile and submarine, but its view was transformed into support when the Soviet Navy introduced first the SS-N-8 missile (4,200nm, 6,760km) followed shortly afterwards by the SS-N-18 (4,846nm, 7,800km). The U.S. Navy then speeded up its program and the first Ohio-class boat was laid down on 10 April 1976. A variety of factors caused delays and the first-of-class, USS *Ohio* (SSBN-726), did not start trials until 17 June 1981.It launched its first successful missile on 17 January 1982 and sailed on its first operational deterrent patrol on 1 October 1982. This was considerably behind schedule and both submarine and missile were subjected to considerable criticism in Congress and the Press at the time, but since then this has proved to be one of the most successful naval weapons systems ever to enter service.

The Ohio-class boats are huge, being only marginally shorter than a Ticonderoga-class cruiser – 560ft (170.7m) compared to 567ft (172.9m) – but with a very much greater displacement, 16,747 tons compared to 9,466 tons. Their immense power, however, lies in their Trident II (D-5) missiles, of which twenty-four are carried, a fifty percent increase on the number of missiles in earlier SSBNs. Each missile is physically capable of carrying sixteen reentry vehicles (RVs), but as a result of the various START agreements now only carries four.

All Ohio-class SSBNs are in commission, split equally between the east

Above: Ohio-class SSBNs are the most powerful war machines ever built.

and west coasts of the United States, with nine based at Bangor, Washington, and nine at King's Bay, Georgia. Each boat in commission has two crews (designated Blue and Gold) and operates on a cycle of a 70-day patrol followed by a 25-day refit and crew changeover, and then another 70-day patrol, the cycle being broken only in the ninth year when there is a 12-month major overhaul, which includes recoring the nuclear reactor and modernisation of all systems. Each patrol consists of a transit to the patrol area, following which the ship cruises at about 3kt, making maximum use of the various layers in the sea to hide its presence from foreign submarines or sea-bed sensors. Once at operating depth communications to and from the ship are difficult but by no means impossible and elaborate systems are in place to enable vital command messages to be passed. One such system is the very low frequency (VLF) system operated by the U.S. Navy's E-6 Mercury aircraft. Under present procedures there are five ships on patrol at any one time, with five others in transit either to or from the patrol areas, and all ten are fully capable of launching their missiles, if and when required to do so.

Eighteen Ohio-class SSBNs were built, joining the fleet between 1981 and 1997, of which eight were armed with the Trident I C-4 missile and ten with the Trident II D-5 missile. As of 2002, the plan is to retire the first four ships (SSBN-726 to SSBN-729) and to rearm the second four (SSBN-730 to

SSBN-733) with Trident II D-5 missiles. This will leave the Navy's deterrent force comprising 14 boats, with each of the 24 missiles carrying five warheads, for a grand total of 1,680 warheads. Of these warheads, some 400 are W-88s with a 300-475kT yield, while the remainder are W-76s with a yield of some 100kT.

One plan for the four ships to be removed from the strategic missile role is for them to be rearmed with Tomahawk missiles, effectively converting them from SSBNs to SSGNs. This would involved installing rotary launchers in the missile tubes, each launcher containing seven Tomahawks. Final decisions on this plan and how many tubes would be converted have yet to be made, but just one such SSGN with 20 tubes converted would carry 140 cruise-missiles, a formidable arsenal by any standard.

In early 2002 the future of some elements of the Ohio-class is uncertain. There are periodic proposals either to reduce the active force to twelve ships, or to reduce the crewing of all fourteen to one crew each. This would produce a totally new deployment cycle and reduce the numbers available on station at any one time; it would also drastically reduce both the manpower requirement and the annual operating costs. The cost of the Ohio/Trident program has been huge, but in combination they provide a strategic system of the most exceptional national value, and will continue to do so for many years to come.

Below: There are 24 hatches, each covering a single Trident II (D-5) missile.

Above: The long-term fleet will comprise 14 Ohio-class SSBNs.

Combat Aircraft

The combat element of the United States' aviation forces are composed of fighter and attack fixed-wing aircraft and attack helicopters, which over the past twenty years have repeatedly shown that they provide a versatile striking force which can defeat any enemy. These forces are capable of rapid deployment to any part of the world and they have repeatedly shown that their power and effectiveness are such that they can rapidly gain and sustain air superiority over regional aggressors. Once they have achieved that air superiority they open the way for air attacks on other enemy targets, while providing security for friendly forces to exploit the air for intelligence-gathering, command-and-control, resupply, movement, logistic support, and other functions relating to the conduct of the campaign.

At all times the Air Force, Navy, Marine Corps, and Army maintain a proportion of their tactical aircraft forward deployed in foreign countries or at sea, and the nearest forces to a new crisis will obviously be the first to be committed. But these forward deployed forces can be reinforced by aircraft based in the United States if and when the need arises. The Air Force is capable of deploying significant forces on an expeditionary basis to locations where runways and limited local support are available. Navy and Marine air wings similarly can be employed in distant contingencies on very short notice, but in their case they possess the unique ability to carry out combat operations from the sea and are thus independent of access to regional land bases. In addition, the Marine Corps has the ability to establish limited basing facilities ashore for fighter/attack aircraft, using unprepared land sites, which are made usable with lightweight metal matting, catapults, and arresting gear, although such sites for AV-8s and helicopters (and, in the future, the MV-22 and JSF) will need even less preparation. In the case of the Army, all but a very few aircraft are capable of operating from improvised air strips.

The United States' aviation assets are huge and far outmatch, both in quantity and quality, those of any other single nation. Current aviation combat forces consist of some 20 Air Force fighter wing-equivalents (FWEs) with 72 aircraft each; 11 Navy carrier air wings, operating 46 fighter/attack aircraft apiece; and four Marine air wings, which are task-organized and include varying numbers and types of aircraft. In addition, the Army currently operates some 1,340 armed helicopters.

The Air Force completed its transition to the new expeditionary deployment concept in FY 2001 in which fighter/attack aircraft and selected additional

elements have been grouped into ten Aerospace Expeditionary Force (AEF) packages for deployment purposes. Each AEF unit is prepared to deploy for a ninety-day period on a fixed, fifteen-month cycle. Although individual AEFs may differ in composition, each is intended to provide comparable combat power to theater commanders, and each provides air superiority, ground attack, command, control, intelligence, surveillance, and reconnaissance capabilities for sustained operations. Additional AEFs would be deployed in the event that a contingency escalated into a major theater war. Through the expeditionary concept, the Air Force will be able to substantially improve the way it packages forces for deployment. This gain will be realized without corresponding changes in force levels or force structure.

Most of the aircraft consist of some very well tried types, such as the F-14 and F-15 heavy fighters, F-16 light fighter, F/A-18 and AV-8 attack aircraft, and the various types of attack helicopter which have been in service for several decades, although modifications and modernization have kept them abreast with current technology. In most cases replacements are on the horizon – for example, the F-22 Raptor and F-35 JSF – but experience suggests that their arrival may be neither so prompt nor as smooth as currently predicted. One particularly noticeable trend is that the airframe, which is the part visible to the naked eye, is actually the least difficult and usually the least expensive component in the system, while the invisible elements, such as the electronics and the data systems are not only considerably more expensive but are also far more difficult to integrate. Indeed, where delays or cost over-runs occur it is often these less visible factors that have caused them.

Another marked trend in both combat and support aviation is a deliberate effort to reduce the number of individual types. Thus, whereas from the 1950s to the 1980s there were large numbers of different types in almost every aircraft category, there is now a diminishing number, leading to cheaper acquisition, and easier and more cost-effective logistic support while in service. This in turn reduces the cost-of-ownership – ie, the expense of operating, maintaining and modifying aircraft throughout their time in service. The final trend to be mentioned here is the length of time that types are remaining in service. Once about ten years was the norm, but now it is more like thirty to forty years.

Below: The F/A-18 Super Hornet: among the finest fighters in the world.

Bell AH-1F HueyCobra, AH-1W SuperCobra and AH-1Z

Bell AH-1F HueyCobra, AH-1W SuperCobra and AH-1Z
Type: attack helicopter.
Manufacturer: Bell Helicopter Textron.
Weight: weight 12,200lb (5,534kg); maximum gross 16,800lb (7,620kg).
Dimensions: length 45.6ft (13.9m); height 13.1ft (4.0m); rotor diameter 48.0ft (14.6m).
Powerplant: two General Electric T700-GE-401 rated at 1,725shp (1,286kW).
Performance: maximum airspeed 190kt (219mph/ 352km/h); maximum range (20 minutes reserve fuel) 350nm (530 miles/854km); endurance 3 hours 30 minutes.
Armament: maximum weapon load 3,914lb (1,775kg) (see text).
Crew: two (pilot/commander; gunner/co-pilot).
Specifications for AH-1W

Bell started to study the possibilities of armed helicopters in the 1950s and the company's first product was a modified version of the AH-47 Sioux, with a streamlined nose housing a pilot and gunner in tandem, with stub wings for weapon mounts and a chin turret. It was quickly apparent that the Sioux was grossly underpowered for this mission so the company turned to an adaptation of the larger and much more powerful AH-1 Huey, which appeared in 1965 as the company-funded Model 209 HueyCobra. At that time the U.S. Army had just identified an urgent need for an armed helicopter in Vietnam and had set in train a development project that would culminate in the large, complicated, and very expensive Lockheed AH-64 Cheyenne. However, seeing that the HueyCobra was immediately available, an order for 110 was placed in April 1966. The Cheyenne was canceled in 1972 and as the AH-1 was still the only aircraft available – but a very good one. It was ordered in ever larger numbers by the Army (1,075 AH-1G), while the Marine Corps developed the twin-engined AH-1T SeaCobra. From this was developed the much more powerful

AH-1W SuperCobra, with deliveries starting in 1986. This now serves in large numbers with the Marines, and is also in service with a large number of overseas armed forces.

The original AH-1G retained most of the dynamic components of the UH-1B/C Huey, but introduced a new narrow fuselage with stub wings to carry weapons and to help offload the rotor in cruising flight. All models had the pilot seated above and behind the co-pilot/gunner who manages the nose sight system and fires the chin turret. The pilot normally fires the wing stores and can also fire the chin turret when it is in its stowed (fore/aft) position, which it reverts to as soon as the gunner releases the slewing switch. The gunner can also fly the aircraft and fire the wing stores in an emergency.

The SuperCobra can carry a wide variety of weapons, the actual mix depending upon the mission, and the load depending upon fuel carried, range required, and ambient conditions. The aircraft carries both TOW and Hellfire anti-armor missiles and is being qualified to carry the Maverick missile. The SuperCobra was the first attack helicopter to qualify to carry and launch both the Sidewinder air-to-air missile and the Sidearm anti-radiation missile, both of which use the same LAU-7 rail launcher. The SuperCobra can also fire a range of rockets, for example 70mm rockets armed with submunition warheads or the larger 127mm Uni rocket bombs. The aircraft carries a three-barrel 20mm Gatling gun with 750 rounds of ammunition for close range (up to 1.25 miles/2km) engagements. The Night Targeting System (NT), jointly produced by Tamam Division of Israel Aircraft Industries Ltd and Kollsman, integrates a Forward Looking Infrared (FLIR) which provides automatic target tracking with a laser designator/rangefinder and video recorder.

The aircraft is powered by twin General Electric T700-GE-401 turboshaft engines providing a total of 3,380shp (2,410kW). In standard conditions and

Below: The USMC has constantly updated the AH-1.

with an air-to-air missile load the SuperCobra can take off and climb out at more than 13.5ft/sec (4.1m/sec) on only one engine. It can also hover Out-of-Ground Effect (OGE) at 3,000ft (914m) with a load of four TOW and four Hellfire missiles, full turret ammunition, and rockets.

The "H-1 Program" for the AH-1W is currently in the development phase, which, if successful, will lead to a new and even more capable version, the AH-1Z. This will involve the remanufacture of the Marine Corps' entire fleet of AH-1W SuperCobra and UH-1N utility helicopters, one of the most notable features being the replacement of the famous twin-bladed, semi-rigid, teetering rotor by a new and very advanced four bladed, hingeless, bearingless rotor system. First flight of the AH-1Z took place in December 2000 and the flight test program should be completed by summer 2003, following which deliveries to the USMC will begin in 2004. The improvement in flight characteristics provided by the four-bladed configuration will lead to significant increases in the flight envelope, maximum speed, vertical rate-of-climb, and payload, coupled with dramatic reductions in the rotor vibration level. In addition to this work, Lockheed Martin is developing a longer range Target Sight System (TSS) for the AH-1Z, which includes a FLIR based on a 3-5 micron staring array, CCD TV, and eyesafe laser rangefinder/designator. Longbow International (a joint venture of Lockheed

Martin and Northrop Grumman) is also developing the Cobra Radar System for the AH-1Z, which is based on the Longbow millimetre wave radar on the AH-64D Apache. This will be housed in a pod, which can be mounted on a wingtip or in a stores position, and will automatically search, detect, classify, and prioritize multiple moving and stationary targets. The H-1 Program also includes provision of a whole range of new electronic warfare systems. Among these will be new radar warning, missile warning, and laser warning systems. Other enhancements will include a new infrared countermeasures system, and a chaff and infrared flare dispenser.

The story of the AH-1 is very similar to that of the B-52 and the Minuteman, in that it was designed in the 1950s but has proved so adaptable that it can be redesigned and improved at regular intervals, enabling it to remain at the forefront of military technology and operational effectiveness for more half-a-century. Also like those other two systems, the AH-1 has been criticized from time to time for complexity and expense, but it has, in fact, proved to be exceptionally cost-effective and remains in front-line service long after its competitors have been forgotten and its critics have fallen silent.

Below: Battle-scarred AH-1W lifts of the deck of USS Tarawa.

Bell OH-58D Kiowa Warrior

Type: scout attack/utility/transport helicopter.
Manufacturer: Bell Helicopter Textron.
Weight: 3,289lbs (1,492kg); maximum combat mission 5,189lb (2,354kg).
Dimensions: length, rotors turning, l 40.9ft (12.5m); height 12.9ft (3.9m); rotor diameter 35.0ft (10.7m).
Powerplant: one Rolls-Royce-Allison T703-AD-700 gas turbine engine, 650shp (485kW).
Performance: maximum cruising speed 138mph (222km/h); vertical rate-of-climb 100ft/min (30.5m/min); maximum range, internal fuel, no reserves, 345 miles (556km); endurance 2h 30m.
Weapons: see text below.
Crew: two (pilot/commander; observer/co-pilot).

The Bell 206 began its long career as the OH-58 Kiowa, one of two entries for the U.S. Army's 1961 Light Observation Helicopter (LOH) program, which was won by the Hughes OH-6. Following much acrimony, the competition was reopened and in March 1968 the Bell entry was declared the winner, resulting in an order for 2,200 aircraft. This launched the JetRanger program, and led to the OH-58B and the OH-58C with uprated engine and other improvements. This in turn led to the Army Helicopter Improvement Program (AHIP) the outcome of which was the OH-58D Kiowa Warrior.

The Armed OH-58D Kiowa Warrior has a single engine driving a twin-bladed rotor, and has been deployed in support of United States armed forces around the world including inHaiti, Somalia, Bosnia, and the Gulf of Arabia. During

Desert Storm and Desert Shield over 115 Kiowas flew a total of some 9,000 hours. The aircraft's primary mission is scout attack role, although it can also be reconfigured to carry out transport and utility roles, using equipment kits installed externally on existing hard points. A cargo-carrying hook below the fuselage is rated to carry loads up to 2,000lb (907kg). The aircraft can also be used for emergency casualty evacuation (CasEvac), carrying two casualties on litters, or to carry some 700lb (320kg) of supplies, both over an operating radius of more than 115 miles (185km). In addition to all this, the OH-58D can be used to transport up to six troops for critical point security missions. The aircraft is itself air-transportable, with two being transported in a C-130 aircraft.

The OH-58D carries a wide variety of weapons, the actual mix and all-up weight depending upon the mission, range, and ambient conditions. Among these weapons are: Hellfire missiles; Hydra 70/CASA 80mm rockets; Stinger air-to-air missiles; TOW, Bofors RBS-70, or HOT anti-tank missiles; and a variety of machine guns, including the 0.50in (12.7mm) and 7.62mm Minigun.

The OH-58D was the first U.S. Army helicopter to have an all-glass cockpit, and also carries a countermeasures suite that includes an infrared jammer, radar warning receivers against pulsed and continuous wave radars, and a laser warning detector. A distinctive Mast Mounted Sight (MMS) is situated above the rotor blades and enables the OH-58D to operate by day and night and to engage an enemy at the maximum range of the weapon systems and with the minimum exposure of the helicopter.

Below: Two OH-58Ds on the flightline, with OH-58As parked on right.

Boeing AH-6J, MH-6J, and A/MH-6 "Little Bird"

Type: light attack helicopter.
Manufacturer: Boeing (formerly McDonnell -Douglas; formerly Hughes).
Dimensions: rotors turning, length 30.8ft (9.4m), fuselage 24.9ft (7.6m); height 8.5ft (2.6m); fuselage width 6.2ft (1.9m); rotor diameter 26.3ft (8m) .
Weight: maximum gross 3,000lb (1,361kg); normal takeoff 2,403lb(1,090kg); empty 1,875lb (896kg).
Powerplant: Rolls-Royce/Allison 250-C30 turboshaft, 425shp.
Performance: maximum level speed 150mph (241km/h); range with normal load 300 miles (485km); hover out-of-ground effect 6,000ft (1,830m); endurance 2h 30m; vertical climb rate 27ft/sec (8.4m/s).
Payload: external load 1,216lb (550kg); 2/3 troops internally, or 6 on external platforms in lieu of weapons.
Weapons: see text below.
Crew: two (pilot/commander; observer/co-pilot).
Specifications for AH-6J Light Attack Helicopter.

A highly modified version of the McDonnell Douglas 530 series commercial helicopter, the AH-6J is a gas-turbine-engined, dual-control, light attack helicopter, which is primarily employed in close air support of ground troops, target destruction raids, and armed escort of other aircraft. The AH-6J is usually flown by two pilots on most overland flights, but the two pilots become mandatory for overwater operations.

The AH-6J is capable of mounting a variety of weapons systems, including the M134 7.62mm Minigun (a six-barrel, air-cooled, Gatling-type weapon); M261 7-round and M260 19-round rocket launchers for 2.75in FFAR rockets; AGM-114 Hellfire anti-tank missiles (maximum of four); and the .5in (12.7mm) machine gun. However, the normal aircraft configuration consists of two

Below: Despite its small size, the MH-6 can carry six troops externally.

Right: Special Operations Forces train with "Little Bird."

7.62mm Miniguns with 1,500 to 2,000 rounds per gun, and two seven-round 2.75in (70mm) rocket pods.

The MH-6J is basically identical to the AH-6J, but is modified to transport up to eight people, the two crew plus six combat troops sitting on the sills facing outwards. In this configuration it is capable of conducting overt and covert infiltrations, exfiltrations, and combat assaults over a wide variety of terrain and environmental conditions. It is also used for command-and-control and reconnaissance missions. The aircraft can be rapidly configured for fast-rope and STABO operations, while special racks can be fitted to enable two motorcycles to be carried. Some aircraft are equipped with Forward Looking Infrared Radar (FLIR), a passive system that provides an infrared image of terrain features and ground or airborne objects of interest. Each aircraft is equipped with the AN/APR-39 Radar Warning Receiver (RWR) system, which detects and identifies hostile search/acquisition and fire control radars, and provides audio and video alerts to the flight crew.

One particular advantage of the AH-60/MH-60's very small size, is that they can be deployed by any Air Force transport aircraft. A C-141 is capable of transporting up to six MH-6s and a C-130 is able to transport up to three MH-6s, with a rapid upload/offload capability. On arrival at the destination MH-6s can be offloaded, restored to flight configuration, fueled and take off within fifteen minutes. Self-deployment is unlimited, provided that refueling facilities are available at a maximum of 270nm (410 miles/660km) intervals.

The A/MH-6 MELB (Mission Enhancement Little Bird) is a variant of the AH-6J optimized for support of short-range operations in hostile areas. Among its roles are fire support and personnel recovery missions and it includes the necessary equipment for shipboard operations. Production began in FY 2000, and a total of forty MELBs have been built. It has an upgraded six-bladed main and four-bladed tail rotor system;

Boeing/BAe AV-8B Harrier II and Harrier II Plus

Type: STOVL attack aircraft.
Manufacturer: Boeing (USA)/British Aerospace (UK).
Weight: normal take-off 22,950lb (10,410kg); maximum short takeoff 31,000lb (14,061kg); maximum vertical takeoff 18,950lb (8,595kg).
Dimensions: length 46.3ft (14.1m); wingspan 30.3ft (9.3m); height 11.6ft (3.6m).
Powerplant: one Rolls-Royce Pegasus F-402-RR-408, 21,500lb (9,751kg) dry thrust.
Performance: maximum level speed, clean, sea-level 661mph (1,065km/h); range, ferry, 2,418nm (3891km); combat radius (12 x Mk82 bombs, 1 hour loiter, STO) 103nm (167km); maximum rate-of-climb at sea-level 14,715ft/min (4,485m/min); service ceiling <50,000ft (15,240m)
Payload: maximum internal fuel 7,759lb (3,519kg), maximum external fuel 8,070lb (3,661kg).
Armament: one fuselage-mounted 25mm gun system. Typical ordnance loads are six Mk 82 500lb bombs, or four AIM-9L/M Sidewinder missiles; maximum ordnance 9,200lb (4,173kg);
Crew: one.
Specifications for AV-8B Harrier II

In the late 1940s and throughout the 1950s and '60s there were many attempts to develop a system which would enable fixed-wing aircraft to take-off and land vertically, thus breaking the link which tied them to large, expensive, and increasingly vulnerable airfields. Some aircraft sat on their tails, while others had one set of engines for vertical lift and another set for forward flight. But it was the Rolls-Royce Pegasus engine that solved the problem, with a single

engine fitted with rotating nozzles which enabled it to power the aircraft in both vertical and horizontal regimes. This led to the P.1127 vertical takeoff aircraft, which was designed and developed in the United Kingdom by Hawker Aircraft, later British Aerospace (BAe), the first flight taking place on 19 November 1960.

The U.S. Marine Corps became interested at an early stage in the project and purchased 102 of the first production version, the AV-8A Harrier, together with eight TAV-8A two-seat trainers. Although it introduced the revolutionary concept of a fixed-wing, vertical takeoff and landing fighter to the battlefield, this version had some shortcomings, especially with payload and range. As a result, McDonnell Douglas, British Aeropsace and the engine manufacturer, Rolls-Royce, began a development program which resulted in the AV-8B Harrier II. Although superficially similar to the AV-8A, this is actually a totally new aircraft, which entered service from 1984 onwards. The Marines have purchased 276 AV-8Bs and 17 TAV-8Bs, the two-seat trainer version, with others being purchased by the British Royal Air Force and the Italian and Spanish Navies.

The Marines operate four versions of the AV-8B. The initial version was the AV-8B (also known as the AV-8B Day Attack (DA)), which was the baseline aircraft, powered by the Rolls-Royce F402-RR-406 engine and equipped with the Hughes ASB-19 Angle-Rate Bombing Set (ARBS), the first of which was delivered in November 1983. From the 167th aircraft, production switched to the AV-8B Night Attack (NA), with the first being delivered in November 1989. This version has night-vision goggle compatible cockpit controls/displays, Navigation Forward Looking Infra-red (NAVFLIR), Digital Map Unit (DMU), and

Below: AV-8B Harrier II Plus is the world's most effective V/STOL aircraft.

the ARBS with a laser spot tracker. The next version, fielded in 1993, was the AV-8B Night Attack/Radar (NA/R), also known as the Harrier II-Plus, which has all the capabilities and avionics of the NA version, but in addition integrates the APG-65 radar, which is also used by the Marine Corps' F/A-18 Hornets; this extends the capabilities of the aircraft in air-ground and air-to-air defense modes. The fourth version is the TAV-8B two-seat trainer. Starting in 1994, seventy-three of the original AV-8Bs were remanufactured and brought up to the same standard as the -Radar aircraft, being designated AV-8B REMAN. Current work concerns the NA/Radar aircraft which are being upgraded to incorporate an Automatic Target Hand-off System (ATHS) and Global Positioning System (GPS).

The aircraft can carry a wide range of stores from its seven stations. These include various types of dumb and smart bombs, such as the Mk 83 1,000lb (454kg) bomb, GBU-12 500lb (277kg) bomb, GBU-16 LGB (laser-guided bomb), and cluster bombs. They can also carry a wide range of missiles, including the AIM-9 Sidewinder for air-to-air combat, as well as 2.75in (70mm) and 5in (127mm) free-flight rockets for ground attack.

The primary missions of the Marine Corps' AV-8B squadrons are to support ground troops by attacking and destroying land and air targets, and to escort helicopters, but they can also be given many other missions at the orders of the relevant commander. Specific tasks include: close air support; deep air support, including armed reconnaissance and air interdiction; offensive and defensive

anti-air warfare; and to operate and deliver ordnance at night. To achieve these tasks, the AV-8Bs are required to operate from any appropriate sea platform, to be capable of air-to-air refueling, and to operate from forward land bases, ranging from established airfields to remote tactical landing sites.

Operationally, the AV-8B has provided the Marines with an extremely capable aircraft, which can operate from ship platforms or from rudimentary airstrips, where it can provide rapid response to requests from the forward troops and without long transit times. For example, during Operation Desert Storm, AV-8Bs were the first U.S. Marine Corps tactical aircraft to arrive in theater, where they operated from an unused airfield and a small forward-based airstrip, as well as from ships in the Persian Gulf. The 86 AV-8Bs involved were in combat for 42 days, during which they flew 3,380 combat sorties, delivering over six million pounds of ordnance during 4,112 hours of combat flying. Over the entire period of Desert Storm, AV-8B squadrons achieved an aircraft readiness rate greater than 90 percent.

The AV-8B is unique in its ability to make extremely short take-offs and to land vertically, something which no other operational fixed-wing aircraft can do. In any future major war, hostile air forces are bound to make airfields and carriers their primary targets, which gives the AV-8B an edge and a degree of survivability which will be unmatched until the Joint Strike Fighter (JSF) enters service.

Below: AV-8B assigned to 15th MEUSOC leaves USS Peleliu for Afghanistan.

Boeing (McDonnell Douglas) AH-64 Apache and Longbow

Type: attack helicopter.
Manufacturer: Boeing (McDonnell Douglas).
Weight: empty 11,015lb (4,996kg); primary mission gross weight 14,694lb (6,665kg); maximum takeoff 17,650lb (8,006kg).
Dimensions: length 48.1ft (14.7m); height 16.8ft (5.1m); rotor diameter 48.0ft (14.6m).
Powerplant: two General Electric T700-GE-701 turboshafts, each 1,696shp (1,265kW).
Performance: maximum airspeed 227kt (365km/h); cruising 182kt (293km/h); hover ceiling (IGE) 13,400ft (4,084m), (OGE) 10,200ft (3,109m); maximum range (internal fuel) 428nm (689km); g limits +3.5 to -0.5.
Armament: missiles, rockets, and guns (see text).
Crew: two (pilot and copilot/gunner).
Specifications for US Army AH-64D

Helicopters entered military service in the mid-1940s but were initially employed in the transport and casualty evacuation roles and it was not until the mid-1950s that the need for an armed helicopter was fully recognized. The U.S. Army's first attempt to develop such an aircraft – the Lockheed AH-56 Cheyenne – turned into a very expensive failure, partly because it was large and extremely complicated, but also because it was far ahead of its time and stretched the technology of the day way beyond its limits. As a result, the Army turned to the AH-1 Hueycobra, a modified version of the UH-1 transport helicopter, as an interim measure, but the requirement remained for a

Below: Apache Longbow with characteristic radome above the rotor head.

Above: AH-64 armed with mix of freeflight rockets and Hellfire missiles.

specialized attack helicopter which could fly all types of front-line missions, by day or night and in all weathers. So, a new project was started in 1972 with Bell and Hughes submitting designs, and the latter was declared the winner in December 1976, although production was not authorized until 1982. Hughes was subsequently taken over by McDonnell Douglas and that company has, in its turn, been bought by Boeing.

Today, the U.S. Army has more than 800 Apaches in service and over 1,000 have been exported to a wide variety of countries around the world. The Apache was first used in combat in 1989 in the U.S. military action in Panama and later in the Gulf War. It has also supported low intensity and peacekeeping operations world-wide, including in northern Iraq, Bosnia, and Kosovo.

The U.S. Army version of the AH-64 is powered by two General Electric T700-GE-701C gas-turbine engines, rated at 1,890shp each, enabling the aircraft to cruise at a speed of 145mph (233km/h), with a flight endurance in excess of three hours. Combat radius is approximately 93 miles (150km), but the addition of a single external 230gal (870) fuel tank enables this to be extended to some 186 miles (300km), although this is dependent upon a number of factors, including weather, temperature, and payload. Ferry range on internal fuel is 430 miles (690km), but this can be considerably extended by the addition of up to four 230gal (870) external tanks. The AH-64 is air transportable in the C-5, C-141 and C-17.

The AH-64D Longbow Apache is equipped with the Northrop Grumman millimeter-wave Longbow radar, which incorporates an integrated radar frequency interferometer for passive location and identification of radar emitting threats. This operates in the millimeter band which ensures not only that it is unaffected by poor visibility or ground clutter, but also, because of its very narrow beamwidth, that it is also resistant to countermeasures. The AH-64D's primary weapon system is the Lockheed Martin/Boeing AGM-114D Longbow Hellfire air-to-surface missile which has a millimeter-wave seeker to allow the missile to perform in full fire-and-forget mode. Range is 5-7.5miles (8-12km). The Apache can also be armed with air-to-air missiles (Stinger, Sidewinder, Mistral, and Sidearm) and 2.75in rockets. The Longbow Apache carries the combination of armaments necessary for the particular mission and in the close support role a typical loadout would be sixteen Hellfire missiles on four 4-rail launchers and four air-to-air missiles. A 30mm automatic Boeing M230 Chain Gun is located under the fuselage. It provides a rate of fire of 625 rounds per minute

and the helicopter can carry up to 1,200 rounds of ammunition.

The Longbow Apache can effect an attack in thirty seconds. The radar dome is unmasked for a single radar scan and then remasked. The processors determine the location, speed, and direction of travel of a maximum of 256 targets. The Target Acquisition Designation Sight – TADS (AN/ASQ-170) – and the Pilot Night Vision Sensor – PNVS (AN/AAQ-11) – were developed by Lockheed Martin. The turret-mounted TADS provides direct-view optics, television, and forward looking infra-red (FLIR) with three fields of view to carry out search, detection, and recognition and Litton laser rangefinder/designator. PNVS consists of a FLIR in a rotating turret located on the nose above the TADS. The image from the PNVS is displayed in the monocular eyepiece of the Honeywell integrated Helmet And Display Sighting System, HADDS, worn by the pilot and co-pilot/gunner.

The Apache is equipped with an electronic warfare suite consisting of: AN/APR-39A(V) radar warning receiver from Litton and Lockheed Martin; AN/ALQ-144 infra-red countermeasures set from BAE Systems (formerly Sanders, a Lockheed Martin company); AN/AVR-2 laser warning receiver from Raytheon (formerly Hughes Danbury Optical Systems); AN/ALQ-136(V) radar jammer developed by ITT; and chaff dispensers.

Below: In the AH-64 the pilot is to the rear, observer/gunner in front.

Boeing (McDonnell Douglas) F/A-18 Hornet/Super Hornet

Type: multi-role attack and fighter aircraft.
Manufacturer: Boeing (McDonnell Douglas).
Weight: empty 23,050lb (10,455kg); normal takeoff, fighter mission, 36,710lb (16,652kg); normal takeoff, attack mission, 51,900lb (23,537kg).
Dimensions: length 56.0ft (16.8m); height 15.3ft (4.6m); wingspan 40.4ft (13.5m).
Powerplant: two F404-GE-402 turbofans, each 16,700lb (78.7kN) with afterburning.
Performance: maximum level speed at high altitude, clean <1,033kt (1,190mph/1,915km/h); ceiling <50,000ft (15,240m); range with external tanks, fighter, 1,379nm (1,586 miles/2,537km), attack, 1,333nm (1,533 miles/ 2,453km).
Armament: 1 x M61A1/A2 Vulcan 20mm cannon; external, combinations of AIM-9 Sidewinder, AIM-7 Sparrow, AIM-120 AMRAAM, Harpoon, HARM, Shrike, SLAM, SLAM-ER, Walleye, Maverick missiles; Joint Stand-Off Weapon (JSOW); Joint Direct Attack Munition (JDAM); general purpose bombs, mines and rockets.
Crew: F/A-18A/C/E – one; F/A-18B/D/F – two.
Specifications for F/A-18C/D.

The F/A-18 has its origins in the Northrop YF-17, one of two contenders for the Air Force's Air Combat Fighter (ACF) program of the 1970s, which was won by the General Dynamics YF-16. The basic Northrop design was dramatically improved and navalized to produce what was, to all intents, a totally new aircraft, and then submitted as an entry for the Navy's ACF

Below: VFA-131 Wildcats F/A-18 assigned to USS Eisenhower.

Above: F/A-18C of Marine Corps' VFMA-251 is prepared for patrol over

program, the initial intention being to produce two separate versions – the F-18 fighter and the A-18 attack aircraft. However, it was found possible to combine both roles in one aircraft, which was then ordered to replace the Navy's A-7 and the Marines' F-4s. This aircraft was planned as a fully navalized aircraft but, recognizing that it had considerable export potential, a separate land-based version, designated F/A-18L, was planned. When it was discovered that foreign air forces were quite happy to buy the naval version as it stood, this proposal was dropped. A pre-production batch of eleven aircraft was ordered, with the first flying in November 1978 and the remainder all completed by March 1980, with production deliveries beginning in May 1980.

The F/A-18 multi-mission, twin-engined aircraft is produced in single-seat (F/A-18A/C/E) and two-seat versions (F/A-18B/D/F). It is a true multi-role platform, being capable of performing a number of missions, including: air superiority, close and deep air support, forward air control, fighter escort, suppression of enemy air defenses (SEAD), reconnaissance, and strike missions by both day and night. It replaced the F-4 Phantom II fighter and A-7 Corsair II attack aircraft, as originally intended, but in the 1990s proved fully capable of replacing the A-6 Intruder as well. The F/A-18 uses a digital fly-by-wire control system which not only gives excellent handling qualities and enables pilots to convert to the type with relative ease, but also makes it an exceptionally maneuverable aircraft, which can hold its own against any adversary. Once in service it proved both a valuable asset and popular with its crews, its only drawback being limited range when loaded with maximum external stores.

In September 1987, following delivery of over 400 F/A-18As and Bs, production switched to the improved F/A-18C (single-seat) and F/A-18D (dual-seat) models, which could carry the Advanced Medium Range Air-to-Air Missile (AMRAAM) and the infrared imaging Maverick air-to-ground missile. In 1989 production switched to the F/A-18C/D Night Attack Hornet, with improved night attack capabilities, carrying a navigation forward looking infrared (NAVFLIR) pod, a raster head-up display, night vision goggles, special cockpit lighting compatible with the night vision devices, a digital color moving map and an independent multipurpose color display.

The modular design of the Hornet has resulted in it being particularly easy to upgrade and throughout its service there have been regular modifications to its avionics, sensors, and weapon systems. However, by the early 1990s it was becoming apparent that the ever-increasing load was starting to reach the limits, partly because of space, but also because of the capacity of the air-cooling and electrical systems. This has led to the development of the F/A-18E/F "Super Hornet" which is 4.2ft (1.3m) longer than earlier Hornets, with a 25 percent increase in wing area and a 33 percent increase in internal fuel, all of which combine to give a 41percent increase in mission range and a 50 percent increase in endurance. Power is provided by two General Electric F414-GE-400 turbo-fan engines, raising

thrust from 36,000lb to 44,000lb.

The F/A-18E/F has two additional weapons stations, making a total of eleven:
two on the wing tips for missiles, six underwing stations (three per wing) for air-to-ground weapons or fuel tanks, two fuselage stations for Sparrows or sensor pods, and a centerline station for fuel or air-to-ground weapons. These enable the aircraft to carry a total external load of some 17,750lb (8,032kg). Finally, as in earlier versions, a 20 mm M61A1 Vulcan cannon is mounted internally in the nose.

Although it is not a "headline" capability, the carrier recovery payload of the F/A-18E/F has been increased to 9,000lb (4,082kg). This means that more unused weapons or unburnt fuel can be recovered to the carrier rather than jettisoned into the sea, a valuable consideration for the battle group commander and his logistics staff. The F/A-18E/F's

Left: The "AG" tail code and "Wildcats" on the droptanks announce proudly that this F/A-18C serves the Navy's VFA-131 aboard USS Eisenhower.

larger fuselage and increased power also give volume, cooling capacity, and electrical power for future enhancements. The Navy intends to procure at least 548 Super Hornets, and possibly as many as 1,000, the actual number depending upon the Joint Strike Fighter (JSF) program. The E/F achieved IOC in 2001 and the numbers in the fleet will increase rapidly from now on.

The ever-flexible Super Hornet may also take on another new role since it is being considered as a replacement for the Navy's EA-6B Prowler. Under a plan currently under consideration the Navy would buy a modified version of the F/A-18E/F for close-in jamming; designated the F/A-18G, it has already been nicknamed the "Growler."

The Hornet has been battle tested and has proved itself to a highly

reliable and versatile strike fighter. Its first combat duty was in the 1986 strikes against Libya when F/A-18As, flying from USS *Coral Sea* (CV 43), launched HARM missiles against Libyan air defense radars and missile sites, effectively silencing them during the attacks on Benghazi facilities. Then, during the Gulf War, squadrons of U.S. Navy and Marine and Canadian F/A-18s operated around the clock, setting new records for reliability, survivability and ton-miles of ordnance delivered. The the tone was set on the first day when two F/A-18s, each carrying four 2,000lb bombs, shot down two Iraqi MiGs and then proceeded with their original mission, which was to deliver their bombs on ground targets.

Below: Latest Hornet, the F/A-18F on final approach.

Boeing (McDonnell Douglas) F-15 Eagle/Strike Eagle

Type: tactical fighter.
Manufacturer: Boeing (McDonnell Douglas Corp).
Weight: empty 28,600lb (12,793kg); normal takeoff 44,630lb (20,244kg); maximum takeoff 58,470lb (26,521kg).
Dimensions: length 63.8ft (19.4 m); height 18.7ft (5.7m); wingspan 42.8ft (13.1m).
Powerplant: two Pratt & Whitney F100-PW-220 turbofan engines with afterburners, each rated at 14,670lb static thrust (65.26kN) dry, 23,830lb (106.0kN) with afterburner.
Performance: maximum level speed, clean, at 36,000ft (10,975m) <1,433kt (1,650mph/2,655km/h); ceiling 65,000ft (19,697m); range 3,450 miles (3,000nm).
Armament: one M-61A1 20mm multi-barrel internal gun, plus four AIM-9L/M Sidewinder and four AIM-7F/M Sparrow missiles, or combination of AIM-9L/M, AIM-7F/M and AIM-120 missiles.
Crew: one.
Specifications for F-15C

The F-15 Eagle is the U.S. Air Force's current all-weather, air superiority fighter and is designed to achieve its mission through a combination of maneuverability, acceleration, and long range, coupled with superior weapons and avionics. The design originated in the mid-1960s when the Air Force undertook a study into the requirements which would have to be met by a new, dedicated air superiority fighter, with particular emphasis on the lessons to be derived from the air campaigns in the various Middle Eastern wars and in Vietnam. Known as the Fighter Experimental (FX) project, this study led to a formal requirement for an aircraft which would combine unparalleled

maneuverability with state-of-the-art avionics and weaponry, and various companies submitted bids, the winner being McDonnell Douglas with its F-15 design. The prototype made its first flight in July 1972 and, after an unusually trouble-free flight development program, the first production F-15A aircraft was delivered in January 1976. Total production of the F-15A was 365 aircraft, before production switched to the F-15C.

The F-15B (originally designated TF-15A) first flew in July 1973 and the first production aircraft was delivered in November 1974. This two-seater version of the F-15A was primarily intended for conversion training, but retained all the combat and weapon-carrying capability of the single-seater. The pilot under instruction sat in the front cockpit, where he had a full set of instruments, and flight and weapons controls, while the instructor sat in the rear cockpit, where most the controls and instruments were duplicated. The exceptions were the weapons-related controls, which were available only to the front-seater.

Next in the line were the single-seat F-15C and the parallel two-seat F-15D, which started to enter the Air Force inventory in 1979. There were minimal external differences between the F-15A and F-15C, but internally the later aircraft had the Production Eagle Package 2000 (PEP 2000) improvements, including capacity for an additional 2,000lb (900kg) of additional internal fuel, provision for carrying exterior conformal fuel tanks, and increased maximum takeoff weight of 68,000lb (30,600kg).

Although conceived solely as an air superiority fighter, it was realized from the start that the F-15 had potential as a ground attack aircraft and this led in 1987 to the appearance of the F-15E Strike Eagle, specially configured for the

Below: F-15E clearly shows its conformal fuel tanks snug against the fuselage.

deep strike mission, which required it to penetrate far into enemy territory to attack high value targets. A two-seater, Strike Eagle had a Weapon Systems Operator (WSO) in the rear cockpit and incorporated an entirely new air-to-ground avionics suite. The F-15E's missions include strategic strike and interdiction, although it can also perform close air support and escort missions. It is equipped with two LANTIRN pods, with an AAQ-13 navigation pod on the starboard intake and the AAQ-14 targeting pod to port; these considerably enhance the aircraft's night delivery capability for precision-guided munitions. The F-15E structure is rated at 16,000 flight hours, double the lifetime of earlier F-15s.

Conformal Fuel Tanks (CFT) were introduced with the F-15C to extend the

aircraft's range. They are carried in pairs, one under each wing, and, as their name implies, fit closely to the side of the aircraft. The shape of the CFT minimizes drag and enables more warlike stores to be carried on the hardpoints which would otherwise carry fuel pods, but, unlike such pods they cannot be jettisoned in combat. In general, fitting CFTs is the norm on F-15Es and the exception for F-15C/Ds.

One of the problems with the earlier F-15s still in service is that their avionics, fire-control, and data-handling systems were designed and built some

Below: F-15Es of USAF 19th Fighter Squadron, 3rd Fighter Wing.

twenty-thirty years ago, which in electronics terms is a bygone age. Thus, not only is the equipment less capable than is obtainable today, but many of the components are now virtually unobtainable. Thus, there is an on-going multistage improvement program to ensure that the F-15 will remain fully capable in any future campaign.

The F-15 air superiority versions can be armed with combinations of four different air-to-air weapons: AIM-7F/M Sparrow missiles or AIM-120 Advanced Medium Range Air-to-Air Missiles (AMRAAM) on its lower fuselage corners, and AIM-9L/M Sidewinder or AIM-120 missiles on two pylons under the wings. There is also an internal 20mm Gatling gun in the starboard wing root. The F-15E can carry up to 24,250lb (11,000kg) of tactical weapons, including free-fall

Above: F-15's nodding intakes maintain optimum rate of airflow to the engines.

and guided bombs and Maverick and HARM missiles. As built, it could also carry various types of nuclear bomb, but these have all been withdrawn.

F-15Cs, Ds and Es were deployed to the Persian Gulf in 1991 in support of Operation Desert Storm where they proved their superior combat capability with a confirmed 26:0 kill ratio. The position on the F-15 fleet in 2002 is that all remaining F-15As have been transferred to the Air National Guard. and there are some 300 F-15Cs remaining assigned to operational units. The present F-15E force level is 132 which will be sustained until about FY 2016, when the numbers will start to be reduced as they are replaced .

Boeing Sikorsky RAH-66 Comanche

Type: reconnaissance/attack and air combat helicopter.
Manufacturer: Boeing Sikorsky.
Weight: empty 8,951lb (4,060kg); takeoff (primary mission) 11,632lb (5,276kg).
Dimensions: length (fuselage) 43.3ft (13.2m), rotor turning 46.8ft (14.3m); width (overall) 11.0ft (3.4m); rotor diameter 40.0ft (12.2m).
Powerplant: two LHTEC T800-LHT-801 turboshafts, each 1,563shp (1,165kW); 5-blade main rotor; "fan-in-fin" tail rotor.
Performance: maximum airspeed 177kt (204mph/328km/h); cruising 161kt (185mph/298kmh); tactical radius (internal fuel) 150nm (173 miles/278km); self-deployment (internal fuel) 1,260nm (1,450 miles/2,332km).
Armament: maximum weapon load 3 Hellfire or 6 Stinger missiles or other weapons in each of two weapons bays, plus 4 Hellfires or 8 Stingers on optional stub-wings; 1 x XM-301 three-barrel 20mm cannon in undernose turret
Crew: two (pilot/commander; gunner/co-pilot).

The RAH-66 Comanche is similar in size to the AH-64 Apache with which it will work in corps and heavy divisional helicopter battalions, while it will replace the AH-1 and OH-58 in light divisional attack helicopter battalions and air cavalry troops. The first prototype was rolled out in May 1995 and made its initial flight in January 1996; the second prototype's first flight was in March 1999 and these are being followed by six pre-production aircraft, which are scheduled to undertake lengthy and comprehensive troop trials. The aircraft's primary role is to detect and designate targets for the AH-64 Apache attack helicopter at night, in adverse weather, and in battlefield obscurants, and to achieve this the RAH-66 will be equipped with a night-vision flying system, helmet-mounted displays,

Below: RAH-66 is under development; IOC is scheduled for 2006.

Above: RAH-66 is the world's first helicopter designed to be stealthy.

electro-optical target acquisition and designation systems and a fully integrated communications, navigation and avionics system.

The Comanche is the first combat helicopter designed to incorporate stealth technology. To achieve the targets set by the Army, the fuselage has a faceted configuration, and on most missions all armament will be carried internally. According to official statements, the frontal radar cross-section (RCS) is 360 times smaller than that of the AH-64, 250 times smaller than that of the OH-58D, and 32 times smaller than OH-58D with mast-mounted sight. In fact, the RCS of the entire helicopter is less than that of the AGM-114 Hellfire missile it fires. Detachable stub wings can be fitted to carry weapons or auxiliary fuel tanks, but such additions will inevitably degrade the RCS. The targeting system includes a second generation forward-looking infrared (FLIR) sensor, low-light-level television (LLTV), laser rangefinder/designator, and the Apache Longbow millimeter-wave radar system. Like all modern attack helicopters, the RAH-66 has features intended to degrade the effectiveness of infrared-guided missiles; in particular, the efflux from the aircraft's twin T800 engines is ducted through long, thin slots, then ejected beneath the chine running each side of the tail. As a result, total IR emissions are approximately 25 percent that of the AH-64D, thus enabling the aircraft to enter service without a built-in IR jammer, although provision is made for the Advanced Threat Infrared Countermeasures (ATIC) system to be fitted later, as an upgrade, if required.

The acoustic signature has been reduced by fitting a five-bladed, all-composite main rotor system, with noise-reducing anhedral tips. In addition, the eight-bladed tail rotor is of shrouded "fan-in-fin" type. When approaching head-on, the RAH-66 is six times quieter than the AH-64.

Great attention has been given to survivability. The cockpit is fitted with side armor, and an optional armor kit is available for the cockpit floor, while the crew seats are designed to cope with the stresses of a 38ft/sec (11.6m/sec) vertical crash landing. The nav/attack system consists of a nose-mounted sight with IR and TV channels, plus a laser range-finder/designator, and all aircraft are fitted to carry an enhanced version of the Longbow millimetric-wave radar carried by the AH-64D Longbow Apache, although only a third of the fleet will actually be equipped with this sensor. Defensive aids include radar and laser warning receivers, plus an RF jammer.

The upper part of the tail folds down for air transportation and once this has been done and the main rotor removed, eight Comanches can be loaded into a single C-5 Galaxy. On arrival and removal from the C-5, the main rotor can be re-installed, the tail unfolded, and the helicopter ready for flight in just twenty minutes.

The armament subsystems consist of the XM-301 20mm cannon, and up to 14 Hellfire anti-tank missiles, 28 Air-to-Air Stinger (ATAS) anti-aircraft missiles, or 56 2.75-inch Hydra 70 air-to-ground rockets carried internally and externally. Up to four Hellfire and two ATAS missiles can be stowed in fully retractable weapons bays, and the gun can be rotated to a stowed position when not in use. This design feature reduces both drag and radar signature. The XM-301 cannon is a new three-barrel 20mm weapon, each barrel being 5.3ft (1.6m) long and coverage, relative to dead ahead, is +15deg to -45deg in

elevation and ± 120deg in azimuth, with positive stops to ensure safe clearances of the fuselage and rotor disc. This gun system is driven by an electric motor and gearbox, which accelerate the gun to its firing rates of 750 or 1,500 rounds per minute within 0.25 seconds.

The U.S. Army plans to buy 1,096 Comanches. Before production is begun, the programme will undergo several reviews to assess aircraft weight, in-flight vibration levels, and progress with integrating the aircraft's radar and other mission equipment. Initial operational capability is expected in December 2006.

Below: No fewer than eight RAH-66 can be transported in one C-5A Galaxy.

Lockheed AC-130H/U Gunship

Type: close air support, air interdiction and force protection aircraft.
Manufacturer: Lockheed/Boeing Corporation.
Weight: empty 72,792lb (33,063kg); maximum takeoff 155,000lb (69,750kg).
Dimensions: length 97.8ft (29.8m); height 38.5ft (11.7m); wingspan 132.6ft (40.4m).
Powerplant: four Roll-Royce Allison T56-A-15 turboprops; each 4,910 shaft horsepower.
Performance: maximum speed (sea-level) 300mph (Mach 0.4), (at 20,000ft/6,100m) 325kt (374mph/602kmh); ceiling with 100,000lb (45,360kg) payload 33,000ft (10,060m); range with internal fuel approximately 1,300nm

(1,500 miles/2,410km).
Armament: 40mm cannon and 105mm cannon (AC-130U, 25mm gun).
Crew: thirteen (five flight crew (pilot, co-pilot, navigator, flight engineer, loadmaster), eight mission crew (fire control officer, electronic warfare officer, TV operator, infrared detection set operator, four aerial gunners).
Specifications for AC-130U.

Among the AC-130 gunship's primary missions are close air support of troops in contact with the enemy, convoy escort, and urban operations. Among its other missions are air interdiction, against either preplanned targets or targets

Left: AC-130 gunship deploys flares to decoy heat-seeking missiles.

of opportunity It can also be used in force protection operations, such as the defense of air bases and other operationally important facilities.

The first operational gunship was the AC-47, an armed version of the legendary C-47 twin-engined transport, which was brought into service early in the Vietnam War. This proved so effective that an armed version of the four-engined C-130A Hercules transport was developed; designated the AC-130A, it was popularly known by its radio callsign of "Spectre." During the Vietnam War AC-130 gunships were credited with many life-saving close air support missions and also destroyed more than 10,000 enemy trucks. The next conflict in which AC-130s took part was Operation Urgent Fury in Grenada in 1983, where they suppressed enemy air defense systems and attacked ground forces, making a significant contribution to the success of the assault on Point Salines Airfield. Next, AC-130s played a vital part in Operation Just Cause in Panama in 1989 when they destroyed Panamanian Defense Force Headquarters and numerous command and control facilities. During Operation Desert Storm, AC-130s provided close air support and air base defense for ground forces, and they were used again during operations in Somalia, providing close air support for United Nations ground forces. Later, gunships played a pivotal role in supporting the NATO mission in Bosnia-Herzegovina by conducting air interdiction missions against key targets in the Sarajevo area, and most recently they have taken part in U.S. operations in Afghanistan.

The AC-130 gunship is a basic C-130 modified with side-mounted guns and various sensors that make it highly adaptable to a variety of special missions. These weapons are integrated with sophisticated sensor, navigation, and fire control systems to provide either surgically accurate firepower or area saturation during extended loiter periods, both by day and night, and in adverse weather. The sensor suite, consisting of a television sensor, infrared sensor, and radar enable the gunship to identify friendly ground forces and targets at any place and under any conditions, either visually or electronically.

The AC-l30 operates best during cover of darkness, since its low altitude and relatively slow speed make it vulnerable to ground fire during daylight. If daylight operations are essential the threat to the AC-130 can be reduced by flying above an overcast, although the AC-130U must then rely on the radar as its only sensor. Mission execution and desired objectives are seriously degraded by radar-guided anti-aircraft artillery, surface-to-air missiles, and some IR-homing MANPAD (man-portable air defense) systems. If radar threats are known or suspected, preemptive jamming or SEAD (suppression of enemy air defenses) is required. SEAD is preferable.

The original AC-130A was armed with two belt-fed Mk 61 20mm Vulcan cannon in the forward cabin, and two MXU-740 7.62 Miniguns, also belt-fed, above the undercarriage fairing. Then, further aft was a pair of clip-fed 40mm Bofors. Sixteen were converted to this role.

The -A model was followed by eleven

AC-130Es which had the same armament as the -A, but with increased armor protection, improved avionics and greater ammunition stowage. One of these was lost, but the ten survivors were upgraded to AC-130H with more powerful engines and some at least were also given a 105mm howitzer. One of the -Hs was lost in the Gulf War and another over Somalia in 1994.

Thirteen AC-130Us were delivered for full operational capability with the Air Force's 16th Special Operations Squadron in FY 2001, but further work is already in hand to improve the flight decks, and to develop more effective ammunition that will enable the aircraft to fire from beyond the range of antiaircraft weapons. The AC-130U is armed with a single L/60 40mm Bofors, a single M102 105mm howitzer, and a single 25mm GAU-12 25mm cannon on a trainable mount. This is a lighter armament than in previous versions, but greatly improved sensors and more effective fire control systems ensure that the amount of firepower delivered and its accuracy are both greater. The AC-130U employs synthetic apertures strike radar for long-range target detection and identification. The gunship's navigational devices include the inertial navigation systems and global positioning system. The AC-130U employs the latest technologies and can attack two targets simultaneously. It also has twice the munitions capacity of the AC-130H. The gunship weapons do not have a hard-kill capability against heavy armor or bunkers. However, the 105mm has Superquick fuzes with both point detonation and 0.05sec delay, concrete penetrators, and proximity fuzes for airburst. All 20mm, 25mm, and 40mm ammunition has impact detonation fuzes. When the AC-130Us are fully operational the surviving AC-130Hs will be transferred to Air Force Reserve units, and the remaining AC-130As will be retired.

Below: AC-130U Spooky II of the USAF's Special Operations Command.

Lockheed Martin (General Dynamics) F-16 Fighting Falcon

Type: single-seat, single-engined supersonic jet air superiority and multi-role fighter.
Manufacturer: Lockheed Martin Corp (General Dynamics).
Weight: empty 19,020lb (8,627kg); normal takeoff 28,500lb (12,928kg); maximum 42,300lb (19,187kg).
Dimensions: length 49.3ft (15.0m); height: 16.9ft (5.1m); wingspan 32.7ft (9.8m); wing area 300sq.ft (27.88m^2).
Powerplant: one General Electric F110-GE-100 two-spool afterburning turbofan rated at 28,982lb (13,146kg) maximum and 17,260lb (7,829kg) military thrust.
Performance: maximum speed 1,500 mph (Mach 2) at altitude, Mach 1.2 at sea level; initial climb rate 50,000ft/min (254m/sec); ceiling above 50,000 feet (15,250m); sustained ceiling 61,500ft (18,745m); operational radius 490 miles (788km) with four AAMs and one external fuel tank; ferry range more than 2,000 miles (1,740nm).
Armament: one M-61A1 20mm six-barrel cannon with 511 rounds; external stations can carry up to six AIM-9 Sidewinders, AIM 120 Amraam, R550 Magic 2, MICA, or Python 3 AAMs, or in combination.
Crew: one.

The F-16 is a compact and highly maneuverable multi-role fighter aircraft, which has proved its worth in both air-to-air combat and air-to-surface attack in numerous campaigns. Officially named the Fighting Falcon, in U.S. service it is better known to its flight and ground crews as either the Electric Jet, or, more usually, the Viper. In its air combat role, the F-16's maneuverability and combat radius exceed those of all potential threat fighter aircraft, it can locate targets in

Below: F-16 with LANTIRN pods, Mavericks, and wingtip Sidewinders.

Above: Among the many payloads carried by the F-16 are "iron" bombs.

all weather conditions and it can detect low-flying aircraft in radar ground clutter. In its air-to-surface role, the F-16 can fly more than 500nm (860km), deliver its weapons with great accuracy, even during non-visual bombing conditions, defend itself against attack by enemy aircraft, and then return to its base.

The cockpit and its bubble canopy give the pilot unobstructed forward and upward vision, and outstanding views over the side and to the rear. The seat is angled at 30 degrees, giving the pilot much greater comfort and gravity force tolerance than in the traditional 13 degree seat, and he has excellent control of the aircraft through its "fly-by-wire" system, in which he uses a side stick controller to send commands down electrical wires, rather than the conventional center-mounted stick and a system of cables and mechanical linkages.

The aircraft has a comprehensive avionics outfit, including a highly accurate inertial navigation system, UHF and VHF radios, and an instrument landing system. It also has a warning system and modular countermeasure pods to be used against airborne or surface electronic threats. The fuselage has space for additional avionics systems.

The F-16's origins lie in the Cold War situation in Europe in the 1960s, where had war broken out, NATO tactical air forces would have been heavily outnumbered by great numbers of less well-equipped Warsaw Pact fighters. Numerical parity was not possible, so the United States initially decided to use technical superiority to defeat superior numbers, ie, to counter quantity by quality. But far away from NATO, U.S. aircraft were in combat over North Vietnam, where the sophisticated F-4 Phantom II was having a hard time against the much more basic MiG-17 and MiG-21, and this caused a fundamental rethink, leading to the concept of the "hi-lo" mix, in which a limited number of very capable and expensive fighters would be backed by large numbers of austere, affordable aircraft optimized for close combat. The hi-tech part of the mix was already underway, in the form of the very advanced F-15

Eagle, so USAF launched the Light Weight Fighter (LWF) competition to meet the lo-tech requirement, setting only a few performance minima and military requirements in order to give the design teams maximum freedom for radical solutions. Five companies responded and in April 1972 General Dynamics and Northrop were each given orders for two proof-of-concept machines.

The fly-off against the Northrop YF-17 took place in late 1974, with the General Dynamics YF-16 being declared the winner in January 1975, but even at that early stage customers were asking for more capability. As a result, a Westinghouse APG-66 multi-mode radar was added, as well as carrying capacity for air-to-surface weapons, while wing and tail area were increased, and the fin made taller and the fuselage longer. Not surprisingly, the weight increased by nearly 2,000lb (907kg), and this became a continuing trend. By the 1980s what had started as a lightweight fighter had become a multi-role middleweight.

The first major variant to enter service was the F-16C, with the advanced APG-68 multi-mode radar, and improved avionics and displays. To counteract weight growth, later aircraft were powered by either the F100-P-229 or F110-GE-100 engines. Then, from Block 40 onwards, the analog fly-by- wire system was replaced by a digital system, while from Block 60 (the most recent build standard) onwards, conformal fuel tanks were fitted along the fuselage above the wings to restore the range, although this did little to improve wing loading.

The F-16B is the two-seater version of the F-16A, with tandem cockpits,

each about the same size as that in the A model, with room for the second cockpit being created by reducing the size of the forward fuselage fuel tank and avionics growth space. On training missions, the student pilot occupies the forward cockpit with the instructor pilot in the rear. Similarly, the F-16D is the two-seater version of the F-16C.

Many F-16 variants have emerged, a number of which never got beyond the prototype, sometimes even the project, stage. Among these were the F-16/79, an austere export-version powered by the General Electric J79, and the F-16ADF, an air defense fighter version modified to carry AIM-7 Sparrow AAMs. A tail-less cranked delta configuration was adopted for the F-16XL and F-16F, but neither entered service, while the "big-wing" Agile Falcon was designed in the late 1980s to offset the creeping weight growth, but this, too, was canceled.

USAF F-16 multi-mission fighters were deployed to the Persian Gulf in 1991 in support of Operation Desert Storm, where more sorties were flown than with any other aircraft. These fighters were used to attack airfields, military production facilities, Scud missile sites, and a variety of other targets. In the spring of 1999, during Operation Allied Force in the Balkans F-16s flew a variety of missions including suppression of enemy air defense, offensive counter air, defensive counter air, close air support, and forward air controller. Mission

Below: F-16 with Raytheon AIM-120 AMRAAM missile under port wing.

results were outstanding as these fighters destroyed radar sites, vehicles, tanks, MiGs, and buildings. Although the F-16 now operates mainly as a bomb truck, it has not failed to make its mark in its designed function, air combat. The first air-to-air victory was by an Israeli pilot, who downed a Syrian Mi-8

Above: Following 11 September, F-16 patrols skies above New York City.

helicopter on 28 April 1981; since then Israeli F-16s have claimed a total of 44 air combat victories.

Lockheed Martin F-117A Nighthawk

Type: single-seat, single-engined strike fighter.
Manufacturer: Lockheed Martin Corp.
Weight: empty approximately 30,000lb (13,610kg); maximum takeoff 52,500lb (23,800kg)
Dimensions: length 65.9ft (20.1m); wingspan 43.3ft (13.2m); height 12.5ft (3.81m); wing area 913sq.ft (84.82m^2).
Powerplant: two General Electric F404-GE-F1D2 turbofans (non-afterburning), each approximately 10,800lb static thrust (48.0kN).
Performance: maximum level speed, high altitude, clean condition <Mach 1.0; maximum speed at optimum operating altitude approximately Mach 0.9; combat radius with maximum ordnance approximately 600nm (690 miles/1,110km).
Armament: approximately 5,000lb (2,270kg) of stores carried internally.
Crew: one.

In the early 1970s there was a growing perception of the need to develop "stealth" techniques to overcome detection of aircraft by radar and infra-red sensors, as a result of which DARPA began work on possible fighter and bomber designs. Despite its triumphs with the U-2 and SR-71 programs, Lockheed's famous "Skunk Works" was left out of these activities, but hearing of them on "the grapevine" it submitted its own proposal, which was so promising that it led to a contract to build and test two technology demonstrators in a program known as " HAVE BLUE" which took place in 1977-78.The main competition came from a Northrop design which had some similarities – for example, by using flat-faceted planes to deflect radar

Below: F-117A about to take off into its natural environment – the night sky.

Above: A mission completed, an F-117A is slowed by its braking parachute.

waves – but there were also some major differences, with the Northrop design having its twin tails canted inwards and the single air intake positioned on the top of the aircraft. The Lockheed entry proved so successful that it led directly to the development of the F-117A Nighthawk, thus defeating the Northrop entry, and in 1978 President Carter authorized development of a production stealth fighter under the codename "Senior Trend."

The F-117A design keeps RCS to a minimum by extensive use of

faceting, in which flat panels and straight lines dominate the aircraft's configuration rather than the traditional curves. These faceted panels are coated with radar-absorbent materials and mounted on a skeletal sub-frame. The highly swept wing is of two-spar construction, and has a faceted airfoil. The original ruddervators caused flutter problems, which resulted in a speed restriction being imposed on the aircraft, but these have been replaced by a modified design made from thermoplastic graphite composites, which give the additional strength needed. The cockpit canopy and most access panels have serrated edges to suppress radar reflection. The engines are fed by rectangular air intakes covered by screens with slots measuring 1.0in (2.5cm) long by 0.6in (1.5cm) wide, which prevent radar energy from entering the intake. To reduce the infrared signature, part of the incoming air bypasses the engine and is then mixed with the engine efflux to lower its temperature, before being ejected through narrow-slot exhausts in the rear fuselage. These are 5.4ft (1.7m) long but only 4in (10cm) deep and have 11 vertical guide vanes. All ordnance is carried in an internal weapon bay 15.3ft (4.7m) long and 5.8ft (1.8m) wide and covered by two large doors hinged on the centerline; but after it was found that when lowered, these doors greatly increased the RCS, changes have been made to minimize the length of time for which they are opened for weapon-release.

Nothing is ever gained without cost and the faceted airframe and the arrow-shaped wing planform render the aircraft virtually unflyable so it has a computer-aided quadruplex fly-by-wire control system. A Texas Instruments Forward-Looking Infra-Red (FLIR) sensor with dual fields of view is mounted in a cavity just below the front of the canopy, while a Downward-Looking Infra-Red (DLIR) and laser designator is mounted in another cavity beneath the forward fuselage to starboard of the nosewheel bay. Both cavities are covered by fine mesh screen to prevent the entry of radar energy.

The designation "stealth *fighter*" is something of a misnomer; since the F-117A is essentially a strike aircraft designed to fly close to a target at subsonic speed, launch a guided missile or "smart" bomb, and then turn away for its return to base; it would no match for a traditional fighter in terms of speed or agility. To avoid such confrontations, it normally operates at night, when conditions make it virtually undetectable. In terms of radar penetration, the F-117A has met its specifications, but at the price of restricted speed and maneuverability, shortcomings that its successors, such as the F-22 Raptor and the Joint Strike Fighter (JSF), are intended to overcome.

Although several developed versions have been proposed, none resulted in an order. F-117A+ was a development of the basic F-117A which would have taken advantage of more recent technologies to produce an aircraft with improved survivability in the face of high-threat environments, while the A/F- 117X (originally known as the F-117N Seahawk) was a proposed long-range naval strike/attack aircraft based on the F-117A. If the

Below: Aft view of F-117 shows the thermoplastic graphite ruddervators

Above: Engine intakes are covered by mesh screens, preventing radar "entry."

A/F-117X had become a firm programme, the Skunk Works planned to offer a land-based F-117B which would have used the redesigned wing and horizontal tail surfaces of the naval variant, and been fitted with GE-F414 afterburning turbofan engines, and all- weather sensors. Three less drastic upgrade schemes have kept the F-117A combat-effective, the first being the replacement of the original Delco M362F computers by IBM AP-102 units in the Weapon System Computational Subsystem (WSCS); the first modified aircraft flew in October 1986 and the entire fleet had been updated by 1 January 1992. Next came the Offensive Capability Improvement Program (OCIP) which added an improved flight-management system, a digital moving map, digital situation displays, new cockpit instrumentation with Honeywell color multi-function displays, a digital auto throttle, and a pilot-activated recovery system. The first upgraded aircraft was delivered in November 1990 and the last in March 1995. The most recent modification scheme replaces the FLIR and DLIR sensors with a new turret-mounted Infra-Red Acquisition and Designation Sensor (IRADS), while another modification adds a ring-laser gyro inertial navigation system and a Global Positioning System (GPS) satellite navigation receiver. There is no two-seat trainer version and pilots have to rely on a sophisticated ground trainer for initial and continuation training.

The F-117A's first action was a low-key affair with two aircraft attacking a Panamanian Army barracks during the 1989 invasion. In Desert Storm, however, a total of forty-two F-117As took part, flying from a base in Saudi Arabia, from where they regularly attacked targets in and around Baghdad and then elsewhere in Iraq, ultimately flying a total of 1,271 missions. In 1999 twenty-four F-117As deployed to Italy in support of Operation Allied Force. Little information was released about their operations in that theater, but one F-117A was shot down, with some reports suggesting it was victim of a SAM strike, and others that it was a fluke hit by conventional anti-aircraft artillery.

All F-117As are concentrated in Air Combat Command's 49th Fighter Wing (formerly the 4450th Tactical Group) which is located at Holloman Air Force Base, N.M. It has been operational with the F-117A since October 1983 and currently has fifty-four aircraft on strength.

Above: Everything about the F-117 is intended to deceive the enemy.

Lockheed Martin F-22A Raptor

Type: single-seat, twin-engined Mach 2+ air-superiority fighter
Manufacturer: Lockheed Martin.
Weight: empty 31,670lb (14,365kg); maximum takeoff approx .60,000lb (27,200kg).
Dimensions: length 62.1ft (18.9m); height 16.7ft (5.08m); wing span 44.5ft (13.6m); wing area 840sq.ft (78.04m^2).
Powerplant: two Pratt & Whitney F119-PW-100 turbofans each of 35,000lb (155.7kN) class, with pitch-vectoring nozzles.
Performance: maximum. speed, altitude <Mach 2, sea-level Mach 1.2; ceiling <50,000ft (15,250m); range 1,735nm (2,000 milkes/3,210km).
Armament: one 20mm M61A-2 six-barrel rotary cannon with 460 rounds. Air-to-air role, six AIM-120C Advanced Medium-Range Air-to-Air Missiles (AMRAAM), plus two AIM-9 Sidewinders. Air-to-ground role, two 1,000-pound Joint Direct Attack Munitions (JDAM), two AIM-120C AMRAAM and two AIM-9T Sidewinders. Maximum weapon load 3,914lb (1,775kg).
Crew: one.

In the early 1980s USAF began concept studies to replace the F-15, which by then had been in service for almost a decade. At the time, the Soviet Union, which posed the major threat to Western security, was known to be developing a new generation of very agile and highly effective fighters, a threat which became reality with the appearance of the Mig-29 Fulcrum and Su-27 Flanker. The requirements for the new USAF fighter were clear: it had to operate deep into hostile airspace and outfly and outfight the opposition; in addition, it had to be easily maintainable, operate from damaged or austere bases, and (with the lessons of the F-14 and F-15 still fresh in the minds of Congressmen planners, and operators) be affordable. These requirements were translated into priorities for what became known as the Advanced Tactical Fighter (ATF) program and which can be summarized as stealth, speed, and agility for the mission, hi-tech

Below: F-22 launches AMRAAM missile, closely watched by an F-15 crew.

Above: Missiles are carried internally to reduce radar cross-section (RCS).

for maintenance, and a maximum weight limit of 50,000lb (22,680kg) for affordability.

Inevitably, there had to be trade-offs where stealth was concerned, since there could be no compromise on the traditional fighter virtues of speed, agility, acceleration, and rate-of-climb. Stealth could however be used to complement them, since in air combat, the priorities are to be the first to detect the enemy and the first to shoot, and a high level of stealth would enable the ATF to do both of these. Stealth would also foil hostile early warning systems and, even when detected, degrade the ability of surface-to-air weapons to engage successfully. Stealth would also reduce the need for electronic countermeasures, thus reducing the inevitable emissions which betray the position of the transmitting aircraft.

Speed was essential, since it reduces the reaction time of the defenses, makes tracking more difficult, allows rapid closure on a target, and, should it prove necessary, also permits rapid disengagement. Studies showed that Mach 1.4 was about the minimum required, but the problem was that speeds appreciably above Mach 1 required afterburning engines, which emit a huge and "unstealthy" infrared signature and also consume fuel at a prodigious rate. The answer was found in "supercruise," in which the aircraft is so designed that it can exceed Mach 1 by a significant margin using only military thrust. This also has the advantage of much greater fuel economy, thus greatly extending the operational radius using internal fuel.

The stealth requirement impinged on almost every aspect of the ATF's design. For example, the requirement stated that a minimum of eight AAMs were needed, all of them to be carried internally. The answer was for six AMRAAM to be mounted ventrally, being pneumatically expelled on launch, while the two Sidewinders were installed in side bays and swung out on trapezes for launch. All these combined to result in a big aircraft, but where stealth is concerned size is rather less important than shaping and a very precise external finish; and all of the new fighter's surfaces were carefully angled to deflect the reflections of incoming radar impulses away from the emitter.

The first of two YF-22s, powered by General Electric engines, flew on 29 September 1990, followed by the second, powered by Pratt & Whitney engines, on 30 October 1990. There then followed a fly-off against the rival Northrop YF-23, which also flew with the two competing engines, the outcome being that Lockheed Martin was awarded the Engineering/Manufacturing/ Development (EMD) contract for the F-22A in August 1991, while Pratt & Whitney won the engine contract. Several changes were made to the original design, notably the reduction of leading edge sweep from 48 to 42 degrees, and in yet further reductions in the radar cross-section. By now officially named Raptor, the first EMD aircraft flew in September 1997.

The production F-22A has a rhomboidal planform wing with 42-degree sweepback on the leading edge, and 17-degree forward sweep on the trailing edge. The leading edge is slatted, while on the trailing edge there are ailerons outboard and flaperons inboard. The angles of the all-moving tailerons are matched to those of the wing, which reduces the RCS, while the large twin fins and rudders are outward-canted, and have a secondary function as airbrakes. The engine inlets are trapezoidal in shape, and raked to match the wing leading edge and canted outwards at the same angle as the fins. Internally, the ducts are serpentine and lined with radar-absorbent material, thus preventing hostile radar emissions from reaching the compressor face and being reflected. The exhaust nozzles are two-dimensional convergent-divergent design and incorporate pitch-only vectoring (±20 degrees) to improve field performance in

taking-off and landing, and for increasing the pitch/turn rate in aerial combat.

External stores inevitably compromise the stealth characteristics and will be carried in two circumstances. First, for ferry flights where maximum point-to-point range is required, the aircraft will carry four 600-gallon fuel tanks and no external weapons. For combat air patrol (CAP) missions where air superiority has already been established the aircraft will carry two 600-gallon fuel tanks on the inboard pylons and four missiles, two on each of the outboard pylons.

The avionics suite of the F-22 is highly integrated, allowing the pilot to concentrate on the mission, rather than on managing the sensors as in current fighters. The AN/APG-77 radar, EW suite, and communications/identification are managed by single system that presents only relevant data to the pilot, and controls the level of electromagnetic emission (such as radar and radio transmissions) according to the tactical situation.

Final assembly of the F-22 is taking place at Lockheed Martin Aeronautical Systems in Marietta, Georgia. To test the "stealthiness" of each F-22 when it comes off the assembly line, the company has built a 50,000sq.ft radar cross-section verification building. USAF plans to procure 339 production F-22s, and production is scheduled to run until 2013, but this could be extended by export orders. Test and training F-22s will be assigned to the Air Force Flight Test Center at Edwards AFB, California, the Air Force Fighter Weapons School at Nellis AFB, Nevada, and the 325th Fighter Wing at Tyndall AFB, Florida, but the operational locations for the F-22 force have not yet been announced.

Below: Every aspect of the F-22's design is intended to promote "stealth."

Lockheed Martin P-3C Orion

Type: land-based antisubmarine warfare/antisurface warfare/maritime surveillance aircraft.
Manufacturer: Lockheed Martin.
Weight: empty 61,491lb (27,890kg); normal takeoff 135,000lb (61,235kg); maximum takeoff 142,000lb (64,410kg).
Dimensions:length 116.6ft (35.6m); wingspan 99.5ft (30.4m); height 33.6ft (10.3m).
Powerplant: four Allison T-56-A-14 turboprop engines (each 4,900 shp).
Performance: maximum airspeed 411 knots (466mph/745kmh); cruise 328 knots (403mph/644kmh); ceiling 28,300ft (8,626m); maximum mission range 2,380nm (2,739 miles/4,408km); range for three hours on station at 1,500ft (457m) 1,346nm (1,550miles/2,494km); maximum endurance approximately 11 hours.
Armament: total 20,000lb (9,000kg), including: Harpoon (AGM-84D), SLAM (AGM-84E), Maverick (AGM- 65), Mk 46/50 torpedoes, rockets, mines, depth bombs, and special weapons.
Crew: Eleven.

The Lockheed Electra turboprop-engined civil airliner had a fairly undistinguished and short commercial career, but the airframe was selected as the basis for a successor to the piston-engined P-2V Neptune, then the U.S. Navy's standard land-based ASW and maritime patrol platform. Surprisingly, the new type, originally designated P-3V Orion, has been an outstanding success, entering service in July 1962 and still in front-line service forty years later. During that time its designation has changed from P-3V to P-3 and three major models have been produced – P-3A, P-3B, and P-3C – of which the latter is the only one now in active service in the ASW mission with the U.S. Navy, although there are numerous specialized sub-types. The last Navy P-3 came off the

Below: A USN P-3 accompanies Japanese P-3 over a U.S. Navy task group.

Above: The successful P-3 was developed from the mediocre Orion airliner.

production line at the Lockheed plant in April 1990, but many hundreds have also been built for export.

The P-3C has advanced submarine detection sensors such as Directional Frequency And Ranging (DIFAR) sonobuoys and Magnetic Anomaly Detection (MAD) equipment. The avionics system is integrated by a general purpose digital computer that supports all of the tactical displays and monitors, automatically launches ordnance, and provides flight information to the pilots. In addition, the system coordinates navigation information and accepts sensor data inputs for tactical display and storage. There are ten underwing hard points, three under each outer wing and two beneath the inboard engine and fuselage, plus a large bomb-bay. Some aircraft are equipped to launch AGM-84 Harpoon and all can carry underwing rocket pods, torpedoes and depth bombs, but the B57 nuclear depth charge, in common with all other tactical nuclear weapons, has been withdrawn from service.

All current P-3Cs have undergone the P-3C Update III program, which was introduced in 1986. This included the UYS-1 Proteus advanced acoustic signal processor, which dramatically increased the ability to find and identify submarines, and a more modern sonobuoy communications suite. Some new-build aircraft were delivered to this standard, while existing P-3Cs were progressively upgraded in a retrofit program. The most recent enhancement is the Anti-Surface Warfare Improvement Program [AIP] which was completed in FY2000. This involved improvements in command, control, communications, and intelligence (C3I) facilities; updated radar, infrared, and electro-optical sensors; Over-The-Horizon Targeting (OTH-T) capability; and enhanced survivability. These aircraft can also carry and launch the Maverick Missile System. A small number of active and reserve P-3C Update III aircraft are being given the Counter Drug Update Equipment (CDUE), which enables them to house a number of specialized equipments and sensors on an "as required" basis.

There have been several studies for P-3C successors. One 1980s study was for a virtually new aircraft, the P-3G (later P-7A Long Range Air ASW-Capable Aircraft), but this was canceled. Next was the P-3C Upgrade IV program, which was also canceled. In 1999 Lockheed Martin was awarded a $30million contract to conduct a Service Life Assessment Program (SLAP), whose aim is to identify the modifications required to keep the P-3 in service until at least 2015.

Lockheed Martin S-3B Viking

Type: carrier-based antisubmarine warfare/maritime surveillance/tanker aircraft.
Manufacturer: Lockheed Martin.
Weight: empty 26,650lb (12,090kg); normal takeoff 42,500lb (19,277kg); maximum gross takeoff: 52,539lb (23,643 kg).
Dimensions: length 53.3ft (16m); wingspan extended 68.7ft (20.6m); wingspan folded 29.5ft (9.0m); height overall 22.8ft (6.9m); height tail folded 15.3ft (4.7m).
Powerplant: two General Electric TF-34-GE-400B turbofan engines each 9,275lb4,207kg) static thrust (41.3kN).
Performance: maximum airspeed, clean, sea-level 450kt (518mph, 829km/h); cruising speed at optimum altitude 350kt (403mph/649kmh); ceiling 40,000ft (12,192m); range <2,300nm (2,645 miles/4,232km); maximum endurance 7.5 hours.
Armament: maximum 3,958lb (1,781kg) including AGM-84 Harpoon, AGM-65 Maverick, AGM-84 SLAM missiles, torpedoes, rockets, and bombs.
Crew: four

The S-3 Viking was developed in response to the U.S. Navy's mid-1960s VSX (carrier-based, fixed-wing, antisubmarine, experimental) requirement, with the first prototype (YS-3A) flying in January 1972 and the type entering squadron service in 1974. The S-3 was designed to meet the threat posed by increasingly quiet and ever deeper running Soviet submarines, which it did exceptionally well, but with the end of the Cold War in the early 1990s it has had to adapt to new missions. The S-3B is an all-weather, carrier-based jet aircraft, its primary mission being to provide protection against threats posed to U.S. Navy Carrier Battle Groups by hostile surface or submarine combatants. It has, however,

Below: Among the duties of the ubiquitous S-3B is air-to-air refueling.

Above: Everything hangs down as an S-3B makes a final approach to a carrier.

proved to be an extremely versatile aircraft and can undertake a wide variety of other missions, including day/night surveillance, electronic countermeasures, command/control/communications warfare, search and rescue (SAR), and, when fitted with a "buddy/buddy" pack, it can also serve as an air-to-air refueler. In addition, although it was originally designed for over-sea operations, it has also shown itself to be capable of overland operations, including pinpoint bombing and tracking Scud launchers.

The S-3B is powered by two General Electric turbofans mounted in pods. It has hydraulically folding wings, but in this case the wings fold asymmetrically so that they lie alongside each other, thus reducing the overall volume occupied in the hangar. In addition, the top half of the tailfin folds to port. There is a four-person crew, comprising pilot, co-pilot/navigator, both seated on the flightdeck, and the Tactical Coordinator (known as "Tacco") and Sensor Operator ("Senso") seated behind them. All sit in McDonnell Douglas ejector seats and both Tacco and Senso have small windows enabling them to see the outside world.

The S-3B Viking has two internal weapons bays and two underwing hardpoints, immediately outboard of the engine pods. It can carry three types of missile: AGM-84 Harpoon antiship missile, AGM-65 Maverick IR missile, and AGM-84E SLAM (Stand-off Land Attack Missile). It also carries up to four Mk 46 or Mk 50 torpedoes and various types of bomb. When serving as a tanker, the aircraft carries a refueling pod under the port wing and a standard 300-gallon fuel tank under the starboard wing.

Other versions of the S-3 include the US-3A carrier on-board delivery (COD) aircraft (six in service), Outlaw Viking, which is equipped for Over-the-Horizon Targeting (OTH-T), and Grey Wolf, which has special electronic surveillance equipment for littoral operations such as tracking Scud launchers.

Lockheed Martin F-35 Joint Strike Fighter

Type: single-seat, single-engined supersonic multi-role fighter.
Manufacturer: Lockheed Martin.
Weights: empty 26,477lb (12,010kg); maximum takeoff 50,000lb (22,680kg).
Dimensions: span 35ft 1.25in (10.70m); length 50ft 10in (15.50m); height n/a; wing area 460sq.ft (42.70m^2).
Powerplant: one Pratt & Whitney F135 two-spool afterburning turbofan rated at 35,000lb (15,876kg) maximum; military thrust classified.
Performance: maximum speed Mach 1.7; supercruise Mach 1.4; rate of climb classified; service ceiling classified but probably about 50,000ft (15,239m); operational radius 620 miles (1,000km).
Armament: one 20mm M61A-2 cannon with 400 rounds or one 27mm Mauser BK 27 cannon; four AIM-120C AMRAAM or ASRAAM AAMs in internal bay.
Crew: one.

The Joint Strike Fighter project will produce a multi-role fighter, optimized for air-to-ground strike operations, but with a significant air-to-air capability, for service with the U.S. Air Force, U.S. Navy and U.S. Marine Corps, as well as such allies as choose to join the program, currently only the UK, although the Netherlands is also known to be very interested. There were two contestants, both of whom flew prototypes, Boeing with the YF-32, a vectored-thrust design, and Lockheed Martin with the YF-35, which

employs a lift-fan. After an intensely fought competition the issue was decided on 21 October 2000 when it was announced that the winner was the Lockheed Martin design, which is now under full development as the F-35. There will be four versions, but all will have the same fuselage, identical wing sweep, canopy, radar, and avionics, as well as a common engine, the Pratt & Whitney F119, a derivative of that being used in the USAF's F-22 Raptor.

The USAF currently plans to buy 1,763 F-35s, which will replace the F-16 and A-10 as a strike aircraft, and will serve alongside the F 22 Raptor. This Air Force version will not be required to have a hovering capability, nor will it operate from aircraft carriers, which means that it will not require the strengthened airframe and undercarriage associated with carrier operations. The result is that the USAF version will be the simplest of all currently planned versions, but the Air Force is adamant that the aircraft must offer a significant advance on the current highly capable and very popular F-16.

The U.S. Navy plans to operate 480 F-35s. This version will have leading edge flaps, a larger area wing, a stronger internal structure , an arrester hook, and an undercarriage which is not only stronger but also has a longer stroke, all of which are necessary for carrier landings. The Navy places great stress on the importance of survivability.

The U.S. Marine Corps also expects to purchase 480 F-35s in a version

Below: Full-size mock-up of the winner in the keenly fought JSF competition.

which will have a short takeoff/vertical landing capability (STOVL), plus full controllability in all axes while hovering, to replace the current AV-8B and F/A-18A/C/D. Unlike the USAF and Navy version, this will not have an internally mounted machine gun, but will have an external mounting so that a gun can be fitted, if required. The British Royal Navy and Royal Air Force are also part of the

Above: At least 3,000 F-35s will be built, including 150 for the UK.

JSF program and expect to purchase a total of approximately 150 to replace RN Sea Harrier F/A2s and RAF Harrier GR7/GR9s; the British version will be very close to that of the Marine Corps.

Northrop Grumman A-10 Thunderbolt II

Type: A-10, close air support; OA-10, airborne forward air control.
Manufacturer: Northrop Grumman (Fairchild Republic).
Weight: empty 21,541lb (9,771kg); maximum takeoff 51,000lb (22,950kg)
Dimensions: length 53.3ft (16.2m) ; height 14.7ft (4.4m); wingspan 57.5ft (17.4m).
Powerplant: two General Electric TF34-GE-100 turbofans, each 9,065lb (4,112kg/40.4kN) static thrust.
Performance: maximum airspeed clean 381kt (439mph/706kmh); ceiling 45,000ft (13,636m); combat radius 695nm (800 miles/1,290km); ferry range 2,131nm (2,454 miles/3,949km).
Armament: one 30mm GAU-8/A seven-barrel Gatling gun; plus maximum of 16,000lb (7,200kg) weapons on eight underwing and three under-fuselage hardpoints, including Mk 82 and Mk 84 series bombs, incendiary cluster bombs, combined effects munitions, mine dispensing munitions, AGM-65 Maverick missiles and laser-guided/electro-optically guided bombs, infrared countermeasure flares, electronic countermeasure chaff; jammer pods; 2.75-inch (7cm) rockets; illumination flares, and AIM-9 Sidewinder missiles.
Crew: one.

The A-10 Thunderbolt II is a simple and rugged twin-engine jet aircraft and the first Air Force aircraft specifically designed for the close air support of ground forces. The A-10 was originally conceived in the Vietnam War era as a counter-insurgency (COIN) aircraft which would bring rapid fire to bear on fleeting targets, while having a high degree of survivability against ground-based air defense weapons. The war ended before the A-10 could deploy to Southeast Asia, but development continued as a "tank-buster" for deployment in a war between NATO and the Warsaw Pact. The A-10 has excellent maneuverability at low air speeds and altitude, and can loiter near the forward battle area up to nearly two hours, operating comfortably under 1,000ft (303m) ceilings with 1.5 mile (2.4km) visibility. Its short takeoff and landing capability permits it to fly in and out of locations close to the front line. The pilot sits in a cockpit which is sited well clear of the wings and the large bubble canopy gives excellent all-around visibility; he also has night-vision goggles, enabling him to conduct missions during darkness.

The A-10 can survive hits from armor-piercing and high explosive projectiles of up to 23mm caliber, which was the standard front-line air defense caliber of the former Warsaw Pact. Many of the primary structural sections are duplicated, while the hydraulically operated flight controls are not only duplicated, but also have a manual back-up. Many parts of the aircraft are protected by titanium armor and the fuel cells are self-sealing with additional protection from internal and external foam.

Weapons delivery systems include a head-up display (HUD) showing airspeed, altitude, dive angle, navigation information and weapons aiming references; a Low Altitude

Safety and Targeting Enhancement system (LASTE) for computing impact point freefall ordnance delivery; and Pave Penny laser- tracking pods under the fuselage. The aircraft also have infrared and electronic countermeasures to handle surface-to-air-missile threats, as well as recently installed Global Positioning System.

For years the major overseas deployment of the A-10 was to England where the type, reinforced by more from reserve squadrons in CONUS, was committed to the battle on the Central Front in Europe. It was never tested in this role and a process of transferring the A-10 to forward air controller duties as the OA-10 had started when the Gulf War broke out. The UK-based aircraft were quickly despatched to the Gulf where they made an outstanding contribution, flying in precisely the role for which they had been designed, and destroying vast numbers of Iraqi tanks and other vehicles. The aircraft flew 8,100 sorties. Two A-10s, directed by an OA-10, destroyed twenty-three enemy tanks in one day. In 2002 there are 371 A-10 and OA-10s in service: 213 with active force squadrons, 56 with the Reserve, and 102 with the Air National Guard.

Below: A-10 carrying Maverick and Sidewinder missiles, and iron bombs.

Northrop Grumman F-14A/B/D Tomcat

Type: two-seat, twin-engined, bisonic all-weather, variable-sweep, carrier-based interceptor fighter.
Manufacturer: originally Grumman, now Northrop Grumman.
Weight: empty 41,780lb (18,951kg); normal takeoff 61,200lb (27,760kg); maximum 70,000lb (31,752kg).
Dimensions: length 61.9ft (18.9m); height 16.0ft (4.9m); wingspan, minimum sweep 64.1ft (19.6m), maximum sweep 38.2ft (11.7m); wing area 565sq.ft (52.50m^2).
Powerplant: two General Electric F110-GE-400 two-spool turbofans, each rated at 16,610lb (7,534kg) military thrust, 27,080lb (12,283kg) with afterburner.
Performance: maximum speed, at altitude with four AIM-120 AMRAAM Mach 2.34, with full external stores Mach 1.88; maximum speed at sea-level Mach 1.2; operational ceiling 53,000ft (16,154m); tactical radius 444nm (510 miles/821km).
Armament: one 20mm six-barrel M61A-1 cannon (675 rounds); missiles, typically four AIM-120 AMRAAM, four AIM-9 Sidewinders.
Crew: two.
Specifications are for F-14D.

During the late 1950s, one of the most dangerous threats to U.S. Navy battle groups was long range antishipping missiles capable of being launched by fast, high-flying jet bombers of the Soviet Air Force and Soviet Naval Aviation. One of the most effective solutions appeared to be to destroy the bombers before they could launch their weapons, but given the technology of the day this was an almost impossible requirement to meet. What was needed was a carrier-based interceptor which could loiter for extended periods far from the fleet,

Below: Afterburners alight, an F-14 powers away from a carrier take-off.

Above: The F-14 is one of only a few swing-wing fighters in service.

Above: A pair of F-14s prepare to land aboard USS Eisenhower.

with a weapon system able to destroy multiple targets at unprecedentedly long ranges. It required supersonic speed to be able to reinforce existing patrols quickly, and a secondary requirement was the ability to carry out combat air patrols and to escort air strikes. At this point politics intervened when Robert McNamara, then Secretary of Defense, perceived a possible commonality between the Navy requirement and one from the USAF for a large, fast tactical fighter, capable of supersonic speeds at low level and operating from semi-prepared runways. So, he compelled the U.S. Navy to meet this long-range fighter requirement with a navalized version of the General Dynamics F-111. In December 1962 Grumman was given the task of navalizing the F-111; the result, the F-111B, flew in May 1965. It was too heavy, lacked maneuverability, had engine problems, and could not land on naval carriers; those apart, its performance was inferior to the F-4 Phantom in all departments. After many tribulations the doomed program was terminated in December 1968, but, in anticipation of such an outcome, the Navy and Grumman had already started studies for an advanced carrier fighter, which was designed around the weapon control system developed for the F-111B, and the contract for the F-14A Tomcat was awarded in January 1969, with the prototype flying for the first time in December 1970.

The F-14 is large by contemporary carrier standards and, like the F-111, it has a variable-sweep wing. In this case, the wings pivot on spherical bearings, with the sweep angle automatically varying to give optimum performance according to the flight regime (there is also a manual over-ride). In-flight sweep range is 20 to 68 degrees at a rate of change of 7.5 degrees per second. Slats and flaps occupy most of the leading and trailing edges, with spoilers on the upper surfaces, while at supersonic speeds vanes are deployed from the wing

gloves. Wing folding is not required, since an "oversweep" angle of 75 degrees is used to reduce parking area. The rear fuselage takes the form of a large "pancake," which not only provides plenty of space for fuel, but also gives a 40 percent increment to the total lifting area. Twin, outward-canted fins are set atop each engine, with small ventral strakes below.

The fire control system is the Hughes pulse-Doppler, multi-mode AWG-9 radar, capable of conducting fire-control solutions for six targets, while simultaneously tracking 24 others. Although designed in the 1960s, the AWG-9 remains extremely effective and is kept up-to-date by new software. Primary weapons are air-to-air-missiles: six AIM-54 Phoenix long-range, six AIM-7 Sparrow medium range, and four AIM-9 Sidewinder short range.

Powerplant installed on the F-14A was the twin Pratt & Whitney TF30-P-412 turbofans, the same as those that had proved so troublesome on the F-111, primarily because they were sensitive to disturbed airflow, which was largely overcome in the F-14 by separating the nacelles from the fuselage, with a straight line from inlet to nozzle. However, improvements have been made which makes them more effective, one major advance coming in the mid-1990s when the Digital Flight Control System was installed which prevents the pilot conducting unsafe maneuvers, thus reducing his workload. A total of 556 F-14As were produced.

Production of the F-14A-Plus (later F-14B) began in 1987. This is powered by the far sturdier and less sensitive General Electric F110-GE-400, and also has many other improvements. In all, 70 F-14Bs were produced.

The final variant was the F-14D, first flown in September 1990, with new avionics, including the APG-71 radar and a glass cockpit, F-110 engines, Airborne Self Protection Jammer (ASPJ), Joint Tactical Information Distribution

System (JTIDS), and Infrared Search and Track (IRST). Only 55 F-14Ds, some new, others rebuilds, were produced.

There has been a succession of upgrade programs, which will continue for several years yet. Thus, all F-14s have the LANTIRN targeting system that enables laser-guided bombs to be delivered in precision strikes during air-to-ground combat missions, while the Tactical Air Reconnaissance Pod System (TARPS) makes the F-14 the Navy's only manned tactical reconnaissance platform.

Various new aircraft based on the F-14 have been considered over the years, particularly by Grumman. These included the Quickstrike F-14, which required minimal changes, and this was followed by the Super Tomcat 21, which would have had enlarged wing-gloves and tailplane, which would have resulted in improved handling and increase in tankage, thus allowing a considerable increase in mission duration. A strike version of the Super Tomcat 21 was also proposed. None of these came to fruition.

In air combat, success has been meager, due to lack of opportunity. Two Libyan Su-22 Fitters were shot down over the Gulf of Sidra in 1981; two Libyan MiG-23 Floggers in the same area in January 1989; and an Iraqi Mil Mi-8 in the Gulf in 1991. Under current plans the Navy intends to retire the F-14 force progressively, starting with the F-14A by 2003-4, F-14B by 2007, and the F-14D by 2008.

Left: F-14's wing-sweep angle is automatically controlled.

Sikorsky S-70 family/SH-60B Sea Hawk/ SH-60F Ocean Hawk

Type: combat ASW helicopter.
Manufacturer: Sikorsky Aircraft Corporation.
Weight: empty 13,648lb (6,191kg); ASW mission takeoff 20,244lb (9,182kg); maximum takeoff (utility role) 21,88lb (9,926kg).
Dimensions: length 64.8ft (19.6m); height 11.9ft (3.6m); rotor diameter 53.7ft (16.4 m).
Powerplant: two General Electric T700-GE-700 or T700-GE-701C engines, 1,690shp (1,260kW).
Performance: maximum speed at 5,000ft (1,525m) 126kt (145mph/234kmh); operational radius 50nm (57.5miles/92.5km) for 3 hour loiter, or 150nm (173 miles/278km) for 1 hour loiter.
Armament: three Mk 46 or Mk 50 torpedoes, plus .50 caliber machine guns in doorways.
Crew: four.

The Sikorsky S-70 was developed to meet a U.S. Army-Navy requirement for a medium-lift helicopter for missions such as utility transport and ship-based ASW. It has since been produced in large numbers and in an ever-increasing variety of sub-types to meet new or changing requirements. This extremely versatile aircraft is now used by the Navy, Army, Air Force, and Coast Guard (and also by many foreign armed forces) for a wide variety of duties, including antisubmarine warfare, search-and-rescue, drug interdiction, antiship warfare, troop transport, Presidential transport, cargo lift, and special operations, and it is thus necessary to outline the complete family.

The original version for the U.S. Army was the transport/utility UH-60A Black Hawk, which was followed in production by the UH-60L, with an uprated powertrain; 1,463 of both types will be built. The SH-60B Sea Hawk was the Navy's version, which shared some 83 percent of the parts of the UH-60A;

Below: SH-60B launches a Kongsberg AGM-119B Penguin anti-ship missile.

Above: SH-60B makes a dusk landing at the end of an ASW mission.

intended for ASW duties aboard destroyers and frigates, 260 were ordered. The EH-60C was a specialized electronic warfare aircraft for the Army; 66 built. The Air Force entered the program with the HH-60D Night Hawk, an extremely well-equipped version for combat rescue and Special Operations Forces, particularly at night and in bad weather; one UH-60A was converted, but the project proceeded no further. The Air Force's attention then switched to a much less sophisticated version, the HH-60E, but this, too, was abandoned and the Air Force finally procured ninety-eight HH/MH-60G Pave Hawk. Meanwhile, the Navy developed another version, the SH-60F Ocean Hawk, intended to provide inner zone ASW protection for carriers. Next in the series were the HH-60H Rescue Hawk and the very similar HH-60J Jayhawk, which were for the Navy and Coast Guard, respectively; both were for combat rescue and covert operations, and both designs were closely based on that of the SH-60F. The MH-60K is a Special Operations Forces version for the Army, and the UH-60L, which has already been referred to, is an uprated UH-60A. The UH-60M was canceled and the UH-60N is a special model for the Marine Corps' Presidential Flight; nine were built. The latest model is the SH-60R for the Navy, which is a common standard for upgraded and modernized SH-60Bs and SH-60Fs.

The Navy's SH-60B Seahawk was developed as an airborne platform to be based aboard cruisers, destroyers, and frigates. It would deploy sonobouys to detect submarines and then launch torpedoes to destroy them. The first of the type, the YSH-60B, flew in December 1979 and the first production SH-60B in February 1983. While maintaining a general similarity with the Army's UH- 60A the naval aircraft has anti-corrosion treatment, T700-GE-401 engines, RAST gear, and the full LAMPS III sonar and magnetic anomaly detector (MAD) suite It also has a hoist under the fuselage for rescue missions. The three man crew comprises pilot, airborne tactical officer (Tacco) and a sensor operator (Senso) In the ASW role the aircraft can act under the direction of the parent ship, serve as an extension of the parent ship's sensors, or act autonomously. The SH-60B also has an antiship capability using the AGM-1188 Penguin missile, and all car carry pintle-mounted machine guns, if required.

The SH-60F Ocean Hawk was developed to operate from carriers to provide inner zone ASW protection, but also to serve as "plane guard" and general utility transport for the carrier. The SH-60F does not have the SH-60B's LAMPS III ASW suite, nor is it fitted for RAST, which is required only for recovery to smaller warships such as destroyers and frigates. In its ASW role it carries up to three Mk 50 torpedoes.

This difference between the SH-60B, SH-60F, and HH-60H has proved something of a limitation in deployment and the survivors of all three types

are now being upgraded to a new common standard, designated SH-60R. The package, formally known as the "SH-60(R) Multi-Mission Helicopter Upgrade," will extend all the helicopters' lives to 20,000 flight hours and will thus give the Navy a multi-mission platform for both antisubmarine and antisurface warfare for the coming twenty-five years. The SH-60R's systems will cope with high numbers of contacts, both air and sea, in confined and shallow waters. The helicopter will be capable of operating with either a carrier group or a surface action group, for which it will be equipped with a new multimode radar, FLIR sensor, ESM system, and a retrievable, active, low-frequency sonar with significantly greater processing power. Two further stores stations will be added, but the MAD equipment will be deleted.

The only other helicopter in the Navy's inventory will be the CH-60, a transport version of the SH-60. Thus, there will be just two sub-types of one main type of helicopter in Navy service, achieving the goal of rationalization which the Navy set itself some years ago.

Below: Sikorsky SH-60 delivers people and mail to a surfaced SSN.

Support Aircraft

As the world's only superpower, the United States needs to be able to deploy its military power anywhere in the world, frequently at very short notice, and often to places where no involvement had been foreseen, as happened in 2001, for example, in Afghanistan. Some problems can be resolved by action by naval or long-range air forces, but there are very few that do not require the rapid deployment of people, ammunition, equipment, and stores. Some of this, in particular the larger and less time-urgent items, can be sent by sea, but a rapid response requires air transport

The United States' armed services each contain a transport element, the bulk of it, of course, in the Air Force, which must first transport the men and women of the armed forces from the United States to the trouble-spot. Then these aircraft must perform the monotonous but absolutely essential task of sustaining them, moving people within the theater, hauling thousands of tons of ammunition, equipment, and supplies to the combat forces, recovering casualties to base hospitals, and taking time-expired troops back to the United States and their replacements to the combat zone.

The transports that carry out these tasks range from the giant C-5 Galaxy to the relatively tiny UH-60, but their missions are all essentially the same –

Right: The C-5 is one of very few transports where the bulkiness of a load is seldom a significant problem. This Galaxy is hauling equipment for Deny Flight, the operation to prevent Iraqi use of specified airspace.

placing the troops in the right place at the time and sustaining them while they are there. Also part of this support force are the tankers, such as the KC-10A, KC-135, and KC-130, whose ability to refuel aircraft ensures that their "customers," particularly combat aircraft, can reach destinations virtually anywhere in the world, or remain airborne for much longer than would be possible on internal fuel alone.

A little-known element of U.S. power projection is the Civil Reserve Air Fleet (CRAF), a scheme maintained by the Pentagon under which U.S. civilian airlines are contracted to maintain certain aircraft and crews at a specified degree of readiness for call-out by the Department of Defense. The actual numbers fluctuate on a monthly basis, but on 1 October 1998, for example, there were 35 carriers enrolled in the CRAF, with 573 aircraft in the international (ie, long-range) segment, 56 in the national (ie, short-range) segment, and 28 aircraft specifically for aeromedical evacuation. Aircraft and crews would be called upon only on an "as required basis" but in general terms there are three stages involved: Stage I, minor regional crises; Stage II, major regional contingencies; Stage III, periods of national mobilization

Bell UH-1N Iroquois (Huey)

Type: utility transport helicopter.
Manufacturer: Bell Helicopter Textron.
Weight: empty 6,143lb (2,787kg); maximum takeoff 11,200lb (5,050kg).
Dimensions: length, fuselage 42.4ft (12.9m); height 14.9ft (4.5m); rotor diameter 48.2ft (14.7m).
Powerplant: 1 Pratt & Whitney Canada T400-CP-400 TwinPac; takeoff 1,290shp (962kW), continuous 1,130shp (842kW).
Performance: maximum cruising speed, sea-level 140kt (161mph/258kmh); economical cruising speed, sea level 100kt (115mph/185kmh); service ceiling 14,200ft (4,330m); hovering ceiling IGE 11,000ft (3,355m).
Armament: two machine guns may be fitted in doorways.
Crew: three (pilot/commander; co-pilot, crewman/gunner).
Specifications for UH-1N.

The Bell Model 212 was developed from the original UH-1, principally by installing a Pratt & Whitney Canada PT6T Turbo Twin-Pac engine, which consists of two turboshaft engines mounted side-by-side, with a combining gearbox, and driving a common output shaft. This not only gives increased power over the single-engine UH-1, but also results in greatly enhanced safety, since, on detecting a loss of power in one engine, sensors in the gearbox automatically cause the other engine to increase its output to compensate, thus enabling the pilot either to make an emergency landing or to complete his mission, depending on the circumstances. First deliveries of the UH-1N were to the U.S. Air Force in 1970, with seventy-nine employed in support of Special Operations Forces. The Marine Corps was the major user, taking 221, of which two were converted to VH-1N VIP transports (another six were newly built to the same standard).

Approximately 100 UH-1Ns remain in service with the Marine Corps where it is used generally for troop transport, liaison, command-and-control, casualty

Above: The UH-1 (Huey) family continues in service with the Marine Corps.

evacuation, and resupply missions, and in particular for the support of amphibious operations, during both the landing and subsequent land combat phases. The current H-1 4BN Upgrade Program is designed to improve the UH-1Ns in service; this will provide a common engine, auxiliary power unit, four-bladed main and tail rotor system, transmission, drive train, and tail boom with the AH-1W and AH-1Z. The four-bladed rotor system will give improved performance, reliability, and maintainability, while the addition of an infrared suppresser will improve survivability.

Below: Current aim of the Marine Corps is to standardize its UH-1 fleet.

Bell Boeing V-22 Osprey

Type: vertical takeoff and landing (VTOL) aircraft.
Manufacturer: Bell Helicopter Textron and The Boeing Company.
Weight: maximum for normal vertical takeoff 47,500lb (21,550kg); STO takeoff 55,000lb (24,950kg); self-deployment 60,500lb (27,443kg).
Dimensions: fuselage length 57.3ft (17.5m); stowed, wing fore and aft 62.6ft (19.1m); width, proprotors turning 84.6ft (25.8m); width, blades folded, 18.4ft (5.6m); maximum height 22.6ft (6.9m).
Powerplant: two Rolls-Royce/Allison T406-AD-400 turboshafts, each 6,150shp.
Performance: maximum speed 377 knots; cruise speed 240kt; service ceiling 26,000ft (7,925m); range, amphibious assault 515nm (780 miles/1,256km); self-deployment range 2,100nm (3,184 miles/5,123km).
Armament: provision for two .50 caliber cabin guns.
Crew: two flight crew (pilot/co-pilot), plus twenty-four troops or twelve litters and attendants, depending on role.
Specifications for MV-22A.

The V-22 is a revolutionary aircraft using a novel tilt-rotor system that combines the vertical lift advantages of a helicopter with the fast forward speed of a fixed wing aircraft. The joint services program is led by the Marine Corps, and

Above: V-22 lands on a carrier; the design promises great flexibility.

planned procurement is 446: Marines, 348; Air Force, 50; Navy, 48. The version for the Marines, the MV-22A, is primarily intended as a replacement for aging CH-46 and CH-53 helicopters and is an assault transport for carrying troops, equipment, and supplies, and will be required to operate from either ships or expeditionary airfields ashore. The Navy model, the HV-22A is required to provide combat search and rescue (CSAR), combat transport for Special Operations troops, and fleet logistic support transport. The Air Force CV-22A is required to support long-range Special Operations missions; it will replace the MH-53J and MH-60J.

The V-22 is a tiltrotor aircraft with a 6,500shp turboshaft engine/transmission nacelle and a 38ft (11.6m) rotor system mounted at each wing tip. The two proprotors are connected to each other by driveshafts, both for synchronization and to provide single-engine power to both engines in the event of one engine failing. The aircraft operates as a helicopter for vertical takeoff and landing, but once airborne the nacelles are rotated forward through 90 degrees for horizontal flight, thus converting it into a high-speed, fuel-efficient turboprop. For stowage aboard ship the rotor blades fold and the wing rotates for maximum compactness.

The first flight occurred in March 1989 and since then a number of prototypes and pre-production models have been completed. The program has been dogged by controversy, which has been heightened by three well-publicized crashes. The first occurred in 1991, with no casualties, the second in 1992 in which seven men died, but the third, in April 2000, was by far the worst, resulting in the deaths of nineteen Marines. There are those who oppose the program, but the greatest requirement for the V-22 lies with the Marine Corps, whose need to replace the small and elderly CH-46 is very urgent.

Left: A platform for parachutists is just one use of this unique aircraft.

Boeing (McDonnell Douglas) C-17 Globemaster III

Type: cargo and troop transport.
Manufacturer: originally McDonnell Douglas, now The Boeing Company.
Weight: maximum peacetime takeoff 585,000lb (265,352kg).
Dimensions: length 174ft (53m); height 55.1feet (16.8 m); wingspan, to winglet tips 169.8ft (51.8m). Cargo compartment 88 x 18 x 12.3ft (26.8 x 5.5 x 3.8m).
Powerplant: four Pratt & Whitney F117-PW-100 turbofan engines, each 40,440lb (18,343kg) static thrust.
Performance: cruise speed at 28,000ft (8,534m) 450 knots (Mach 0.74); service ceiling at cruising speed 45,000ft (13,716m); range at 160,000lb (72,575kg) payload and cruise altitude 28,000ft (8,534m) 2,400nm.
Payload: 102 troops/paratroops; 36 litter and 54 ambulatory patients and attendants; 170,900lb (77,519kg) of cargo (18 pallet positions).
Crew: three (pilot/captain, co-pilot, loadmaster).

The C-17 Globemaster III made its maiden flight in September 1991, with the first production model being delivered in June 1993 and the first squadron being declared operational in January 1995. The Air Force's original plan was to purchase a total of 120, with the last one being delivered in November 2004; of these, 114 will be with active force units at Charleston AFB (W. Virginia), McChord AFB (Washington), and Altus AFB (Oklahoma), and six with the ANG. However, a further fourteen have since been added for Special Operations duty, but their basing has yet to be announced.

The C-17 Globemaster III is capable of rapid strategic delivery of troops and all types of cargo to main operating bases or direct to forward bases in the deployment area. The aircraft is also fully capable of performing tactical airlift and airdrop missions, when required. The C-17 is powered by four Pratt & Whitney F117-PW-100s, the same engine as that used on the Boeing 757 commercial airliner. The engines are fully reversible, with the thrust reversers directing the flow of air upward and forward, thus avoiding ingestion of dust and debris. Elsewhere in the aircraft, maximum use is made of off-the-shelf equipment, either from commercial sources or, in the case of the avionics,

Below: The C-17 Globemaster III strategic cargo and passenger transport.

Above: C-17s can deliver troops or cargo anywhere in the world.

using Air Force-standardized equipment. Great emphasis is placed on reliability and maintainability, current criteria requiring an aircraft mission completion success probability rate of 92 percent and no more than twenty manhours of maintenance per flying hour.

Considering the large size of the aircraft, the crew is very small, just three people: pilot, co-pilot, and loadmaster. Cargo is loaded onto the C-17 through a large aft door and the aircraft can carry virtually any of the Army's air-transportable equipment. The aircraft is capable of taking off and landing on runways 3,000ft (914m) long and 90ft (27.4m) wide, and even on such a narrow runway, the C-17 can turn around using a three-point star turn and its backing capability.

A number of C-17 aircraft are modified to fly SOLL-II missions (Special Operations, Low Level – Image Intensifier) in which the flightcrew wear image intensifying goggles in order to fly at very low level, and land and take off, all in total darkness. This enables them to conduct clandestine formation or single-

ship intrusions into hostile territory in order to either airdrop or airland personnel and equipment. The success of such missions will depend upon minimum lighting and communications, deceptive course changes, and the avoidance of hostile radar, air defenses, and populated areas.

The original specification to McDonnell Douglas required a service life of 30,000 hours, which will almost certainly be exceeded. Meanwhile the aircraft are being regularly upgraded to keep them in line with current and future requirements for threat avoidance, navigation, and communications, including global air traffic management (GATM). Commercially available avionics and mission computer upgrades are being investigated to reduce life-cycle costs and improve performance.

Boeing CH-46D/E Sea Knight

Type: medium-lift assault helicopter.
Manufacturer: Boeing Vertol Company.
Weight: empty, equipped 12,406lb (5,627kg); maximum takeoff 24,300lb (11,032kg).
Dimensions: length, rotors folded 45.7ft (13.9m), rotors spread 84.3ft (25.7m); width, rotors spread 51.0ft (15.5m); height 16.7ft (5.1m).
Powerplant: two General Electric T58-GE-16, each 1,8770shp (1,394kW).
Performance: maximum speed 144 knots (166mph); range 132 nautical miles (151.8 miles) for land assault mission, ferry range 600nm (691 miles/1,112km).
Payload: maximum of 22 troops and 2 aerial gunners, or 15 litters, 2 attendants, or 5,000lb (2,270 kg) stores; maximum slung load 6,300lb (2,871kg).
Crew: four (pilot, co-pilot, crew chief, mechanic).

The CH-46 Sea Knight is one of the oldest aircraft still in frontline service, having been the mainstay of the Marine Corps' medium-lift squadrons since entering service in June 1964. Since that time it has provided the Corps' medium-lift requirements in all combat and peacetime environments, and the survivors (currently some 230) are being maintained until a suitable replacement enters service, which, according to Marine Corps' plans, will be the MV-22A. The CH-46's mission is to provide assault transport of combat Marines, supplies, and equipment during amphibious landings and subsequent operations ashore, in all weathers, and by day or night (the latter with night vision goggles). Additional missions may include combat and assault support for evacuation operations and other maritime special operations; over-water search and rescue augmentation; support for mobile forward refueling and rearming points; and casualty evacuation from the field to suitable medical facilities.

The original version was the CH-46A, with 160 delivered to the Marine Corps and 14 UH-46A to the Navy for vertical replenishment (Vertrep) operations. These were followed by the D model with more powerful engines and modified rotor blades, with 266 CH-46Ds for the Marines and 10 UH-46Ds for the Navy. The final production model was the CH-46F, of which 174 were delivered to the Marine Corps. Virtually all models still flying are now the CH-46E which was a modification aplliied to both the CH-46D and the CH-46F, comprising uprated engines, fiberglass rotor blades, and strenthening of the structure to improve survivability in a crash. A further, more minor, modification has involved fitting enlarged sponsons to increase fuel capacity and thus range/endurance.

Right: Boeing CH-46E Sea Knight from HMM-262 (Medium Helicopter Squadron 262) lands aboard USS Essex (LHD-2). The CH-46, originally designed and built by the Vertol Company, has been in continuous service since 1964.

Boeing CH-47D
and MH-47D/E Chinook

Type: medium-lift helicopter.
Manufacturer: Boeing Vertol Company.
Weight: empty 22,379lb (10,151kg); normal takeoff 46,000lb (20,866kg);
maximum takeoff 50,000lb (22,679kg).
Dimensions: length, fuselage 51.0ft (15.4m), rotors turning 98.9ft (30.1m);
rotor diameter (each) 60.0ft (18.3m); height 18.9ft (5.8m).
Powerplant: two Textron Lycoming T-55-L- 712, each 3,750shp (2,796kW) for
takeoff, 3,000shp (2,237kW) continuous.
Performance: maximum level speed at sea-level 161kt (186mph/298kmh);
cruising speed at optimum altitiude 138kt (159mph/256kmh); maximum
operational radius 100miles (115km); ferry range 1,093nm (1,259
miles/2,028km).
Payload: 55 troops, or 24 litters, or 22,798lb (10,341kg) externally, or 13,907lb
(6,308kg) internally.
Crew: three (pilot, co-pilot, loadmaster).
Specifications for CH-47D.

The CH-47 Chinook is another of those great designs about which everything
seems just right first time and are then capable of being continuously
developed and refined over a long period of service. The design was an
enlarged and improved version of the Vertol CH-46, and the prototype CH-47A
(then designated YHC-1B) flew in September 1961. Since then well over a
thousand have been built and most are still in frontline service in 2002 with the
United States and many other armies and air forces. The most significant
feature of the design is a long unobstructed cabin with a large ramp at the after
end, making it ideal for use by troops, vehicles, light guns, and cargo. This has
been achieved by mounting both rotors and engines above the fueselage, and
by fitting sponsons outside the cabin to carry the undercarriage, fuel tanks, and

Below: MH-47 Chinook self-deploys, using its in-flight refueling capability.

Above: Maximum external payload is 22,798lb (10,341kg) in cargo nets.

other services. The twin rotors are connected by a transfer shaft, so that if one engine has problems the other can power both rotors for a safe landing.

The CH-47 has served in the U.S. armded forces in two main versions, mainly as a medium-lift transport. The Army bought 354 CH-47As, followed by 108 CH-47Bs, which had more powerful engines and increased diameter rotor blades. The CH-47C had even more powerful engines, but also included a number of other significant improvements such as increased fuel tankage; 270 were delivered to the Army, most of which were later refitted with composite blades. Meanwhile, large numbers were being sold to foreign customers and some of the enhancements they had requested were fed back into the U.S. program, resulting in the CH-47D, which entered service with the Army in May 1982. The Army's CH-47D fleet is a mix of upgraded earlier models plus some new-build. The enhancements include engines with better battle survivability, night-vision compatible flightdeck, triple (instead of single) cargo hooks, and a pressurized system, for faster and safer refueling.

The MH-47D and E are heavy assault helicopters based on the CH-47 airframe. Its mission is to conduct overt and covert infiltrations, exfiltrations, air assault, resupply, and sling operations over a wide range of environmental conditions. The MH-47 is capable of operating at night during marginal weather conditions. Using special mission equipment and night vision devices, the aircrew can operate in hostile mission environments over all types of terrain at low altitudes during periods of low visibility and low ambient lighting conditions with pinpoint navigation accuracy. As with other CH-47 types, MH-47s can be transported in C-5 and C-17 transport aircraft (two in each), or can self-deploy over extended distances using ground or air-to-air refueling.

The MH-47E is a further modification for use by Special Operations Forces. It has more advanced avionics and a revised internal fuel tankage arrangement, enabling the aircraft to carry an additional 2,068 gallons (7,828 litres) of fuel, thus reducing the need for auxiliary tanks in the cabin, which reduced the space available for cargo. There are three weapons stations: an M60 7.62 machine gun at the ramp, and two 7.62mm miniguns forward, one in the port-side window, the other in the starboard door. Army SOF currently operate twenty MH-47Es and these are being constantly modified to ehnance their capabilities.

The CH-47 has been constantly in combat in virtually every campaign

Above: The ICH program will extend the life of the CH-47 to 2030.

undertaken by the U.S. Army, starting with deployment to Vietnam in the mid-1960s. In the Bosnia peacekeeping operations, over a six month period, a CH-47D aviation company with sixteen aircraft flew 2,222 hours, carried 3,348 passengers, and transported over 3,200,000lb (1,452,000kg) of cargo.

The Improved Cargo Helicopter (ICH) program is intended to extend the life of the present CH-47D airframes to 2025-2030, giving them the extraordniary service life of sixty years. This will involve the total remanufacture of the aircraft, one major aim being to reduce vibration, which is a major cause of reliability problems and thus of maintenance costs. There will also be a new cockpit and new digital command and communications systems. The ICH will be capable of carrying 16,000lb (4,900kg) of either external or internal cargo. The first ICH is due to be fielded in 2003-04, with a total of 300 being delivered by 2015. The remaining 131 CH-47Ds will not be modernized.

A separate program involves upgrading the engine to the more powerful T-55-714 standard, which offers improvements in hot/high conditions. The ICH and the enhanced engine are intended to keep the Army's CH-47 fleet fully serviceable and up-to-date until the Joint Transport Rotorcraft (JTR) begins to enter service in the 2020-2030 timeframe.

Boeing KC-10A Extender

Type: aerial tanker and transport.
Manufacturer: originally, McDonnel Douglas, now Boeing.
Weight: empty (tanker) 240,065lb (108,891kg); maximum takeoff 590,000lb (265,500kg).
Dimensions: length 181.6ft (54.4m); height 58.1ft (17.4m); wingspan 165.4ft (50m).
Powerplant: three General Electric CF6-50C2 turbofans, each 52,500lb (23.3kN) static thrust.
Performance: maximum speed, clean) 619mph (Mach 0.83); normal cruising speed at 30,000ft (9,145m) 490kt (564mph/908kmh); ceiling 42,000ft (12,727m); range with cargo 3,800nm (4,400 miles/7,080km); without cargo 10,000nm (11,500 miles/18,500km).
Payload: maximum cargo payload 170,000lb (76,560kg); maximum fuel load 356,000lb (160,200kg).
Crew: four (aircraft commander, pilot, flight engineer, boom operator).

The KC-10A Extender is a straightforward development of the successful DC-10 commercial airliner, which entered service in 1971. The KC-10A has 81 percent commonality with the commercial model, but whereas the normal DC-10 has three main fuel tanks in the wings, the military tanker was created by adding three more tanks under the cargo floor. One of these tanks is under the forward lower cargo compartment, the second in the center wing area, and the third under the rear compartment. The combined capacity of these six tanks is 356,000lb (160,200kg).

Inflight transfer of fuel is achieved either by the USAF's advanced aerial refueling boom system, or by a hose-and-drogue centerline refueling system, which is employed by the U.S. Navy and Marine Corps, and virtually all foreign

air forces. In the boom system, the KC-10A's operator controls refueling operations through a digital, fly-by-wire system from a seat in the rear of the aircraft, where he can see the receiving aircraft through a wide window. Once the operator has "flown" the boom into the receptacle on the receiver aircraft, fuel is transferred at a rate of 1,100 gallons (4,180 liters) per minute. With the hose-and-drogue system the KC-10A extends the hose and the receiving aircraft's pilot is then responsible for making the connection; once in place fuel is transferred at 470 gallons (1,786 liters) per minute. The KC-10A is fitted with an Automatic Load Alleviation System and an Independent Disconnect System which greatly enhance safety and facilitate the air refueling process. The KC-10A is equipped with lights for night air-refueling operations, and can itself be air-refueled by another tanker.

The KC-10A's primary mission is aerial refueling, but it can also serve as a transport, for which it is fitted with a large cargo door, while inside the cargo compartment there are powered rollers and winches to permit moving heavy loads. Cargo loads range from 27 pallets in an all-cargo configuration to a mixed load of 17 pallets and 75 passengers. With the latter load normal range is of the order of 4,400 miles (7,040km), which can, of course, be greatly extended by the use of air-to-air refueling. The KC-10A's normal crew comprises a pilot/commander, co-pilot, flight engineer, and boom operator, but additional seats and bunks can be installed for extra crew members, if required.

There are fifty-nine KC-10s in service with active units of the U.S. Air Force, and none with either the Reserves or the ANG. The current planned service life is to 2043 and while the fleet is being constantly modified to enhance its capabilities there is no known discussion of a successor, as yet.

Below: KC-10 uses the USAF's "probe-and-drogue" system to refuel a C-141.

Boeing KC-135 Stratotanker

Type: aerial refueling and airlift.
Manufacturer: Boeing.
Weight: empty 106,306lb (48,220kg); maximum takeoff 322,500lb (146,285kg).
Dimensions: length 136.3ft (415m); wingspan 130.8ft (39.9m); height 41.7ft (12.7m).
Powerplant: KC-135E, four Pratt and Whitney TF-33-PW-102 turbofan engines, each 18,000lb (801kN) static thrust; KC-135R, four CFM International CFM-56 turbofan engines, each 21,634lb (97.9kN) static thrust.
Performance: speed 530mph at 30,000ft (9,144m); ceiling: 50,000ft (15,240m); range 1,500 miles (2,419km) with 150,000lb (68,039kg) of transfer fuel; ferry mission, up to 11,015 miles (17,766km).
Payload: maximum transfer fuel load 200,000lb (90,719kg); maximum cargo capability 83,000lb (37,648kg); 37 passengers.
Crew: four (pilot, co-pilot, navigator, boom operator).
Specifications for KC-135R, unless otherwise indicated.

The Boeing KC-135A was the world's first jet-powered air-to-air refueling aircraft to enter large-scale service, and used the USAF "flying boom" system in which an operator in the refueling aircraft flies (controls) the boom into a receptacle in the receiving aircraft. Designated KC-135A, the type entered service in 1957 and a total of 732 were built, the last being delivered in 1965. The first 582 had a shorter fin, but the remaining aircraft had a taller fin to increase stability during takeoff; this was subsequently retrofitted to all earlier aircraft.

The original KC-135A was powered by four Pratt & Whitney J57 jet engines, a type well-known for its noise, black exhaust, and high fuel consumption. In

the 1980s Boeing carried out a program to re-engine 410 of these aircraft with the CFM-56 turbofan, which was not only more powerful but also quieter and more economical; designated KC-135R, this aircraft can offload 50 percent more fuel, is 25 percent more fuel efficient, and costs 25 percent less to operate than the KC-135A. The KC-135R also has an on-board auxiliary power unit (APU) enabling the aircraft to operate autonomously away from main bases. Under a different modification program, 157 Air Force Reserve and Air National Guard tankers were re-engined with the TF-33-PW- 102 engines. This was achieved mainly by purchasing a large number of surplus Boeing 707 civil airliners and removing their engines. The opportunity was also taken to remove the civil airliners' wide-span tails and transfer them to the military aircraft to maintain stability to compensate for the higher thrust of the engines. The re-engined tanker, designated the KC-135E, is 14 percent more fuel efficient than the KC-135A and can offload 20 percent more fuel, but more importantly it is considerably safer, can use shorter runways, and is much quieter. The present inventory totals 545 tankers, of which 253 are KC-135Rs with the active force, while the Air National Guard (222) and Air Force Reserve (70) operate a mix of KC-135Rs and KC-135Es.

Originally, the KC-135 was capable of refueling using only the flying boom system. However, greater flexibility was needed in order to replenish U.S. Navy and foreign aircraft, as a result of which a hose-and-drogue system was added, which deploys from the boom. A cargo deck above the refueling system can hold a mixed load of passengers and cargo up to a maximum of 83,000lb (37,648km). Some aircraft are fitted with the PACER CRAG navigation suites and do not require a dedicated navigator in the crew.

Below: Boeing KC-135R refuels a B-1B strategic bomber.

Lockheed C-130 Hercules

Type: intratheater airlift transport.
Manufacturer: originally Lockheed, now Lockheed Martin.
Weight: empty 69,300lb (31,434kg); maximum takeoff 135,000 lb (61,236kg).
Dimensions: length 97.8ft (29.3 m); height 38.3ft (11.4m); wingspan 132.6ft (39.7m).
Powerplant: four Rolls-Royce Allison T56-A-15 turboprops, each 4,300shp (3,080kW).
Performance: maximum cruising speed 321kt (370mph/595kmh) at 30,000ft (9,144m); range 4,210nm (4,848 miles/7,802km) with maximum fuel or 1,910nm (2,199 miles/3,539km) with maximum payload.
Payload: maximum passenger loads 92 troops or 64 paratroops or 74 litter patients; maximum allowable cabin load 36,000lb (16,330kg).
Crew: five (two pilots, navigator, flight engineer, loadmaster).

A description of the C-130 would fill several books, so this entry summarises only the transport versions used by the U.S. armed forces. The study for a new transport was initiated in 1951, with the first prototype C-130A flying in 1954, followed by the first production delivery to the USAF in December 1956. A total of 219 C-130As were delivered, powered by four Allison T56-A-1A turboprops with three-bladed propellers, followed by 134 C-130Bs with the Allison T56-A-7 turboprops, four-bladed propellers, additional fuel in the wings, strengthened landing gear and other improvements, most of which were later retrofitted to the C-130As. A U.S. Navy transport version of the C-130B was originally designated GV-1U, later C-130F, while several A models were modified with wheel-ski landing gear for service in the Arctic and for resupply missions to units along the Distant Early Warning line as the C-130D.

The next major transport version was the C-130E with two underwing fuel tanks, and increased range and endurance capabilities; 369 were delivered. A wing modification to correct fatigue and corrosion problems on the USAF's C-130Es has extended the life of the aircraft well into the 21st century, while

ongoing modifications include a Self-Contained Navigation System (SCNS) to enhance navigation capabilities, especially in low-level environments, and a state-of-the-art autopilot, incorporating a Ground Collision Avoidance System. Next came the C-130H which has uprated T56-A-T5 turboprops, a redesigned outer wing, updated avionics, and other minor improvements. Both C-130E and C-130H carry 6,700 gallons (25,363 liters) of fuel in six integral wing tanks, with a pylon under each wing for a 1,300 gallon (4,921 liter) fuel tank. Delivery of some 350 C-130H to the USAF started in 1975 and ended some years later, but was restarted with an order for eight to make up for losses in the Gulf War, being funded in FY96.

USAF units are now equipped with the C-130H, which continues to be upgraded. Most C-130Hs have been fitted with the Night Vision Instrumentation System since 1993. Some aircraft with the ANG and Reserves are fitted for fire-fighting missions; others are fitted for aerial spraying, typically to suppress mosquito-spread epidemics; and another seven, designated LC-130Hs, are modified with wheel-ski gear for use in support of Arctic and Antarctic operations. Another upgrade is the C-130 Avionics Modernization Program (C-130X AMP) which will modify approximately 525 in-service aircraft of approximately 13 different sub-types, to establish a common, supportable, cost effective baseline configuration for all C-130 aircraft, with a new avionics suite.

The current production model, C-130J, has a two-crew flight system, four Rolls-Royce-Allison AE-21-00D3 engines, all-composite Dowty propellers, digital avionics and mission computers, enhanced performance, and improved reliability and maintainability. These result in an all-round improvement in performance and availability. Another new version is the C-130J-30 which is 15ft (4.58m) longer, significantly increasing carrying capacity and range, enabling it to work as a strategic, as well as tactical, transport.

Below: Built in thousands, the C-130 is among the greatest transport aircraft.

Lockheed Martin C-141 StarLifter

Type: strategic cargo and troop transport.
Manufacturer: originally Lockheed, now Lockheed Martin.
Weight: maximum takeoff 323,100lb (146,863kg).
Dimensions: length 168.3ft (51m); height 39.2ft (11.9m); wingspan 160ft (48.7m).
Powerplant: four Pratt & Whitney TF33-P-7 turbofan engines, each 20,250lb (9,113kg) static thrust.
Performance: maximum speed 500mph (Mach 0.74) at 25,000ft (7,620m); range 2,174nm (2,500 miles/4,023km) on internal fuel.
Payload: 200 troops, or 155 paratroops, or 103 litters plus 14 seats, or 68,725 lb (31,239kg) cargo.
Crew: routine flights, five (pilot/captain, co-pilot, two flight engineers, one loadmaster); airdrops, six (as before, plus navigator); aeromedical missions, five, plus five (two flight nurses, three medical technicians).

Although larger and considerably faster, the C-141design drew on Lockheed's experience with the C-130 Hercules, with a large, uncluttered cargo hold 10.3ft (3.1m) wide and 9.1ft (2.8m) high, and a large rear ramp covered by clamshell doors, which could be opened in flight. The prototype C-141A first flew in December 1963 and the type entered service in October 1964, whereupon it was immediately involved in the air-bridge carrying troops and equipment to and from the war in Vietnam. It soon became apparent, however, that the space in the cargo hold was almost always filled well before the aircraft reached its weight limits, a situation known in the Air Force as "bulk-out before weight-out." As a result the entire fleet, apart from four special-role NC-141s, were taken in hand by Lockheed and lengthened by 23.3ft (7.1m), a process which not only increased the capacity of each aircraft, but also increased total fleet capacity by the equivalent of ninety new C-141s. The rebuild also included installing in-flight refueling equipment, which makes the C-141B instantly recognizable by the hump immediately abaft the cockpit. Started in the mid-1970s, the work was completed in June 1982.

Below: The C-141 entered service in 1964 and will remain in the fleet until 2006.

Above: A key capability is transporting paratroops over strategic ranges.

The cargo compartment has over thirty different configurations, ranging from rollers for pallets, through smooth floor for vehicles to aft-facing seats for 166 troops and sidewall canvas seats for some 155 fully equipped paratroops, with all changes being achieved quickly and economically. In the aeromedical evacuation role, the Starlifter can carry about 103 litter patients, 113 walking patients or a combination of the two. The Air Force Reserve provides 50 percent of the Starlifter's airlift crews, and 40 percent of its maintenance capability, and flies more than 30 percent of Air Mobility Command's peacetime worldwide missions. A number of C-141s were modified to carry the Minuteman intercontinental ballistic missile in its special container, up to a total weight of 92,000lb (41,400kg). Some C-141s have been equipped with intra-formation positioning sets that enable a flight of two to thirty-six aircraft to maintain formation regardless of visibility. The C-141 was the first jet transport from which U.S. Army paratroopers jumped; it was also the first to land in the Antarctic.

The current C-141B fleet consists of 241 in the Active Force, 16 in the Air National Guard, and 12 in the Reserve Force, and it is intended to keep these in service until 2006, at the least. All will receive modifications intended to enhance their availability and capability, but in addition the sixty-three aircraft with the lowest equivalent damage hours will undergo major modification, including an all-weather flight control system, ground collision avoidance system, enhanced GPS, and defensive systems to provide protection against shoulder-launched surface-to-air missiles.

The first C-141B was received by the Air Force in December 1979. Conversion of 270 C-141s from A to B models was completed in 1982. High flight-hour aircraft are already being retired, but the remainder are being given modifications aimed at preserving them by reliability and maintainability improvements, and capability improvements necessary for effective use through 2006. In addition, thirteen aircraft will receive additional SOLL-II upgrades under the Special Operations Forces Improvement program.

Lockheed Martin C-5A Galaxy

Type: strategic troop and cargo carrier.
Manufacturer: originally Lockheed, now Lockheed Martin.
Weight: operating, empty 374,000lb (169,643kg); maximum takeoff, peacetime 769,000lb (348,818kg), wartime, 840,000lb (381,024kg).
Dimensions: length 247.8ft (75.3m); height 65.1ft (19.8m); wingspan 222.9ft (67.9m).
Powerplant: four General Electric TF-39GE-1C turbofans; each 43,000lb (191.3kN) static thrust.
Performance: maximum speed 402kt (463mph/741kmh); maximum cruising speed at 25,000ft (7,620m) 480kt (578mph/930kmh); range, empty with maximum fuel 5,618nm (6,469 miles/10,411km).
Payload: maximum wartime 291,000lb (130,950kg) (see notes).
Crew: seven (pilot, co-pilot, two flight engineers, and three loadmasters).

The Lockheed C-5 Galaxy originated in a U.S. Air Force requirement, framed in 1963, for a Cargo Experimental – Heavy Logistics System (CX-HLS) aircraft capable of transporting a 250,000lb (113,400kg) load over a range of 2,600nm (3,000 miles/4,828km) without refueling. The first prototype flew in June 1968 and the first service aircraft became operational in 1970. The aircraft provided air movement on an unprecedented scale, with a cargo hold that was 13.5ft (4.1m) high, 19.0ft (5.8m) wide, and 143.8ft (43.8m) long,. There were also full size doors at each end which enabled huge loads to be accommodated, and also allowed ground crews to work at both ends simultaneously. The maximum load was 270,000lb (122,472kg) which enabled almost every item of equipment in the U.S. Army's inventory to be airlifted, or thirty-six pallets, and the undercarriage had a special "kneeling" facility to bring the aircraft sill down to the level of a truck bed. In addition, seventy-three passengers can be accommodated on the upper deck and a further fourteen on the forward upper deck, plus a relief crew of seven.

A total of seventy-seven C-5As were delivered and the type initially experienced some problems, particularly cost over-runs and in the wing structure, the latter being overcome by fitting a new wing. The last C-5A was delivered in 1967 and the production-line then closed. However, an increase in demand for heavy-lift capacity led to the line being reopened for the production of fifty C-5Bs between 1986 and 1989. The C-5B is externally very similar to the A-model, but it does in fact incorporate many enhancements, not least being a greatly simplified version of the 28-wheel undercarriage. The hauling capacity of the C-5 is enormous. It can accommodate two M1 tanks, an Armored Vehicle Launched Bridge (AVLB), or ten of the Marine Corps LAV-25s, or a Ch-47 Chinook helicopter.

A major effort to update the C-5 fleet began in the late 1990s. This includes avionics modernization and reliability enhancement, the latter including replacement of the engines, pods and auxiliary power units, the new engine being the General Electric F6-80C2L1F turbofan. The airframe structure and covering will also be upgraded to prolong the life of the aircraft well into the middle of the 21st century. Like the C-17 and C-141, the C-5 is capable of conducting clandestine flights into potentially hostile territory to either airdrop or airland troops, equipment or both. These aircraft are fitted with SOLL-II (Special Operations Low-Level - Image Intensifier) which enables them to operate in darkness with minimum lighting. The current inventory is 70 C-5s with the Active force, 11 with the Air National Guard, and 28 with the Air Force Reserve.

Right: The C-5A was built for large loads, including the CH-47 Chinook.

Lockheed Martin MC-130E/H Combat Talon I/II

Type: Special Operations Forces transport.
Manufacturer: originally Lockheed, now Lockheed Martin.
Weight: empty 72,892lb (33,063kg); maximum takeoff 155,000lb (69,750kg).
Dimensions: length, MC-130E 100.8ft (30.7m), MC-130H 99.8ft (30.4m); height 38.5ft (11.7m); wingspan 132.6ft (40.4m).
Powerplant: four Rolls-Royce-Allison T56-A-15 turboprop engines, each 4,910 shp.
Performance: maximum speed at 30,000ft (9,145m) 330kt (380mph/612kmh); ceiling 33,000ft (10,000m); range 4,080nm (4,700 miles/7,560km).
Payload: MC-130E, 53 troops, 26 paratroopers; MC-130H, 77 troops, 52 paratroopers or 57 litter patients.
Crew: MC-130E, nine (two pilots, two navigators, electronic warfare officer, flight engineer, radio operator, two loadmasters); MC-130H, six (two pilots, navigator/ electronic warfare officer, flight engineer, two loadmasters).

Both these aircraft are adaptations of the ever-flexible C-130 Hercules design, the mission of the MC-130E Combat Talon I and MC-130H Combat Talon II being to support U.S. and allied Special Operations Forces by air-dropping and air-landing personnel and equipment by day or night, anywhere in the world and in any weather. The U.S. Air Force's first special operations conversion was the C-130E-1 which was employed during the Vietnam War, one possible task being for the vertical extraction of men from the jungle using the Fulton Strategic/Tactical Airborne Recovery (STAR) system. In this, a Y-shaped framework on the aircraft nose engaged a nylon line held aloft by a helium-filled balloon from a harness worn by the man on the ground. The physical characteristics of the line ensured that the man's initial ascent was vertical,which brought him clear of any trees while the cable was fed back to a winch on the rear ramp, which then hauled the man into the aircraft. Although the system was tested and remains fitted to eight MC-130Es (known as "Clamps") it has never, as far as is known, been used operationally.

The seventeen C-130E-1s were redesignated MC-130E Combat Talon I in the 1970s. This was followed by twenty-four MC-130H Combat Talon IIs, which entered service in the early 1990s. This is basically an improved E-model, with new radar , FLIR, and improved countermeasures, but is otherwise similar in its equipment and tasks. Both versions are capable of accepting inflight refueling, and of air-refueling

Above: Combat Talon aircraft carry a wide variety of mission radars.

helicopters in support of extended operations. Both are also capable of FARP (Forward Air Refueling Point) missions, in which they land, usually in hostile territory, to provide a refueling facility for helicopters involved in long-range special operations.

Combat Talon aircraft have seen extensive operational service in many campaigns. Two of the more famous examples are the Son Tay raid, when an attempt was made to extract prisoners-of-war from a North Vietnamese camp, and the Teheran raid when several MC-130Es set up a FARP at Desert-One.

There are numerous improvement programs in train, most of them aimed at enhancing the low-level flying capabilities. One particular program is intended to reduce the engines' infra-red (IR) signature, since the current equipment is both unreliable and difficult to maintain. The current inventory is thirty-eight of both types: twenty-four MC-130H with the Active force, and fourteen MC-130E with the Air Force Reserve.

Below: Combat Talon air-to-air refuels a SOF Sikorsky H-60 helicopter.

Lockheed Martin MC-130P Combat Shadow

Type: in-flight tanker for Special Operations Forces helicopters.
Manufacturer: originally, Lockheed, now Lockheed Martin.
Weight: empty 72,892lb (33,063kg); maximum takeoff 155,000lb (69,750kg).
Dimensions: length 98.8ft (30.1m); height 38.5ft (11.7m); wingspan 132.6ft (40.4m).
Powerplant: four Rolls-Royce-Allison T56-A-15 turboprop engines, each 4,910shp.
Performance: maximum speed at 30,000ft (9,145m) 330kt (380mph/612kmh); ceiling 33,000ft (10,000m); range 4,080nm (4,700 miles/7,560km).
Payload: MC-130E, 53 troops or 26 paratroops; MC-130H, 77 troops or 52 paratroopers or 57 litter patients.
Crew: eight (pilot, co-pilot, two navigators, flight engineer, communications systems operator, two loadmasters).

The primary mission of the MC-130P Combat Shadow is the inflight refueling of helicopters engaged in special forces operations. The origin of the type was the HC-130N, fifteen of which were built for the support of rescue missions,

equipped with hose reel units under each wing, as well as the Fulton STAR rescue system (see Combat Talon entry). These were followed by a number of new-build aircraft, designated HC-130H(N), which had modernized avionics and the underwing hose units, but without the Fulton gear. Finally came the HC-130P. In the mid-1990s it was decided that the prefix "H" normally indicates an aircraft whose primary role is rescue and that this was not suitable for a type whose main role is in supporting Special Operations Forces. As a result the prefix was changed to the more suitable "M."

The mission of the MC-130P is clandestine formation or single-ship intrusion into hostile territory to provide aerial refueling for Special Operations Forces helicopters. To perform this mission, the primary emphasis is on night vision goggle (NVG) operations, the MC-130P flying such missions at night to reduce probability of visual acquisition and interception by airborne threats. Secondary mission capabilities may include airdrop of small special operations teams, small bundles, and combat rubber raiding craft.

Some aircraft have been modified with the Universal Air Refueling Receptacle Slipway Installation (UARRSI) system for inflight refueling as a

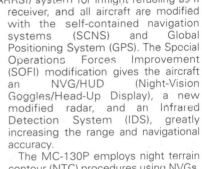

receiver, and all aircraft are modified with the self-contained navigation systems (SCNS) and Global Positioning System (GPS). The Special Operations Forces Improvement (SOFI) modification gives the aircraft an NVG/HUD (Night-Vision Goggles/Head-Up Display), a new modified radar, and an Infrared Detection System (IDS), greatly increasing the range and navigational accuracy.

The MC-130P employs night terrain contour (NTC) procedures using NVGs, flying at about 500ft (152m) above ground level, using terrain masking. The range of the mission depends on several factors: length of time on the low-level route, enroute weather, winds, and the air-refueling offload requirements. Portions of the profile may be flown at high altitude to minimize fuel consumption. NTC procedures will be used to avoid enemy detection in a non-permissive environment to get the aircraft to the objective area. Current inventory is twenty-eight, with twenty-four in the Active force and four with the Air National Guard.

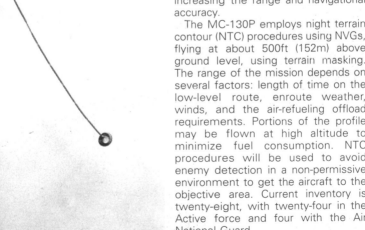

Left: MC-130P's primary mission is inflight refueling of SOF helicopters.

Sikorsky CH-53E Super Stallion

Type: heavy transport helicopter.
Manufacturer: Sikorsky Aircraft Division of United Technologies Corp.
Weight: empty 33,338lb ((15,072kg); maximum takeoff 69,750lb (31,640kg).
Dimensions: length, fuselage 67.5ft (20.3m); length, rotors turning 88.3ft (26.5m); height 24.9ft (7.2m); main rotor diameter 72.3ft (21.7m).
Powerplant: three General Electric T64-GE-416 turboshafts, each 4,300shp (3,266kW).
Performance: speed 160kt (184mph/294kmh); ceiling 12,450ft (3,795m); range 578nm (665 miles/1,064km); ferry range 886nm (1,338 miles/2,153km).
Payload: 37 troops, or 24 litter patients plus 4 attendants, or 8,000lb (3,600kg) cargo.
Crew: three (two pilots, one aircrewman).
Specifications for CH-53E.

The CH-53D Sea Stallion, which entered service with the U.S. Marine Corps in the mid-1960s, is a heavy-lift helicopter, powered by two General Electric T64 turboshafts. It is capable of lifting 7 tons (6.4 metric tonnes), or 37 passengers in its normal configuration and 55 passengers with centerline seats installed. There are currently 54 in active units and 18 with reserve units, and the fleet has been regularly upgraded , recent improvements including an elastomeric rotor head, external fuel tanks, crashworthy fuel cells, new radios, and defensive electronic countermeasure (ECM) equipment.

By the mid-1970s the Marine Corps required much greater lifting power, but from an aircraft that was still able to operate from its amphibious platforms. Rathe

han produce a new design, Sikorsky devised the much simpler solution of fitting a third engine to the existing airframe, which solved the problem very satisfactorily, resulting the the CH-53E Super Stallion. The CH-53E entered service in 1981 and since then has been the Corps' heavy-lift helicopter, operating from LHAs (Landing-ship, Helicopter, Assault), LPHs (Landing Platform, Helicopter, and now LHDs Landing-ship, Helicopter, Dock). The helicopter lifts 16 tons (14.5 metric tons) at sea level, transporting the load 50 nautical miles (57.5 miles) and returning. Among the heavier loads routinely caried are Light Armored Vehicles (LAVs) which weigh 26,000lb (11,804kg). The aircraft has an endurance of 4 hours 30 minutes, but is equipped with a refueling probe enabling it to refuel in flight. There are 160 in service.

In just one example of its capabilities, during Operation Eastern Exit in January 1990, two CH-53Es flew from their ship standing offshore to Mogadishu, capital of Somalia, where they landed at the American Embassy to rescue American and foreign diplomats. Each leg, outward and return, was some 460nm (532 miles/856km) long. The entire operation took place under cover of darkness and involved two air-to-air refuelings for each aircraft. The mission was entirely successful.

There are various ongoing programs to increase service life, enhance reliability, and reduce maintenance, and thus cut the operating costs until the CH-53E is replaced, which is currently intended to start in 2015. Such a Service Life Extension Program (SLEP) could be applied to both CH-53Es and CH- 53Ds.

Below: Marines board a CH-53E, with rotors "turning and burning."

Sikorsky MH-53J/M Pave Low

Type: long-range Special Operations Forces helicopter.
Manufacturer: Sikorsky Aircraft Division of United Technologies Corp.
Weight: empty 23,569lb (10,691kg); maximum takeoff 42,000lb (19,050kg); war emergency 50,000lb (22,680kg).
Dimensions: length, fuselage 67.5ft (20.3m); length, rotors turning 88.3ft (26.5m); height 24.9ft (7.2m); main rotor diameter 72.3ft (21.7m).
Powerplant: two General Electric T64-GE-100 turboshafts, each 3,936shp (2,935kW).
Performance: maximum peed, clean, sea-level 170kt (196mph/315kmh); cruising speed at optimum altitiude 150kt (173mph/278kmh); service ceiling 20,400ft (6,220m); hover ceiling IGE 11,700ft (3,565m); range on internal fuel 468nm (540 miles/868km).
Armament: maximum of three 7.62mm miniguns or 0.5in machine guns.
Payload: 38 troops or 14 litters; external 20,000lb (9,000kg) cargo hook.
Crew: six (pilot/captain, co pilot, two flight engineers, two gunners).

The most powerful helicopters flown by the U.S. Air Force in the Vietnam War were the CH-53 heavy transports and HH-53 combat rescue helicopters, the latter being universally known by their radio callsign "Jolly Greens." In 1969

an HH-53B was fitted with a low-light TV system to give it some night-flying capability; designated Pave Low I, this was followed by the more ambitious Pave Low II, which led into the definitive Pave Low III. After trial installations in two aircraft, a total of nine CH-53Cs were converted into HH-53H Pave Low III aircraft. But then a special forces commitment was added together with yet more new equipment, as a result of which the nine MH-53Hs and thirty-two other HH- and CH-53s were modified and designated MH-53J. The modifications included improved Pave Low avionics, satellite communications and structural improvements and all were also adapted for shipboard operations, with automatic folding for the main rotor blades and tail rotor pylon. The MH-53J is also equipped with armor plating and has three gun positions, all of which can mount either 7.62mm miniguns or .50in machine guns.

The MH-53M Pave Low IV is a modified MH-53J that has been fitted with the Interactive Defensive Avionics System/Multi-Mission Advanced Tactical Terminal (IDAS/MATT), which enhances the aircraft's defensive capabilities, providing instant access to the total battlefield situation, through near real-time Electronic Order of Battle updates. It also provides improved threat avoidance and the ability foir airborne route re-planning, where necessary.

The primary mission of the MH-53J/M is to conduct covert, low-level, long-range undetected penetration into denied areas, by day or night, in adverse weather. The tasks include infiltration, exfiltration, or resupply of Special Operations Forces, such missions being conducted by airdrop, airlanding, or using the heavy-lift sling. Six of the older MH-53Js are being de-modified to TH-53Bs exclusively for use in training.

MH-53Js have flown in a host oif U.S. military operations over the past twenty years, including Operation Just Cause (Panama, 1989), Desert Storm (Gulf, 1991), Provide Comfort and Southern Watch (Gulf, 1992), and Provide Promise and Deny Flight (Balkans, 1992 onwards). In 1997 MH-53Js airlifted Americans out of Zaire and Albania, and in 1998 they returned to Saudi Arabia in support of the buildup to convince Iraq to comply with U.N. weapons inspections.

The current Air Force inventory comprises thirteen MH-53Js and twenty-five MH- 53Ms, all in the active force. There are none of either type in either the Air National Guard or the Air Force Reserve.

Left: MH-53 Pave Low helicopter; note nose radome, inflight refueling probe.

Sikorsky MH-60G/HH-60G Pave Hawk/MH-60K

Type: Special Operations Forces helicopter.
Manufacturer: Sikorsky Aircraft Division of United Technologies Corp.
Weight: maximum takeoff 22,000lb (9,979kg).
Dimensions: length 64.8ft (19.8m); height 16.8ft (5.1m); rotor diameter 53.6ft (16.4m).
Powerplant: two General Electric T700-GE-700 turboshafts, each 1,622shp (1,210kW).
Performance: maximum level speed, clean, sea-level 160kt (184mph/296kmh); cruising speed, 4,000ft (1,220m) 145kt (167mph/268kmh); service ceiling 19,000ft (5,790m); ferry range 1,200nm (1,380 miles/2,220kmh).
Armament: two 7.62mm miniguns.
Crew: four (two pilots, one flight engineer, and one gunner).

There are a number of versions of the UH-60 whose primary role is the support of Special Operations Forces. These are currently the Air Force's MH-60G and the Army's MH-60K, but, in addition, the Air Force's HH-60G, essentially a combat rescue aircraft, can also have an SOF role. The MH-60G Pave Hawk is a twin-engined, medium-lift helicopter, whose main wartime missions are infiltration, exfiltration, and resupply of SOF by day or night and regardless of weather conditions. It is operated by the Air Force Special Operations Command, which is one of the components of the U.S. Special Operations Command. The MH-60G is equipped with an all-weather radar which, among other uses, enables the crew to avoid inclement weather. To extend its range, the aircraft is also equipped with a retractable in-flight refueling probe and additional internal auxiliary fuel tanks can also be carried, if necessary. A rescue hoist has a 200ft (60.7m) cable and 600lb (270kg) lift capacity, and external loads can be underslung on an 8,000lb (3,600kg) capacity cargo hook. Pave

Above: Crewmen mount a Minigun in an MH-60 Blackhawk.

Hawks are equipped with folding rotor blades and a tail stabilator, both for shipboard operations and to ease air transportability.

The HH-60G is very similar to the MH-60G, but its primary mission is independent combat search and rescue (CSAR) operations in combat areas up to and including medium-threat environments. The actual rescues can be made by landing or by a variety of other means, including rope ladder or hoist. The hoist can be operated from heights of up to 200ft (61m) and can recover up to three men at a time or a single patient on a Stokes litter. The basic crew normally consists of five: pilot, co-pilot, flight engineer, and two PJs. The aircraft can also carry eight to ten troops.

The MH-60K is the Army's standard special operations helicopter. It is capable of providing long-range airlifts far into hostile territory in adverse weather conditions. Modifications include two removable 230-gallon external fuel tanks, two .50 cal. machine guns, an air-to-air refueling probe, and an external hoist. The MH-60K can also be armed with two M134 7.62mm miniguns. A new avionics suite includes interactive Multi-Function Displays (MFDs), Forward-Looking Infrared (FLIR), digital map generator, and terrain-avoidance/terrain-following multi-mode radar. Survivability equipment includes radar and missile warning systems and IR jammers. The MH-60K has full shipboard operability. It is powered by two General Electric T700-GE-701C 1843 shp turboshaft engines.

Left: MH-60 with numerous radars and antennas, and refueling probe.

Special Electronic and Reconnaissance Aircraft

The cutting edge of an air force's capabilities is popularly considered to be its fighters and bombers, which are broadly termed "combat" aircraft and which demonstrably fight or deliver hardware. On the other hand, reconnaissance and electronic warfare aircraft are generally considered to be of secondary importance, not least because the aircraft involved in such missions rarely carry guns or missiles and their physical appearance lacks the "glamor" of a true fighting machine. However, such a view is the result of a misconception, because in real war just one such aircraft on a single mission may prove crucial to the success of the campaign, perhaps even to the war itself. As a result, the U.S. armed forces operate a large and growing number of such aircraft, which range in size and sophistication from the large E-3 to the tiny RC-12. But what they have in common is that they are packed with electronic equipment, which is almost invariably very considerably more expensive than the airframe, while their wings, fuselage, and tailplane are festooned with antennae of varying size and shapes.

Two other factors that most of these systems have in common are that the installation has been created by adapting an existing airframe and that they have exceptionally long service lives. Thus, the C-135/707 airframe lives on in the E-3, E-6, and E-8, while the A-6 was converted without great difficulty into the EA-6, and has since served the U.S. Navy and Marine Corps for some forty years.

One important aspect of the work of these aircraft is that they are increasingly producing their information in real-time. Thus, whereas in the past a photographic reconnaissance aircraft had to land to enable its film to be taken to be processed and interpreted, today the information is transmitted in digital electronic form as it is gained, thus saving a great deal of time. This, in turn, enables the information to be interpreted and in the hands of the operations staff much more rapidly so that they can respond in a timely and appropriate manner.

In only a very few cases are these aircraft autonomous, but are, rather, just one part of a much larger system that consists of a variety of collection platforms, which are interlinked both with each other and with further elements on the ground. Thus, for example, while the Beech RC-12 is labeled the Guardrail intelligence collector, it is, in fact, necessary to have three aircraft in the air simultaneously to provide the required area coverage, while in order to give the 24-hour coverage which is an inescapable factor on the modern battlefield, this in turn requires twelve aircraft working a three-way shift cycle. Nor is that all, since there is also a network of ground stations of various types, which are involved in processing information, communicating it to those commanders who need it, and providing maintenance support for the system.

Right: In a national emergency, America's war-fighting could be directed from the E-4B.

Boeing E-3 Sentry

Type: airborne warning and control system (AWACS).
Manufacturer: The Boeing Company.
Weight: maximum takeoff 347,000 pounds (156,150kg).
Dimensions: length 145.5ft (44.0m); height 41.3ft (12.5m);span 130.8ft (39.7m). Radome diameter 30ft (9.1m); depth 6ft (1.8m).
Powerplant: four Pratt & Whitney TF33-PW-100A turbofans, each 21,000lb (9,450kg) static thrust.
Performance: optimum cruising speed 360mph (Mach 0.48); service ceiling <29,000ft (8,788m); endurance, internal fuel <11 hours.
Armament: None.
Crew: twenty-one (four flight crew, thirteen-nineteen AWACS mission specialists).

The Boeing E-3 Sentry introduced a totally new concept of airborne warning and control to air and land warfare. When first mooted, the idea of a huge rotating saucer-shaped dome on top of the rear fuselage of a high-performance airliner was greeted with a mixture of amazement and scorn. The project went ahead despite its critics and has proved to be a great success. The airframe is a modified version of that used for the Boeing 707/320B commercial airliner, together with its engines and avionics, and to this has been added a rotating, disc-shaped dome, 30ft (9.1m) in diameter, and 6ft (1.8m) deep, which weighs 3,395lb (1,540kg). This is held 14ft (4.2m) above the rear fuselage by two struts and is canted forwards at a very small angle (approximately 3 degrees). The dome rotates at a speed of six revolutions per minute in the air and must be kept rotating at about 0.25rpm on the ground, in order to maintain the lubrication of the bearings.

The dome contains the transmitting and receiving elements of the Westinghouse AN/APY-2 radar, which provide coverage of the earth's surface up into the stratosphere, over land or water, and out to a range of more than 250 miles (375km) for low-flying targets and much further for aircraft flying at medium to high altitudes. The radar includes an

Identification Friend or Foe (IFF) sub-system and these sensors, in conjunction with a powerful computer, enable the operators to perform surveillance, identification, weapons control, battle management, and communications functions in real time. Tracks are classified into land, air or sea, friendly or hostile, and data downlinks enable all the information to be passed to U.S. military command and control centers in rear areas or aboard ships, or, in time of crisis, to the National Command Authorities.

Missions normally last for some 8-10 hours, but air-to-air refueling and on-board rest facilities enable much longer missions to be undertaken when necessary. The E-3 is unarmed. At first sight, the E-3, orbiting in its racetrack pattern at some 30,000ft (9,145m) might appear vulnerable, but it does, in fact, have a greater chance of survival than a fixed, ground-based radar system, with its on-board sensors giving early warning of any direct threat, enabling the aircraft to take evasive action or to call up support from friendly fighters.

The first of two AWACS prototypes, then designated EC-137D, flew in February 1972, with the first production aircraft flying in October 1975 and IOC achieved in 1978. A total of thirty-four E-3As were built (which included the two EC-137Ds upgraded to production standard), and twenty-four of these were then upgraded to E-3B standard, which involved enhanced sensors and accommodation for five more crew members. Then in 1984 the ten remaining E-3As were upgraded to E-3C standard, which also involved extra crew positions and enhanced sensors. One aircraft was lost in 1995 in Alaksa, leaving thirty-three in service today.

The USAF E-3 fleet is being regularly modernized to keep the airframe, engines and electronics up-to-date. The Block 30/35 Modification Program was completed in 2001, which included enhanced Electronic Support Measures (ESM), installation of Joint Tactical Information Distribution System (JTIDS) and Global Positioning System (GPS), and an increase in

Below: Boeing E-3 AWACS, an aircraft which revolutionized war-fighting.

computer memory to accommodate these enhancements. In a separate program all aircraft are undergoing the Radar System Improvement Program (RSIP) which involves major improvements to the radar's hardware and software, which will greatly improve the E-3's radar electronic countermeasures (ECM) and also enhance the system's availability and reliability.

A major program is under consideration, which, if implemented, will transfer many of the command and control tasks from the aircraft to the ground. This will transform the aircraft from an airborne command center into a surveillance platform, with only the flight crew and two technicians aboard the aircraft and the remainder relocated to ground-based command centers. This will achieve significant manpower and training savings and will also make a great deal of space available in the aircraft for additional sensors and electronic equipment. If it comes to fruition, twenty-seven of the present thirty-three aircraft will be converted at a cost of US$1.52 billion.

E-3s are among the first assets to be deployed in any crisis. In

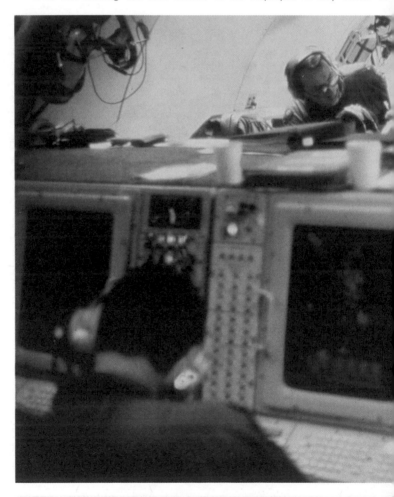

Operations Desert Shield/storm, for example, they flew more than 400 missions, logging more than 5,000 hours of on-station time, to provide radar surveillance and control for more than 120,000 Coalition sorties. The support provided ranged from giving senior leadership time-critical information on enemy actions to participating in 38 of the 40 air-to-air kills recorded during the conflict. In addition, they provided, for the first time in the history of aerial warfare, a recording of the entire air campaign.

Such a high-value system has only been released to a few, carefully selected allies: NATO (17), France (4), Saudi Arabia (5) and the United Kingdom (6), while Japan operates the same AWACS system, but installed on a Boeing 767 platform.

All E-3s undergo a carefully designed maintenance program which is intended to keep the fleet in frontline service. Under present plans there will be no further major modifications after 2018 and all but five of the present aircraft will be retired in 2025.

Below: Operators and analysts at work inside a USAF Boeing E-3 Sentry.

Boeing E-4B

Type: national emergency airborne command post (NEACP).
Manufacturer: The Boeing Company.
Weight: maximum takeoff 800,000lb (360,000kg).
Dimensions: length 231.3ft (70.5m); height 63.4ft (19.3m); span 195.7ft (59.7m).
Powerplant: four General Electric CF6-50E2 turbofans, each 52,500lb (233.6kN) static thrust.
Performance: maximum level speed at 30,000ft (9,150m) 523kt (602mph/969kmh); ferry range 6,000nm (7,730 miles/12,600km); endurance, unrefueled 12 hours, with refueling <48hr; cruise ceiling < 40,000ft (12,000m).
Armament: None.
Crew: <100.

The Boeing E-4B uses the commercial Boeing 747-200 airframe, but with considerable internal alterations to suit it for its role as the United States' National Emergency Airborne Command Post (NEACP). This means that in case of national emergency or the destruction of ground command and control centers, the aircraft will provide a modern, highly survivable, command, control, and communications center to direct U.S. forces, execute emergency war orders, and coordinate actions by civil authorities. Its most recent use in this role was on 11 September 2001 when President Bush spent some hours airborne taking command of U.S. resources until the extent of the terrorist attacks was known.

There are two deck levels, with the upper deck providing rest and sleeping accommodation for off-duty personnel. The main deck is divided into five functional areas: a National Command Authorities (NCA) work area, conference room, briefing room, an operations team work area, and a communications area. Apart from the president and his immediate staff, the E-4B crew comprises between 110 and 120 people, including a joint-service operations team, two complete flight crews (aircraft commander, co-pilot, navigator, flight engineer), a maintenance and security component, and a communications team, but others may be added, as necessary.

Above: Boeing E-4B airborne over the U.S. national capital, Washington D.C.

The E-4B has state-of-the-art electronic and communications equipment and is fitted with shielding against nuclear and thermal effects. Its electrical and electronic systems are also shielded against the effects of electromagnetic pulse (EMP), one of the major effects of a high airburst nuclear weapon, to which such a high-flying aircraft would otherwise be very vulnerable. The aircraft also carries advanced satellite communications systems to provide worldwide communications coverage. One of the many communications facilities aboard the aircraft is one which would enable the president to break into terrestrial TV and radio broadcasts in order to speak direct to the nation.

There are four E-4Bs, which are based at Offutt AFB in Nebraska, but one is

always forward deployed and at a high state of readiness, so as to be available to the president at very short notice, wherever in the world he might be.

From 1994 onwards, and with the approval of the president and the Joint Chiefs of Staff, the E-4B has had the additional task of supporting the Federal Emergency Management Agency (FEMA) by flying an immediate response team to the site of a national disaster, such as an earthquake, fire, hurricane or typhoon. The E-4B would then continue as the FEMA command and control center until the emergency team's own equipment and facilities have been established. This reduces FEMA's response to such a disaster from a matter of days to one of hours.

Left: High in U.S. airspace, an E-4B NEACP aircraft refuels from a KC-135 tanker.

Boeing E-6A/B Mercury

Type: E-6A – communications relay for fleet ballistic missile submarines; E-6B – communications relay for fleet ballistic missile submarines and airborne command post for U.S. strategic forces.
Manufacturer: The Boeing Company.
Weight: maximum takeoff 342,000lb (154,400 kg).
Dimensions: length 150.3ft (45.8m); height 42.4ft (12.9m); span 148.3ft (45.2m).
Powerplant: four CFM-56-2A-2 high-bypass turbofans; each 22,000lb (97.9kN) static thrust.
Performance: maximum level speed at optimum altitude 530kt (610mph/980kmh); maximum cruising speed at 40,000ft (12,200m) 455kt (523mph/840kmh); ceiling <40,000ft (12,200m); range with 6 hours loiter time, no refueling 6,600nm (7,600 miles/12,144km); endurance without refueling <15 hours, with multiple flight refueling 72 hours.
Armament: None.
Crew: E-6A – fourteen; E-6B – twenty-two.

When ballistic missile submarines (SSBNs) are on patrol the depth of water makes it difficult to pass messages to them from the National Command Authority, except by Very Low Frequency (VLF) radio, which requires an airborne relay station equipped with very long trailing-wire antennas (TWA). This

requirement was originally met by a modified Hercules, the EC-130Q, in a system known as TAke Charge And Move Out (TACAMO). Work on a replacement began in 1983 and the selected contractor, Boeing, based its airframe on the E-3, the prototype flying in 1987 and the first production models being delivered to the Navy in 1989.

The E-6A was designed and entered service solely for the U.S. Navy's TACAMO mission, which is described in more detail below. The aircraft and its systems are hardened against the effect of electromagnetic pulse (EMP) and can fly for over fifteen hours without refueling or up to a maximum of seventy-two hours with several in-flight refuelings. The E-6A carries a normal crew of fourteen, consisting of five naval officers and nine enlisted naval aircrew.

When the Air Force's EC-135 command posts were approaching retirement it was decided to replace them by modifying the E-6A to become a dual-mission aircraft. This involved adding battlestaff positions and other specialized equipment, so that it can be used as either a TACAMO aircraft, or as an airborne national command post (ABNCP), or both. To carry out the ABNCP duties the E-6 carries an additional eight people and is fitted with an airborne launch control system (ALCS), which enables it to launch U.S. land-based intercontinental ballistic missiles, in the event that other communications between the NCA and

Below: The first E-6A TACAMO on its first flight on February 19, 1987.

the missiles fail. The first E-6B aircraft was accepted in December 1997 and the E-6B became fully operational in October 1998. The last E-6A will complete conversion in 2003.

The E-6A's primary mission is to broadcast on the VLF band which requires two vertically polarized very long trailing wire antenna (TWA). One of these is 4,000ft (1,220m) long and is deployed from a winch in the tail-cone, while the second is deployed from under the rear fuselage, and is considerably longer – 26,000ft (7,925m). When it is required to transmit, the antennae are first deployed horizontally behind the aircraft but then the pilot puts the aircraft into a steep bank at a predetermined speed and rate-of-turn, which results in the

Above: Primary mission of the E-6 is to provide VLF radio links to SSBNs.

greater part of the two TWAs hanging vertically and thus acting as relatively efficient end-fed antennae. However, some problems have been experienced with this procedure and there have been incidents where there has been contact between the wire and the tail, resulting in safety restrictions being imposed on the angle of bank and thus reducing the length of TWA that is actually hanging vertically. This is being addressed by the E-6A Orbit Improvement Program, which involves installing auto-throttles and software improvements to the Flight Management Computer System (FMCS).

Lockheed Martin EC-130H Compass Call/Rivet Fire

Type: tactical command, control, and communications countermeasures (C³CM) aircraft.
Manufacturer: originally Lockheed, now Lockheed Martin.
Weight: empty 69,300lb (31,434kg); maximum takeoff 135,000lb (61,236kg).
Dimensions: length 97.8ft (29.3m); height 38.3ft (11.4m); span 132.6ft (39.7m).
Powerplant: four Rolls-Royce Allison T56-A-15 turboprops, each 4,300shp (3,080kW).
Performance: maximum cruising speed 321kt (370mph/595kmh) at 30,000ft (9,144m); range 4,210nm (4,848 miles/7,802km) with maximum fuel or 1,910nm (2,199 miles/3,539km) with maximum payload.
Crew: thirteen (two pilots, navigator, flight engineer, plus nine specialist operators).

The EC-130H Compass Call is a version of the Lockheed C-130 Hercules adapted for use as a tactical command, control, and communications countermeasures (C³CM) platform. Electronic attacks on hostile command and control systems provide friendly commanders with an immense advantage before and during the air campaign. Among the means the Compass Call uses is noise jamming to prevent communication or to degrade the transfer of information essential to enemy command and control of weapon systems and other resources. Although the aircraft's primary mission is support of tactical air

operations it can also provide jamming support to ground force operations. Modifications to the aircraft include an electronic countermeasures system (Rivet Fire), air-refueling capability, and associated navigation and communications systems. External indications of the aircraft's role are two blisters, one each side of the rear fuselage, and a gantry under the tail which is used to deploy wire antennae.

Ten such aircraft were built and all continue to serve. They have been regularly upgraded in service, the most recent being Block 30, which is intended to improve system reliability and currency, although a funding problem has deferred completion until 2004-05. Even though this has not been completed Blocks 35 and 40 upgrades are already planned.

The EC-130H carries a combat crew of thirteen people, of whom four are the flightcrew. The other nine operate the Rivet Fire equipment and comprise: electronic warfare officer/mission crew commander (EWO/MCC), a mission crew supervisor (MCS), six operators, and an airborne maintenance technician. Compass Call assets are deployed worldwide, often at very short notice, in support of all the unified commands. There are five in each of two squadrons and three as attrition reserves.

Below: Compass Call is a command-and-control version of the C-130; it can also provide jamming support for ground forces.

Boeing/Raytheon RC-135V/W Rivet Joint

Type: electronic reconnaissance aircraft.
Manufacturers: Boeing (airframe), Raytheon (electronics).
Weight: maximum takeoff 297,000lb (133,633kg).
Dimensions: length 135ft (41.1m); height 42ft (12.8m); span 131ft (39.9m).
Powerplant: four Pratt & Whitney TF33-P-5 turbofans, each of 16,050lb (7,280kg) static thrust.
Performance: maximum speed <500mph (Mach 0.66); unrefueled range 3,900 miles (6,500km).
Armament: none.
Crew: .five (three pilots, two navigators) plus 21-27 specialists, but usually a minimum of 3 electronic warfare officers, 14 intelligence operators, and 4 inflight/airborne maintenance technicians.

Some 820 aircraft of the C-135 family were built for the U.S. armed forces, of which the great majority were tanker (KC-135) or transport (C-135) variants. A total of thirty-nine were also built as Airborne Command Posts (ABNCP); designated EC-135, their role ended with the Cold War and since then they have been either scrapped or converted to other roles.

A number were built as reconnaissance aircraft; with the prefix "R" these are usually recognizable by the odd-shaped noses and many extra external antennae and fairings hiding exotic sensors. It is known that there are three discrete types, but so highly classified are their roles and equipment that there may be more, as yet unrecorded, variants. The RC-135S Cobra Ball (two built) is intended to detect and track foreign missile launches and may also be used to detected Scud launchers (????????). The mission of the RC-135U Combat Sent (two built) is to detect hostile electronic signals to assist planners in tasking and locating the main ELINT assets. Only one RC-135X Cobra Eye was built, its task being to photograph missiles, but it has since been converted to RC-135S standard. The remaining fifteen are Rivet Joint stand-off jammers, comprising eight RC-135V and six RC-135W; fouteen were built for the role and one C-135 was converted in the late 1990s.

Both these Rivet Joint types are fitted with sophisticated intelligence gathering equipment, designed to enable military specialists to monitor the electronic activity of potential and actual adversaries. This involves ELINT and COMINT intercepts of hostile activity at ranges of up to about 150 miles (240km) in order to give information about the location and intentions of enemy forces. They are also required to originate voice broadcasts, the highest priorities being imminent threat warnings direct to aircraft in danger and "combat advisories" to warn general areas. They also operate data and voice links to provide target information to ground-based US air defense forces.

Like all USAF aircraft the RC-135s are being constantly upgraded. Current known programs for the Rivet Joint system include Tactical Common Data Link (TCDL), High- and Low-Band Subsystem (LBSS) various antenna improvements, the installation of more advanced direction-finding (DF) equipment, and enhanced data links. The aircraft themselves are also being upgraded, being fitted with CFM-56 engines, a "glass cockpit" and more efficient air-conditioning. One surprising and long overdue upgrade is the installation of an airline-type toilet to replace the very unsatisfactory and

Above: RC-135W Rivet Joint, showing just some of its many antennas.

unpopular current arrangement. The interior seats thirty-two people, including the cockpit crew, electronic warfare officers, intelligence operators, and in-flight maintenance technicians. All RC-135s are assigned to Air Combat Command and are permanently based at Offutt Air Force Base, Nebraska, where they are operated by the 55th Wing, using various forward deployment locations worldwide.

Lockheed Martin EC-130E Rivet Rider (Commando Solo)

Type: airborne radio and television broadcasting system.
Manufacturer: originaly Lockheed, now Lockheed Martin.
Weight: empty 69,300lb (31,434kg); maximum takeoff 135,000 lb (61,236kg).
Dimensions: length 97.8ft (29.3m); height 38.3ft (11.4m); span 132.6ft (39.7m).
Powerplant: four Rolls-Royce Allison T56-A-15 turboprops, each 4,300shp (3,080kW).
Performance: maximum cruising speed 321kt (370mph/595kmh) at 30,000ft (9,144m); range 4,210nm (4,848 miles/7,802km) with maximum fuel or 1,910nm (2,199 miles/3,539km) with maximum payload.
Crew: flight crew plus mission operators.

Commando Solo (initially known as Volant Solo) is the name given to a USAF airborne electronic broadcasting system, which is operated by four EC-130E Rivet Rider aircraft. The Commando Solo mission primarily involves psychological operations and civil affairs broadcasts over standard civil frequencies. These audio broadcasts can be made over long-wave, short-wave, and very high frequency (VHF) bands, using either AM or FM modes, as well as TV. However, under certain circumstances, broadcasts may also be made on military frequencies. The aircraft normally operate alone and fly at their maximum altitude to ensure that their broadcasts cover the widest possible geographical area, following an orbital track, which is offset from the desired target audience. Apart from its wartime

Above: Latest version of Rivet Rider with four antennas on vertical fin.

applications, this system can also be used to support disaster relief operations, by making public information broadcasts or issuing instructions for evacuation operations. Other uses include the temporary replacement of existing transmitters or expanding their areas of coverage. These aircraft are operated by 193 Special Operations Wing, Air National Guard, part of the USAF's Special Operations Command.

The aircraft have one oversized blade antenna under each wing outboard of the outer engines; originally there was a third, extending forward from the vertical fin, but this has now been replaced by two new antennae projecting laterally from the fin. A trailing wire antenna can also be deployed from a winch in the tail, with a second which is hung vertically from the belly and maintained directly below the aircraft by a 500lb (227kg) weight.

Among the operations undertaken by these aircraft are Desert Shield and Desert Storm during which, among other tasks, they broadcast a station known as "Voice of the Gulf," which was intended to convince Iraqi soldiers to surrender. More recently, Commando Solo broadcast radio and television messages to the citizens and leaders of Haiti during Operation Uphold Democracy (1994), and in Operation Joint Guard the system operated in support of SFOR operations in Bosnia-Herzegovina. It latest operations have been over Afghanistan.

Left: Earlier version with blade antenna forward of fin.

Lockheed Martin EP-3E (ARIES II)

Type: land-based signals intelligence (SIGINT) aircraft.
Manufacturer: originally Lockheed, now Lockheed Martin.
Weight: empty 61,491lb (27,890kg); normal takeoff 135,000lb (61,235kg); maximum takeoff 139,760lb (63,395kg).
Dimensions: length 116.6ft (35.6m); height 33.6ft (10.3m); span 99.5ft (30.4m)
Powerplant: four Allison T-56-A-14 turboprop engines (each 4,900 shp).
Performance: maximum airspeed 411kt (466mph/745kmh); cruise 328k (403mph/644kmh); ceiling 28,300ft (8,626m); mission range 2,380nm (2,740 miles/4,410km); range for three hours on station at 1,500 feet (460m) 1,346nm (1,549 miles).
Armament: none.
Crew: twenty-four (five flight crew plus nineteen mission crew).

In the 1960s the U.S. Navy conducted its SIGINT (Signal Intelligence) missions using specially-modified Super Constellations, but these were replaced in 1969-74 by EP-3A ARIES I (Airborne Reconnaissance Integrated Electronic System) aircraft, which equipped two squadrons, each of nine aircraft. In the 1990s these were replaced by a further twelve P-3Cs, which were converted under a program known as CILOP (conversion in lieu of procurement) to EP-3E ARIES II standard, the last of the new aircraft being delivered in 1997. Eleven of these aircraft remain in service.

The EP-3E ARIES II has a large radome under the forward fuselage, a ventral radome, numerous small antennae, and a shortened tailboom. Internally it houses direction-finding (DF) equipment; signals gathering, analysis and

recording equipment; and their own real-time communications equipment.

The EP-3E ARIES II is a four-engined, low-wing aircraft powered by four Allison T56-A-14 turboprop engines, which is capable of over 12 hours' endurance and has a range in excess of 3,000nm. The normal crew is twenty-four strong – a flight crew comprising three pilots, one navigator, one flight engineer, and three tactical evaluators, plus a mission crew of sixteen operators, technicians, and mechanics.

EP-3Es have been heavily engaged in reconnaissance in support of NATO forces in Bosnia, and joint forces in Korea and in Operation Southern Watch, Northern Watch, and Allied Force. Normally these operations are shrouded in secrecy, but one hit the world's headlines on 1 April 2001 when it was involved in a major incident with two fighters of the Chinese PLA-Air Force. The Navy aircraft was on a routine patrol in international airspace off Hainan Island when it was intercepted and one fighter flew too close, miscalculated its speed and in trying to slow down pitched up and hit one of the EP-3's propellers. Considerable damage was caused to both aircraft; the Chinese aircraft crashed, killing its pilot, but the EP-3 pilot managed to recover his crippled aircraft to Hainan, where he made an emergency no-flaps, three-engine landing. Once on the ground the crew found that the radome was missing, there was much debris wrapped around the tail, and one propeller was missing. After a high-level dispute, followed by negotiations, first the crew and then the aircraft were returned to the United States.

Below: The exterior of this EP-3E is covered in antennas of all descriptions.

Lockheed Martin ES-3A Shadow

Type: twin-engined, carrier-based ELINT/SIGINT aircraft.
Manufacturer: originally Lockheed, now Lockheed Martin.
Weight: empty 26,650lb (12,090kg); normal takeoff 42,500lb (19,277kg); maximum gross takeoff: 52,539lb (23,643 kg).
Dimensions: length 53.3ft (16m); height overall 22.8ft (6.9m), height tail folded 15.3ft (4.7m);span extended 68.7ft (20.6m), span folded 29.5ft (9.0m).
Powerplant: two General Electric TF-34-GE-400B turbofan engines, each 9,275lb (4,207kg) static thrust (41.3kN).
Performance: maximum airspeed, clean, sea-level 450kt (518mph/828.8kmh); cruising speed at optimum altitude 350kt (403mph/649kmh); loiter speed at 20,000ft, 210kt; ceiling 34,000ft (10,360m); range 2,300+ nautical miles (2,645 miles/4,232km); maximum endurance 7 hours.
Armament: none.
Crew: four.

The ES-3A Shadow is a variant of the S-3 Viking carrier-based ASW aircraft. It was developed to provide indications and warnings of hostile electronic emissions for the carrier battle group commander as a replacement for the EA-3B Skywarrior, which served with the fleet for some forty years. It is a high-

winged, twin turbojet-powered, carrier-based electronic reconnaissance mission aircraft equipped with folding wings, a launch bar, and a tailhook.

The heart of the ES-3A Shadow is an avionics suite based on the ARIES II system of the land-based EP-3E Orion (see previous entry). The aircraft's fuselage is packed with sensor stations and processing equipment, and more than sixty antennae have been identified on the aircraft's exterior. The crew comprises a pilot, co-pilot, and two systems operators. The advanced sensor, navigation and communications systems allow the crew to collect extensive data and distribute high-quality information through a variety of channels to the carrier battle group, giving the battle group commander a clear picture of potential airborne and surface threats. Missions flown by the detachment include over-the-horizon targeting, strike support, and reconnaissance. The ES-3A is configured as an airborne refueling platform and can be utilized in the airborne tanking role.

In a highly controversial, budget-driven decision, the ES-3A was removed from service in 1999/2000; the two squadrons were disbanded and all aircraft placed in storage. They remain there and will become progressively more out-of-date as time passes, but while in service they were a highly regarded and considered to be a valuable asset to the carrier battle group.

Left: Lockheed Martin ES-3A Shadow lands on carrier USS George Washington (CVN-73), while deployed in the Persian Gulf during Operation Southern Watch. Note the antennas on wingtips, as well as both above and below the fuselage.

Lockheed Martin U-2S

Type: high-altitude reconnaissance aircraft.
Manufacturer: originally Lockheed, now Lockheed Martin.
Weight: maximum takeoff 40,000lb (18,140kg).
Dimensions: length 63.0ft (19.2m); height 16.0ft (4.9m); span 103.0ft (31.4m).
Powerplant: one General Electric F-118-101 turbofan, 17,000lb (7,710kg) static thrust.
Performance: maximum speed <475mph (Mach 0.58); ceiling <70,000 feet (21,212m); range <6,000nm (11,280km).
Armament: none.
Crew: one.

First flown on 1 August 1955, the U-2 was developed to meet a CIA requirement for a highly specialized reconnaissance aircraft able to overfly targets in the Soviet Union at altitudes in excess of 70,000ft (21,000m). The aircraft would rely primarily on height for survivability, but the need for stealth was also appreciated and a low radar cross-section (RCS) was included in the design goals, although in practice the technology of the time made it unattainable. Reconnaissance flights over the Soviet Union began in July 1956, but it soon became obvious that Soviet radars were able to track the aircraft. Thereffre Lockheed re-examined methods of reducing the RCS, but this still proved impractical, although one technique that was tried was the use of a new paint scheme containing radar-absorbing "iron-ball" ferrite pigment.

Fewer than thirty overflights had been completed when the U-2 flown by Francis Gary Powers was shot down near Sverdlovsk on 1 May 1960 and this "U-2 Incident" was the direct cause of the collapse of the summit meeting between President Eisenhower and Soviet Premier Nikita Khrushchev which had been due to take place shortly afterwards. A furious Eisenhower ordered overflights to cease immediately, but even so U.S. intelligence experts had some 1.2 million feet of photographic film covering more than a million square miles of Soviet territory, which gave them an unprecedented view of Soviet aircraft, tactical missile, and nuclear deployments.

Surveillance of the Soviet Union by U-2s continued, but this time with the aircraft flying missions along the Soviet border, using sideways-looking sensors to look deep into Soviet territory. A small batch of U-2s supplied to Taiwan carried out overflights of China between 1959 and 1974, but four were shot down and in 1974 the CIA ended its involvement in the U-2 program and the twenty surviving aircraft were handed over to the USAF.

Around fifty-five U-2As were built and at least seven were reworked as U-2Bs, receiving structural strengthening and the more powerful Pratt & Whitney J75-P-13 turbojet. The follow-on U-2C (a mixture of reworked and new-build aircraft) introduced a slightly extended nose, a long dorsal equipment fairing, increased fuel capacity, enlarged intakes, and the J75-P-13B engine. The U-2D had a modified instrument bay housing either specialized sensors or a second crew member, while the U-2E was a CIA version with advanced ECM systems. At least four U-2As were modified into U-2Fs by addition of a USAF-style refueling receptacle.

The aircraft returned to production in 1968 in its U-2C form. This was powered by the same F5-P-1B engine as the earlier aircraft, but had a strengthened airframe, improved handling, greater range and payload, and a less cramped cockpit. Wingspan was increased by 23ft (7m), the outboard 5.9ft (1.8m) of each wing folding inwards for storage. One of the most obvious new features of the U-2C were the underwing equipment pods which were replaced in 1978 by still larger underwing fairings pods known as "superpods." In fact, although the result bore a superficial resemblance to the earlier U-2 models, this was a completely new design and some seventeen U-2Cs were produced.

Next in the series was TR-1A, which was structurally identical to the U-2C and was ordered in 1979 as a source of "day or night, high-altitude, all weather stand-off surveillance of a battle area in direct support of U.S. and allied ground and air forces." The first example flew on 1 August 1981 and was delivered to the USAF in the following month; the type operated mainly from USAF bases in England, starting in February 1983. The last production aircraft were delivered in October 1989 and in 1992 the USAF dropped the designation TR-1, and classified all operational aircraft as U-2C.

In May 1988 the USAF gave Lockheed a contract to demonstrate and flight test a General Electric F118-GE-101 turbofan engine, which was lighter, produced more thrust, and burned less fuel than the older J75-P-1B turbojet. The first re-engined U-2C aircraft flew for the first time on 23 May 1989. The upgrade proved successful, and was applied to the entire fleet. Other upgrades improved the aircraft's sensors and added a Global Positioning System (GPS) satellite-navigation system that would record geographical co-ordinates directly on the collected images. The re-engined single-seat aircraft are designed U-2S, while the trainer is the U-2ST.

The first production single-seaters and trainers were delivered in October 1994, with the first operation taking place one year later. This aircraft is capable of collecting multi-sensor photo, electro-optic, infrared and radar imagery, as well as performing other types of reconnaissance, but requires a skilled pilot. Its

Below: All TR-1s and U-2s were redesignated U-2R in 1992, then U-2S.

high aspect ratio wings give the U-2 glider-like flying characteristics and make the aircraft extremely challenging to control in certain regimes, especially when landing. The high-altitude mission means that the pilot must wear a full pressure suit, which adds to the challenge of flying the aircraft. An official USAF description of the U-2 notes that it "can be a difficult aircraft to fly due to its unusual landing characteristics."

The aircraft that the Soviets once dubbed "the black lady of espionage"

Above: U-2 of 9th Reconnaissance Wing, Beale Air Force Base, California.

has outlived its supersonic SR-71 replacement. On 11 August 1994, U-2C number 0338 became the first U-2 to achieve 20,000 flying hours, and the type is expected to remain in service for many years. There are currently thirty-five aircraft in the Air Force inventory, of which four are two-seat trainers.

Northrop Grumman E-2C Hawkeye

Type: carrier-borne, all-weather, airborne early warning, command-and-control aircraft.
Manufacturer: originally Grumman, now Northrop Grumman.
Weight: basic 40,200lb (18,090kg); maximum takeoff 53,000lb (23,850kg).
Dimensions: length 57.5ft (17.5m); height 18.3ft (5.6m); span 80.6ft (28m).
Powerplant: two Allison T-56-A427 turboprops. each 5,000shp (3,700kW).
Performance: maximum speed 323kt (372mph/598kmh); maximum cruising speed at optimum altitude 311kt (358mph/576kmh); endurance with maximum fuel 6.1 hours; ceiling 30,000ft (9,100m).
Armament: none.
Crew: five (pilot, co-pilot, combat information officer, air control officer, radar operator).

Airborne radar first became operational during World War II and development continued into the post-war era, leading to the concept of carrier-borne aircraft which would combine the function of airborne early warning with that of command-and-control. These two tasks were originally performed by two separate aircraft, but were eventually combined by the U.S. Navy in one aircraft, the Grumman E-1 Tracer, a variant of the S-2 Tracker anti-submarine aircraft, fitted with a huge fixed, saucer-shaped radome above the fuselage. This entered service in 1954, but it was replaced ten years later by the E-2A Hawkeye (originally designated W2F), which was the first carrier-based aircraft designed from the outset for the all-weather airborne early warning and command and control function. This entered service in 1964. The early models,

Above: E-2C Hawkeye "eyes of the fleet" taking off from a carrier.

E-2A and E-2B, are no longer in service, all current models being the E-2C version, which entered service in the 1970s and has been constantly upgraded ever since.

The E-2C provides all-weather airborne early warning and command-and-control functions for the U.S. Navy's carrier battle groups, but is also able to perform additional missions, such as the coordination of surface surveillance, control of strike and interception missions, guidance of search-and-rescue operations, and communications relay. It is a high-wing, twin-engined aircraft, with the antenna of its APS-145 radar contained in a 24ft (7.3m) rotadome above the fuselage. This radome causes peculiar airflow which, combined with the need to keep height to a minimum, has led to the unusual four-finned tail unit.

The E-2 has been the "eyes of the fleet" for almost forty years, having made its combat debut during the Vietnam War. Hawkeyes directed F-14 Tomcat fighters flying combat air patrol during the two-carrier battle group joint strike against terrorist-related Libyan targets in 1986. More recently, E-2Cs provided the command and control for successful operations during the Gulf War, directing both land attack and combat air patrol missions over Iraq and providing control for the shoot-down of two Iraqi MiG-21 aircraft by carrier-based F/A-18s in the early days of the war. E-2 aircraft also have worked extremely effectively with U.S. law enforcement agencies in drug interdiction. Today, E-2Cs and AEGIS cruisers work together to provide total air superiority over the American fleet.

Left: E-2C shows its very complicated wing-folding system.

Northrop Grumman E-8C Joint STARS

Type: airborne battle management aircraft.
Manufacturer: Northrop Grumman Corp.
Weight: empty 171,000lb (77,565kg); with maximum fuel 336,000lb (152,408kg).
Dimensions: length 152.9ft (46.6m); height 42.5ft (13.0m); span 145.8ft (44.4m).
Powerplant: four Pratt & Whitney TF33-102C (JT-3D), each 19,000lb (84.5kN) static thrust.
Performance: maximum cruising speed at 25,000ft (7,620m) 525kt (605mph/973kmh); optimum orbiting speed (depending on altitude) 390-510kt (Mach 0.52-0.65); ceiling: 42,000ft (12,800m); range with maximum fuel 5,000nm (5,758 miles/9,266km); endurance, unrefueled 11 hours, refueled 20 hours.
Armament: none.
Crew: standard mission, 21 (flight crew – 3; mission crew – Army 3, Air Force 15); protracted mission 34 (flight crew 6, mission operators 28).

The Joint Surveillance Target Attack Radar System (Joint STARS) is an Air Force-Army program with a long and complicated history. The program (originally known as "J-STARS" but later changed to "Joint STARS") had its roots in two separate projects which started development in the late 1970s, the Air Force Pave Mover and the Army SOTAS, but these were brought together in 1982 into a joint program, with the Air Force designated the lead service.

There then followed two years of discussion of the most appropriate platform and precisely what capabilities the system should have. This was resolved by a Chiefs of Staff decision that the platform would be a rebuilt Boeing 707 airliner and that the system would be based on SAR (synthetic aperture radar), with MTI (moving target indication), and weapons guidance capabilities. A contract was then placed for two development and ten production aircraft.

In April 1988 it was decided that the first two development aircraft only would be rebuilt ex-commercial Boeing 707s (designated E-8A) and that the remainder would be new-build aircraft using a modified E-3 airframe; the decision was justified on the grounds of the Boeings' lack of remaining service life and the difficulties of converting such old airframes. The new-build aircraft was designated E-8B, and it was also decided to increase the number of airframes from 10 to 22 (although the Air Force considered that over 30 would be needed). The first flight of a fully equipped prototype E-8A took place in December 1988, but in late 1989 there was a sudden and dramatic increase in the cost of the proposed new-build E-8Bs, since there would be a three year gap on the production line at Boeing, between completing the last existing order in 1991 (an E-3D for the British Royal Air Force) and the start of E-8B production in 1994-95.

Thus, the program was reconsidered yet again and a number of other platforms were considered, including the Boeing 757 and 767 and the McDonnell Douglas MD-11, but all were extremely expensive and could not be integrated with the new Joint STARS system in time to meet the intended IOC of 1997. As a result, it was decided to produce a revised version of the original proposal, again using rebuilt Boeing 707s, but now designated E-8C, and approval for the construction of five was given in 1993. The first E-8C flew in March 1994 and served as the pre-production test-bed, while the two E-8A test

Above: Joint STARS airborne platform is a converted Boeing E-8C.

aircraft will be upgraded to C standard and will be the last to be delivered. The first E-8C was accepted by the 93rd Air Control Wing at Robins AFB, GA, on 11 June 1996 and the second on 13 December 1996.

In September 1996 approval was given for full production of nineteen aircraft, but problems were emerging. The early aircraft had been pressed into operational service and, although in many ways they had done well, there had also been shortcomings. The system as a whole had shown a lack of reliability, while the aircraft had proved incapable of climbing to the required altitude, which was 36,000ft (10,973m) under normal conditions and 42,000ft (12,800m) maximum. In addition, the aircraft was so heavy and the engines lacking in power that when loaded with the maximum 140,000lb (63,504km) fuel it required for takeoff an 11,000ft (3,353m) runway when the NATO standard was 8,000ft (2,438m).

Joint STARS consists of an airborne element – an E-8C (converted Boeing 707) aircraft with a multi-mode radar system – and a ground element of Army-operated, vehicle-mounted Ground Station Modules (GSMs). The aircraft carries a phased-array radar antenna in a 26ft (8m) canoe-shaped radome under the forward part of the fuselage, which provides targeting and battle management data to all Joint STARS operators, both in the aircraft and in the GSMs. These operators can then call on aircraft, missiles or artillery for fire support. The radar is reported to have a range in excess of 155 miles (250km) and can cover an estimated $386,100^2$ miles $(1,000,000km^2)$ in a single eight-hour sortie. The radar operates in Wide Area Surveillance (WAS) and Moving Target Indicator (MTI) modes, and is designed not only to detect, locate, and identify slow-moving targets, but also to differentiate between wheeled and tracked vehicles. A further facility is the Synthetic Aperture Radar/Fixed Target

Indicator (SAR/FTI) which produces a photographic-like image or data map of selected geographic regions, showing the precise locations of critical non-moving targets such as bridges, harbors, airports, buildings, or stationary vehicles.

When the Gulf War broke out the two E-8A pre-production aircraft (which were actually still owned by Northrop Grumman) were pressed into service for Operation Desert Storm, flying forty-nine combat sorties, and in some ways did very well. It was Joint STARS for example that detected an Iraqi follow-up force heading for Khafji and at the end of the war detected the huge Iraqi exodus from Kuwait; both targets were dealt devastating blows as a result of Joint STARS detection. The project then reverted to the more normal routine of development, but the next major test was due in November 1995 when Joint STARS was despatched to Europe to support Operation Joint Endeavor in Bosnia. One of the E-8As and a production E-8C took part from December 1995 to March 1996 and again in October-December 1996.

The aircraft are currently being produced, with the aim of reaching a figure of fourteen by 2004, but a whole series of upgrades have already been set in

train, perhaps the most important being to replace the present JT3D-3B engines with the more powerful and economical JT3D-7 engines, which will enable the E-8C to operate from standard runways at full load, and to reach the required altitude. According to recent reports, however, the program is in some doubt, since the purchase of the full number of engines has not yet been funded. Other modifications concern the system and include enhancements to the radar, signal processor, communications system, and target acquisition and identification systems.

Meanwhile, Boeing has suggested once again that a more modern airframe should be considered, with particular reference to the Boeing 767-200 Extended Range, because such an aircraft would provide a longer life, greater room for growth, greater flight range, greater fuel efficiency, higher operational availability, and lower program life-cycle costs.

Below: Boeing proposes that Joint STARS' platform should be modified 767-200.

Northrop Grumman EA-6B Prowler

Type: carrier-borne electronic countermeasures (ECM) aircraft.
Manufacturer: originally Grumman, now Northrop Grumman.
Weight: empty 31,572lb (14,321kg); normal carrier takeoff 54,461lb (24,703kg); maximum takeoff 61,500lb (27,450kg).
Dimensions: length 59.8ft (17.7m); height 16.7ft (4.9m); span 53.0ft (15.9m).
Powerplant: two Pratt & Whitney J52-P408 engines, each 11,200lb (49.8kN) static thrust.
Performance: maximum speed 710kt (817mph/1,315kmh); ferry range, 5 drop-tanks 2,085nm (2,400miles/3,861km); with maximum external load 1,000nm (1,150 miles/1,840 km); service ceiling, clean 41,200ft (12,550m); crew endurance approximately 8 hours.
Armament: .AGM-88B/C HARM missile(s).
Crew: four (pilot plus three electronic countermeasures officers).

The Grumman A-6 Intruder two-seat carrier-borne attack aircraft entered service with the U.S. Navy and Marine Corps in the early 1960s and was finally replaced by the F/A-18 Hornet in the late 1990s. The EA-6B Prowler was a relatively straightforward development of the A-6 with a new, 4.5ft (1.4m) longer forward fuselage accommodating a crew of four, extensive electronic systems and the capability to carry anti-radiation missiles; 177 were produced up to 1991. For

the past thirty years a detachment of EA-6Bs has been included in every carrier air wing, their mission being to protect the carrier battle group and other U.S. military assets by detecting and, where appropriate, jamming hostile radars and communications transmissions, or by attacking the transmitters with missiles such as HARM. The Marine Corps EA-6Bs, which can operate from either carriers or unsophisticated forward air bases, provided the same support for Marines ashore. In the mid-1990s, however, a reorganisation of defense assets resulted in the retirement of USAF EF-111 Raven and F-4G Wild Weasel tactical jammer aircraft and the assumption of their role by the EA-6B. This has led to the formation of five new EA-6B squadrons, four of which are dedicated to supporting USAF Aerospace Expeditionary Force wings.

The heart of the EA-6B system is the AN/ALQ-99 Tactical Jamming System which consists of an underwing pod housing electronic receivers and two jamming transmitters, each covering one of seven frequency bands; the pod also contains its own integral electrical system driven by a turbine, which is spun-up by the slipstream. The EA-6B has five hardpoints, two under each wing and one in the belly, and can carry any combination of five ALQ-99 pods, fuel tanks or HARM anti-radiation missiles, depending on the requirement of the mission.

The EA-6B's ALQ-99's first task is to collect data to enable the enemy's

electronic order of battle (EOB) to be compiled and then disseminated via a real-time downlink to the command-and-control system. The next task is to jam enemy electronic systems, particularly radar in support of friendly air and ground operations. Third, the EA-6B can contribute to the SEAD (suppression of enemy air defenses) campaign by using its HARM missiles. Atop the EA-6B's tail fin is a large pod (known colloquially as the "football") which houses a number of Systems Integration Receivers (SIR), with four more in bulges on the fin. The SIRs, each covering a discrete frequency band, detect hostile radar emissions at long range and the emitter information is processed by the central mission computer, with detection, identification, direction-finding, and jammer-set-on-sequence operations performed automatically or by the crew.

Marine Corps EA-6Bs can operate from carriers, established airfields, or from expeditionary airfields (EAF). In addition to the equipment aboard Navy EA-6Bs, the Marine aircraft are part of the Tactical Electronic Processing and Evaluation System (TERPES), which provides post-mission analysis of EA-6B electronic surveillance data for reporting and updating electronic orders of battle.

The crew of the Prowler consists of the pilot and three electronic countermeasures officers (ECMOs). ECMO1 sits in the starboard front seat where he is

Left: EA-6B ready for take-off; note underwing ALQ-99 pod.

responsible for navigation, communications, and defensive electronic countermeasures. ECMO2 and ECMO 3 sit in the after cabin where they operate the ALQ-99 tactical jammer system.

The EA-6B is being progressively upgraded, the latest standard being Block 89, the main elements of which are greatly improved radios and navigation systems, together with enhancements to the AGM-88 HARM missile. An Improved Data Modem (IDM) also enables EA-6Bs to pass targeting data to HARM-equipped F/A-18s, or to exchange relevant data with other EA-6Bs or USAF RC-135 Rivet Joint aircraft.

The EA-6B force is due to continue to serve for at least another eight years, with retirement starting in about 2010, by which time this outstanding aircraft will have had a career of more than forty years of service in support of Navy, Marines and, more recently, Air Force

operations. The most recent known plans for replacement are that there will be a three-layer airborne ECM system. The outer layer would be provided by the Air Force employing ECM versions of the B-52 or B-1 (EB-52/EB-1), with the inner layer provided by unmanned air vehicles (UAVs) such as the Northrop Grumman Global Hawk or General Atomics Predator. For the middle layer, the Navy and Marines would develop a direct successor to the EA-6B, which would be an ECM version of the F/A-18E/F Hornet (which has unofficially been given the name "Growler"). In the nearer-term, however, the EA-6B fleet will continue to be upgraded to keep abreast of developing threats and maintain aircraft safety.

Below: The EA-6B has been a great success and will serve on until 2010.

Raytheon (Beech) RC-12 Guardrail

Type: utility transport/reconnaissance aircraft.
Manufacturer: Beech (airframe), Raytheon (system).
Weight: empty 7,334lb (3,327kg); maximum 15,500lb (7,031kg).
Dimensions: fuselage 43.8ft (13.3m); height 15.0ft (4.6m); span 57.8ft (17.6m).
Powerplant: two Pratt & Whitney Canada PT6A-41 turboprops; each 850shp (634kW).
Performance: maximum level speed 14,000ft (4,265m) 260kt (300mph/481kmh); maximum cruising speed 30,000ft (9,145m) 236kt (272mph/438kmh); range 1,584nm (1,824 miles/2,935km).
Armament: none
Crew: two to four.
Specifications for RC-12D.

The U.S. Army has procured numerous versions of the Beech King Air/Super King Air/Model 1900-series of twin-engined light aircraft, starting with the RC-12A (King Air 100). Some are used as utility transports, but many are electronic reconnaissance aircraft (prefixed "R"), whose appearance is characterized by a multiplicity of antennas, and which are designated "Guardrail." The Army employed the original Guardrail system in many missions, including collection coverage along the Inner-German Border (the Cold War frontier between the Federal Republic and the East Germany) from 1972 to 1990, in Korea from 1974 to the present, and in Central America from 1983 to 1994.

In the early 1990s a revised system was fielded known as the Guardrail Common Sensor (GR/CS), which is an Army, corps-level, signals/electronic intelligence (SIGINT/ELINT) collection/location/dissemination system deployed aboard RC-12K/N/P/Q aircraft. Key features of GC/RS are that it integrates COMINT and ELINT reporting, enhances signal classification and recognition, speeds up Direction Finding (DF), and improves emitter location; it also includes an advanced integrated cockpit for the pilot. The outcome is that GR/CS provides near real-time SIGINT and targeting information to tactical commanders throughout the corps area. Typically, each GC/RS system comprises twelve aircraft, with three airborne at any one time flying in "race-course" orbits some diustance behind and parallel to the forward line of own troops (FLOT) in order to intercept hostile comminications (eg, tactical ground radio) and non-communications (eg, radar) transmissions. The information is then transmitted to the ground-based Integrated Processing Facility (IPF), and Commanders Tactical Terminals (CTTs), of which there are usually nine, but can be up to thirty-two. Also airborne are two or three Airborne Relay Facilities (ARFs), providing radio relay facilities; this involves a specially- equipped RC-12 with just one pilot and no other crew or operators.

The Guardrail systems currently in service include the Guardrail V (RU-12H aircraft), the Guardrail Common Sensor Minus (RC-12H aircraft), and the Guardrail Common Sensor (RC-12K/N/P aircraft). Guardrail Common Sensor (GRCS) combines the Improved Guardrail V (IGRV) Communication Intelligence (COMINT) sensor package with the Advanced Quicklook electronics signals (ELINT) intercept, classification, and direction-finding capability, and a Communication High Accuracy Airborne Location System (CHAALS). GRCS shares technology with the Ground-Based Common Sensor, Airborne Reconnaissance Low, and other airborne systems.

Below: Guardrail is the Army's major tactical electronic warfare platform.

Unmanned Aerial Vehicles (UAVs)

Following their successes in the first months of the war in Afghanistan, Unmanned Aerial Vehicles (UAVs) will be one of the most exciting areas of technological advance in the U.S. military machine over the next ten years. UAVs have been around for many years, an early pioneer being Dr. F. W. Buck of Flagler, Colorado, who designed "Aerial Torpedoes" during World War I. Biplanes launched by compressed air from the roof of an automobile, they flew a straight course until a timing device shed the wings and the machines dived to the ground. These were pilotless bombs, but the next step was the drone, designed to replace sleeves towed by airplanes as targets for anti-aircraft gunners, a system that was invented in the mid-1930s by Reginald Denny, a former Hollywood movie star. Denny used model airplane technology to develop a radio-controlled target drone, which took off , flew simple maneuvers and then landed, under the orders of a ground controller holding a small transmitter. By 1943 it was in wide-scale service with the U.S. Army and Navy.

The 1946 Northrop KD2R5 was in all essentials a small airplane and over 50,000 were built for practice with guns and missiles. The next step came in the 1960s in answer to the requirement for airborne intelligence-gathering systems at both strategic and tactical levels which did not put aircrew at risk. Several target drones were adapted, among the most successful being the Ryan Firebee-series. At this stage the drones were controlled by simple on-board computers, followed a programmed track over hostile territory, and had to be returned to base for their intelligence "take" to be recovered, processed,

and analyzed. Methods of recovery included parachute, flying into a net, being "captured" in mid-air by specially equipped aircraft, or in a very few cases by a normal airplane-type landing.

Many technical difficulties were encountered and there were some spectacular and expensive failures, such as the U.S. Navy's QH-50 ASW torpedo-carrying drone. Since 1964 the Defense Department has initiated eleven UAV projects, of which only three have achieved actual production status, and people began to ask why it was costing so much money to develop what appeared to be little more than a military adaptation of the radio-controlled models flown by enthusiasts all over the country at every week-end. However, when something goes wrong in a manned airplane the pilot can often take corrective action to bring it back to base, but in a UAV most faults will lead to a crash. Further, the UAV is just one element in a complex system of sensors, data-handling devices, and communications links, and it is frequently this overall complexity that causes many of the problems.

Today the Department of Defense is developing UAVs in three main categories, Tactical, with a range less than 125 miles (200km); Endurance, with a range over 125 miles; and Shipboard. Meanwhile, a whole new area is opening up with the appearance of Unmanned Combat Airborne Vehicles (UCAVs) and Micro Air Vehicles (MAVs).

Below: Predator UAV is not small; wing-span is no less than 48.7ft (14.8m).

Fire Scout

Type: vertical tactical unmanned aerial vehicle (VTUAV).
Manufacturer: Northrop Grumman Ryan.
Weight: empty 1,457lb (661kg); takeoff 2,550lb (1,157kg).
Dimensions: length (folded) 22.9ft (7.0m); rotor disk diameter 27.5ft (8.4m).
Powerplant: Rolls-Royce Allison 250-C20W turboshaft; 420shp.
Performance: maximum speed 125kt (144mph/232kmh); combat radius 110nm (125 miles/200km); on-station endurance 3 hours; operating altitude 20,000ft (6,100m).
Launch: vertical take-off (ship/land).
Recovery: vertical landing (ship/land).
Armament: none.
Payload: 200lb (90kg).

The U.S. Navy used a small number of Pioneer UAVs and its first attempt to find a replacement was in a joint project with the Army, named Outrider. The Navy then withdrew from that project and formulated its own requirements for a second generation UAV. In outline, these were for a vertical takeoff and landing (VTOL) aircraft, with a payload capacity of 200lb (90kg), and the ability to spend three hours on patrol at an altitude of 20,000ft (6,100m) at a distance of 125 miles (200km) from the parent ship. The aircraft had to be capable of landing on a cruiser or destroyer flightdeck in a 25kt (29mph/46kmh) wind. There were three finalists in the competition, Bell, Sikorsky, and Ryan Schweizer Helicopters, with the latter being judged the winners.

The design, named FireScout, is based on that of the Schweizer 330SP

Hunter

Type: multi-role, short-range, tactical UAV (TUAV).
Manufacturer: IAI/TRW
Weight: empty 1,300lb (590kg); maximum takeoff 1,600lb (725kg).
Dimensions: length 22.9ft (7m); height 5.6ft (1.7m); span 29.1ft (8.9m).
Powerplant: 2 x Moto Guzzi 750cc pusher/puller; each 60shp.
Performance: maximum speed 109kt; cruise 70kt; ceiling 15,000ft (4,750m); combat radius 67nm (78 miles/125km); endurance 8-10 hours.
Launch: runway takeoff with or without rocket booster.
Recovery: conventional landing with hook.
Armament: none.
Payload: 200lb (91kg).

This battlefield system, originally known as the Short-Range UAV but subsequently named Hunter, was designed by Israeli Aviation Industries (IAI) at a time when the IDF's reputation for use of UAVs was high. The type was selected for development and production by the U.S. Army, a number were bought by Belgium, and a single system was trialed by the French Army. The U.S. program began in 1988 with the intention of procuring fifty systems of eight UAVs each, plus the associated ground and electronic equipment, for a cost of $US1.2 billion. The development history was troubled, involving no fewer than twenty crashes; production was extremely slow, and by the time the project was canceled in 1996 total program costs were expected to be of the order of $US2 billion.

Each system comprised eight Hunter UAVs, plus their associated Modular Mission Payloads, but these were supported by a considerable array of ground equipment. This included: two Ground Control Shelters, one Mission Planning

Right: Model 379 Fire Scout is one of few rotary-wing UAVs.

helicopter, which was itself based on that of the Hughes 300 helicopter, but the FireScout has a new fuselage and fuel system, a remote-control flying system, and the necessary UAV electronics and sensors. The first prototype flew with a human pilot for its initial tests and flew autonomously for the first time in January 2000, but crashed in November of that year, although further prototypes are now flying.

Above: Hunter did not enter full production, but some models are in service.

Shelter, one Launch and Recovery Shelter, two Ground Data Terminals, four Remote Video Terminals, four Air Data Relays, plus launch and recovery equipment and ground support equipment. The Hunter has a general configuration not much different from the Pioneer, except that it is bigger and has twin engines, consisting of two 60-horsepower Moto-Guzzi piston engines arranged on both ends of center fuselage in a "push-me-pull-you" configuration.

RQ-1 Predator

Type: long-range surveillance, reconnaissance, and target acquisition UAV.
Manufacturer: General Atomics Aeronautical Systems Inc.
Weight: empty 950lb (43kg); maximum takeoff 2,250lb (1,021kg).
Dimensions: length 27.0ft (8.2m); height 6.9ft (2.1m); span 48.7ft (14.8m).
Powerplant: Rotax 912 four-cylinder engine; 81hp.
Performance: cruise speed 70-120kt (84-140mph/135-225kmh); range 400nm (454 miles/731km); 16 hours on station; ceiling 25,000ft (7,620m).
Launch: runway, wheeled.
Recovery: runway, wheeled.
Armament: none (see text).
Payload: 450lb (204kg).
Specification for RQ-1A.

The RQ-1 Predator is a USAF-operated system which is normally employed in moderate risk areas. Each system comprises four airborne platforms with their related sensors, a ground control station (GCS), a satellite communication suite and fift-five people, all of which must be collocated on the same airfield, with a hard surface runway measuring 5,000 x 125ft (1,524 x 38m). The aircraft carries three cameras transmitting full motion video – one in the nose, normally used by the flight controller, a daylight TV camera, and a low light/night infrared camera – together with a synthetic aperture radar for looking through smoke, clouds or haze. The cameras produce full motion video and the synthetic aperture radar produces still-frame radar images. The UAV and its sensors are controlled by the GCS, which is manned by four people. The GCS, which is mounted in a shelter, is the largest single component in the system; it is air-transportable in a C-130.

The satellite suite consists of a 20ft (6.1m) satellite dish and associated support equipment, which provides communications between the ground

Above: An RQ-1 Predator flies past a nuclear-powered aircraft carrier.

station and the aircraft when it is beyond line-of-sight and also links into networks disseminating secondary intelligence. The RQ-1 can operate at 25,000ft (7,620m), but typically flies at around 15,000ft (4,570m), with a normal mission involving a 400nm transit, followed by 14 hours on station.

In April 2001, the U.S. Air Force tested a Predator armed with three Hellfire anti-armor missiles. The tests were carried out with the Predator flying at a height of 2,000ft (610m), a speed of 70kt (80mph/130kmh), and at a range of about 3 miles (5km). The first two trial shots used missiles with inert warheads, the target being illuminated first by a ground-based laser and then by the Predator's own laser designator. On both being successful, a third engagement using the Predator's laser-designator and a missile with a live warhead resulted in a direct hit. The next step in this particular program is to increase the Hellfire launch altitude from 2,000ft (610m) to 15,000ft, where there is much less chance of the UAV being shot down. There are current proposals to adapt the Predator to carry either twelve Hellfire missiles or short-range, heat-seeking AIM-9 Sidewinder missiles for use against such targets as helicopters and low-flying aircraft. Such an aircraft would be a form of interim UCAV (see X-45A below).

Currently in development is the Predator-B which is intended to fill the gap between the capabilities of RQ-1 Predator and Global Hawk. Despite the similarity of the names, this new aircraft bears little resemblance to the RQ-1 Predator, since it is somewhat larger, powered by a turboprop and has a much higher ceiling of approximately 50,000ft (15,240m). It is intended that it should fly the outward leg at high altitude, thus avoiding bad weather, and then drop down to about 15,000ft over the operational area. A separate development of the original Predator is the I-Gnat, which is used by the CIA, and one of which was shot down over Afghanistan.

Left: Predator at a mountain airstrip; the larger bulge houses a satellite dish.

RQ-2 Pioneer

Type: reconnaissance, surveillance, targeting acquisition (RSTA) UAV.
Manufacturer: Pioneer UAV Inc.
Weight: maximum takeoff 416lb (188.7kg).
Dimensions: length 14.0ft (4.3m); height 3.3ft (1m); span 16.9ft (5.2m).
Powerplant: one 2-stroke, 2-cylinder gasoline engine; 26hp.
Performance: speed 100kt (115mph/185kmh); cruise 65kt (75mph/120kmh); ceiling 15,000ft (4,572m); range <100nm (115 miles/185km); endurance <3 hours.
Launch: runway, wheeled (with or without rocket assistance), or pneumatic catapult.
Recovery: runway with hook, or net.
Armament: none.
Payload: 100lb (45kg).

The U.S. Navy was impressed with reports of the successful use of UAVs in the early 1980s and ran a competition for an interim system to provide imagery intelligence (IMINT) for spotters for naval gunfire support from its battleships, as well as to provide a UAV capability for the Marine Corps. Winner of the competition was a partnership of Mazlat (Israel) and AAI (USA) with an improved version of the Scout, an existing Israeli UAV. This first generation U.S. UAV, named Pioneer, had a twin boom configuration, with a pusher propeller driven by a 26hp two-stroke twin-cylinder piston engine, and a fixed tricycle landing gear. The sensors were mounted in a turret underneath the fuselage

A total of nine systems, each with eight aircraft and the associated ground

Shadow 200

Type: tactical UAV (TUAV).
Manufacturer: AAI.
Weight: maximum 328lb (149kg).
Dimensions: length 11.2ft (3.4m); span 12.8ft (3.9m).
Powerplant: UEL AR741 208cc piston engine; 38hp.
Performance: maximum speed 115kt; cruise speed 65-85kt; endurance 6-8 hours; radius 43nm (49 miles/78km); ceiling 15,000ft (4,570m).
Launch: runway, wheeled, or hydraulic rail launcher.
Recovery: runway, wheeled, net or parachute.
Armament: none.
Payload: 60lb (27.2kg).

The Shadow 200 is the latest in the U.S. Army's lengthy search for a viable UAV-based tactical, day or night reconnaissance, surveillance, and target acquisition system. The aircraft is a high-wing design with twin tailbooms and a fixed tricycle undercarriage. It is powered by a small 38hp gasoline engine driving a pusher propeller and is launched either by a conventional wheeled takeoff from a runway, or from a trailer-mounted rail launcher, with a hydraulic catapult. The aircraft can either make a conventional wheeled landing on flat ground about the length of a soccer field, or can be recovered using a deployable arresting hook on the aircraft and ground-based cables.

Each Shadow 200 tactical UAV system comprises three UAVs plus ground support, all of which is mounted in vehicles and trailers. There are two Ground Control Stations (GCS), which use ruggedized hardware and well-proven software to reduce development risk; each GCS is mounted in a shelter on the

Right: The Navy's RQ-2 is a U.S.-built version of the Israeli Scout.

equipment, were procured by the Navy and the Marines. Deliveries started in July 1986 and first deployment was aboard the battleship USS *Iowa* (BB-61), with three more systems being delivered to the Marine Corps in 1987. The Army joined the program in 1990, with one system on loan from the Navy.

Pioneers have been used in combat since the late 1980s, including the Persain Gulf tanker crisis in the late 1980s and the Gulf War, when over 300 combat reconnaissance missions were flown. More recently it has flown in operations over Bosnia, Haiti, and Somalia.

It had been intended that Pioneer would be replaced in the late 1990s by newer systems, but this has not yet taken place, so nine systems (each of eight aircraft) remain active in 2002: Navy – five; Marines – three; training – one. Some thirty Pioneers were the result of an additional procurement order in the mid-1990s to an enhanced standard with slight increases in aircraft weight and fuel capacity. A new, more capable and more reliable sensor payload was approved in 1998. Thus, as so frequently happens with "interim" systems, the Pioneer has soldiered on for far longer than was ever intended and has outlasted many of the systems which were supposed to replace it.

Above: The U.S. Army's latest UAV is the Shadow 200.

back of a standard military truck. There are also two Portable Ground Control Stations (PGCS), which are packaged in ruggedized transit cases to enable easy transport and rapid set-up and tear-down in the field. The PGCS, in conjunction with the Portable Ground Data Terminal, has full functionality to launch and recover the air vehicle, operate the payload, and receive and display payload data. The Remote Video Terminal provides forward battle commanders with a capability to view the area of operation using a flat panel display in near-real time. The system requires minimal operator training. The Ground Data Terminal has transceivers and an antenna system designed for lightness, mobility, and ease of shipment. No tools are needed for setting it up.

The system incorporates a number of technical improvements arising from lessons learned during UAV deployments, particularly during Operation Allied Force in Kosovo. The Army plans to buy forty-four Shadow 200 systems, but as of early 2002 a firm production order had not been announced.

Tier II Plus UAV (Global Hawk)

Type: high-altitude, long-endurance UAV.
Manufacturer: Teledyne/Ryan.
Weight: maximum takeoff 25,600lb (11,612kg).
Dimensions: length 44.3ft (13.5m); height 15.1ft (4.6m); span 116.1ft (35.4m).
Powerplant: Rolls-Royce-Allison turbofan.
Performance: maximum cruising speed 340kt (391mph/630kmh); ceiling 65,000ft (19,812m); ferry range 13,500nm (15,525 miles/25,000km); endurance 36 hours.
Launch: runway; wheeled.
Recovery: runway, wheeled.
Armament: none.
Payload: 2,000lb (kg).

The RQ-4A Global Hawk is a high-altitude, long-endurance UAV which provides field commanders with high resolution, near-real-time imagery of large geographic areas and can image an area the size of Illinois (40,000 nautical square miles) in just 24 hours. To achieve this it carries cloud-penetrating, Synthetic Aperture Radar/Ground Moving Target Indicator, electro-optical, and infrared sensors and through the use of satellite and ground systems can relay the imagery in near-real-time to battlefield commanders.

The RQ-4A has been under development since 1994. It is a large aircraft with a mission-ready weight of 25,600lb (11,612). A typical mission would be to fly 1,200 miles (1,931km) to the operational area, where it would remain on patrol for 24

hours before the flight home again. The entire flight from taxi out to taxi back, and including routes, heights, and sensor activity, is programmed into the computer before take-off. The ground-based operators monitor the aircraft's activities and can change navigation and sensor plans during flight, where necessary.

Global Hawk currently is undergoing flight-testing at the Air Force Flight Test Center at Edwards Air Force Base, Calif., with 1,255.5 hours flown during 103 successful sorties. The Global Hawk Program, Reconnaissance Systems Program Office, Aeronautical Systems Center at Wright-Patterson AFB, Ohio, assumed total program control on 1 October 1998. On 20 April 2000 Global Hawk Air Vehicle No. 4 deployed to Elgin AFB, Fla., to participate in two exercises that included its first trans-oceanic flight to Europe, and first mission flown in one theater of operations while being controlled from another. In April 2001 a prototype Global Hawk flew non-stop to Australia, a distance of 7,500 miles (12,000km). It remained in the area for six weeks during which it carried out eleven sorties before returning to the USA, again in a non-stop flight.

The system is capable of both direct line-of-sight communications with the ground station by a common data link or beyond line-of-sight through a satcom link. In the future users detached from the ground station could directly receive imagery data from the Global Hawk.

In March, 1999, one of the Global Hawks lost control and crashed, which caused some two months' delay in the testing program. However, at least one aircraft has been deployed to Afghanistan since September 2001, where it has proved a considerable success.

Left: Global Hawk has an inter-continental range and a 36-hour endurance.

X-45A Unmanned Combat Aerial Vehicle (UCAV)

Type: experimental unmanned combat aerial vehicle (UCAV).
Manufacturer: The Boeing Company.
Weight: empty 8,000lb (3,629kg).
Dimensions: length 27ft (8.2m); span 34ft (10.4m).
Powerplant: Honeywell F124 turbofan.
Performance: classified.
Launch: runway, wheeled.
Recovery: runway, wheeled.
Armament: missiles, smart bombs.
Payload: 3,000lb (1,361lb).

Although strictly an experimental program, the Boeing X-45A UCAV is included here to give some indication of the way in which developments are progressing. Two X-45As are being built and tested as part of an undertaking by the USAF, the Defense Advanced Research Projects Agency (DARPA), and Boeing. Total cost is $131 million, of which Boeing is funding $21 million. The first prototype began flight testing in spring 2001 and was joined by the second in early 2002; if successful, the program could lead to a definitive UCAV entering service in the 2010-15 timeframe.

According to current plans, the UCAV will be programmed for each mission, being given a "script" by the mission controller which will tell it where the targets are expected to be and how to attack them. The mission will then be carried out either autonomously, with or without en route revisions, or totally managed by the controller. Even in the autonomous condition, it would be usual for the mission controller to have the ability to give a final "go/no-go" decision before each attack.

The X-45A is a stealthy, tail-less, aircraft with highly swept wings, and a manta-shaped fuselage. It is powered by a Honeywell F124 turbofan. This is situated in the center of the fuselage, is fed by an intake on the top of the fuselage, and is set back from the nose in the position where the pilot's cockpit would normally be. The aircraft is designed to carry a payload of some one-and-a-half tons to targets some 1,000 miles (1,600km) distant, and carries video cameras, a Global Positioning System (GPS) and radar for precision-targeting attacks. It is envisaged that most operations would consist of coordinated attacks by "squadrons" of

UCAVs, thus confusing, perhaps even overwhelming, the defenses.

Advocates of the UCAV state that the lack of a pilot and the associated cockpit have a number of significant advantages. First, the aircraft can operate in nuclear, biological or chemical environments without any risk to a human crew. Second, it reduces the need for expensive training and personnel administration. Third, the mission commander is situated in the control center where a full range of communications plus access to the latest intelligence is constantly available.

Below: The technician lends scale to the X-45; UAVs are growing ever larger.

X-47 Pegasus

Type: unmanned combat aerial vehicle (UCAV).
Manufacturer: Northrop Grumman.
Weight: empty 5,500lb (2,495kg).
Dimensions: length 27.9ft (8.5m); span 27.8ft (8.5m).
Powerplant: Pratt & Whitney JT15D-5C-TF; 3,190lb (1,447kg) static thrust.
Performance: endurance <1hr.
Launch: runway; wheeled.
Recovery: runway; wheeled.
Armament: none.
Payload: 1,000lb.

The Northrop Grumman X-47 Pegasus unmanned combat aerial vehicle is a technology demonstrator designed to evaluate technologies and concepts for a carrier-capable, naval UCAV (UCAV-N), which is under consideration for introduction into service in the 2010-2015 timeframe. If built, this UCAV-N will be designed to fly three types of mission: surveillance, strike, and suppression of enemy air defenses (SEAD). The single X-47 flight test aircraft was formally rolled out in July 2001 and started its twelve-flight test program later in the year. The major significance of the X-47 is that it is the first UAV/UCAV project to involve fixed-wing take-offs and landings from an aircraft carrier. Previous naval UAVs have either been rotary-winged or have been recovered by nets, but the X-47 will be the first to land in a conventional manner. Iit should be noted that this is a skill in which the Grumman element of Northrop Grumman has more expertise than any other aerospace company in the world.

Micro-Air Vehicles (MAVs)

Among the most exciting current development programs concerns Micro-Air Vehicles (MAVs), which are defined as being less than 6in (150mm) in any dimension and capable of performing useful missions at an affordable cost. This concept appears to have its origins with DARPA, which was investigating means of surveillance in hostage situations, and first examined methods of microwave imaging through building walls. When this proved impracticable they came up with the idea of flying something inside to look around, which, of necessity, had to be extremely small, very quiet, have a reasonable endurance, and be able to carry some means of surveillance.

In the case of the military, missions for such MAVs might include reconnaissance, surveillance, battle damage assessment, targeting, emplacing sensors and communications relays, or for detecting chemical, nuclear or biological substances. The vehicles will need to conduct real-time imaging, have ranges of up to 6 miles (10km) and speeds of up to 30mph (48kmh) for missions lasting between twenty minutes and two hours.

If the technology can be developed, these tiny flying objects could conduct short-range reconnaissances for small units, particularly in the increasingly important urban environment; for example, to see what is behind that wall, or if a soldier/terrorist is lurking around the next corner.

The current programs are focusing on the technologies and components required to enable these systems to work. Some systems under investigation are fixed-wing, others use the helicopter principle, while several projects are even looking at flapping wings. Among the major challenges to be faced are power supplies for the motor, sensors, and communication systems, flight stability, and navigation and control systems, all of them on a tiny scale never

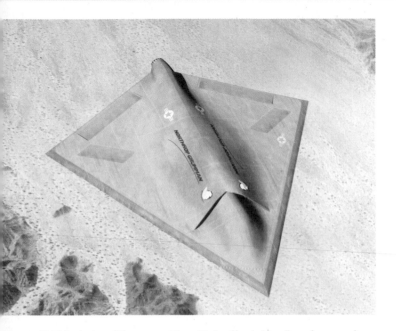

Above: X-47 is designed for conventional takeoffs and landings from carriers.

Right: One of many revolutionary MAV designs now on the drawing board.

previously considered. One company is known to be working on a gas-turbine with 1.4lb (0.6kg) thrust, while another is developing a solid oxide fuel cell.

One known project is Micro-Bat, which is said to weigh 0.5oz (14gm) and fly at 10mph (16kmh). Its wings are made from titanium-alloy frames covered in Mylar, which is a polysester film coated with metal to increase its strength. Power is provided by a 1.5V nickel-cadmium battery. There is an antenna which receives signals from a remote operator, and via which it transmits recordings and pictures from a micro-camera. This project is the brainchild of the the California Institute of Technology, Pasadena, Califirnia. Another project is the Robot Fly (Robofly), which is the size of a fingernail with a wingspan of about 0.8in (20.3mm) and a weight of about 0.04oz (100milligrammes) – about the same as a fat bluebottle. It has a stainless steel body and Mylar wings.

The DoD has already allocated $12million and in late 2001, U.S. Secretary of Defense Donald Rumsfeld urged research scientists to speed up development of such MAVs, which could then be used on missions such as tracking down Osama bin Laden and his colleagues in the caves of Afghanistan. So, this is a serious area. of research.

Air-to-Air Missiles

Air-to-air missiles (AAMs) were first developed in World War II and early types employed command guidance, in which they were directed from the launch aircraft, with commands being passed either by wire or by a radio link. By the 1950s, technology had moved on to guidance systems in which the missile carried its own guidance systems, the two generally used being semi-active radar homing (SARH) and infra-red (IR).

.S. air-to-air missiles have been four families, of which two, AIM-7 Sparrow and AIM-9 Sidewinder, trace their origins to development work which began immediately after the end of World War II, with both entering service in 1956. Of the other two, AIM-54 Phoenix entered service in 1974, while AIM-120 AMRAAM is much more recent, having been fielded in 1991. There have, of course, been other missiles, but these are the most successful, and all four remain in service today.

In general terms, the air-fighting requirement has been met by three categories of missile, one for distant, beyond-visual range (BVR) engagements, one for close-in dogfighting, and the third to cover the area in between. From the 1950s to the mid-80s the United States enjoyed a degree of superiority in all three of these categories. This, coupled with the excellence of its aircraft designs, ensured that they would predominate in any air battle. Over the past fifteen or so years, however, that superiority has become increasingly open to challenge as foreign aircraft and missile designs have undergone dramatic improvements, with the benchmark in possible adversaries now being the Russian-built but widely exported MiG-29, armed with AA-10 and AA-11 missiles.

In order to restore the margin that U.S. aircraft had previously enjoyed, the Air Force decided in the early 1990s to conduct the Air Superiority Missile Technology (ASMT) program to examine the development of revolutionary air-to-air missiles to counter the new breed of foreign aircraft. An important

element within this program is the Dual-Range Missile (DRM) which is intended to meet all the requirements, from BVR to close-in dogfighting, in one missile. All the technological areas involved are being closely scrutinized, including guidance and control techniques to enhance the close-in combat capability, terminal seekers with extended acquisition range, advanced propulsion units for greater range, and greatly improved maneuverability to enable the missile to counter increasingly agile fighters. The program started in 1992 and in June 1997 McDonnell Douglas (now part of Boeing) received a contract to design, develop, and demonstrate an advanced flight control system that will enable the DRM to meet these requirements.

Among the revolutionary capabilities being examined is the ability to launch the missile "over-the-shoulder," thus enabling pilots to attack targets approaching them from behind. This would require the missile to reverse its course within less than 2-3 seconds of launch. One of the flight control systems being examined to achieve this exceptional agility consists of a number of small, side-thrusting reaction jets integrated into the aft section of the missile, which would bleed propulsive gas from the rocket motor.

Meanwhile development of the existing weapons systems continues apace. The Air Force and Navy continue to procure AMRAAM, with performance being enhanced in a number of areas, including kinematics and lethality. Sidewinder is also being improved with AIM-9X due to enter service shortly. An incremental advance, it combines the motor, fuze, and warhead of the current AIM-9M with a new seeker and airframe, and it also has the ability to be cued by a helmet-mounted sight to a target outside the aircraft radar's field of view.

Below: AIM-120 AMRAAM at the moment of ignition on an F-16.

AIM-7 Sparrow

Type: medium-range, air-to-air, tactical missile.
Manufacturer: Raytheon (formerly General Dynamics).
Weight: approximately 500lb (225kg)
Dimensions: length 12ft (3.6m); diameter 8.0in (20.4cm); wingspan 3.3ft (1.0m).
Powerplant: Hercules Mk58 solid-propellant, dual thrust, rocket motor.
Performance: range approximately 30nm (34.5miles/55.5km).
Guidance: semi-active on either continuous wave or pulsed Doppler radar energy
Warhead: annular blast fragmentation warhead 88lb (40kg) high explosive.
Platforms: (AIM-7M/7P) Navy – F-14 and F/A-18; Air Force – F-15, F-16; Marine Corps – F-4, F/A-18.
Specifications for AIM-9P.

The AIM-7 Sparrow is a radar-guided air-to-air missile powered by a solid-propellant, dual-thrust rocket motor, and has a high-explosive/continuous rod warhead. It is very widely used as an air-to-air missile (Sparrow AIM-7 series) and as a ship-launched surface-to-air missile (NATO Sea Sparrow RIM-7 series). It has an all-weather capability and can attack high-performance aircraft and missiles from any direction and at any altitude. The missile is designed for either rail or ejection launching and its hydraulically operated control surfaces, under control of the guidance system, direct the missile on a proportional navigational course to the target. During Operation Desert Storm, the AIM-7 proved to be one of the most potent weapons used, with twenty-two Iraqi fixed-wing aircraft and three helicopters being downed by air-launched missiles.

The Sparrow story started as long ago as 1946, when the U.S. Navy began the development of Project Hotshot, which led to a missile that entered service in 1953. This was a beam-rider, with antennae around the body to pick up the

Above: F-16s armed with AIM-7 Sparrow, flying out of Aviano, Italy.

signals from the fighter radar beam, which was locked on to the target, with the missile's guidance system working all the time to keep the missile in the center of the beam. This version (subsequently designated Sparrow I) entered Navy service in 1956 as AIM-7A. Experience during the Vietnam War showed this concept to be of very limited value unless the target was proceeding in level flight and at a more or less constant speed. Sparrow I was developed by Douglas, starting in 1955, as the armament for the proposed F5D-1 Skylancer but the Navy canceled the project in 1956, although some work was then continued as the armament for the proposed Canadian Arrow, but the missile was canceled for a second and final time in 1958. Meanwhile work had started on a Sparrow II, which used almost the same airframe as Sparrow I but with semi-active radar homing, and this was much more successful, entering service in 1958 as AIM-7C.

AIM-7D introduced the Thiokol pre-packaged liquid-fuel motor, and this version was adopted by the USAF for use on their F-4C Phantom II, by a number of foreign air forces, and for naval use as the NATO Sea Sparrow shipborne short-range air defense system (also known as the Basic Point Defense Missile System/BPDMS). Next came AIM-7E with a Rocketdyne solid-fuel motor, which increased burn-out speed to about Mach 3.7. Many thousands of AIM-7Es were carried by F-4s in Vietnam, but political constraints, particularly concerning range, prevented all but a few being

Left: F-16C Fighting Falcon launched AIM-7 during certification trials.

fired. This led to the development of AIM-7E2 "dogfight" version, which had a much shorter minimum range and increased maneuverability. This version also introduced plug-in control surfaces, which meant that they could be simply pushed into place by the ground crew without the use of tools. Some 34,0000 AIM-7C, D and E were produced.

The AIM-7F was an almost completely new missile, one major step forward being that improved avionics enabled the warhead to be moved to the front, which not only enhanced the terminal effects upon the target, but also created extra space for a larger motor, thus increasing the range. AIM-7F entered service in 1976 as the primary medium-range air-to-air missile for the Air Force's F-15 Eagle.

AIM-7M, which entered service in 1982, had improved reliability and performance over earlier models at low altitudes and in electronic countermeasures environments. It also had a significantly more lethal warhead. The latest software version of the AIM-7M is the H-Build, which has been produced since 1987 and incorporates additional improvements in guidance. The F-15 Eagle and F-16 Fighting Falcon fighters carry the AIM-7M Sparrow. The parallel shipborne version, RIM-7M, is deployed aboard Spruance-class DDGs armed with the NATO Sea Sparrow Missile System (NSSMS). The major differences between AIM-7M and RIM-7M are that the latter has folding wings,

clipped fins, and a remotely armable rocket motor. The prime shipboard mission of NSSMS is to neutralize the threat of high performance, anti-ship missiles. Most AIM-7Ms are being upgraded to AIM-7P Block II (see below) or are being allowed to waste out as training missiles.

The current frontline version is AIM/RIM-7P which began as a retrofit program to AIM/RIM-7M and exists in two versions, known as Blocks I and II. The AIM/RIM-7P Block I provides low altitude guidance and fuzing capability and approximately 600 earlier versions of Sparrow were upgraded to the AIM-7P Block I configuration. AIM/RIM-7P Block II provides increased memory, greater software reprogramming capability, and mid-course up-link improvements to the rear receiver. AIM/RIM-7P was produced by both retrofitting AIM-7M missiles, starting in 1993, and also by new production. All the modifications required to upgrade AIM/RIM-7M to -P standard are in the guidance section and as there was no physical or operational change involved the changeover in the fleet was a very smooth process.

The AIM/RIM-7R was the most recent configuration and added a dual-mode radio frequency/infrared (RF/IR) seeker capability, but the program was canceled in 1997 while still in the development phase.

Below: Sparrow has proved a great success in almost 20 years' service.

AIM-9 Sidewinder

Type: air-to-air missile.
Manufacturer: Raytheon.
Weight: 188lb (85.0kg).
Dimensions: length 119in (302cm); diameter 5in (13cm); finspan 24in (61cm).
Powerplant: ATK Tactical Systems Mk 36, solid-propellant, single-thrust rocket motor with thrust vector control (TVC).
Performance: supersonic Mach 2.5; range 10 to 18 miles (16-29km) depending on altitude.
Guidance: solid-state, infrared homing.
Warhead: annular blast-fragmentation.
Platforms: full capability – F/A-18C/D/E/F, F-15C/D/E, F-16C/D, and F-22; reduced capability – F-14B Upgrade, F-14D, AV-8B, and AH-1W. Also backward compatible to aircraft/launchers only capable of AIM-9M analog communication.

The Sidewinder was designed by a team at the Navy Weapons Center (then NOTC), China Lake, in the late 1940s, and the latest version, AIM-9X, will begin to enter service in 2002 – a remarkable lifespan by any standard. The naval scientists were the first in the world to develop the idea of passive IR homing guidance and their revolutionary missile, then designated XAAM-N-7, was first launched in 1953 and entered service in 1956, designated N-7 by the Navy and GAR-8 by the Air Force. The missile was basically simple: a 5in (12.7cm) aluminum tube, which housed the rocket motor, with a homing head and warhead at the front end and four fixed tail fins, each equipped with a rolleron at the back. The Sidewinder was elegant in its simplicity, having just twenty-four moving parts and "fewer electronic components than the average

Below: AIM-9 Sidewinder; the world's most successful air-to-air missile.

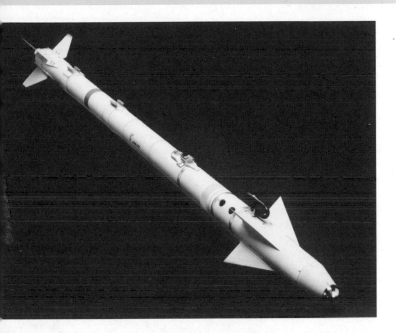

Above: Latest in a long line, the AIM-9X fire-and-forget dogfight missile.

domestic radio," which meant that it was remarkably cheap to produce, while the IR guidance meant that it could be carried by virtually any aircraft, regardless of whether or not it was fitted with radar. It was also the first "fire-and-forget" missile. On the other hand, the IR homing meant that the pilot had to set up a tail-chase, preferably at high altitude and with good visibility, and the seeker had a distressing tendency to try to home on the sun or, at low altitudes, reflections from lakes. Nevertheless, when it was first used in combat by the Republic of China (Taiwan) Air Force in October 1958 Sidewinders shot down fourteen MiG-17s in one day (this was also the first use of *any* AAM in combat).

The prototype, designated AIM-9A (AIM = Air Intercept Missile), led to the first production version, AIM-9B, which entered service in 1956. It was only effective at close range and could not engage targets close to the ground, nor did it have nighttime or head-on attack capability, but despite these shortcomings 80,900 were produced for the U.S. forces. AIM-9C was a Semi-Active Radar Homing (SARH) version by Motorola (1,000 built), while the AIM-9D had an improved IR seeker, higher speed, and better maneuverability; 950 were built for the Navy. AIM-9E was a -9B rebuilt with a new cooled, wide-angle seeker; about 5,000 were built for the Air Force. AIM-9G was an upgraded AIM-9D with a new capability to lock on and launch against a target offset from the axis of the launch aircraft (2,120 for the Navy), while AIM-9H was very similar in performance but replaced the tube-technology with solid-state electronics and introduced a new warhead (3,000 for the Air Force).

AIM-9J was an upgraded conversion of the AIM-B and E with a new front end to give increased maneuvering capability for dogfighting, together with greater speed and range. Deliveries began in 1977 to equip the F- 15 and other Sidewinder-compatible aircraft. A further minor upgrade was originally designated AIM-9J1 but was later redesignated AIM-9N. Some 21,000 AIM-9B and -E were upgraded to AIM-9J and AIM-9N standard, starting in 1977.

AIM-9L added a more powerful solid-propellant rocket motor as well as tracking maneuvering ability, while improvements in heat sensor and control systems gave an all-aspect attack capability and improved guidance characteristics. This was the first model to be able to attack from all angles, including head-on, and an improved active optical fuze increased the missile's lethality and resistance to electronic countermeasures. A conical scan seeker increased seeker sensitivity and improved tracking stability. The AIM-9L was configured with an annular blast fragmentation warhead. Production and delivery of the AIM-9L began in 1976 and 11,700 were delivered.

Developed from AIM-9L, AIM-9M had further improvements, particularly in infra-red counter-countermeasures (ECCM) and the motor, to give higher all-round performance. Deliveries began in 1983 and a further sub-variant – AIM-9M-9 – has expanded infrared counter measures detection circuitry. AIM-9M is the only variant currently in service and is also the start-point for the AIM-9X plans (see below). Next to appear after the AIM-9M was the AIM-9P, which was an improved version of the J model,

out with increased engagement boundaries and greater range.

AIM-9X is the latest version to be deployed on U.S. Air Force, Navy, and Marine Corps fighters as a fire-and-forget "dogfight" missile, complementing longer range radar guided missiles such as AMRAAM. It is intended to restore U.S. pre-eminence in short-range air combat particularly against the Russian-built MiG-29 with its AA-10/AA-11 missiles. AIM-9X will retain the warhead, fuze, and rocket motor of the current AIM-9M in order to capitalize on the large numbers already in service, and will be first deployed on F-15C/D and the F/A-18C/D.

The major new elements in AIM-9X are new titanium wings and control fins, longer hangers (to increase separation between the aircraft and the missile) and a new Guidance Section. The AIM-9X seeks and homes in on IR energy emitted by the target. When an IR-emitting source enters the seeker field of view, an audio signal is generated by the electronics unit. The pilot hears the signal through the headset, indicating that the AIM-9X has acquired a potential target. One method of cueing the AIM-9X to the target's IR energy source is referred to as boresight, whereby the missile is physically pointed toward the target via the pilot maneuvering the aircraft. The IR energy gathered by the missile seeker is converted to electronic signals that enable the missile to acquire and track the target up to its seeker gimbal limits. A second method of cueing the AIM-9X to the target's IR energy is the Sidewinder Expanded Acquisition Mode (SEAM), in which the AIM-9X seeker is slaved to the aircraft radar. On target acquisition, a seeker interlock in the missile is released and the missile seeker begins tracking the target. A third method for cueing the AIM-9X to the target's IR energy is through use of the pilot's helmet-mounted sight. For aircraft fitted only with analog interfaces, the AIM-9X gives the appearance of an AIM-9M.

About all that the AIM-9X of 2002 has in common with AIM-9B of 1956 is the overall principle of IR-homing and the diameter of the main tube, but the story is one of great success, with steady and determined updating keeping the missile at the forefront of design for five decades.

Left: Below carrier flightdeck, and experienced crew prepares AIM-9M air-to-air missiles for fitting to Navy fighters.

AIM-54A/B/C Phoenix

Type: long-range air-launched air intercept missile.
Manufacturer: Hughes/Raytheon.
Weight: AIM-54A 1,000lb (454kg); AIM-54C 1,040lb (472kg); AIM-54
ECCM /Sealed Missile 1,023.0lb (464kg).
Dimensions: length 13.0 feet (3.9 m); diameter 15.0in (38.1cm); wingspa
3.0ft (0.9m).
Powerplant: Hercules Mk 47 Mod 1 solid-propellant rocket motor
Performance: maximum speed >3,000mph (4,800kmh); range >100nr
(115 miles/184km).
Guidance: semi-active and active radar homing.·
Warhead: high explosive; 135lb (60.8kg); proximity fuse.
Platform: Navy F-14.

The AIM-54 Phoenix missile provides air defense cover over an area o
some 12,000 square miles (31,000m^2) from near sea-level to the limits o
altitude attained by aircraft or tactical missiles. It is deployed only on the
Navy's F-14 Tomcats and, while it is an exceptionally versatile weapor
system, it is also very expensive. Development began in 1960, at which
stage the project was designated AAM-N-11, and it was intended to be the
long-range, air-to-air, defensive armament for the F-111B, the naval versior
of the joint F-111 project. When that ill-fated project was canceled
development of the missile continued to become the primary weapon fo
its replacement, the F-14 Tomcat. The AIM-54 Phoenix is carried in clusters
of up to six missiles on the Tomcat, and can be launched singly, in ripple o
simultaneously, under all weather conditions and in heavy jamming
environments.

Below: F-14 launches an AIM-54 Phoenix air-to-air missile.

Above: AIM-54 has a range of over 100nm, speed of over 3,000mph.

Four versions of the AIM-54 have been produced of which three remain in service. AIM-54A was the original version, which became operational in 1974; production ended in 1980, but some remain in the inventory and are being expended in training and not replaced. The AIM-54A was given several modifications, one of which enhanced its capabilities against low-lying targets over water and another improved its resistance to certain ECM threats. AIM-54B differed only in minor detail, having sheet metal instead of honeycomb wings and tails, and improved hydraulics; it was in production from 1977 until 1980 and none remain. Next came the AIM-54C which offered a number of significant improvements most of them designed to increase its capability against aircraft and cruise missiles, but it also received a new solid-state radio system and digital electronics. In addition, it was re-engineered to give greater reliability and a 15 percent reduction in parts; production started in 1986.

The last model to be produced was AIM-54 ECCM/Sealed which has

improved electronic counter-countermeasure capabilities, but the mos
significant change was that it is self-contained and no longer require:
coolant conditioning from the aircraft while airborne and prior to launch
hence the name. Production started in 1988, but has now ended. The Nav

Above: Fully armed with six AIM-54s, the F-14 is a potent killing machine.

has accepted AMRAAM for service with its Hornet and Super Hornet force but retains AIM-54 for its F-14s.

AIM-120 AMRAAM

Type: medium-range, air-to-air tactical missile.
Manufacturer: Hughes/Raytheon.
Weight: 335lb (150.8kg).
Dimensions: length 12ft (3.7m); diameter 7.0in (17.8cm); wingspan 20.7in (52.6cm).
Powerplant: Hercules solid-fuel, boost-sustain, rocket motor
Performance: speed >Mach 4; range >17.4nm (20 miles/32.2km).
Guidance: inertial mid-course, active radar terminal homing.
Warhead: blast fragmentation; proximity fuze; high explosive; 45lb (20kg).
Platforms: Navy – F/A-18; Air Force – F-15, F-16.

The Vietnam War was the first conflict in which missiles were used in significant numbers. One of the many lessons learnt was that, to ensure his survival, a future fighter pilot would have to deal with not just one but a number of targets simultaneously. This was not possible with the AIM-7 Sparrow, which required the launching pilot to maintain a constant radar lock on the target until the missile hit it. Thus, the new missile needed to be both autonomous, enabling the pilot to maneuver immediately following launch, as well as fast and highly maneuverable to keep pace with improvements in performance by hostile aircraft. This led to an operational requirement for a new missile – the AIM-120 Advanced Medium-Range Air-to-Air Missile (AMRAAM) – which was stated in the early 1970s. This required the missile to have a higher performance and lethality than any conceivable advanced version of Sparrow, but within a package that was smaller, lighter, more reliable, and cheaper. The

joint USAF/USN program was led by the Air Force and the conceptual phase was completed in 1979, with Hughes and Raytheon being selected to continue into the validation phase. This was completed in 1981 and Hughes was declared the winner. The production contract was placed in 1987 and AMRAAM became operational in 1991.

The AMRAAM is a large missile, 12.0ft (3.7m) long and 7.0in (17.8cm) in diameter, and weighs 335lb (150.8kg) at launch. It is powered by a Hercules solid-fuel rocket motor, which accelerates it rapidly to a speed in excess of Mach 4, and has a range well in excess of 20 miles (32.2km). At close ranges the missile assumes control on being launched, leaving the pilot to maneuver and engage other targets. In a long-range engagement, however, the missile uses inertial guidance, updated as necessary by a data-link from the launch aircraft, but changes to autonomous mode as soon as its internal monopulse radar acquires the target. The chances of a target escaping once it has been acquired are very slim, but in the event that the target uses jamming, the missile has a fall-back "home-on-jam" mode. The missile is fitted with an active-radar proximity fuze which detonates the 45lb (20kg) high-explosive warhead.

The first live launch of an AIM-120 was in December 1992 when an F-16 shot down an Iraqi Air Force MiG-25 Foxbat over southern Iraq. Today, the AIM-120 is operational on all U.S. high-speed fighters, with the exception of the Navy's F-14 Tomcat, which have retained their AIM-7 Sparrows, although all Navy Hornets and Super Hornets are fully equipped to fire AIM-120.

Below: AIM-120 AMRAAM is large: 12ft (3.7m) long, and weighs 335lb (151kg).

Air-to-Surface Missiles

The development of air-to-surface weaponry for the U.S. armed forces has reflected a number of basic trends over the past twenty-thirty years, of which the most important undoubtedly is the increase in precision. During World War II great strides were made in increasing the accuracy of gravity bombs, but essentially no matter how sophisticated the sighting arrangements there could be no absolute guarantee of success with a single bomb or bomber. The answer lay in using a number of aircraft each dropping a number of bombs, which was clearly an inefficient use of resources, especially in aircraft and, even more importantly, in aircrew. Recently, however, great strides have been made in improving accuracy, not only be developing totally new weapons, but also by developing and fitting relatively inexpensive attachments to gravity bombs. Although not applied in every system, one of the major elements is the Global Positioning System (GPS) which is proving invaluable, since it provides information not only instantaneously but also with an unprecedented degree of accuracy.

In fact, the situation now is that bombs are so accurate that almost any target can be hit, although two types remain a problem. First, as shown in the Gulf War and recent operations in Afghanistan, deeply buried facilities such as command posts, ammunition depots, and communications centers are very difficult to attack. Despite recent advances, greater research is clearly needed into penetrations which can drive through concrete, rock or even just hard-packed earth in order to destroy such installations. Second, highly mobile targets remain a problem, the difficulty being not so much to attack them, but

rather in carrying out the attack in a timely manner, while the enemy is still in the same position. This is not so much a technical matter as one of procedures and the rapid passage of intelligence and commands.

A further major development is in the stand-off capability, which means that neither bombers nor attack aircraft now need to fly directly over a target, thus enabling them to avoid the enemy's air defenses. In addition, the development of long-range unmanned stand-off weapons, such as air-launched cruise missiles, means that targets deep inside enemy territory can be attacked from the first day, whereas in the past they could be approached only after enemy defenses on the periphery had been progressively taken out.

Moreover, the weapons enable the air forces to suppress the enemy's air defenses (SEAD) very quickly after the outbreak of hostilities, thus clearing the way for air attacks over the entire enemy territory at minimal risk to aircrew.

As in other fields, some totally new weapons have come into service but a number of the older ones have proved themselves capable of accepting modifications and upgrades which have kept them in the frontline for two to three decades.

Thus, the combined air forces of the United States now have the weapons which will enable them to gain the upper hand against almost any foreseeable enemy.

Below: Marine Corps AV-8B launches air-to-surface AGM-65 Maverick.

AGM-62 Walleye I/II

Type: TV-guided glide bomb.
Manufacturer: Martin Marietta/Hughes.
Weight: Walleye I – 1,127lb (511kg); Walleye II – 2,403lb (1,090kg).
Dimensions: length Walleye I – 11.5ft (3.5m), Walleye II – 13.1ft (4.0m); diameter (both) – 2.9ft (0.3m); wingspan (both) – 3.9ft (1.2m).
Powerplant: none.
Performance: range Walleye I – 16nm (24.3 miles/39km), Walleye II – 35nm (40miles/65km).
Warhead: Walleye I – 822lb (373kg), Walleye II – 2,000lb (908kg).

The AGM-62 Walleye is a guided bomb, which (apart from the original model) employs a television camera in the missile's nose to transmit pictures during its flight, enabling the airborne operator to guide it to its target with a considerable degree of accuracy. The system was developed by the Navy at China Lake in the early 1960s, the production contract was placed in 1966, and it entered service in 1967. Walleye is intended for use against fairly large, static targets, such as fuel tanks, tunnels, bridges, radar sites, port facilities, and ammunition depots.

In general terms, Walleye produces excellent results in good visibility against targets which are not only lightly defended, but also have a strong contrast with their background. During Desert Storm, for example, F/A-18 pilots reported that a target was sometimes indistinguishable from its own shadow, particularly in the low-light conditions at dawn and dusk, which made it difficult to designate the actual target, rather than its shadow.

The initial version, Walleye I, was a "fire-and-forget"system in which the TV tracker in the bomb sent pictures to the TV monitor in the aircraft. The pictures were used to designate the target. Once the system had locked on, the fuze was set and the weapon released, after which it guided itself to the target and the aircraft turned to another task.

This was followed by the Walleye I Extended Range Data Link (ERDL) which used the same bomb, but the electronics were revised so that the missile continued to transmit a continuous video display to the operator up to the time of impact, while the operator was able to guide the weapon throughout its flight, either correcting errors or even selecting a new target. This control could be exercised by either the original aircraft or a second aircraft fitted with a suitable data-link pod.

The Walleye II weapon is essentially the same as the Walleye I except that it is some

2ft (0.61m) longer, enabling it to carry a considerably larger warhead. It also has improved electronics. Walleye II Extended Range Data Link (ERDL) is the same as the Walleye II but with larger wings and added data link functions; these enable the weapon to be launched with longer slant ranges to a target.

The weapon system may be used in either one- or two-aircraft operations. In a single-aircraft operation, the launch aircraft carries both the weapon and the pod, and the aircraft performs both launch and control functions. In the two-aircraft operation, one aircraft carries and launches the weapon, but a second carries the pod. and controls the flight, and can update the weapon aim point all the way to impact. All Walleyes are believed to have been withdrawn to storage, but have not been disposed of.

Below: Walleyes may be long in the tooth, but could be called upon to hit large targets.

AGM-65 Maverick

Type: air-to-surface guided missile.
Manufacturer: Raytheon Systems Co.
Weight: launch AGM-65B 462lb (207.9kg), AGM-65D 485lb (218.3kg), AGM-65E 777lb (353.2kg), AGM-65F 804lb (365.5kg), AGM-65G, 670lb (301.5kg), AGM-65K 793lb (360.5kg).
Dimensions: length 8.17ft (2.49m), diameter 12in (310mm); wingspan 2.33ft (7.11m).
Powerplant: Thiokol TX-481 solid-propellant rocket motor.
Performance: speed approx 620kt (715mph/1,150kmh); range <12nm (17miles/27km) but see notes.
Warhead: AGM-65B/D 125lb (56.3kg), AGM-65E/F/G/K 300lb (135kg).
Guidance: AGM-65B/K electro-optical television; AGM-65D/F/G imaging infrared; AGM-65E laser guided.
Platforms: A-10, F-15E, F-16.

The AGM-65 Maverick is a very successful tactical, air-to-ground guided missile, which entered service in 1972 and has only recently gone out of production, although modernization of older models continues, particularly to meet export orders. Its role is close air support, interdiction, and suppression of enemy air defenses (SEAD), providing stand-off capability and a high hit probability against a wide range of tactical targets, including armor, air defenses, ships, transportation equipment, and fuel storage facilities. Maverick was used during Operation Desert Storm and, according to the Air Force, hit 85 percent of its targets.

The Maverick has a cylindrical body with long-chord delta wings and tail control surfaces, an aerodynamic design based on that of the earlier AIM-4 Falcon, one of the world's first successful air-to-air missiles. The center body is of modular design, enabling weapons to be assembled to meet different requirements by using combinations of three different guidance packages and two different warheads, which are then attached to the common Thiokol rocket

Below: Infrared-guided AGM-65 Maverick air-to-surface missiles.

Above: Four versions of Maverick; – IR (USAF), laser, TV and IR (Navy).

motor section. The front end houses the seeker section, which can be either an electro-optical (E/O) imaging, imaging infrared (IIR), or a semi-active laser (SAL) guidance package. The missile's center section houses the warhead, which is either a 125lb (56.3kg) shaped-charge with a contact fuze for use against targets such as tanks, or a 300lb (135kg) penetrator with a delayed-action fuze, which allows the warhead to penetrate the target using kinetic energy before firing.

Maverick is currently carried by A-10, F-15E, and F-16 aircraft, usually in three-round, underwing clusters, although it can also be hung singly. The missile also has a "launch-and-leave" capability that enables a pilot to fire it and let it guide itself to the target, while he either takes immediate evasive action or attacks another target. Maverick can be launched at any height from high altitudes to tree-top level, and can hit targets ranging from a distance of a few thousand feet to 13nm at medium altitude.

Maverick A had an electro-optical television guidance system, with the view seen by the camera being displayed on a cockpit television screen. The pilot selected the target, centered cross hairs on it, locked on, then launched the missile. Maverick A has been phased out of service primarily because it is so old that the spare parts are simply no longer available; indeed, before production of the spares ended in 1988-89, the USAF logistics organization made a "lifetime" buy of spares, and even that has run out!

Maverick B was similar to the A model, but had new optics, a stronger gimbal mount, and revised electronics, and the television guidance system had a screen magnification capability that enabled the pilot to identify and lock on to smaller and more distant targets. The Maverick B was in production from May 1980 to May 1983 at a rate of 200 per month. Developed in the late 1970s, Maverick C was the first to have a semi-active laser, but was canceled in favor of Maverick E, which had a larger warhead. Maverick D has an IIR guidance system, which overcame the daylight-only, adverse weather limitations of the E/O systems. When slaved to an aircraft-mounted sensor such as FLIR, a laser pod or the APR-38 radar warning system it can lock-on at at least twice the range otherwise possible, especially in mist, rain or at night.

Although the Navy and Air Force withdrew from the SAL program, the Marines developed it as the Maverick E, which is essentially Maverick C with the heavier warhead. Still in service, Maverick E is used to attack fortified ground installations, armored vehicles, and other surface combatants. It operates in conjunction with ground or airborne laser designators, with the missile seeker, searching a sector 7 miles (11km) across and over 10 miles (16km) ahead. Maverick F used by the Navy has a 300lb (136kg) penetrating warhead and an infrared guidance system optimized for ship tracking and attack. Maverick G has the same guidance system as the D, but with software modifications to track larger targets and the same heavyweight penetrator as Maverick F.

The Maverick G was canceled, and the latest version of the missile is the Maverick K, which is still in development. This is being produced by taking a

Maverick G and replacing the IR guidance system with charge-coupled device (CCD) guidance system, which would give greater reliability and the ability to operate in lower light levels, married to the larger warhead. A major factor in this program is cost and numerous efforts are being made to keep these down to the lowest possible level.

If despatched in free flight the range of the Maverick would be about 12nm (14 miles/23km) but the operational range is more realistically about 8nm (9 miles/14km), which is the maximum possible with the seekers and, in particular, to achieve lock-on. As is clear from the above, Maverick has been in service for many years and one of the problems associated with this otherwise very successful weapon system is that it imposes a heavy workload on the pilot, especially of fast jets such as the F-16.

Below: AV-8B launches an AGM-65E laser-guided Maverick.

AGM-86B ALCM/ AGM-86C CALCM

Type: air-to-ground cruise missile.
Manufacturer: The Boeing Company.
Weight: 3,150lb (1,429kg).
Dimensions: length 20.8ft (6.3m); diameter 24.5in (622mm); height 4.0f
(1.2m); wingspan 12.0ft (3.7m).
Powerplant: Williams Research Corp. F-107-WR-10 turbofan engine; 600lb
(272kg) static thrust.
Performance: speed approx 500kt (576mph/927kmh); range <600nm (690
miles/1,112km).
Guidance: Litton INS element integrated with multi-channel onboard GPS.
Warhead: conventional blast/frag warhead; Block 0 ca 2,000lb(907kg); Block
ca 3,000lb(1,360kg).
Platform: B-52H.
Specifications are for AGM-86C.

The AGM-86 Air-Launched Cruise Missile (ALCM) armed with a 200k
nuclear warhead is part of the U.S. strategic deterrent force, while the
conventionally armed versions, AGM-86C/D CALCM, are among the mos
effective weapons of their type in the national arsenal. Development of the
ALCM began in June 1974 and six of the initial model, AGM-86A, were test
flown in 1976, followed in 1977 by the slightly larger and longer range AGM
86B which was ordered for the USAF and became operational in Decembe
1982. During the program Boeing manufactured 1,739 production AGM
86B missiles, the last in September 1986; no further missiles have been
manufactured and all later -B/C/D models are conversions from the origina
stock of AGM-86B.

All versions of AGM-86 are launched only from B-52H bombers, which carr
six missiles on each of two externally mounted pylons and eight internally on

Below: AGM-86Bs can be carried on internal rotary launchers or on wing racks

Above: AGM-86s on an underwing pylon.

rotary launcher, giving a maximum capacity of twenty missiles per aircraft. Immediately following release, the wings unfold, tail surfaces and engine inlet deploy, and the engine starts.

In a new program starting in mid-1986, a number of AGM-86B missiles were converted to carry a high explosive blast/fragmentation warhead in place of the nuclear warhead, becoming the AGM-86C Block 0 Conventional Air-Launched Cruise Missile (CALCM). This modification also replaced the B model's terrain contour-matching guidance system and integrated a GPS capability with the existing inertial navigation computer system.

In 1996-97, a further 200 CALCMs were produced from surplus AGM- 86Bs . Designated Block I, these incorporate a larger and improved conventional payload (approximately 3,000lb/1,361kg)) and an improved avionics package, which was also backfitted into all Block 0 missiles, so that all AGM-86Cs are electronically identical. Under a separate contract, precision accuracy kits are being produced to retrofit the entire CALCM Block 0/1 inventory. This work is taking place in 2002-3.

Next version was the Block 1A with upgraded avionics which includes a third-generation GPS receiver, advanced navigation software, and a GPS anti-jam system for a significant increase in immunity to electronic jamming. A total of 132 missiles were converted in this program. A further fifty missiles are being converted to AGM-86D standard, which has both the avionics upgrade and a new, penetrating warhead for use against hardened and buried targets. Boeing has proposed a new, extended-range version of CALCM for the Air Force's Extended Range Cruise Missile requirement.

The AGM-86B missile has been in service since 1982, during which time more than 100 practice launches have been made, with about a 90 percent success rate. Over 200 AGM-86Cs have been launched in various regional conflicts, demonstrating its ability to deliver a large conventional warhead with exceptional accuracy over distances of 6-700nm. In its first action in 1991, seven B-52s flew from their base at Barksdale, Louisiana, launched 35 AGM-86Cs at high-priority targets in Iraq, and then returned to the United States, in the longest known aircraft combat sortie in history, covering more than 14,000 miles in 35 hours' flying time.

AGM-88 HARM

Type: air-to-surface anti-radiation missile.
Manufacturer: Raytheon (Texas Instruments).
Weight: 800lb (360kg).
Dimensions: length 13.7ft (4.1m); diameter 10in (254mm); wingspan 3.7ft (1.1m).
Powerplant: Thiokol dual-thrust, solid propellent, rocket motor
Performance: speed <661kt (760 mph/1,216kmh); range <57nm (80miles/91km).
Warhead: WAU-7/B, 150lb (68kg); blast/fragmentation.
Guidance: radar homing.
Platforms: A-6E, F-16, F/A-18.

One of the major campaigns in the early days of any modern war is the suppression of enemy air defenses (SEAD), which is the essential prelude to achieving air superiority and in which anti-radar missiles (ARM) play a pivotal role. By the early 1970s, the two in-service anti-radiation missiles, AGM-45 Shrike and AGM-88A Standard ARM, were beginning to lose their edge, so in 1972 the Naval Weapons Center, China Lake, started research on a High-speed Anti-Radiation Missile (HARM). Their main objectives were much higher speed and quicker lock-on, so that targets could be hit before they switched off. The outcome was AGM-88 HARM which began flight tests in 1976 and entered service in 1983.

    The new missile's first real test came in the attack on Libyan targets in the Gulf of Sidra in 1986, and it was later used extensively by the Navy and the Air Force in Operation Desert Storm in 1991, with considerable success. Due to the technological backwardness of the Taliban regime, however, there has been

Above: HARM's mission is the suppression of enemy air defenses (SEAD).

little need for it in the war in Afghanistan.

The AGM-88 can detect, attack and destroy a target with only minimal involvement from the aircrew. Guidance is provided through reception of signals emitted by a ground-based threat radar and it has the capability of discriminating one target from a number of emitters. The missile is powered by a dual-thrust rocket motor, using a smokeless, solid propellant.

The original version, AGM-88A, had a warhead containing some 25,000 pre-formed steel fragments and used Block I software. Block II software provided guidance and fuzing improvements and was used in both AGM-88A missiles and AGM-88B missiles. One of the problems associated with AGM-88A was that whenever the software needed altering or upgrading the entire guidance section had to be returned to the factory, which was clearly unacceptable operationally. The main advance in the AGM-88B was that the guidance section was redesigned so that the software could be changed in the field. AGM-88C, fielded in the 1990s, incorporated a new warhead containing 12,845 tungsten fragments and an improved explosive charge to give greater overall lethality, as well as a new capability against high power GPS jammers. AGM-88Cs were fielded with Block IV software, but this was replaced by Block V in 1999.

The AGM-88D program will involve upgrades of both software and hardware, including replacing the original mechanical gyros by a GPS-based system to improve missile accuracy and increase kill probability, and which will also further reduce the possibility of fratricide (ie, attacking a friendly radar). Under current plans production of the retrofit kits will start in 2003. Yet further developments are being studied in the Advanced Anti-Radiation Guided Missile (AARGM) program, which might be fielded in the 2005 timeframe.

Left: AGM-88 HARM being attached to the pylon of an EA-6B Prowler.

AGM-114K Hellfire II/ Longbow Hellfire

Type: helicopter-launched anti-tank missile.
Manufacturer: Martin Marietta.
Weight: basic 100lb (45.4kg); Longbow 108lb (49.0kg).
Dimensions: length, basic 5.33ft (1.6m), Longbow 5.77ft (1.8m); diameter (all) 7in (17.8cm); wingspan (all) 12in (305mm).
Powerplant: single-stage, single-thrust, solid-propellant motor.
Performance: speed approx 825kt (950mph/1,530kmh); range <2.7nm (3.1 miles/5km).
Warhead: shaped charge 14.8lb (6.7kg).
Guidance: lazer/aradr homing.
Platforms: USN – SH-60B, HH-60H, CH-60S; USMC – AH-1W; Army – AH-64; USAF – Predator and Predator-B.

The AGM-114 Hellfire Air-to-Ground Missile System (AGMS) provides anti-armor capability for attack helicopters and, in a recent development, also for some Unmanned Aerial Vehicles (UAVs). The missile entered service in 1983 and has undergone many updates, one of the most striking being that while all versions use a laser seeker, the most recent adds a radar-frequency seeker. Hellfire II and Longbow Hellfire are the latest production versions, the combination of Hellfire II's precision guidance and Longbow Hellfire's fire-and-forget capability providing the battlefield commander with flexibility across a wide range of mission scenarios, permitting fast battlefield response and a degree of mobility not afforded by other anti-armor weapons.

AGM-114A Basic Hellfire was the original Army version, with 31,616 produced, but it is no longer in service and stocks are being expended in live-fire training. The AGM-114B was the equivalent version for the Navy and

Below: Loading Hellfire missiles aboard an Army AH-64 Apache helicopter.

Above: Hellfire has been tested on "Hummer" and Improved TOW vehicles.

Marine Corps. The naval version differed in having an additional electronic arm/safety device required for shipboard use. The AGM-114C/D/F were experimental versions; none entered production. Next came AGM-114F Interim Hellfire missile with a tandem warhead designed to defeat reactive armor; a small number were ordered by the Army, but none by the Navy; production ended in 1994.

The current version, AGM-114K Hellfire II, has been in production since 1993, and features tandem warheads for defeating reactive armor, electro-optical counter-countermeasures, semiactive laser seeker, and a programmable autopilot for course selection. The weapon can also be employed against concrete bunkers and similar fortifications. The missile is powered by a single-stage, single-thrust, solid-propellant motor, with arming taking place some 164- 328yd (150-300m) from the launcher. Maximum velocity is about 825kt (950mph).

There are two engagement methods: autonomous and remote. In an autonomous engagement the launch aircraft conducts the entire operation from target location, through identification, firing, guidance until the target is destroyed. In contrast, in a remote engagement the aircraft simply acts as a launcher, despatching the missile to the general location of the target, where another aircraft or a ground observer, designating with a laser, guides the missile to its intended target. This remote engagement requires coordination, but has the advantage that the launch aircraft can remain masked behind terrain, greatly reducing its visible launch signature, thereby increasing aircraft survivability.

The Longbow Hellfire missile is an adverse weather, "fire-and-forget" version of the Hellfire missile. The Longbow fire-control radar system locates, classifies, and prioritizes targets for the Longbow Hellfire missile and is being integrated into the Army's entire AH-64D Apache attack helicopters and into one-third of its RAH-66 Comanche armed reconnaissance helicopters.

The main advantages of the Longbow missile are: adverse weather capability (rain, snow, fog, smoke, and battlefield obscurants); millimeter wave countermeasures survivability; fire-and-forget guidance, which allows the Apache Longbow to launch and then remask, thus minimizing exposure to enemy fire; an advanced warhead capable of defeating reactive armor configurations projected into the 21st century; and reprogrammability to adapt to changing threats and mission requirements.

AGM-122A Sidearm

Type: helicopter-launched anti-radiation missile.
Manufacturer: Motorola.
Weight: 195lb (88.5kg).
Dimensions: length 9.42ft (2.87m); diameter 5in (127mm); wingspan 2.07ft (0.63m).
Powerplant: single-stage rocket motor.
Performance: maximum speed Mach 2.3; range about 18,000yd (16,460m) from high-altitude launch.
Warhead: 10lb (4.5kg) blast fragmentation.
Guidance: semi-active radar homing.
Platforms: AH-64D, AH-1W, AV-8B.

The AGM-122 Sidearm anti-radar missile was developed quickly and cheaply from the ubiquitous AIM-9 Sidewinder by the Naval Weapons Center at China

Lake for use by the F-8 Crusader naval fighter. A more advanced version was then developed as the AGM-122A for use by the Marines to arm their A-4 Skyhawks, AV-8 Harriers, and AH-1 attack helicopters for use against hostile radars serving air defense gun and missile systems. The weapon has also been adopted by the Army for use aboard its AH-64 Apache attack helicopters.

The Sidearm is based on the AIM-9C Sidewinder airframe, tailplane, Mk 17 propulsion system, and WDU-17 warhead, but there are minor modifications to the canard control surfaces. The control electronics are modified to command a pitch-up immediately following release, so that the missile can be launched from a very low-flying aircraft and also to ensure that the missile approaches its target in a high-speed dive. The guidance section is also modified to enable it to detect and track a radiating, ground-based radar.

Below: AGM-122 (her on AH-1) is designed to destroy hostile ground radars.

AGM-130 air-launched stand-off weapon

Type: air-launched stand-off weapon.
Manufacturer: The Boeing Company.
Weight: launch 2,917lb (1,313kg).
Dimensions: length 12.9ft (3.9m); diameter 18in (457mm); wingspan 4.92ft (1,5m).
Powerplant: rocket motor.
Performance: speed high subsonic; range classified; ceiling <30,000ft (9,090m).
Guidance: television or imaging infrared seeker.
Warhead: AGM-130A – MK-84 blast/fragmentation warhead; AGM-130C – BLU-109 penetrator.
Platform: F-15E.

The GBU-15 (GBU = guided bomb unit) was developed during the Vietnam War to provide both a stand-off capability to protect the aircrew and to give much greater accuracy. This was achieved by taking a Mk 84 bomb and adding the seeker head from a Maverick missile, together with a data link, which enabled the missile to be guided from a second aircraft fitted using a two-way data link. In its turn, the AGM-130 was created by taking the GBU-15 as the base unit and adding a rocket motor to give extended range, and an altimeter to give height control. On release from the aircraft, the rocket motor fires and on termination of thrust it is jettisoned. The AGM-130 carries a television camera and an imaging infrared seeker which provide a visual presentation of the target as seen from the weapon, which is passed via

Above: AGM-130s; note the underslung, jettisonable rocket motor.

a data link to the aircraft, which carries an AQ.-14 pod and is fitted with a cockpit screen. The seeker can be locked onto the target before or after launch, following which guidance is automatic, or the weapon can be manually

controlled by a weapon systems officer, using the two-way data link. There are two variants which differ only in the warhead: AGM-130A with a Mk 84 blast/fragmentation warhead, and AGM-130C with a BLU-109 penetrator.

A more recent development is the Adverse Weather AGM-130, which has a 24-hour capability using a new INS/GPS guidance system coupled with a state-of-the-art Imaging Infrared Focal Plane Array Seeker. The guidance system consists of a tightly coupled INS/GPS which flies the AGM-130 to the vicinity of the target by day or night and in any weather conditions and places the target in the seeker's field-of-view with approximately 2-3 miles (3.2-4.8km) still to go. The weapon system operator then locks the seeker on to the specific aiming point.

Left: F-15E launching an AGM-130 stand-off weapon.

AGM-142 Popeye (Have Nap)

Type: medium range, conventional stand-off missile.
Manufacturer: Lockheed Martin (Marietta)/Rafale (Israel).
Weight: 3,300lb (1,497kg).
Dimensions: length 15.8ft (4.8m); diameter 1.8ft (0.5m); wingspan 6.5ft (2.0m).
Powerplant: solid-fuel rocket motor.
Performance: range <50nm (57 miles/93km).
Warhead: blast fragmentation 750lb (340kg) or penetration 770lb (350kg).
Guidance: television and imaging infrared (IIR) (man-in-the-loop).
Platforms: B-52H.

This cruise missile originated in Israel but was adopted by the U.S. Air Force under the Have Nap program as the AGM-142, being produced in the USA by Precision Guided Systems United States (PGSUS), a joint company set up by Lockheed Martin Missiles and Rafale of Israel. The significant feature of AGM 142 is that in addition to autonomous control it also has a "man-in-the-loop" capability. It is intended to conduct precision attacks against high value, fixed targets, including electricity generating facilities (eg, transformers, generators cooling towers); oil-production facilities (eg, cracking -plants, distillation towers) electronic sites (radars, communications towers); and research and development facilities. The critical importance of the "man-in-the-loop" feature

s that it enables specific buildings, such as control centers, to be selected, thus causing maximum destruction or disruption to the system as a whole. The missile is launched from stand-off ranges by a B-52H bomber, which may then either control the attack itself or pass control to another aircraft.

Construction of the AGM-142 is modular, with two types of guidance and two types of warhead, which can be assembled in any combination. Guidance is either by television or an imaging infrared seeker, while the warheads are either a blast fragmentation warhead for use against soft targets or a penetration warhead for use against hardened targets.

Popeye has also been purchased by Turkey, and Israel and Turkey have cooperated in developing a Popeye II missile (USAF = Have Lite), which is smaller and uses more advanced technology, with a range of 94 miles (150km). Israel is also developing a turbojet-powered version (Turbo-Popeye) which appears to be an equivalent of the USAF's Air-Launched Cruise Missile (ALCM).

AGM-142 is a very capable weapon system, but it was not used during Desert Storm, one possible reason being that it might have been thought at the time that there could be policy implications in launching an Israeli-made weapon against an Arab country.

Below: USAF F-16 carrying the Israeli-designed AGM-142 Popeye missile.

AGM-154A/B/C Joint Standoff Weapon (JSOW)

Type: unpowered, stand-off bomb.
Manufacturer: Raytheon.
Weight: approximately 1,250lb (567kg).
Dimensions: length 13.3ft (4.1m); wingspan 8.8ft (2.7m).
Powerplant: none (see notes).
Performance: range, low altitude launch (unpowered) 12nm (24km), high altitude launch (unpowered) 40nm (64 km); range, powered >120nm (200km)- see notes.
Warhead: BLU-97 or BLU-108.
Guidance: GPS/INS.
Platforms: AV-8B, B-1, F-15E, F-16, F/A-18C/D, F/A-18E/F, P-3, S-3.
Specifications apply to AGM-154A Baseline version

AGM-154A Joint Standoff Weapon (JSOW) has recently entered service to replace current weapons such as Paveway, Skipper, and Maverick. In its current non-powered versions it has a gliding range of 12nm (24km) from a low altitude launch, increasing to 40nm (64km) at high altitude. It employs a tightly coupled Global Positioning System (GPS)/Inertial Navigation System (INS) for midcourse navigation, and imaging infra-red (IIR) and datalink for terminal homing. It is capable of day/night and adverse weather operations. The basic airframe (also known as the "truck) is of square cross-section, with a spinal hump which houses the folded wings and the power supply. The conical nose houses the terminal seeker, behind which is the guidance package and then a long weapons bay taking up most of the fuselage. Behind that is an electronics package and then the tail and control surfaces.

There are three variants. AGM-154A carries 145 BLU-97/B Skeet submunitions, each having a shaped charge to destroy armor, a fragmenting case for material destruction, and a zirconium ring for incendiary effects. AGM-154B, the specialized anti-armor version for the Air Force, carries six BLU-108/B submunitions, each of which releases four projectiles that use infrared sensors to detect targets; upon detection, the projectile detonates, creating an explosively formed, shaped charge capable of penetrating armor targets. AGM-154C carries the BLU-111/B variant of the MK-82, 500lb (227kg) general-purpose bomb and is designed to attack point targets.

The original requirement was for a powered weapon, but this was dropped in order to meet the cost criteria. However, space has been left in the tail for either a rocket or a turbofan, and an example powered by a Williams International J75 engine (as used to power several types of target drones) was successfully tested in 1995.

Below: F/A-18 carrying four AGM-154 Joint Stand-Off Weapons (JSOW).

AGM-158 Joint Air-to-Surface Standoff Missile (JASSM)

Type: air-launched cruise missile.
Manufacturer: Lockheed Martin.
Weight: 2,250lb (1,134kg).
Dimensions: length 14.0ft (4.3m).
Range: <200nm (230 miles/371km).
Powerplant: Teledyne Continental J402-CA100-2 turbojet; approx 600lb (272kg) static thrust.
Guidance: see text.
Warhead: 1,000lb (454kg).
Platforms: B-1, B-2, B-52, F-15E, F-16, F/A-18E/F, F-117, P-3C, S-3B.

The Navy and Air Force have had a long-standing requirement for a stand-off weapon (cruise missile) capable of attacking various types of deep target and of being launched from outside the enemy's air defenses, thus protecting the aircrew. Originally, this was to have been met by the Tri-Service Stand-off Attack Missile (TSSAM), but that project was canceled when its costs escalated to an unacceptable level. This resulted in 1996 in the setting up of the Navy/Air Force Joint Air-to-Surface Standoff Missile (JASSM) program. JASSM is a cruise missile which is launched from a maximum range of some 200nm

(230 miles/371km) and is intended to attack hardened, medium-hardened, soft, or area targets. Having been launched, the wings extend and the turbojet starts, following which it follows a low-level, circuitous route under the guidance of an inertial navigation system (INS) aided by a new antijam-protected GPS. Once in the area of the target, the terminal guidance system, which consists of an imaging infrared (IIR) seeker and a pattern-matching target recognition system, takes over to guide the missile in for a high-precision direct hit.

Power is provided by the Teledyne Continental J402 turbojet engine, which is an upgraded version of the J402 already in use in the Harpoon. Initial production versions of the JASSM will be powered by the J402-CA-100-2 model, but later versions will have the J402-CA-100-9B engine which incorporates advanced aerodynamic components for a further improvement to engine performance.

Several upgrades are already under consideration, one of which involves replacing the original warhead with an advanced penetrator, which would have either a dense metal case or contain dense metal ballast for maximum penetration. This was under development before the start of the war in Afghanistan, but with the problems caused by the caves, its importance will be greatly enhanced. Total production is expected to be at least 3,700 missiles.

Left: Crew of an F-16 watch as the JASSM they have launched powers away en route to its distant target.

BLU-82 Blast Bomb

Type: blast bomb.
Weight: 15,000lb (6,804kg).
Dimensions: length 11.8ft (3.6m); diameter 54in (1,372mm).
Guidance: ballistic.
Warhead: aluminum powder; 12,600lb (5,715kg).
Platform: MC-130 .

The devastating explosive power of the BLU-82 has gained it considerable notoriety. It was originally one of a series of bombs developed during the Vietnam War, under the codename Commando Vault, for clearing helicopter landing zones and artillery gun positions in dense jungle, which was otherwise a very manpower-intensive and vulnerable task for ground troops. The BLU-82 was the largest in this series, indeed being so big that it could not be accommodated in the bomb bay or on the hardpoints of any dedicated bomber or attack aircraft. Therefore, then as now, it could only be carried in the hold of an MC-130 Hercules, where it is mounted on a standard cargo pallet and extracted (still on the pallet) from the aircraft's rear door by a drogue parachute. The minimum altitude for release is 6,000ft (1,830m) above ground level, due to possible blast effects on the aircraft.

The bomb contains 12,600lb (5,715kg) of conventional explosive (a mix of aluminum powder, ammonium nitrate, and polystyrene) and it is not, as is sometimes alleged in the popular media, a fuel-air explosive (FAE) weapon. To ensure maximum effect, the weapon must be detonated some 2-3ft (0.6-0.9m)

Above: Largest non-nuclear bomb in use today, BLU-82 is carried by MC-130.

above the ground, which is achieved by fitting an M904 contact fuze attached to a 4ft (1.2m) length of metal pipe projecting from the nose. The blast effect is some 1,000psi (700,000kgf/m^2) immediately adjacent to the impact point, but decreases with distance. This above-ground explosion also minimizes the crater.

A number of BLU-82s were used in the Vietnam War and one was dropped on Son Tay Island during the recovery of the crew of the SS *Mayaguez* in May 1975. Eleven BLU-82s were dropped during Desert Storm, initially to discover whether the bomb could be used to clear mines, but later for their psychological effect on Iraqi troops. Several have also been used in Afghanistan, where they were intended to destroy caves and tunnels, although, again, their psychological effect also had considerable significance.

The BLU-82 is not the largest non-nuclear bomb ever used – that distinction belonging to the British World War II Grand Slam which weighed 22,000lb (9,980kg) – but it is certainly the largest bomb in use today. It should also be noted that although the BLU-82 is frequently referred to as the "Daisy Cutter bomb" this was originally the generic term applied to any bomb using this type of above-ground fuzing.

Left: This BLU-82 was dedicated to the crew of Special Ops AC-130 lost during the Gulf War.

BLU-107 Anti-Runway Weapon (Durandal)

Type: anti-runway weapon.
Manufacturer: Matra (France).
Weight: 483lb (219kg).
Dimensions: length 8.8ft (2.7m); diameter 8.7in (221mm); wingspan 1.5ft (0.46m).
Powerplant: solid-fuel rocket.
Performance: speed at impact approximately 490kt (560mph/900kmh); minimum release altitude 195ft (60m).
Warhead: 220lb (100kg) high-explosive.

One of the major reasons for the Israeli success in the 1967 Middle East War was their destruction of Arab aircraft on their bases and of the runways. This led to the development of a series of anti-runway bombs, of which the Durandal was one of the best. It had been designed to meet a French Air Force requirement and was subsequently acquired by the USAF.

The weapon is delivered by an aircraft flying at a speed of between 400

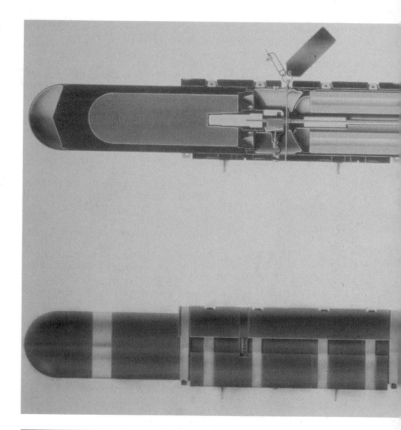

and 650mph (644-1,050kmh) at a minimum height of 195ft (60m).On release, a brake parachute slows the weapon until the main parachute can deploy, which brings the speed down to about 56mph (90kmh), at which point the weapon pitches forward to point directly at the runway. Once at the optimum angle, the parachute is released and the rocket motor fired, accelerating the bomb downwards to hit the runway at some 560mph (900kmh), where the kinetic energy and the hardened steel penetrator combine to drive it through some 16in (406mm) of unreinforced concrete. A one-second delay fuse then detonates the warhead, resulting in a crater some 100sq ft ($9m^2$) in area, but with the "heave" causing significant damage over some 2,000sq ft ($200m^2$), all of which requires repair before the runway can be used again by high-speed aircraft. In the late 1990s the United States transferred 523 BLU-107s each to Greece and Turkey, but a small stock remains.

Below: Durandal was the winner of a long competitive evaluation.

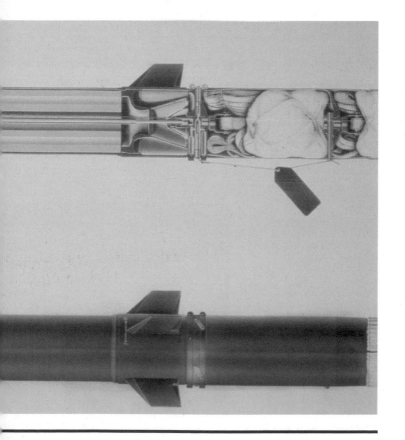

GBU 31/32 Joint Direct Attack Munitions (JDAM)

Type: guided air-to-surface weapon.
Manufacturer: The Boeing Company.
Weight: JDAM plus warhead GBU-31(v)1/B – 2,036lb (925.4kg); plus GBU-31(v)3/B – 2,115lb (961.4kg); plus GBU-32(v)1/B – 1,013lb (460.5kg).
Dimensions: length JDAM plus warhead GBU-31(v)1/B – 12.73ft (60.1cm), plus GBU-31(v)3/B – 12.36ft (58.5cm), plus GBU-32(v)1/B – 9.96ft (47cm); wingspan GBU-31 – 25in (10cm), GBU-32 – 19.6in (7.7cm).
Powerplant: none.
Performance: range maximum about 13nm (15 miles/24km); ceiling <45,000ft (13,677m).
Guidance: GPS/INS.
Platforms: current – B-1B, B-2A, B-52H, F-16C/D, and F/A-18C/D ; planned – AV-8B, A-10, F-14A/B/D, F-15E, F/A-18E/F, F-22, F-35 (JSF), F-117, S-3.

Among the lessons learnt from Operation Desert Storm was that there was a deficiency in air-to-surface weapon capability, where poor weather conditions had limited the effectiveness of precision guided munitions (PGM), while the well-known fact that unguided weapon accuracy is degraded when delivered from medium and high altitudes was also relearnt. As a result, development of an "adverse weather precision guided munition" – officially known as the Joint Direct Attack Munition – started in 1992, with the first weapons delivered in 1997 and operational testing taking place in 1998-99. During these tests, some 450 JDAMs were dropped, including in snow, rain, and cloud conditions, but despite these conditions they achieved an unprecedented 95 percent system reliability, with a 10.5yd (9.6m) accuracy rate.

JDAM consists of a new guidance tail kit which is strapped to an existing, unguided free-fall bomb, thus converting it into an accurate, all-weather "smart" munition. Current weapons are the 2,000lb (907kg) BLU-109/Mk 84 or the 1,000lb (453kg) BLU-110/Mk 83. The new tail unit contains an inertial navigational system (INS) and a global positioning system (GPS) guidance control unit. Once released from the aircraft, the JDAM autonomously navi-gates to the designated target coordinates, which will have been loaded into the aircraft before takeoff, or manually set by the aircrew before weapon release. In its most accurate mode, when GPS data is available, the JDAM system provides a circular error probable (CEP) of 14yd (13m), while if GPS data is not available it will achieve a 33yd (30m) CEP. JDAM can be launched from very low to very high altitudes in a dive, toss and loft or in straight-and-level flight with an on-axis or off-axis delivery. JDAM enables multiple weapons

Above: JDAM is designed to increase accuracy in poor weather conditions.

to be directed against single or multiple targets on a single pass.

The B-2 bomber made its operational debut using JDAM during Operation Allied Force, when the bombers flew nonstop, roundtrip flights from Whiteman Air Force Base, Missouri, to deliver more than 600 JDAMs. The weapons have since been used in Afghanistan, where they have again proved to be both very accurate and highly reliable, and repeatedly demonstrated their effectiveness in virtually any weather condition.

The Department of Defense plans to buy some 62,000 JDAM kits for the Air Force and a further 25,500 for the Navy up to 2009 at a unit cost (in FY01 dollars) of $21,000 per tail kit. The JDAM also has significant growth potential and anticipated upgrades include integrating the weapon into additional aircraft, extending the range, evolving smaller weapons, and improving on the already exceptional accuracy by adding low-cost terminal guidance. Growth of the JDAM family of weapons is being expanded to the Mk 82 500lb (227kg) version, which began development in late 1999. Also, the Navy is currently studying the effects of adding enhancements such as improved GPS accuracy, a precision seeker for terminal guidance, and additional warheads.

Below: Some 500 JDAMs were dropped over former Yugoslavia, many from B-2s.

GBU-36/B, GBU-37B GAM (GPS-Aided Munitions)

Type: Global Positioning System-Aided Munition (GAM)
Manufacturer: Northrop Grumman.
Powerplant: none.
Performance: range <5nm (4.4miles/7.0km); circular error probable (CEP) 40-60ft (12-18m).
Warhead: GPU-36B Mk 84 general-purpose bomb; GPU-37B BLU-103 penetrator bomb (see text).
Guidance: GPS/INS.
Platform: B-2.

The Global Positioning System-Aided Munition (GAM) was developed as an interim measure to improve the accuracy of two of the weapons carried by the B-2 bomber. It is, in essence, an "add-on" tail unit, which combines a GPS receiver and a control module to steer the bomb to its target, rather than rely on free-fall, which is known to be inaccurate. Identical kits are added to two bombs. GBU-36B is the GAM-modified Mk 84 LDGP (low-drag, general-purpose) 2,000lb (907kg) bomb. The Mk 84 was designed in

the 1950s for use against a wide variety of ground targets.

GBU-37B is the GAM-modified BLU-113 4,000lb (1,814kg) penetrator ("bunker-buster"). This weapon was created in seventeen days during the Gulf War when there was an immediate requirement for a weapon to destroy Iraqi underground command bunkers, some of which were known to be very deeply buried. The basis of the bomb is a surplus Army 8in (203mm) gun tube, weighing some 4,600lb (2,086kg), which is filled with 630lb (286kg) of high-explosive, and was originally fitted with a GBU-27 laser guidance kit on the nose. This has now replaced by the GAM tail. If released from high altitude, the BLU-113 is credited with penetrating up to 100ft (30m) of earth or 20ft (6m) of concrete. Designing a fuze to survive the high speed impact and subsequent penetration is not easy, and the weapon is presently fitted with the FMU-143 tail fuze. The GBU-37 entered service with the B-2 in late 1997 and is currently the only all-weather, near-precision "bunker-buster" available.

Below: GBU-37B is a modified artillery shell, fitted with GPS guidance.

Paveway II (GBU-10)/
Paveway III (GBU-24/27/28) LGBs

Type: add-on guidance kits for gravity bombs.
Manufacturer: Texas Instruments.
Weight: bomb unit 2,100lb (953kg).
Dimensions: length 14.1ft (4.3m); diameter 1.5ft (0.5m); wingspan, closed 2.5ft (0.8m), open 5.5ft (1.7m).
Powerplant: none.
Performance: speed, high sub-sonic; range, low-altitude launch approximately 1,650yd (1,510m), high-altitude launch 20,000yd (18,300m).
Warhead: Mk 84 conventional high-explosive/fragmentation warhead, 1,970lb (894kg); explosive 945lb (429kg).
Guidance: semi-active laser-homing.
Specifications for Paveway II GBU-10C/D/E/F.

A lesson learnt in World War II, and again in Korea and Vietnam, is that while free-fall bombs are cheap they are also inaccurate and the only way to destroy pinpoint targets was to drop a large number of bombs. Research begun in the mid-1960s to overcome this led to a series of bombs known as Paveway (PAVE

Above: GBU-10Es are prepared for first strike on Iraqi forces in Desert Storm.

= precision avionics vectoring equipment). The designation Paveway I, applied in 1978, was for an add-on kit consisting of a unit added to the nose, weighing some 30lb (13.6kg) and with new shorter tail fins. The nose section housed a laser receiver and control elements, and homed the bomb onto a target being marked by an air- or ground-based laser designator. This resulted in a great increase in accuracy and required no modifications to the launch aircraft, which, as an added benefit, was able to exit the area after launch, unless it was itself acting as the marker. The system worked at night and in poor visibility; the minimum cloud base for successful operation was 2,500ft (760m).

Paveways I and II function in similar manner. The laser seeker at the extreme nose detects laser energy reflected from the "illuminated" target at different strengths on each of its four internal quadrants. This strength differential generates error signals which are passed to the computer located just forward of the canard control fins. The computer then translates these inputs into commands to the four canard control fins, seeking always to reduce the error to zero, at which point the weapon is falling directly towards the target. One of the characteristics of this early system was that the computer moved the control surfaces on the "bang-bang" principle; ie, they were always deflected fully one way or the other. As a result, the missile followed a somewhat wobbly path, which was relatively inefficient and reduced range.

The Paveway II system entered service in 1980. It

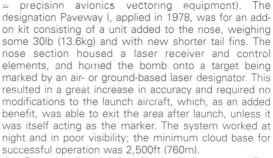

Left: Paveway III LGBs on F-16; this version uses the Mk82 500 pound (227kg) warhead.

was based on the same concept but with a simpler and cheaper guidance package, and a folding wing group (comprising spring-open extensions to the fixed tail fins for extra maneuverability and additional horizontal range) added at the tail. Paveway II weapons still in service are the GBU-10C/D/E/F, based on the 2,000lb (907kg) Mk 84 bomb, and the GBU-10G/H/I/J, based on the BLU-109B Improved 2,000lb Penetrating Warhead. Also in the original Paveway II program were the GBU-12B/C/D (500lb Mk 82 bomb) and the GBU-16A/B (1,000lb Mk 83 bomb), but none remains in service.

Development of Paveway III started in 1980, and the first weapons entered service in 1987. It is an improved version of Paveway II designed for use in the degraded weather and high-threat scenario of European operations. It is, therefore, fitted with high-lift folding wings at the rear, a microprocessor-based control system, a digital autopilot, and an improved scanning seeker. The main benefit of the microprocessor is that it moves the control surfaces proportionally (ie, only as far as required as opposed to the earlier "bang-bang" system). Paveway III also has a small rocket booster. Taken together, these improvements combine to increase range for a low-level launch to 3-5nm (3.5-5.8 miles/5.6-9.3km) compared to 1-2nm (1.2-3 miles/1.9-3.7km) for Paveway I/II. The result is a weapon of far greater operational flexibility than its predecessors and the ability to release it at low level, in either level flight or a

Below: Paveway III – GBU-24 (top); GBU-27 (center); GBU-28 (bottom).

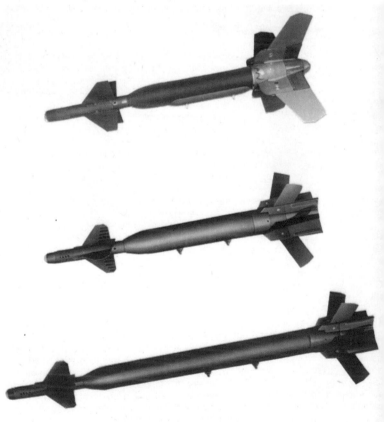

Above: GBU-24 aboard USS Carl Vinson; note the wing folded into the nearest fin.

zoom climb, although it can also be released at higher altitudes in dives as steep as 60 degrees.

The latest development is the Advanced Unitary Penetrator (AUP), which is designed to provide at least twice the penetration capability of existing 2000lb (907kg) bombs. Penetration capability is directly proportional to the warhead's sectional density (weight ÷ cross-section) which is maximized in the AUP by reducing the explosive payload and using heavy metals in the warhead case. The AUP retains the carriage and flight characteristics of the BLU-109, and is compatible with the GBU-24, GBU-27, and GBU-15/AGM-130 series of precision-guided bombs. Thus, the AUP will be capable of delivery from a wider inventory of aircraft, including stealth platforms.

GBU-24E/B is a precision-guided hardened target penetrator used to destroy hardened aircraft hangers and underground bunkers. It integrates a Global Positioning System and a ring laser gyro inertial measuring unit (IMU) to the already fielded GBU-24B/B with the existing laser guidance. A new guidance and control unit has been modified to incorporate GPS electronics, GPS antenna, IMU, and software for precision GPS/INS guidance. Testing of this system began in late 1999.

GBU-27 is a GBU-24 modified for delivery by the F-117 stealth strike/fighter. The operator illuminates a target with a laser designator and then the munition guides to a spot of laser energy reflected. The GBU-27 uses a BLU-109 improved performance 2,000lb bomb developed in 1985 under the project name HAVE VOID and has a modified Paveway II guidance control unit which provides "terminal trajectory shaping" for optimum impact angle against various target structures, by hitting an aircraft shelter vertically, for example, but a bridge support horizontally. A Paveway II tail assembly with folding wings completes the bomb. The F-117 can carry two GBU-27s in two weapons bays and is reportedly capable of hitting a 35sq ft (1m^2) target from an altitude of 25,000ft (7,620mm).

Wind Corrected Munitions Dispenser

Wind Corrected Munitions Dispenser
Type: strap-on error-correction guidance kit for dumb bombs.
Manufacturer: Lockheed Martin.
Weight: n.k.
Dimensions: n.k.
Powerplant: none.
Performance: ballistic.
Warhead: CBU-87, CBU-89, CBU-97.
Platforms: B-1, B-52, F-15E, F-16, F-117.

During the latter part of the Cold War the primary means of air attack against Warsaw Pact targets would have involved fast, low-altitude deliveries, but in the regional conflicts in the Gulf, Bosnia, and now Afghanistan, the Air Force has used medium/high-level deliveries to protect air crew from anti-aircraft attacks. There are, however, problems associated with delivering "dumb" bombs from such altitudes. First, their accuracy decreases as release altitude increases, mainly due to winds encountered during the descent, and, second, each discrete target requires a separate pass. One solution is electro-optical "smart" bombs, but their performance is severely degraded in cloud, smoke or dust. The Wind Compensated Munitions Dispenser (WCMD, known colloquially as "Wick-Mid") is intended to overcome these problems, and is currently being

Zuni 130mm Rocket

Type: folding-fin aircraft rocket (FFAR).
Weight: 110.9lb (50.3kg).
Dimensions: length 9.11ft (2.78m); diameter 5in (127mm).
Powerplant: Mk 71 low-smoke rocket motor.
Performance: maximum speed approximately 2,370ft/sec (1,616mph/2,600kmh).
Warhead: Mk 33 flare (length 33.0in (84cm), weight 45.9lb (21kg)).
Guidance: unguided.
Platforms: F-14, F/A-18; AH-1.
Specifications for Mk 33 warhead; length and weight vary according to warhead (see text).

The unguided 5.0-inch rocket is designated as the 130mm rocket, although the actual caliber is 127mm. It was originally developed for air-to-air use (carried by aircraft such as the F-4 Phantom and F-8 Crusader) and also for anti-submarine use (on S-2 Tracker and S-3), but actually it is most widely used in the air-to-ground role. There is a variety of warheads, but the most often used today are marking flares.
   The bare rocket (tube plus fins plus motor) is some 6.67ft (2.03m) long and weighs about 66lb (31kg), but the overall length and weight depend upon the warhead fitted, which in turn depends upon the tactical requirement. Current operational warheads include: Mk 24 (general-purpose); Mk 32 (anti-armor/anti-personnel); Mk 33 (flare); Mk 34 (smoke); Mk 34 (incendiary); Mk 63 (H fragmentation). As examples, the rocket fitted with the Mk 24/1 warhead is 8.01ft (2.44m) long and weighs 11.4lb (5.2kg), while with the Mk 63 it is 92.25ft (2.81m) long and weighs 124lb (56.2kg). There are also a number of practice warheads available, including the Mk 6, Mk 62, and WTU- 11.

Right: An F-16 carrying a variety of weapons, including (port outer weapon with a red tail) a Wind-Corrected Munition, and an AIM-9 on each wingtip.

applied to weapons such as CBU-87 CEM (Combined Effects Munition), CBU-89 GATOR, and CBU-97 SFW (Sensor Fuzed Weapon).

The WCMD is a tail kit which corrects for wind effects and errors during the weapon's ballistic fall, thus turning a "dumb" bomb into a "smart" weapon, and is currently demonstrating an accuracy of some 30ft (9m). The WCMD can be used from a wide range of altitudes and in adverse weather, and also enables aircraft to use tactics such as level-, dive-, and toss-bombing, as well as bombing on coordinates. To minimize errors due to inaccuracies in aircraft heading, velocity, and position, all aircraft will have Global Positioning System (GPS) but the WCMD itself does not require GPS. It is also possible to give different targets to different bombs in the same aircraft, thus reducing the number of passes that have to be made. The Air Force plans to modify 40,000 tactical munitions dispensers at a cost of $8,937 per unit – a remarkable bargain.

Right: Navy ordnanceman adjusts the tailfins on a Zuni 5in (130mm) rocket.

Four rockets are carried in the LAU-10 reusable rocket pod, which is made of treated paper, covered with a thin aluminum skin, which can be carried at speeds up to Mach 1.2. The rockets can be launched singly or in ripple.

Zuni rockets were involved in two notorious accidents in the 1960s. The first was aboard USS *Forrestal* on 29 July 1967. An aircraft was being prepared for a mission when a Zuni was accidentally fired and hit another aircraft, starting a fuel fire. Some 90 seconds later the intense heat detonated a bomb, which breached the flight deck, resulting in burning fuel descending into the hangar, where various bombs, warheads, and rocket motors exploded. Casualties were 134 killed and 161 wounded, with 21 aircraft destroyed.

Only two years later, on 15 January 1969, there was another tragedy, aboard USS *Enterprise*, when an aircraft engine starter unit was allowed to direct its exhaust onto a Zuni pod. The rockets exploded, piercing the aircraft's fuel tanks, which started a major fire. Three more Zuni rockets, fitted with shaped charge warheads then exploded, blasting holes in the flightdeck, allowing burning fuel to descend into the hangar. This time losses were 28 dead, 344 wounded, and 15 aircraft destroyed. Following these two accidents the most stringent safety precautions were applied and there has been no recurrence.

Surface Warships

The strategic interests of the United States make it imperative that she should dominate the Atlantic and Pacific Oceans in order to protect herself and to guarantee access to the rest of the world, both to trade with partners and to project power in defense of national interests. However, the United States' concerns are global and cannot be confined to those two oceans; she needs to exercise maritime power in every ocean and major sea, and to ensure freedom of passage through the major choke points. This was achieved during the Cold War when the U.S. Navy and Marine Corps, assisted to a certain extent by allies, faced down every attempt by the Soviet Navy to achieve maritime parity, let alone superiority.

The Cold War has been over for a decade, but national interests require that the United States maintains strong and capable naval and marine forces with a global reach. Today's surface fleet is intended to do just that. Many of the ships of the Cold War Navy have been retired, are in reserve or have been "cascaded" to friendly countries, and the result is a leaner and meaner fighting force.

It is said that as soon as he is warned of an overseas crisis the U.S. president's first question is: "Where are the carriers?" These ships, with their unparalleled power and global reach, are at the core of the surface Navy. Each carries an air wing composed of some seventy ultra-modern aircraft which can dominate the oceans and project U.S. power into the littoral areas and deep inland, as has recently been shown in Afghanistan.

A major development is the reduction in numbers of classes, making standardization and logistic support easier and more cost-effective. There are now one class of cruiser (Ticonderoga), two classes of destroyer (Spruance and Arleigh Burke), and one class of frigate (the Oliver Hazard Perry). There are also reductions in amphibious shipping with the San Antonio-class replacing four different types, while within a decade the Wasp-class will be the only major amphibious units. Now deep in reserve are the last two battleships, *Iowa* and *Wisconsin*; once symbols of naval might, they were ships of which America was justly proud, but their day is done. Thus, it is very improbable that any crisis

could occur to justify the enormous expense of overhauling them, modernizing their systems, and assembling and training the huge crews needed to send them to sea again.

During the Cold War uninformed critics made adverse comparisons between U.S. warships, with their clear decks and uncluttered masts, and Soviet ships whose decks were crowded with weapons systems and their masts festooned with antennae. Such people thought this showed a weakness in the U.S. approach, but the opposite was the case. U.S. systems were, in almost all cases, far superior, but their capabilities were not so visually striking. It is the same today, with empty decks hiding vertical launchers which can despatch dozens of Tomahawk missiles deep into hostile territory or Standard SAMs against incoming aircraft or missiles, while the masts carry just a few sensors, hiding the sophisticated electronics, most importantly the Aegis system, which is unequaled in any other navy.

Left: The symbols of U.S. naval power – carriers to strike and supply ships to sustain.

Kitty Hawk-class

Type: aircraft carrier, conventionally powered (CV).
Completed: 1961-68.
Number in class: four (three in service).
Displacement: 61,351 tons light; 81.985 tons full load
Dimensions: length 1,068.9ft (325.8m); beam 130.0ft (39.6m); draught 40.0ft (12.2m).
Powerplant: four shafts; Westinghouse geared steam turbines; eight Foster-Wheeler boilers; 280,000shp; 33kt; 8,000nm at 20kt.
Aircraft: Typical 2002 air wing, 70 aircraft: 11 x F-14B Tomcat interceptors; 36 x F/A-18C Hornet fighter-bombers; 4 x EA-6B Prowler airborne electronic warfare; 4 x E-2C Hawkeye AEW; 8 x S-3B Viking ASW; 7 x SH-60F/HH-60H Seahawk helicopters; 1 x C-2A Greyhound carrier on-board delivery.
Armament: 3 x Mk 29 launchers for Sea Sparrow SAMs; 3 x 20mm Mk 15 Phalanx CIWS.
Complement: 5,096.
Specifications for Kitty Hawk (CV 63) in 2000.

The three remaining conventionallypowered "super-carriers" are very powerful fighting units, in combat capability second only to the U.S. Navy's nuclear-powered carriers. There were originally four ships, with minor differences between the first pair – Kitty Hawk (CV-63) and Constellation (CV-64), both completed in 1961 – and the second pair – America (CV-66) and John F Kennedy (CV-67), completed in 1965 and 1968, respectively – but they are usually considered together since they have common hulls, propulsion systems, and flightdeck layouts.

The Navy's first "super-carriers" were the four ships of the Forrestal-class, completed between 1952 and 1955 and displacing 78,000 tons. They were followed by Enterprise (CVN-65), the first nuclear-propelled carrier, but the enormous expense involved caused Congress to call for more non-nuclear carriers, which resulted in Kitty Hawk and Constellation. These were ordered as repeats of the Forrestal-class, but with improved aircraft handling arrangements – in particular, increased flightdeck area and a different elevator layout. In the Forrestal-class the port side elevator was located at the forward end of the angled deck, making it unusable when aircraft were landing, but in the Kitty Hawks it was repositioned to the after end of the overhang, where it no longer interfered with flying operations. In addition, the center of the three elevators on the starboard side was repositioned ahead of the island, enabling two elevators to serve the forward catapults, thus greatly speeding up the launching process. A further improvement to the elevators themselves was that an additional angled section at the forward end of the platform enabled them to accommodate longer aircraft. This flightdeck and elevator arrangement was so successful that it has been used, with only minor modifications, in all subsequent U.S. "supercarriers."

The third ship of the class, America (CV-66), was laid down four years after Constellation and incorporated further improvements, one of them being that she was fitted with a bow anchor in anticipation of an SQZ-23 sonar dome being installed at the foot of the stem, although in the event this was never fitted. It was planned by the Navy that the fourth carrier, due to be laid down in FY64, should be nuclear-powered, but Congress, still shaken by the expense of the first nuclear carrier, Enterprise, flatly refused to fund it and the ship was built as a conventionally powered carrier to a modified Kitty Hawk design, the most obvious visual change being a narrower funnel canted outwards to carry exhaust fumes clear of the flightdeck.

These carriers have been modified and modernized throughout their service

Above: USS Kitty Hawk (CV-66) transits the Suez Canal.

careers, one area in particular being the armament. The first two ships mounted two Mark 10 launchers for Terrier missiles, but it was later realized that these merely duplicated similar weapons aboard the escorts which would always accompany the carriers, so these were not fitted in the second pair, being replaced by three octuple launchers for the BPDMS (Basic Point Defense Missile System). All three surviving ships are now armed with three Mark 29 launchers, each with eight Sea Sparrow SAMs, and three 20mm Mark 15 Phalanx CIWS (close-in weapons systems), and at least one, *Kitty Hawk*, is to receive two General Dynamics RIM-116A RAM (Rolling Airframe Missile) systems. Similarly, the radar, command-and-control, and other electronic systems have been regularly upgraded.

It was planned to modernize all four under the SLEP (service life extension program), which involved 28 months' work and was intended to extend each ship's life by some 10-15 years. This included fitting more powerful catapults, upgrading the aircraft facilities, modernizing all electronics, and extensive refurbishment of the hull, propulsion system, and electrics. In the event, only two received the full SLEP, *Kitty Hawk* (1988-91) and *Constellation* (1990-93), while the third, *John F Kennedy*, received a shorter, less comprehensive, 14-

month "Complex Overhaul" (1994-95). She was then transferred to the reserve in 1994, but continued to deploy and officially returned to operational status in 2000. As of early 2002, there are reports that she may transfer her homeport to Yokosuka, Japan, in 2008 and serve on until 2018, although both proposals seem somewhat optimistic. In 2002 *Kitty Hawk*, the oldest active ship in the Navy, is in the Pacific Fleet, having been homeported at Yokosuka since 1998; she is due to be deactivated in 2008. *Constellation*, serving with the Atlantic Fleet, will deactivate in 2003, transferring to the "mobilization reserve." The fourth carrier, *America*, was not updated at all and was stricken in August 1996.

Together with the four earlier Forrestal-class conventionally powered carriers, the four Kitty Hawk-class ships provided a vital contribution to the Navy's order-of-battle throughout the Cold War. They provided the same air wing as the nuclear carriers, but at considerably less cost and, while it is highly improbable that the Navy will ever build another non-nuclear carrier, these have given many years of unique and invaluable service.

Below: USS Constellation (CVN-64); she transfers to reserve status in 2003.

Enterprise-class

Type: aircraft carrier, nuclear powered (CVN).
Completed: 1961.
Number in class: one.
Displacement: 73,858 tons light; 92,325 tons full load.
Dimensions: length 1,088.9ft (331.6m); beam 257.2ft (78.4m); draught 39.0f
(11.9m).
Powerplant: Four shafts; eight Westinghouse A2W nuclear reactors; four sets
Westinghouse geared steam turbines; 280,000shp; 33.6kt.
Aircraft: typical 2002 air wing, 70 aircraft: 11 x F-14B Tomcat interceptors; 36
x F/A-18C Hornet fighter-bombers; 4 x EA-6B Prowler airborne electronic
warfare; 4 x E-2C Hawkeye airborne early warning; 7 x S-3B Viking ASW; 7 x
SH-60F/HH-60H Seahawk helicopters; 1 x C-2A Greyhound carrier on-board
delivery.
Armament: 3 x Mk 29 launchers for Sea Sparrow SAMs; 2 x RAM Mk 31 SAM
systems; 3 x 20mm Mk 15 Phalanx CIWS.
Complement: 5,828.

Authorized in the FY58 program, *Enterprise* (CVN-65) was laid down in February

1958 and completed in the remarkably short time of 3 years 9 months. She cost nearly twice as much to build as her oil-fuelled contemporaries of the Kitty Hawk-class, but convincing arguments were advanced to justify nuclear propulsion, including reduced life-cycle costs due to infrequent refuelings, and the ability to conduct lengthy transits and continuous operations in high threat areas at a high sustained speed. Also, the elimination of ship's bunkers made possible a 50 percent increase in aviation fuel. The technology of the time meant that no fewer than eight Westinghouse A2W nuclear reactors were required, feeding thirty-two Foster-Wheeler heat-exchangers, which, in their turn, provided the steam to power four Westinghouse geared steam turbines. The carrier's design speed is 33kt, although she actually achieved just over 35kt on trials.

In size and layout *Enterprise* was similar to the Kitty Hawk-class, but internally the entire center section of the ship below hangar deck level was taken up with machinery, while she had four rudders, compared to two in all other "super-carriers." As built, *Enterprise* had a unique box-shaped island, with four huge planar arrays (known as "billboards") for the electronically scanned SPS-32/33 radars, but this was removed and replaced by a more conventional

island in a subsequent refit. Like the other nuclear carriers, *Enterprise* does not need to replenish her own fuel stocks while at sea, but the total of 8,500 tons of aviation fuel means that she must restock about once every twelve days when her air wing is flying at intensive rates.

Enterprise has been regularly refitted and updated, including: January 1979-March 1982, January 1991-July 1995 (which included refueling), and, most recently, August-December 1999. Although militarily very effective, the costs of these nuclear carriers are high, as illustrated by two of these refits: the one in 1991-94 costing $3.1billion, while the less extensive undertaking in 1999 cost $80million (both at "then-year" prices").

Enterprise began her service career in the Atlantic Fleet, but was transferred, together with her nuclear-powered escort group, to the Pacific Fleet during the Vietnam War. She remained in that area for many years, but then returned to the Atlantic, where she now serves, being homeported at Norfolk, Virginia. She normally operates in the Atlantic or Middle Eastern waters but, like all the big carriers, she can redeploy anywhere in the world at only a few days' notice. Known affectionately to her crew as the "Big E," she is expected to remain in service until 2013.

Left: USS Enterprise – known to the fleet as "Big E."

Nimitz-class

Type: aircraft carrier, nuclear-powered (CVN).
Completed: 1984-2002.
Number in class: nine.
Displacement: 77,607 tons light; 98,235 tons full load.
Dimensions: length 1,091.9ft (332.8m); beam 256.9ft (78.3m); draught 39.0ft (11.9m).
Powerplant: four shafts; two General Electric A4W/A1G nuclear pressurized-water reactors; four sets geared steam turbines; 280,000shp; 31kt.
Aircraft: Typical 2002 air wing, 70 aircraft: 11 x F-14B Tomcat interceptors; 36 x F/A-18C Hornet fighter-bombers; 4 x EA-6B Prowler airborne electronic warfare; 4 x E-2C Hawkeye airborne early warning; 7 x S-3B Viking ASW; 7 x SH-60F/HH-60H Seahawk helicopters; 1 x C-2A Greyhound carrier on-board delivery.
Armament: 3 x Mk 29 launchers for Sea Sparrow SAMs; 2 x RAM Mk 31 SAM systems; 3 x 20mm Mk 15 Phalanx CIWS.
Complement: 5,621.
Specifications for Ronald Reagan (CVN -76).

These nine nuclear-powered "super-carriers" are the mightiest warships ever built. Together with *Enterprise* and the remaining conventionally powered Kitty Hawk-class, each one deploys a seventy-strong airwing, which is far ahead in modernity, performance and capability of all but a few national air forces in their entirety. Moreover, these ships can patrol the world's oceans and serve as bases for air campaigns unconstrained by political difficulties or the security problems associated with so many land bases, their nuclear power giving them unlimited range, while their vast size, coupled with at-sea replenishment of expendables such as food, ammunition, and aviation fuel, enable them to remain on station for many months at a time.

Below: CVNs do not need refueling, but do need aviation fuel and ammunition.

Above: Nuclear carriers have more airpower than most national air forces.

The Nimitz-class carriers belong to two sub-groups, the first comprising three ships: *Nimitz* (CVN-68), *Dwight D Eisenhower* (CVN-69), and *Carl Vinson* (CVN-70), which were completed in 1975, 1977 and 1982, respectively. The second group comprises the remaining six: *Abraham Lincoln* (CVN-72), *George Washington* (CVN-73), *John C Stennis* (CVN-74), and *Harry S Truman* (CVN-75), which were completed in 1986, 1989, 1992, 1995 and 1998, respectively, and the mightiest of them all, *Ronald Reagan* (CVN-76), being delivered in December 2002.

The Nimitz-class was intended to replace the Midway-class of conventionally powered carriers, which had joined the fleet in 1945-47 and it was planned to use the same basic hull design as that of the *Enterprise* (CVN-65) while the flightdeck layout, torpedo protection and electronic systems would be virtually identical to those of *John F Kennedy* (CV-67). There had, however, been great advances in nuclear technology since *Enterprise* was built, which meant that just two nuclear reactors could produce virtually the same power as the eight in that first CVN, while the nuclear cores would only need to be replaced about every 13-15 years; ie, three times during the projected 50-year life-span of the ships. The two new reactors also occupied much less volume, thus freeing up a great deal of internal space, enabling the inside arrangement of the new ships to be greatly improved. The propulsion machinery was divided into two separate units, with the magazines between and forward of them, while there was also a 20 percent increase in volume available for aviation fuel, munitions, and general stores.

The hull and decks are constructed of high-tensile steel, and there are numerous longitudinal as well as 23 transverse bulkheads, and 10 firewall bulkheads, creating more than 2,000 internal compartments. In addition, 0.3in (65mm) thick Kevlar armored plate has been installed to cover vital spaces. However, passive protection is not sufficient on its own, and thirty damage-control teams are available at all times, while a 15 degree list can be corrected within twenty minutes. It has been calculated that these carriers are capable of absorbing three times the damage inflicted on the Essex-class carriers by Japanese attackers in the desperate naval battles of 1944-45. The second group (*Roosevelt* – CVN-71 – onwards) incorporates numerous further improvements, including increased passive protection, with more Kevlar armor over the vital compartments, and better hull protection.

When built, it was anticipated that each carrier would have a useful life of fifty years. This looks likely to be achieved, although it has been announced that *Eisenhower* is to be retired in 2017 (after only forty years).

The future revolves around the "CVN-77-class," which, under current plans, will consist of three carriers, entering service in 2008, 20013 and 20018, respectively. Few firm details are available, but it seems likely that they will be very similar to the present Nimitz-class in size and overall layout, particularly of the flightdeck. It is, however, intended to fit new and much more efficient propulsion systems, probably new nuclear reactors coupled with electric drive, together with the latest electronic and electrical systems. There will also be great efforts to lower the crew number from its present 5,600-odd to about 5,100.

The air wing in both the current and future "super-carriers" will probably

remain similar in overall effectiveness to the present systems. There are reports that, as individual aircraft capability increases, there may be a slight reduction in numbers, although current estimates for the Air Wing 2015 still show a strength of some 70-plus aircraft. Fighter strength will comprise 12 Lockheed Martin F-35 Joint Strike Fighters (as opposed to the 14 originally planned), plus 36 Hornets, sub-divided into 24 F/A-18E single-seat and 12 F/A-18F twin-seat fighter/attack versions. There will also be some 14-16 of the planned Common Support Aircraft (CSA), which is intended to provide a single airframe capable of carrying different sensor and avionic suites in order to meet the requirements for airborne early warning, or anti-submarine warfare, or electronic counter-measures, as well as carrier on-board delivery and airborne refueling, thus replacing the current S-3B, ES-3A, E-2C, and C-2A aircraft. The Air Wing 2015 will also include six helicopters, probably a mix of CH-60 and SH-60R sub-types.

Below: Nuclear-powered aircraft carrier, USS George Washington (CVN-73).

Ticonderoga-class

Type: guided-missile cruisers (CG).
Completed: 1983-94.
Number in class: twenty-seven.
Displacement: 7,019 tons light; 9,589 tons full load.
Dimensions: length 565.9ft (172.5m); beam 55.1ft (16.8m); draught 24.6ft (7.5m).
Powerplant: four shafts; COGAG; four General Electric LM-2500 gas-turbines; 100,000shp; 30+kt; 6,000nm at 20kt.
Armament: 2 x Mark 26 twin-arm launchers for Standard SM-2 MR SAM; 8 x launchers for Harpoon SSM; 2 x 5in (127mm) gun (1 x 2); 2 x 20mm Vulcan Phalanx CIWS; 2 x 25mm Bushmaster cannon; 6 x 12.8in (324mm) ASW TT
Aircraft: one or two LAMPS-III ASW helicopters.
Complement: 380.
Specifications for Ticonderoga (CG-47), as built.

In the 1970s the major threat to U.S. and NATO fleets, but particularly to U.S. aircraft carrier battle groups, was perceived as omni-directional saturation missile attacks launched from a combination of Soviet surface warships, submarines, and aircraft. Conventional radar systems would have been overwhelmed by such a combination of threats, so the Aegis system was

developed specifically to counter it. This is based on a planar array system, with each of the four SPY-1 fixed antennae covering one quarter of the airspace around the ship. The constant 360-degree coverage is then achieved by sequential illumination of the 4,096 transmitting elements using electronic control, rather than by mechanical rotation of the entire antenna, as used by conventional systems, the return signals being detected by 4,352 receiving elements. The system, which remains the most sophisticated air defense system in the world, automatically detects and then tracks air contacts out to ranges in excess of 200 nautical miles.

The Ticonderoga-class cruisers use the same basic hull and gas-turbine propulsion system as the Spruance-class destroyers and were originally designated Guided Missile Destroyers (DDG). The Ticonderogas were, however, redesignated as Guided Missile Cruisers (CG) on 1 January 1980. The ships were built in two major groups. The first group of five, *Ticonderoga* (CG-47) to *Thomas S Gates* (CG-51), are armed with two Mark 26 twin-arm launchers, each served by a below-decks, rotating magazine containing 44 Standard SM-2(MR) missiles. These ships also have the earlier, less capable version of the Aegis system. The remaining ships, from *Bunker Hill* (CG-52)

Below: USS Antietam (CG-54); note the huge antennas of the Aegis system.

onwards, are armed with two Mark 41 vertical launcher groups, one forward, the other aft, containing a total of 122 missiles; the types of missile can be varied according to the mission, but the majority will usually be Standard SM-2(MR) SAMs, with the balance being made up by Tomahawk anti-ship/land-attack missiles. This ability to launch Tomahawk missiles is a very significant advance over the first five ships which can only handle Standard SAMs. All ships have two 5.0in (127mm) guns (one forward, one aft), eight Harpoon anti-ship missile canisters on the transom, and a flightdeck and hangar for the LAMPS-III helicopter. All also have two 20mm Vulcan Phalanx CIWS which are mounted on platforms immediately abaft the forward stack, one on each side. Another noticeable difference from the Spruance-class is that the Ticonderogas are fitted with a large bulwark, which is necessary because the greatly increased displacement causes the hull to sit rather deeper in the water; without the bulwark the foredeck would be extremely wet.

A variety of plans have been made for the future of these ships, the eldest of which has been in service for some twenty years. One proposal was for the first five (CG-47 to CG-51) to be retired in 1995-96, but this was canceled. The next proposal was for these same ships to have had their Mark 26 twin-arm launchers replaced by Mark 41 vertical launch groups, but this, too, has been canceled. While all five are scheduled to remain in service it is unclear whether they will be upgraded and, if so, to what standard.

The ships from CG-52 onwards are being upgraded as part of the Cruiser Conversion program, in which a modernized combat system will enable the

Above: Missile launch from USS Shiloh (CG-67) Mark 41 vertical launcher.

ships to counter incoming tactical ballistic missiles. The program also includes replacement of the present 5in/54-caliber guns by the new "Mk 45 Gun System Technical Improvement Program" (also known as the Mk 45 Mod 4), which will include a new gunshield with reduced RCS, improved rate of fire, and a new 62-caliber barrel, together with new, enhanced range rounds. This will enable the ships to meet the Marine Corps' requirements for greater shore bombardment capability. Their Phalanx CIWS mounts are also being replaced by the lightweight RAM (Rolling Airframe Missile), with each mount carrying eleven missiles. In addition, since replenishment of missiles in the Mark 41 VLS has proved impracticable at sea, the crane systems are being deleted, enabling three more missiles in each of the two mounts to be carried.

Build standards are designated "baselines," starting with Baseline 0 (CG-47, CG-48). Baseline 1 (CG-49 to -51) added the RAST helicopter recovery system and improved SAMs, data displays, and EW suites. Baseline 2 (CG-52 to -58) replaced the Mk 26 launchers with the Mk 41 VLS, while Baseline 3 (CG-59 to -64) has the SPY-1B radar and new computers. Baseline 4 (CG-65 to -73) has the SPY-1B(V) radar and even more advanced computers and displays. The latest is Baseline 6, which will replace the computers in Baselines 2-4 ships. Only a few of the ships currently in service still carry their SQR-19 towed arrays, the remainder having been removed and placed in storage.

Spruance-class

Type: destroyer (DD).
Completed: 1975-81.
Number in class: thirty-one (twenty-four in service).
Displacement: 7,410 tons light; 9,250 tons full load.
Dimensions: length 563.3ft (171.7m); beam 55.0ft (16.8m); draft 20.5ft (6.3m).
Powerplant: two shafts; COGAG; four General Electric LM-2500 gas-turbines; 80,000shp; 30kt; 6,000nm at 20kt.
Armament: 8 x Harpoon SSMs; 1 x Mark 41 Vertical Launch System for 61 Tomahawk SSM and VLASROC ASW missiles; 1 x Mark 29 launcher for NATO Sea Sparrow SAM; 2 x 5in (127mm) guns (2 x 1); 2 x 20mm Mark 15 Phalanx CIWS; 4 x 0.5in (12.7mm) MG; 6 x 12.8in (324mm) ASW TT.
Aircraft: one or two helicopters.
Complement: 393.
Specifications for Spruance (DD 963), as built.

By the early 1970s, the Gearing- and Sumner-class destroyers were reaching the end of their useful lives, despite regular updates and modifications. After much discussion, the U.S. Navy settled on the Spruance-class design to replace them. At the time they joined the fleet, the design epitomized the Navy philosophy of the time, which concentrated on three features. The first of these was for large hulls and a block superstructure in order to maximize internal volume. The second was for machinery which combined power and fuel economy with ease-of-maintenance and, when necessary, ease-of-replacement. The third was a weapon system which combined high technology and combat effectiveness with modular design, so that individual elements could be repaired or replaced easily. Taken together, it was hoped that these measures would minimize "platform" costs and maximize "payload" during the ships' anticipated thirty-year life.

Their appearance was, however, greeted with a storm of criticism. The first cause of these adverse comments was that the ships were extremely expensive and double the size of the ships they were replacing. The criticism then intensified when the ships entered service, since to the amateur observer they appeared to have very little armament – only two guns and the ASROC launcher – and few sensors, particularly when compared with contemporary Soviet ships, whose decks were covered with weapons and whose masts were festooned with antennae of every description. The Spruance-class has, however, overcome such ill-informed criticism and has given many years of excellent service. It has gradually become clear that the apparently few launchers on the deck are served by large magazines which are hidden from view below decks, while the antennae serve radars, sensors, and other electronic devices which are far more capable and flexible than those in Russian ships. Finally, the inherent flexibility of the design has been shown by the ease with which it was adapted to become the Ticonderoga-class cruiser for the U.S. Navy and the Kidd-class air defense destroyer for Iran.

The first seven ships were completed with Mark 26 rail launchers forward, but these were replaced from the eighth ship onwards by the Mark 41 Vertical Launcher System (VLS). This VLS is capable of launching Tomahawk land-attack missiles and Vertical-Launch ASROC, and is also capable of a significantly higher rate of fire, giving the ships much greater operational flexibility. As a result the first seven ships were retired in FY97, even though they had many years of service left; of these, one is earmarked as a possible museum ship, one is being retained as a source of spares, and the remainder are being scrapped.

The remaining ships have undergone many modernizations and modifications. Twelve are currently being fitted with RAM (rolling-airframe missile) launchers on the stern. *Arthur W Radford* (DD-968) was fitted with an

Below: Spruance is an outstanding design; this is USS John Young (DD-973).

Advanced Enclosed Mast Sensor System in 1997. This is a very large, flat-sided, experimental mainmast, totally enclosing the antenna arrays. This structure, which is 88ft (26.8m) high and weighs 35.7 tons (36.3 tonnes), is intended to reduce the radar cross-section and to provide easier maintenance for the sensors inside. *Radford* was badly damaged in a collision with a merchant ship in 1999 and was rebuilt at a cost of $US32.7million.

The Spruances have a large hangar which is sited almost amidships and is integrated with the after exhaust uptakes. This accommodates a single Sikorsky SH-60 LAMPS-III ASW helicopter, but Congress tried to force the Navy into building an "air-capable" ship, *Hayler* (DD-997), which would have had facilities for four helicopters. This proved to be such an expensive project, however, that the ship, the last Spruance to be built, was completed almost to the standard design, although it does have some differences; for example, it is the only ship in the class to have the SPS-49 air-search radar.

In the early 1970s the (then) Shah of Iran ordered four modified versions of the Spruance-class and the allowances made in the Spruance design for spaciousness and modular installation made redesign to meet the Shah's requirements an easy matter. The ships were optimized for air defense with

Mark 26 twin-arm SAM launchers in place of the ASROC and Sea Sparrow launchers in the Spruance-class, although, since the Mark 26 could launch the ASROC missile, very little capability was actually lost. The Iranians also required additional air-conditioning and sand filters for operations in the Gulf, but following the revolution and Ayatollah Khomeini's accession to power the order was canceled. The ships were eventually acquired by the U.S. Navy as the Kidd-class and served from 1981 to the late 1990s when they were offered for sale. Various navies examined the possibilities very closely, including those of Australia and Greece, but in the end both turned them down. In late 2000 the Taiwanese declared an interest in the ships, declaring that the increasing threat from mainland China, coupled with the U.S. Navy's known reluctance to release Aegis technology, made these ideal ships for its navy and President Bush approved this proposal in early 2001.

One curious feature of the Spruance-class ships is that, while they are equipped with a Mark 41 VLS and are capable of launching several types of missile, they are not classified as "guided missile" ships. As a result, they are designated DD and not DDG.

Below: Spruances displace 9,250t, more than most World War II cruisers.

Arleigh Burke-class

	Flight I Block I	Flight I Block II	Flight IIA
Type	guided-missile destroyer (DDG)		
Completed	1991-97	1998-99	2000-2008 (est)
Number in class	21	7	29

Displacement
  light
  full load
	6,624 tons
	8,315 tons
		6,914 tons
		9,033 tons
			n.k
			9,238 tons

Dimensions
  length
  beam
  draft
	504.6ft (153.8m)
	66.6 ft (20.3m)
	20.7ft (6.3m)
		504.6ft (153.8m)
		66.6ft (20.3m)
		21.7ft (6.6m)
			509.5ft (155.3m)
			66.6ft (20.3m)
			21.7ft (6.6m)

Propulsion
  shafts
  gas-turbines
  power
  speed
  range
	2
	4 x General Electric LM-2500
	90,000shp
	30+kt
	4,400nm at 20kt		

Armament
  launchers
  missiles
  harpoon
  gun
  CIWS
  TT
	2 x Mark 41 VLS
	90
	8
	1 x 5in (127mm)
	2 x 20mm Phalanx
	6 x 324mm Mk 32
			2 x Mk 41 VLS
			96
			-
			1 x 5in (127mm)
			2 x 20mm Phalanx
			6 x 324mm Mk 32

Aircraft	-	-	2 x SH-60R
Complement	337	372	380

Like the Spruance-class, the Arleigh Burke-class, designed as a replacement for the aging missile destroyers, was the subject of much debate before the design was finalized and authorized by Congress. One of the design criteria was that the Arleigh Burkes would provide about 75 percent of the air defense capability of a Ticonderoga-class cruiser at 66 percent of the price, although whether this has been achieved in practice has never been made public. Nevertheless, they are very comprehensively equipped compared with destroyers in other navies, although it should be noted that, with a full load displacement of some 9,000 tons and a length of over 500ft (152m), they are larger than many ships previously categorized as cruisers.

The design has been progressively upgraded as construction continues, the first production standard being "Flight I" which was sub-divided into Block I (21 ships) and Block II (7 ships). Compared with earlier warship designs, the hull form is unusually broad in relation to its length, which has resulted in excellent seakeeping qualities. Both hull and superstructure are made of steel, the only

Above: USS Ramage (DDG-61) one of 21 Arleigh Burke Block I destroyers.

aluminum being used for the funnels, while the structure also includes some 130 tons of Kevlar, of which approximately 70 tons is used around the command-and-control spaces. This was the first U.S. Navy warship to include comprehensive stealth features, with all outside surfaces angled and corners rounded to reduce the radar signature, while infra-red suppressors are fitted to the exhaust uptakes, and the Prairie/Masker device suppresses propeller noises. All electronics are hardened against electromagnetic pulses (EMP), one of the side effects of a nuclear explosion. This was also the first class of U.S. Navy warship to include a comprehensive collective protection system for defense against nuclear fallout or chemical/biological attack, with access to the ship's interior being through double air-locked hatches (of which there are many fewer than in most other ships of this size), and the entire interior is protected by positive pressurization to exclude contaminants. In addition, as much reliance as possible is placed on recirculated air within the ship, with any incoming air being carefully controlled and filtered.

The sensor and weapons control system centers on the Aegis SPY-1D three-dimensional radar, with four planar arrays mounted on the forward superstructure below the bridge and angled outwards at 45 degrees to give 360-degree coverage. As with most modern warships, the Arleigh Burkes are commanded from the operations room which is below the waterline.

One of the surprising decisions about the Flight I ships was that they would not have full helicopter facilities. Thus, there is a flightdeck aft and the ship is provided with refueling and rearming facilities for a visiting helicopter, and there is also a full LAMPS-III data-link to receive operational ASW information, but there is no hangar, with its associated repair and shelter facilities.

The second production standard was Flight I Block II, which consisted of seven ships, from *Mahan* (DDG-72) to *Porter* (DDG-78). In general, these are identical to Flight I Block I ships, but with a number of enhancements. The ships can handle the extended range version of the Standard SAM-SM2(ER) and are fitted with the Joint Tactical Information Data (JTIDS) and other more advanced electronic systems, including the SLQ-32(V)3 EW suite and the Link 16 tactical data information exchange system. The specifications above show that Flight I Block II has a greater full load displacement, which is due to the allocation of greater volume to fuel bunkers, thus increasing the range. The only visible difference between Blocks I and II is that in the former the topmast follows the same angle as the mast, whereas in the latter the topmost is vertical.

Flight I Block II was originally known as Flight II, and a Flight III was planned, which would have been a major advance but it was dropped, principally on grounds of expense. However, the Japanese Kongou-class gives some

Above: Hopper (DDG-70) is named after the great female computer engineer.

mpression of what a U.S. Navy Arleigh Burke Flight III might have looked like and been capable of.

Having lost Flight III, the Navy developed Flight IIA, which is essentially a 5ft (1.5m) longer version of the Flight I, but with a number of significant changes, the most important of which is that it is fitted with two hangars, thus enabling it to embark two SH-60 Seahawk helicopters. The transom has also been extended to enable a dual RAST to be fitted in the flightdeck, which means that the SQR-19 TACTAS towed-array can no longer be shipped. One consequence of this new hangar is that the after pair of SPY-1D arrays have had to be raised by 7.9ft (2.4m) to enable their beams to clear the hangar roofs.

There are several changes with regard to the missiles. First, the Navy has decided that there is little value in the ability to replenish the missile stock at sea, which means that the cranes, which took up the space of three cells in each of the two launcher groups, are no longer required. Thus, six more vertical launch cells per ship are available for missiles – a valuable addition. Also, the vertical launcher can handle the new Evolved Sea Sparrow Missile (ESSM), which is supplied in "Quad Packs" (ie, four ESSMs in each cell normally allocated to one missile); six cells are allocated to ESSM for a total of twenty-four missiles. Once ESSM is available the 20mm Phalanx CIWS mounts will be removed. As with Flight II ships, the deck fittings for Harpoon launchers have been installed but the missiles will not normally be shipped. From 2003 onwards Tactical Tomahawk and Land-Attack Standard Missiles (LASM) will be carried.

Left: USS Russell (DDG-59) shows off its speed and maneuverability.

Oliver Hazard Perry-class

Type: guided-missile frigate (FFG).
Completed: 1979-1989.
Number in class: fifty-one (thirty-seven in service).
Displacement: 2,769 tons light; 3,658 tons full load.
Dimensions: length, 453.0ft (138.1m); beam 45.0ft (13.7m); draft (hull) 14.8ft (4.5m).
Powerplant: one shaft; two General Electric LM-2500 gas-turbines; 41,000shp; 29kt; 4,200nm at 20kt. Plus 2 retractable electric emergency propulsors; total 720bhp; 6kt.
Armament: 1 x Mk 13 launcher (4 x Harpoon; 36 x Standard SAM); 1 x 3in (76mm) OTOMelara gun; 1 x 20mm Vulcan Phalanx CIWS; 2 x 25mm Bushmaster low-angle cannon; 2 or 4 0.5in (12.7mm) MG; 6 x 12.8in (324mm) ASW TT.
Aircraft: one or two helicopters.
Complement: 214.
Specifications for Oliver Hazard Perry (FFG-7), as built.

In the 1970s some expensive and sophisticated specialized ASW and AAW ships were being built to protect U.S. Navy carrier and surface action groups, and the Oliver Hazard Perry-class was intended as the "low-technology" counterpart. The primary mission was ASW protection of amphibious forces, merchant ship convoys, and underway replenishment groups, but strict limits were placed on cost, displacement, and manpower. They were intended to be built in smaller yards, so simple building techniques were employed, for example, by using flat panels wherever possible and keeping internal passageways straight. Propulsion was also simplified, using two gas-turbines to drive one propeller.

The weapon fit also reflected the design philosophy. There was a single Mk 13 launcher on the foredeck with a forty-missile magazine below; usual weapon load was thirty-six Standard SAM and four Harpoon SSM. The gun was an OTOBreda 76mm Compact located atop the superstructure, with a single Mk 15 20mm Vulcan Phalanx CIWS added later to the hangar roof. ASW capability included two triple torpedo tubes and one or two helicopters but, unlike on previous frigate classes, ASROC missiles were not carried.

Propulsion was by two gas-turbines, the ships attaining 25kt on one engine and 28kt on both, although *Perry* achieved 31kt on trials. One unusual feature was two retractable propulsion pods, each containing a 325hp engine, to provide a "get-you-home" facility and to assist in docking.

The original ships had a vertical transom and a flightdeck designed for a single LAMPS I (SH-2F) helicopter. When it

was decided to operate the LAMPS III (SH-60) helicopter from these ships a slightly larger flightdeck was needed, which was achieved by angling out the transom, thus increasing overall hull length from 435ft (138.1m) to 455ft (135.6m). FFG-36 onwards were built with this longer hull and four of the earlier ships were later rebuilt to the same standard.

A total of fifty-one Perry-class frigates were built for the U.S. Navy, but with the end of the Cold War the number has been steadily reducing and in 2002 thirty-seven remain, split between the active and reserve fleets. The others have been passed on to foreign navies including Bahrein, Egypt, and Turkey, while one has been presented as a gift to the Polish Navy. Although built as ocean escorts and with deliberate limits imposed on their capabilities, these ships have proved a major success and of great value to the U.S. Navy as general-purpose warships. Ships of this class have been deployed in the Gulf since the early 1980s and no fewer than fourteen took part in the Gulf War. Six ships were also built for the Royal Australian Navy (Adelaide-class), four in the USA and two in Australia. Six were built in Spain (Baleares-class), while Taiwan (-RoC) is building eight (Cheung Kung-class), the last of which will be completed in 2003.

Below: FFG-7, nameship of a large class of frigates, only a few of which still serve.

Cyclone-class

Type: Patrol Coastal (PC).
Completed: 1993-2000.
Number in class: fourteen (thirteen in service).
Displacement: 341 tons full load.
Dimensions: Length: 170ft (51.8m); beam 25ft (7.6m); draft 7.8ft (2.4m).
Powerplant: four shafts; four Paxman Valenta diesels; 13,400shp; two Caterpillar generators, each 155kW; 30+kt; 3,000nm at 16kt.
Armament: 1 x Stinger SAM (6 x missiles); 1 x 25mm Bushmaster gun in stabilized mount; 1 x 25mm Bushmaster gun in low-angle mount; 5 in any combination of M2-HB 0.50in (12.7mm) heavy machine guns, M60 medium machine guns, Mk 19 grenade launchers, Mk 52 Mod 0 chaff decoy launching system.
Complement: 28, plus 9 SEAL/USCG law enforcement detachment.

U.S.Naval Special Warfare Command (NSW) operates thirteen Patrol Coastal (PC) ships, built by Bollinger of Lockport, Louisiana; thirteen were delivered between 1993 and 1996, followed by the last one (PC-14), which was built at the insistence of the U.S. Congress, in 2000. The PC class has a primary mission of coastal patrol and interdiction, with a secondary mission of support to Naval Special Warfare. Primary employment missions include forward presence, monitoring and detection operations, escort operations, non-combatant evacuation, and foreign internal defense.

The PC class operates in low intensity environments. Naval Special Warfare operational missions will include long-range SEAL insertion/extraction, tactical

swimmer operations, intelligence collection, operational deception, and coastal/riverine support. The Patrol Coastal ships, used successfully by joint operational commanders during both wartime and peacetime operations, have proved particularly effective in counter-drug operations. Indeed, *Thunderbolt* (PC-12) was lent to the U.S. Coast Guard from March to July 1998 to see whether the type was suitable for full-time transfer; the trial was successful, leading to a proposal that seven boats would by transferred to the USCG in the year 2000, but this has not taken place.

The last to be built, *Tornado* (PC-14), was completed with a hull lengthened by 9.0ft (2.74m) to enable it to accommodate the Combat Craft Retrieval System (CCRS) in the stern, by which it launches and recovers either a 36ft (11m) Rigid Inflatable Boat (RIB) or a SEAL Delivery Vehicle. Following the success of this installation, three in-service vessels – *Tempest* (PC-2), *Zephyr* (PC-8), and *Shamal* (PC-13) – have also been converted. This upgrade significantly increases NSW's ability to support surveillance and interdiction missions. PCs normally operate as a two-boat detachment, which allows enhanced support and facilitates the assignment of one Mobile Support Team, MST, every two ships.

First-of-class, *Cyclone* (PC-1) has been stricken, but thirteen remain in U.S. Navy service, with nine operating from Naval Amphibious Base Little Creek, Virginia, and four from Naval Amphibious Base Coronado, California.

Below: Cyclone (PC-1), nameship of a class of 14; 13 are operated by NAVSOC.

Mk V Pegasus-class

Type: Special Operations Craft (SOC).
Completed: 1995-99.
Number in class: twenty.
Displacement: 57 tons (full load).
Dimensions: length 81.2ft (24.75m); beam 17.5ft (5.33m); draft 5ft (1.52m).
Powerplant: two KaMeWa waterjets; two MTU 12V396 diesels (2,285hp each);
48kt; 600+nm at 45kt.
Armament: 1 x Stinger SAM (6 x missiles); 5 in any combination of M2-HB 0.50in
(12.7mm) heavy machine guns, M60 general-purpose machine guns, Mk 19
grenade launchers.
Complement: 6, plus 16 SOF combat-loaded operators with 4 CRRCs.

The Mk V Special Operations Craft (SOC) is the newest vessel in the Naval Special
Warfare inventory, with ten detachments, each of two craft (twenty boats), being
delivered by March 1999. The Mk V SOC's primary mission is medium-range
insertion and extraction for Special Operations Forces in low- to medium-threat
environments. The secondary mission is limited coastal patrol and interdiction
(CP&I), specifically limited duration patrols, and low- to medium-threat coastal

interdiction. Mk V SOCs normally operate away from base in two-craft detachments, with each detachment accompanied by a Mobile Support Team (MST). Each craft is road-mobile on a special transport trailer, and one craft, mounted on its trailer and with its prime mover, can be air transported in a single USAF C-5A Galaxy, with a total of two aircraft for the complete detachment. Once in location, typical employment pattern for the Mk V SOC is a 12-hour mission followed by a 24-hour turnaround, during which the MST will provide technical assistance and maintenance support, but the detachments are not responsible for providing their own security, messing, or accommodation while forward-deployed.

The hull is designed for minimum radar and infrared signature and has a ramp at the stern for launching and recovering four inflated RIBs. Propulsion is provided by two MTU diesels driving two KaMeWa waterjets for a top speed in excess of 50kt and a range in excess of 600nm at 45kt. Current assignment is twelve at Special Boat Unit-1 (SBU-1) at Coronado, California, and eight to SBU-2 at Little Creek, Virginia.

Below: Mark V Special Operations Craft shows its speed and maneuverability.

Patrol Boat, Riverine (PBR)

Type: river patrol boat.
Completed: 1960s.
Number in class: 500+ (twenty-four in service).
Displacement: 8.8 tons.
Dimensions: length 32ft (9.8m); beam (including guard rails) 11.6ft (3.5m); draf
2ft (0.6m).
Powerplant: two Jacuzzi 14YJ water jet pumps; two GM 6V53N diese
engines (215hp each); 24 kt; 300nm at full speed.
Armament: 2 x M2-HB 0 .50in (12.7mm) machine guns; 1 x Mk19 40mm
grenade launcher.
Complement: 4 crew, 6 passengers.

The River Patrol Boat (PBR), whose image is synonymous with that of the
Vietnam War, was designed for high-speed riverine patrol operations in

contested areas of operations, and the insertion and extraction of SEAL Team elements. More than 500 units were built in the 1960s and the type was introduced into service in Indochina in 1966. The PBR hull is made from fiberglass and can be armed with a wide variety of weapons; vital crew areas are protected with ceramic armor. The PBR can operate in shallow, debris-filled water, and is highly maneuverable, being capable of turning 180 degrees within its own length while operating at full power. Engine noise-silencing techniques were introduced early in its service and have been improved over the years. The combination of relatively quiet operation and its surface search radar system make this unit an excellent all-weather picket as well as a shallow water patrol and interdiction craft. The PBR can be mounted on skids and transported in a C-5 aircraft. Current inventory is twenty-four craft.

Below: Designed for the Vietnam War, some 24 PBRs remain in service.

Light Patrol Boat

Type: Patrol Boat, Light (PBL).
Number in class: sixteen.
Dimensions: length 25ft (7.62m); beam 8.6ft (2.6m); draft 18in (46cm).
Powerplant: twin 155hp outboards; 40kt; 150nm.
Armament: three weapons stations, one forward and two aft: combination of .50 cal, or M-60 machine guns.
Complement: 4 to 5 operators and 6 passengers.

The Light Patrol Boat (PBL) is a lightly armed, unarmored Boston Whaler-type craft with a fiberglass hull and reinforced transom and weapons mount areas. It is powered by dual outboard motors, which give it a very high speed of 40kt, and is highly maneuverable. It is useful in interdicting a lightly armed adversary but would not be suitable for engaging heavily armed or well organized enemies. Its most effective functions are in police actions, harbor control, diving and surveillance operations, riverine warfare, drug interdiction, and other offensive or defensive purposes. Sixteen PBLs are located at Special Boat Unit-22 (SBU-22).

The weapon mountings can include .50 caliber heavy machine guns or 7.62mm machine guns mounted on 180-degree mounts, providing an effective weapon employment in any direction. Due to its unique hull design, the PBL is excellent for the riverine environment, allowing it to operate in virtually any water depth. Its two low-profile engines are capable of providing eight hours of continuous operation at a fast cruise speed of 25-plus knots. It displaces 6,500lb fully loaded and is transportable via its own trailer, helicopter sling, or C-130 aircraft.

Right: Two PBLs from Special Boat Unit SBU-26 during Operation Unitas 96.

Rigid Inflatable Boats (RIB)

Rigid Inflatable boats (RIB)
Completed: 1992 onwards.
Number in class: approximately ninety.
Weight: 14,700lb (6,668kg).
Dimensions: length 30ft (9.1m); beam 11ft (3.4m); draft 3ft (0.9m).
Powerplant: two water jets; one Volvo Penta Two Iveco diesel; 35+ knots; 200nm.
Armament: M-60 or M2-HB machine guns, or Mk 19 grenade launchers.
Complement: 3 crew and 8 passengers.
Specifications are for NSW 30ft RIB; see text for other types.

Rigid Inflatable Boats (RIB) have a rigid hull, usually made of fiberglass, and inflatable sponsons, which combine to give a craft which is very light but particularly

Right: RIBs are very fast and highly maneuverable – ideal for Special Operations Forces.

strong. The inflatable sponsons give a high degree of buoyancy, while the deep-vee hull and high-power engines ensure that the craft is capable of both very high speed and excellent maneuverability. Various types are in service, including the elderly

24ft (7.32m) RIB, but the two in widest use are the 30ft (9.14m) and 36ft (11m) models.

The Naval Special Warfare (NSW) 30ft RIB (30RB-series), of which eighteen are in service, is intended for two main missions: the insertion/extraction of SEAL tactical elements from enemy-occupied beaches; and coastal surveillance. The hull is constructed of glass reinforced plastic with an inflatable tubular sponson, made of hypalon neoprene/nylon-reinforced fabric. The 30ft RIB has demonstrated the ability to operate in light-loaded condition in sea state six and winds of 45 knots although, for other than heavy-weather coxswain training, operations are limited to sea state five and winds of 34 knots or less.

The latest NSW RIB (11MRB-series) is deployed either aboard U.S. Navy amphibious ships, or in land-based detachments. It has a 36ft Kevlar-reinforced vinylester deep-vee hull with inflatable nylon-reinforced sponsons and is powered by two 470hp Puckett-Caterpillar turbocharged diesels driving two KaMeWa FF280 water jets. At full load (3 crew plus either 8 passengers or 1.6

Combat Rubber Raiding Craft (CRRC)

Combat Rubber Raiding Craft (CRRC)
Number in class: several hundred.
Weight: 265lb (120kg), without motor or fuel.
Dimensions: length 15.4ft (4.7m); beam 6.3ft (1.9m); draft 2.0ft (0.6m)
Powerplant: one outboard engine, 35-55hp; 18 knots; range depends on fuel carried.
Complement: 8 max.

The traditional craft for all special forces, the Combat Rubber Raiding Craft (CRRC) has inflatable reinforced rubber sponsons and a rubber/canvas floor, and is powered by a single outboard engine mounted on a wooden or light metal transom. It can be delivered to the operational area by ship, by parachute from a fixed-wing aircraft, free-dropped from a helicopter, deck-launched or locked-out from a submarine, or by road using a light truck. It can be used for a wide variety of missions including clandestine surface insertion and extraction of lightly-armed SOF forces, and is capable of passing through surf. It has a low visual electronic signature, and is capable of being cached by its crew once ashore.

Right: The inflatable rubber raiding craft is ideal for covert movement through swamps and along rivers.

U.S. tons/1,500kg of cargo) its maximum speed is 45 knots, and it cruises at 33kt with a range of over 200nm. Thirty-six were delivered to Special Boat Units (SBUs) in San Diego, California, and Norfolk, Virginia, in 1998-99, followed by a further 40 in 2000.

The RIBs are organized into detachments, each of two boats, together with a deployment package, which includes one spare engine between the two boats.. Land-based detachments also include trailers and Ford F800 4x4 truck prime movers. All such detachments, including their transport, are movable by standard C-130 aircraft. In early 2000, NSW validated the Maritime Craft Air Delivery System (MCADS), which allows the RIB to be air-dropped. In this system, the RIB is mounted on a 2,700lb (1,225kg) platform for road and air transportation; they are extracted from the aircraft together, but then separate and descend under separate parachutes. Armament depends upon the mission but can include any small weapon in the Special Operations Forces armory, such as M2-HB machine guns, grenade launchers, and mortars.

Avenger-class

Avenger-class
Type: minesweeper/minehunter.
Completed: 1987-94.
Number in class: fourteen.
Displacement: 1,195 tons light; 1,312 tons full load.
Dimensions: length 224ft (68.3m); beam 39ft (11.9m); draft 12.2ft (3.7 m).
Powerplant: two shafts; four Waukesha L-1616 diesels, 2,400bhp; two Hansome electric motors, 400shp (for hovering); 1 x Omnithruster hydrojet, 350shp (for maneuvering); 13.5kt.
Armament: 2 x 0.5in (12.7mm) M2-HB machine guns.
Complement: 81.

These ships were the outcome of a lengthy program which suffered from more than its fair share of problems. The initial requirement, approved in 1976, was for a class of nineteen ocean-going Mine Countermeasure Vessels (MCMV) to deal with the threat posed by new Soviet deep-water mines, but the program was canceled on the grounds of cost. However, another program was then started which led to the Avenger-class, with the contract for the prototype (MCM-1) being awarded in June 1982, followed by contracts for the remainder of the class being placed between 1983 and 1990.

The Avenger-class MCMVs may not be the largest wooden warships ever built, but they are certainly among the most sophisticated. For strategic reasons they were constructed using only timbers available in North America, so that the keel is a single piece of laminated Douglas fir, upon which are laid transverse laminated white-oak frames, followed by longitudinal girders of laminated Douglas fir. The hull structure is then covered with three inner layers of diagonally-laid 5in (127mm) thick Alaskan cedar planking, followed by an outer layer, also 5in (127mm) thick, of Douglas fir planking. The decks are constructed from tongued-and-grooved, lam-inated Douglas fir and sheathed with Douglas fir plywood, while the superstructure is a mix of laminated and solid woods, with plywood sheathing. Finally, the entire exterior surface is covered with glass-reinforced plastic for environmental protection. The first two ships were powered by Waukesha diesels, but

these suffered from problems, and although these have been solved the remaining ships are powered by low magnetic Isotta-Fraschini engines.

A further problem arose when it was discovered that the entire class needed to be lengthened by 5.9ft (1.8m) to overcome potential stability problems. The first ship was already under construction and the hull had to be lengthened before work could continue, but the others were built from scratch to the new length.

Avenger (MCM-1) and *Defender* (MCM-2) were transferred to the Naval Reserve Force in 1995, followed by *Champion* (MCM-4), *Pioneer* (MCM-9), and *Warrior* (MCM-10) in 1996, and *Sentry* (MCM-3) later. The remaining eight are scheduled to remain with the active fleet: *Guardian* (MCM-5) and *Patriot* (MCM-7) are permanently home-ported in Japan, with a further two in Bahrain, while the remainder are based at Ingleside, Texas.

Below: The Avenger-class are the most sophisticated wooden ships ever built.

Osprey-class

Type: minehunter.
Completed: 1993-99.
Number in class: twelve.
Displacement: 803 tons light; 918 tons full load.
Dimensions: length 188.0ft (57.3m); beam 36.0ft (11.0m); draft 9.5ft (2.9m).
Powerplant: two Voith-Schneider vertical cycloidal propellers; two Isotta-Fraschini ID36SS6V-AM diesels, 1,160bhp; two hydraulic motors (silent running); one 180shp bow thruster; 12kt; 1,500nm at 10kt.
Armament: 2 x 0.5in (12.7mm) M2-HB machine guns.
Complement: 51.

The original U.S. Navy minehunter project was based on a surface-effect ship (SES) but this was canceled in 1986 when the design failed shock testing. Following an international competition, a design contract was placed with Italian company, Intermarine, for a new design based on, but larger than, that company's successful Lerici/Gaeta-class minehunters. This was followed by a construction contract in May 1987 for the lead ship of the new class, whereupon Intermarine SpA established Intermarine USA and purchased the Sayler Marine Corporation in Savannah, Georgia, where eight ships were built. In October 1989, at Congressional insistence, Avondale Marine, Gulfport, Mississippi, was named as the second construction source and they built the remaining four. The program has suffered repeated delays, with the last ship not being completed until 1999. This was due, at least in part, to the engine modifications..

The Osprey-class is fitted with U.S. minehunting equipment, but a significant difference to all other versions of the Lerici/Gaeta design is that it is

Above: Pelican (MHC-53), one of four Osprey-class built by Avondale.

fitted with two Voith-Schneider cycloidal propellers. These do away with the need for a combination of conventional propeller for normal movement and a secondary propulsion system (such as water jets) for use when minehunting. An unusual feature of this particular installation, however, it also has a bow thruster, since the Voith-Schneider system is designed to thrust in any direction and it is not usually considered necessary to fit an additional bow thruster.

The original plan was for all ships to spend their first year of service with the regular fleet, following which all but one would transfer to the Naval

Reserve Force (NRF). This has since been amended and only three are now with the NRF while the remainder are based at Ingleside, Texas, except for two which are home-ported in Bahrein. At various times there were plans to build seventeen of the original design and another to produce a lengthened version, but both were canceled.

The Osprey-class ships were designed as minehunters, but a new device, the Modular Influence · Minesweeping System (MIMS) is now under development to enable them to sweep mines as well as to hunt them. MIMS is a towed influence sweep and includes its own integral sweep-current generator.

Left: Cormorant (MHC-57). These small ships have proved of great value in the never-ending war against mines, which can be laid easily and at very small cost.

Wasp-class

Type: helicopter/dock landing ship (LHD).
Completed: 1989-2005.
Number in class: eight.
Displacement: 28,233 tons light; 40,532 tons full load
Dimensions: length 844.2ft (257.3m); beam 140.1ft (42.7m); draft 26.6ft (8.1m).
Powerplant: two shafts; Westinghouse geared steam turbines; 77,000shp 24kt; 9,500nm at 20kt.
Aircraft: assault mode – 30-32 CH-46 (fewer, if CH-53) helicopters, 6-8 AV-8B Harrier II; carrier mode 20 AV-8B Harrier II; 4-6 SH-60F ASW helicopters.
Armament: 2 x Mk 29 launchers for Sea Sparrow SAM; 2 x RAM system; 2 x 20mm Mk 15 Phalanx CIWS; 4 x 0.5in (12.7mm) M2-HB machine guns.
Complement: ship 1,147; troops 1,893.

The Wasp-class LHDs are the largest amphibious warfare ships in the world, but a basic consideration in their design is that, in addition to serving in the amphibious role, carrying troops and helicopters, they are also required to be capable of Sea Control duties (ie, an aircraft-carrier) with an air wing consisting of twenty Harrier IIs and six ASW helicopters. The basic design is a slightly enlarged version of the Tarawa-class LHA, retaining the advantages of the earlier design but with a number of enhancements, particularly in survivability and aircraft handling. Thus, whereas in the Tarawa-class the command and communications facilities are in the island, in the Wasp-class most have been moved down into the hull where they are much better protected. This has also enabled the island to be reduced in height and footprint. In addition, the flightdeck itself is constructed from HY100 steel, the same as that used for the pressure hulls of nuclear submarines, thus giving much greater protection to all elements below.

A large bulb at the foot of the stem enhances sea-keeping; this had also been planned for the Tarawa-class, but was canceled due to lack of funding. Somewhat surprisingly, these ships are powered by steam turbines after gas-

turbines had been rejected on cost grounds. At one stage consideration was given to installing a skijump to enhance the payload capability of the Harrier II, but this was rejected since it would have reduced the number of helicopter "spots."

The flight deck measures 819 x 106ft (250 x 32m) and has nine helicopter landing spots. Major efforts were made to maximize the area available for aircraft use and, apart from reducing the footprint occupied by the island, the weapons which occupied "cut-outs" in the four corners of the Tarawa flightdeck have been moved, enabling these areas to be restored to flying operations. The flightdeck is served by two deck-edge aircraft elevators, both of which are completely clear of the flightdeck; both also fold for Panama Canal transits. In the Tarawa-class the rising stern door is inset into the after end of the flightdeck, which results in an effect on flying operations out of proportion to its actual size; this is avoided by the bottom-hinged stern door in the Wasp-class.

The normal air group is either thirty CH-46E Sea Knight helicopters, plus up to eight Harrier II, or twenty Harrier II plus up to six SH-60B Seahawks in the Sea Control role. However, almost any type of military helicopter can also be supported, including AH-1W Super Cobra, CH-53E Super Stallion, CH-53D Sea Stallion, UH-1N Twin Huey, or AH-1T Sea Cobra. Space allocated to vehicles is 20,000 cu ft (566 cu m) and a typical load might comprise five M1 tanks, twenty five light armored vehicles, eight M198 guns, sixty-eight trucks and ten logistics vehicles. Cargo capacity is 101,000 cu ft (2,862 cu m). In addition, there are hospital facilities, comprising six fully equipped operating theaters, four dental surgeries, and wards with 600 beds.

The seventh ship, Iwo Jima (LHD-7) was delivered in 2001 and it is planned that LHD-8 (as yet un-named) will be laid down in 2005 and commissioned in about 2008-09. With Congress's refusal to authorize a SLEP for the Tarawa-class, however, it may well be that more of the far better Wasp-class are ordered, instead.

Below: USS Boxer (LHD-4) with large numbers of helicopters, plus AV-8Bs aft.

Tarawa-class

Type: amphibious assault ships (LHA).
Completed: 1976-80.
Number in class: five.
Displacement: 33,536 tons light; 39,967 tons full load.
Dimensions: length 834.0ft (254.2m); beam 131.9ft (40.2m); draft 25.9ft (7.9m).
Powerplant: two shafts; Westinghouse geared steam turbines; 77,000shp; 24kt; 10,000nm at 20kt.
Aircraft: typical air-group – 16 CH-46, 6 CH-53, 4 UH-1N.
Armament: 2 x RAM Mk 31 SAM systems; 2 x 20mm Mk 15 Phalanx CIWS; 8 x 0.5in (12.7mm) M2-HB machine guns.
Complement: ship – 1,058; troops – 1,903.

The Tarawa-class was the outcome of the change in U.S. Navy thinking on amphibious warfare which took place as a result of the Korean War, the Anglo-French Suez landing in 1956, and the lessons of the French experience in the first Indochina War. The amphibious planners of the time concluded that a speed of advance of 20kt was essential for an amphibious task group, leading directly into a rapid delivery of a mass of troops and equipment over the beach. The outcome was a huge ship, much larger than anything that had gone before, basically designed to operate helicopters, but retaining many of the more traditional amphibious ship attributes, with the major exception of any ability to land troops and equipment directly onto the beach. The result was a very large flightdeck combined with a docking well which could handle landing craft up to LCU size, and a complex, automated cargo-handling system of conveyors and elevators. In addition, some of the available space was devoted to extensive command-and-control facilities. Finally, the problem of keeping the troops occupied and fit during lengthy transits or stand-offs was addressed by the provision of training and acclimatization facilities.

The original intention was to build nine of these ships, but only five were actually completed. At one time, there were moves to convert one into a light

Above: USS Tarawa (LHA-1) with twelve AV-8B Harriers on deck.

carrier, but these came to nothing. By the mid-1980s, amphibious warfare policy was becoming a little clearer, and the Tarawa program was halted in favor of the slightly bigger, more-up-to-date Wasp-class.

The large size of these ships results from the need to accommodate both a helicopter hangar and a docking well for the landing craft. The hangar is 268ft (81.6m) long and 78ft (23.7m) wide, and is 20ft (6.8m) high to enable it to accommodate the largest helicopters. The docking well is directly below the

hangar and can accommodate four LCUs, each of which can carry three M1 main battle tanks or 150 tons of cargo. The island accommodates three command organizations together with the appropriate staffs and command, control and communications (C^3) facilities: the ship's own command organization, the Commander Amphibious Task Group, and the Commander Landing Force.

The ships can carry up to 1,703 troops, while the docking well and vehicle decks can be used to accommodate either four LCU Type 1610, or two LCU and two LCM 8, or 17 LCM 6, or 45 LVT tractors, or one LCAC. In addition, four LCPL are carried on davits. The flightdeck measures 834 x 131ft (254 x 42m) overall, but the areas occupied by the island, and the four weapons "cut-outs," are not available.

All five ships are now showing their age – Tarawa (LHA-1) is twenty-six years old – and Congress has refused to authorize a SLEP (Service Life Extension Program). As a result, it seems probable that they will be retired between 2010 and 2013.

Left: USS Saipan (LHA-2) at the U.S. overseas base in Rota, Spain.

San Antonio-class

Type: dock landing ship (LPD).
Completed: 2003-2008.
Number in class: twelve.
Displacement: 25,296 tons full load.
Dimensions: length 684.0ft (208.5m); beam 105.9ft (32.0m); draft 23.0ft (7.0m).
Powerplant: two shafts; four Colt-Pielstick medium-speed diesels, 42,000bhp; 21kt.
Aircraft: typical air group – 2 x CH-53E; or 4 x AH/UH-1; or 4 x CH-46; or 2 x MV-22 Osprey.
Armament: 2 x RAM Mk 31 SAM systems; 3 x 25mm Bushmaster; 4 x 0.5in (12.7mm) M2-HB machine guns.
Complement: ship – 422; troops – 705.

The aim of the San Antonio-class is to replace no fewer than four classes of amphibious vessel: Austin-class dock landing ships (LPD); Newport-class tank landing ships (LST); Anchorage-class landing ships, dock (LSDs); and Charleston-class amphibious cargo ships (LKA). In practice of course, it is not that clear-cut. The Charlestons have already gone into reserve or "reduced operational status," while the Newport-class has been reduced to two full-time in-service ships, with a four more in reserve and the majority already sold or leased to foreign navies. The cargo-carrying duties of the LKAs, plus some of the troop- and equipment-carrying duties of the Anchorage-class LSDs, will naturally fall to the Whidbey Island LSDs and their cargo-carrying version, the Harpers Ferry-class (LSD-CV). But the San Antonio-class, with twelve ships in service by 2008, is important for the U.S. Navy, since its arrival will complete the process – begun many years ago and pursued somewhat haphazardly since – of sharply reducing the number of amphibious ships, standardizing the ship types, and restoring the amphibious capability of moving troops and equipment into hostile territory.

Award of the contract for the lead ship was issued in FY 98 and *San Antonio* (LPD-17) is expected to enter service in 2004. Current estimates of costs are approximately $1.15 billion for the lead ship, with the remaining eleven having an average cost of $750 million each.

The hull and superstructure are made of steel, and all exposed surfaces are sloped and shaped to reduce the radar cross section (RCS), while as many items as possible have been moved inside the superstructure or concealed. Sharp corners have been smoothed, radar "pockets" eliminated, masts raked, and infra-red hotspots cooled. The ship has also been designed with "producibility" in mind, in order to simplify construction and reduce costs.

These LPDs will not have all the attributes of the classes they are replacing. There is, for instance, no over-the-side lift capability, nor can the new class offload over a beach. One of the features of the requirement is that it must be capable of passing through the Panama Canal.

There are three vehicle decks, with an area of 25,000 sq ft (2,323m^2), two cargo/ammunition magazines, 25,000 cu ft (708m^3), a crane for support of boat operations, and a well-deck and stern gate arrangements similar to the Wasp-class, with ship-shore lift being provided by two LCACs and the helicopters. The flightdeck provides landing facilities for two CH-53E, or four AH/UH-1s, or four CH-46, or two MV-22, while the hangar can accommodate one CH-53E Sea Stallion, or two CH-46 Sea Knight, or one MV-22 Osprey, or three UH/AH-1s. The San Antonio-class also has medical facilities, including four operating theaters (two medical, two dental), a 24-bed ward and 100 casualty overflow beds.

Below: LPD-17-class brings new capabilities to the USN's amphibious fleet.

Submarines

The U.S. Navy's nuclear-propelled attack submarines (SSNs) are among the most sophisticated weapons platforms ever produced, able to patrol to greater depths, at greater speeds, and yet far more stealthily than any other submarine in the world. In the early days of SSNs there was a succession of new classes, but from the 1970s to the mid-1990s the Navy's development and production concentrated on only one, the Los Angeles-class. This showed, as has proved to be the case in many other fields, that producing one sound design and then developing it incrementally over many years is much more effective, both militarily and financially, than a succession of new designs, each of which requires great efforts to get into service, and whose teething problems have scarcely been sorted out before attention switches to the next type.

The SSN is the ultimate stealth machine and all but a few outsiders have any inkling at all of where an SSN is going as it leaves its home port, what adventures its crew experiences while at sea, and where it has been when it returns. Thus, rumors circulated during the Cold War of U.S. SSNs operating well inside waters the Soviet Navy would have liked to dominate, such as the Barents Sea and the Sea of Okhotsk, but these were rarely confirmed and even today only snippets of information of what went on has been allowed to leak into the public domain. What is certain is that, short of actually firing torpedoes,

the crews of these SSNs were on active service, repeatedly taking their boats into hostile waters. Possible missions there included detecting and tracking Soviet SSBNs to establish their operational deployment patterns and areas, and seeking to prevent Soviet SSNs from getting anywhere near friendly SSBNs. U.S. SSNs also carried out many clandestine intelligence-gathering missions. Today, the threat and the international situation have both changed, but the SSN remains one of the most important elements of the U.S. arsenal. Indeed, with its Tomahawk missiles it is now able to influence the battle on land as much as it does at sea.

After so many years of development, the Los Angeles-class has now reached its limits and the major effort is now concentrating on the three boats of the Seawolf-class, of which two are in service while the third is due to join the fleet in 2004, and on the future mainstay of the submarine force, the Virginia-class. The first of these extremely sophisticated platforms will be delivered in 2004 and will be followed by up to nineteen more over the next two decades, thus maintaining the dominance achieved by the Navy's SSNs well into the middle of the 21st century.

Below: USS Hartford (SSN-768), one of the Improved Los Angeles-class.

Los Angeles-class

Type: attack submarine, nuclear-powered (SSN).
Total built: sixty-two (see notes).
Completed: 1995-96.
Displacement: surfaced 6,330 tons; submerged 7,177 tons.
Dimensions: length 360ft (109.7m); beam 33ft (10.1m); draft 32.0ft (9.8m).
Powerplant: one shaft; one x S6G pressurized-water nuclear reactor; ca 30,000shp; ca 33kt (submerged); maximum operating depth 1,480ft (450m).
Armament: 4 x 21in (533mm) torpedo tubes; 12 x vertical launch tubes for Tomahawk missiles; 22 torpedoes; mine capable.
Complement: 141.
Specifications are for Improved Los Angeles SSN 771-773.

This was one of the most expensive of all the defense program undertaken during the Cold War, and, with sixty-two units completed, is the largest class of SSNs ever built; indeed, since 1945 only the Soviet diesel-electric Whiskeys and Foxtrots were built in larger numbers. Hull numbers ran continuously from SSN-688 completed in November 1976, to SSN-733, completed in September 1996, a twenty-year production run unprecedented in submarine history; there was, however, a gap in the numerical sequence since numbers #726 to #749 were allocated to Ohio-class SSBNs. The overall cost of the program would be almost impossible to calculate, but the building costs of a single boat (in "then-year" U.S. dollars) were: 1976 – $221million; 1979 – $326million; 1981 – $496million; and 1990 – $900million. (It should, however, be noted that the new Virginia-class will cost an estimated $2billion each and SSN-23 over $3billion.)

The Los Angeles-class boats were much larger than any previous U.S. Navy SSN, primarily in order to accommodate the larger and much more powerful S6G nuclear reactor, which was needed to raise the maximum speed. Officially, the maximum underwater speed was stated to be "20+ knots" but it is widely accepted that the boats were actually capable of some 32kt, making them the first class to exceed the speed of the Skipjacks, built in the late 1950s. It was

Below: Los Angeles-class on the surface, but the depths are its natural habitat.

Above: Rectangular object is scanner for BPS-15 X-band surface search radar.

originally intended to construct them of HY-100 steel but this proved too difficult with the technology that then existed and, in the event, HY-80, was used, except that the pressure hulls of *Albany* (SSN-753) and *Topeka* (SSN-754) were partially fabricated from HY-100 to test the construction processes for the Seawolf-class. The entire bow area of these new boats was taken up by the dome for the BQQ-5 sonar system, while a towed array was carried in a sheath on the outside of hull, a neater and more hydrodynamically efficient arrangement than the large pods on Soviet SSNs. The torpedo tubes were located amidships and used to launch SubRoc ASW weapons, as well as the Mk48 and Mk48ADCAP conventional torpedoes, an armament that was later increased to include Sub-Harpoon and Tomahawk. Despite the increase in size, however, the boats are considered quite cramped, with a number of men having to use sleeping bags. All boats have a Fairbanks-Morse 38D8Q diesel-generator and batteries for emergency propulsion.

Naturally, in a program involving so many boats produced over such a long period, there have been changes, but the class can be divided into three broad groups, plus one boat converted for special purposes. The first group consisted of thirty-one boats (SSN-688 to SSN-718) which, apart from changes of detail, were identical. When the Tomahawk SLCM was introduced, the weapons were stored in the torpedo room and launched from the torpedo tubes. The next eight boats (SSN-719 to SSN-725 and SSN-750) incorporated a major change in the weapons arrangements. When Tomahawks were carried internally and launched from the torpedo tubes this could be done only at the expense of torpedoes, so it was decided that from SSN-719 onwards twelve Tomahawks would be carried in vertical launch tubes positioned between the sonar dome and the pressure hull in space that had previously been occupied by ballast tanks. These boats also had a longer-life core for their nuclear reactors.

More changes were made in the third group – SSN-751 to SSN-773 (23 hulls) – which is referred to as the "Improved Los Angeles" or "688I"class (I =

Improved). The most important of these changes was that they were made
"Arctic capable" by installing a strengthened sail and by relocating the diving
planes from the sail to the bows. In addition, quietening was greatly improved,
the sonar suite was enhanced, and two anhedral stern fins were added, as in
the Seawolf-class. Some of the later units in this group also have shrouded
pump-jet propulsors. All these have the twelve vertical tubes for Tomahawk,
but from SSN-756 onwards they also have a mine-laying capability. The fourth
group comprises just one boat, *Memphis* (SSN-691), which was completed as
a standard SSN in 1977, but in 1981 was re-roled and has since carried out a
large number of trials. It retains its combat capability and is therefore still
designated SSN, although its actual employment would be better indicated by
an auxiliary (AGSSN) designation.

During their Cold War service Los Angeles-class boats carried out missions
in all oceans of the world, the great majority of them of a clandestine nature.
Their activities usually came to light only through mishaps, such as collisions
with Soviet submarines, two known occurrences affecting *Augusta* (SSN-710)
in the Atlantic (October 1986) and *Baton Rouge* (SSN-689) in the Barents Sea
(February 1992). Two came to prominence when they launched Tomahawk
Land-Attack Missiles (TLAM) against Iraq in the Gulf War, *Louisville* (SSN-724)
launching eight and *Pittsburgh* (SSN-720) four. Closer to home, *San Juan* (SSN-
751) collided with *Kentucky* (SSBN-737) off Long Island in March 1998.

During the production run of the Los Angeles-class many plans for

alternatives were considered, one example being in
the early 1980s when Congress forced the Navy to
examine designs for a small, cheaper SSN, but none
of these ever came to anything. Later, when it
became clear just how expensive the successor
Seawolf- and Virginia-classes would be, it was
proposed that production of the 688I should continue
instead, but this, too, came to nothing because there
was no potential for system growth left in what had
become a 25-year-old design.

All Los Angeles-class boats were built for a thirty-
year life, although experience suggests that, with
proper refits, recores of the reactor, and
modernization, they could actually be expected to last
for up to fifty years. However, a mixture of factors,
including the end of the Cold War, the resulting
requirement to reduce operating costs and manning
requirements, and a desire to avoid the costs of
recoring during refits, have resulted in a reduction in
the fleet. The U.S. Navy started to retire ships of the
original Los-Angeles class in the mid-1990s, the past
retirements and future forecast up to 2008 being:
1995 – 2; 1996 – 1; 1997 – 3; 1998 – 3; 1999 – 2; 2000
– 1; 2001 – 3; 2005 – 1; 2006 – 1; 2007 – 1; 2008 – 1.
Thus, by 2008 nineteen will have been retired, all of
them of the original SSN-688 to SSN-750 group,
leaving thirty-four in commission (eleven SSN-688;
twenty-three SSN- 688I). A number of those which
the Navy intends to keep have been modified to
carry one Dry Deck Shelter (DDS) plus a
detachment of SEALs: SSN-688, - 690, -700, -701
and -715.

*Left: 688I-class has forward hydro-planes moved
from fin to bow.*

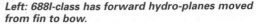

Seawolf-class

Type: attack submarine, nuclear-powered (SSN).
Total built: three.
Completed: 1997-2004.
Displacement: surfaced 7,467 tons; submerged 9,137 tons.
Dimensions: length 353.0ft (107.6m); beam 42.0ft (12.8m); draft 36.0f
(11.0m).
Powerplant: one pump-jet propulsor; one S6W pressurized-water nuclea
reactor, 200Mw; 45,500shp.
Performance: submerged 35+kt; maximum operating depth 1,970ft (600m).
Armament: 8 x 26.5in (673mm) TT (amidships); ca. 50 Mk 48ADCAP torpedoes
or Tomahawk SLCM, or up to 100 mines.
Complement: 133.
Specifications for SSN-21, as built.

The Seawolf-class, the most advanced submarines currently at sea, had a
troubled inception. The project for a Los Angeles-class successor started in the
1980s, its primary mission being to counter what was then the major threat to
the United States by penetrating the Soviet SSBN "bastions" and then
destroying Soviet ballistic missile submarines before they could launch their
missiles. However, there was constant discussion about the requirement and
the enormous costs involved, and then, when these had been resolved, there
was a serious dispute over which yard – Newport News or Electric Boat –
should build it. Once construction of the first-of-class had begun, there were
delays due to welding difficulties and these were followed by problems with
the covers for the flank sonar arrays. At a less important level, traditionalists
were upset by the numbers allocated – SSN-21, -22, -23 – which are totally out
of sequence in the U.S. Navy's excellent and well-established hull-numbering
system, and appears to have arisen out of the project title "SSN for the 21st
Century" which was abbreviated to "SSN-21." The name of the third boat, –
Jimmy Carter (SSN-23) – was also considered inappropriate by many, even

Below: Main control room of USS Seawolf (SSN-21).

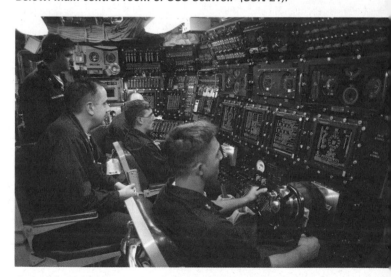

Above: USS Seawolf (SSN-21); note the "fillet" at forward edge of the sail.

hough the ex-president is a former nuclear-qualified officer in the submarine service.

The Seawolf-class hull is of generally the same shape as that of the Los Angeles-class. The designers have gone to great lengths to ensure silent operation, one measure being that the boat is entirely covered in anechoic tiles. The sail is specially strengthened for under-ice operations and incorporates a arge fillet at the forward end, which is designed to improve the waterflow over he structure and reduce noise. A shrouded propulsor – a device pioneered by he British Royal Navy in the 1980s – replaces the customary propeller, and here are six fins, the customary cruciform, plus one at 135 degrees and one at 225 degrees.

The first two boats of the Seawolf-class are 7.0ft (2.1m) shorter than the _os Angeles-class, but with a greater diameter – 42.0ft (12.8m) compared to 33.1ft (10.1m) – resulting in a considerable increase in internal volume. Nevertheless, even this proved insufficient and the third boat, *Jimmy Carter* SSN-23), will incorporate a 27ft (8.23m) plug abaft the sail to enable her to carry a fifty-strong Special Operations Forces detachment and their equipment. There will also be facilities for operating and controlling a variety of remotely-operated vehicles (ROVs). This boat will not now be delivered until June 2004, some 2 years 3 months behind the original schedule and will result in a cost, or this one boat, of $US3.2billion.

The Seawolf-class is armed with eight 26.6in (660mm) torpedo tubes, a new and much larger caliber for the U.S. Navy, which will be mounted in a double-decked torpedo room, which is intended to enable it to engage multiple argets simultaneously. The boats will carry a total of approximately fifty veapons, the actual mix of Tomahawk cruise missiles, Harpoon anti-ship missiles and Mk48ADCAP torpedoes depending upon the operational situation, lthough the normal load-out of Tomahawks is twelve. Mines can also be arried on a basis of two mines replacing each torpedo, up to a maximum of 00. Note that there are no externally mounted vertical launch tubes for

Tomahawk missiles.

It was originally planned to build twelve Seawolf-class boats, a program estimated in 1991 to cost $33.6 billion in current dollars, and a total figure of twenty-nine was under consideration at one time. This meant that some 25 percent of the Navy's entire shipbuilding budget would have been devoted to this one class, whose *raison d'etre* – attacking Soviet SSBNs – disappeared with the end of the Cold War. In the event, only three are actually being built: *Seawolf* (SSN- 21), *Connecticut* (SSN-22), and *Jimmy Carter* (SSN-23). One of the main justifications for the third boat is the need to keep submarine design and construction skills alive rather than the operational need, although it will, of course, be a valuable addition to the fleet.

Work is now well in hand on the new class – the Virginia (SSN-744) – of which thirty are currently planned, with the first due for delivery in 2004. These boats will displace 7,800 tons submerged and will be armed with twelve vertical tubes for Tomahawk missiles, plus four 21in (533mm

torpedo tubes; this is the same number of tubes as in the Los Angeles-class, although thirty-eight weapons (plus the twelve vertical launch Tomahawks) is a considerable increase in load-out. Although intended as a cheaper alternative to the SSN-21-class, the cost of these boats has steadily increased and in 1998 was estimated to be $3.3billion for the first and $2.1billion for the fourth (FY98 dollars). In order to keep nuclear submarine construction expertise alive in two yards, the fore and after sections are being built by Electric Boat and the mid sections by Newport News, with responsibility for final assembly, fitting out, and trials alternating between the two yards.

Even well before the first-of-class was competed, work had started on its successor, currently dubbed "SSXN," which is scheduled to start joining the fleet in the 2020s.

Below: At one time 29 SSN-21s were to be built; only three were completed.

SEAL Submarine Delivery Systems

SEALs (Sea-Air-Land), the Navy's special operations forces, were raised during the 1960s, since when they have earned a fearsome reputation for efficiency and daring. One of their favorite methods of arriving in and departing from operational areas is by submarine, since these vessels can travel long distances at high speed, in great security and without alerting the enemy, and can take the troops to a point close to the hostile shore. They cannot, however, deliver them actually on to the shore and therefore the SEALs need specialized means of transport to cover that gap.

Lafayette-class SSBN conversions

Since the 1950s the U.S. Navy has maintained a small number of former attack and ballistic missile submarines which have been converted to become transports for Special Operations Forces. Over the years these have included *Grayback* (SS-574), a diesel-electric-powered former cruise-missile boat (SSG), which served in this role from 1969 to 1984, followed by two former ballistic missile submarines, *Sam Houston* (SSBN-609) and *John Marshall* (SSBN-611) from 1985 to 1994. The most recent conversions were *Kamahameha* (SSBN-642) and *Polk* (SSBN-645), both former Lafayette-class ships, of which only *Kamahameha* (SSN-642) remains in service in 2002. This ship has a submerged displacement of 8,250 tons and has had its sixteen missile tubes converted so that seven are now variable ballast tanks, three are used as magazines/armories, and the remainder are showers, drying rooms, etc. Missions performed from such boats include reconnaissance and surveillance, combat swimmer attacks, cross-beach infiltration/exfiltration, and reconnaissance in support of amphibious operations (beach feasibility studies, hydrographic survey, surf observation, etc). Any operational U.S. submarine can be employed on such missions, but the specialist conversions are the most effective, providing accommodation for many more troops, with *Kamahameha*

Below: SEAL exits a drydeck shelter aboard USS Silversides (SSN-679).

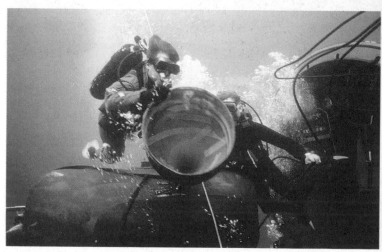

Above: Mk8 SEAL Delivery Vehicle, piloted by men of SEAL Team Two.

able to carry 67 SEALs or 100 Marines. *Kamahameha* has the fittings necessary to mount two portable Dry Deck Shelters (DDS) used to transport and launch SEAL Delivery Vehicles (SDVs) or to lock out combat swimmers; both are described below. The Sturgeon-class former attack submarine *L Mendel Rivers* (SSN-686) can carry SEALs and one DDS.

Dry Deck Shelter (DDS)

The U.S. Navy operates six Dry Deck Shelters, each of which is 38ft (11.6m) long and 9ft (2.7m) in diameter, and weighs 65,000lb (29,500kg). These are land- and air-transportable and can be mounted on any suitably fitted submarine, currently *Kamehameha* (two) and five Los Angeles-class (one each), and, in the future, *Jimmy Carter* (SSN-23) and all Virginia-class (SSN-774 onwards).

The DDS is mounted aft of the submarine's sail and is connected to the submarine's after hatch to permit free passage between the DDS and the pressure-hull while submerged. The SEALs can also exit or re-enter the water from the DDS while the boat is submerged, either to ascend immediately to the surface or to travel on the Swimmer Delivery Vehicle (SDV). The DDS allows for the launch and recovery of an SDV or combat rubber raiding craft (CRRC), with personnel, from/to a submerged submarine. It consists of three modules constructed as one integral unit. The first module is a hangar in which an SDV or CRRC is stowed. The second module is a transfer trunk to allow passage between the modules and the submarine. The third module is a hyperbaric recompression chamber. The DDS provides a dry working environment for mission preparations. In a typical operation the DDS hangar module will be flooded and pressurized to the surrounding sea pressure, and a large door is opened to allow for launch and recovery of the vehicle. A DDS can be transported by USAF C-5/C-17 aircraft, rail, highway, or sealift.

SEAL Delivery Vehicle (SDV) Mk VIII Mod 1

The SDV Mk VIII Mod 1 is a "wet" submersible; ie, it carries combat swimmers in fully flooded compartments, where they are sustained by their individual Underwater Breathing Apparatus (UBA). The SDV has an electric propulsion

system, powered by silver-zinc batteries, which are recharged by the parent submarine. The SDV is controlled by an operator using a control stick, and he also has a computerized Doppler navigation sonar which displays speed, distance, heading, depth, and other piloting functions. The SDV carries a maximum of four swimmers, together with stores, weapons, and mines. Fourteen SDV Mark VIII Mod 0 were originally built, of which three were sold to the UK Royal Marines in 1999; one has been discarded and the remaining ten underwent a SLEP from 1995 onwards, following which they have been designated SDV Mark VIII Mod 1.

Advanced SEAL Delivery System (ASDS)

Whereas the SDV is a "human torpedo" carrying personnel in "wet" conditions, the ASDS is a submarine in its own right, carrying its crew and passengers in dry conditions within a pressure hull. The vessel is 65ft (19.8m) long, with a beam of 6.8ft (2.1m) and a height, 8.3ft (2.5m), and has a submerged displacement of 60 tons. It is propelled by a single 67hp electric motor, which is powered by fourteen silver-zinc cells, which are recharged from the parent submarine, giving it a submerged range of 125nm at 8kt. There are also eight retractable electric thrusters for precise maneuvering. The ASDS has a crew of two. Unlike the great majority of submarines it does not have a sail. There is a lock-out chamber amidships. The first was delivered in 2000, some three years late and, with a cost of $230million, it was considerably over budget. It is planned to procure six of these ASDS, but at a relatively slow rate, with the second being ordered in 2003 and the third in 2005.

Below: SEAL emerges from a dry deck shelter aboard USS Silversides.

Naval Weapons Systems

The U.S. Navy has a wide range of weapons systems in service, but within each category there are remarkably few different types. From the 1950s to the late 1970s there was a general tendency to meet every new requirement with a new weapon system, a procedure that was time-consuming, very expensive and, while it resulted in a few sound and effective systems, there were also a large number of costly failures. From about the mid-1980s onwards, however, the tendency has been that wherever possible new requirements are met by adapting or developing existing weapons systems, with totally new systems being developed only where all other options have been shown to be unworkable. This has proved to be sensible and effective, and missiles such as the Standard and Sea Sparrow have been progressively developed over a period of some thirty years and yet the latest versions still remain firmly at the forefront of

technology. On the other hand, some new weapons have been developed, such as the Rolling Air-frame Missile (RAM), where no other weapon could meet the evolving threat, although close examination of even the RAM shows that it has taken the guidance system from one missile, the warhead from a second, and the propulsion unit from a third in order to reduce development complications.

Each of the Navy's missiles is outstanding in its own field. Thus, Harpoon and Tomahawk are the leading anti-ship and land-attack weapons, with the latter making signal contributions to virtually every conflict in the past twenty years. In air defense, Standard has proved itself almost infinitely adaptable, while Sea Sparrow is used by more navies than any other short-range naval air defense missile.

Guns still have an important role to play in naval warfare, but they are secondary to missiles, although recent developments in very long-range artillery may reverse this trend. The Navy's present heavy gun is the excellent Mark 45 5in (127mm), but there are revolutionary systems, such as electrically powered rail-guns, now under development, which may offer dramatic increases in range, payload, and accuracy.

This review does not investigate the arcane world of naval electronics, except to outline the Navy's Aegis system, which provides individual ships and battle groups with detection, tracking, and fire control capabilities far beyond anything that has gone before. This does not mean that the system is perfect or that new techniques will not be developed to overcome it, but for the time being attacking an Aegis-equipped U.S. naval battlegroup from the air, on the surface, or by submarine will be very difficult, indeed.

Left: Sea Sparrow missile is launched from a carrier's Mark 29 launcher.

RGM-84/AGM-84 Harpoon/ Stand-Off Land Attack Missile (SLAM)

Type: air- and ship-launched anti-ship and land-attack missile.
Manufacturer: Boeing.
Weight: with booster 1,503lb (681.9kg); without booster 1,145lb (519.3kg).
Dimensions: length with booster 15.2ft (4.6m); length without booster 12.6ft (3.8m); diameter 1.1ft (34cm); wing span 2.7ft (83cm).
Guidance: Inertial and active radar.
Powerplant: Teledyne CAE J402-CA-4000 single-spool turbojet; 2.9kN static thrust.
Performance: maximum speed Mach 0.85; range 67nm (124 km).
Warhead: 488.5lb (221.6kg) semi-armor-piercing with contact delay fuze.
Booster: Thiokol or Aerojet rocket.
Specifications for Block 1C version.

The Harpoon anti-ship missile was designed to be launched from surface warships, submarines or (without the booster) from aircraft, and has proved its worth in numerous engagements during the conflicts of the past twenty years. Harpoon was developed in the early 1970s, but successive upgrades have maintained it at the forefront of missile development. The major versions have been Block 1 introduced in 1978, which was followed by Block 1B in 1981 and Block 1C in 1982. It was originally planned that the system would remain in service until about 2015, but there are no known plans for a successor and there are intensive ongoing efforts to ensure that it remains up-to-date, so Harpoon will remain in service well into the 2020s and possibly longer.

Harpoon missiles require minor adjustments according to the method of launch. With the appropriate attachments the AGM-84 missile can be launched from various USAF and USN aircraft, including the USAF's B-52G/H and the Navy's S-3B and P-3C Orion. For such air launches there is no booster and the turbojet engine is usually not started until the missile has been released, which allows the missile to be launched from higher altitudes and to achieve longer ranges. Alternatively, RGM-84 Harpoons can be launched from surface warships, using Mark 6, Mark 7 or Mark 12 canisters, as well as the Mark 112 ASROC launcher, and the Mark 116 Tartar launcher. The UGM-84 missile was also designed to be launched from a standard submarine 21in (533mm) torpedo tube, in which case it was contained within a capsule, which carried it to the surface where the top was blown off and the missile launched. This Sub-Harpoon was withdrawn from service in U.S. submarines in 1997, but for financial rather than operational reasons; it remains in use with a number of foreign navies. Once launched the missile flies at very low ("sea-skimmer") altitude to the general vicinity of the target, where the terminal seeker is switched on, and when it has acquired the target the missile strikes without further action from the firing platform. This autonomous capability enables the firing ship to engage other threats instead of concentrating on one at a time.

The missile consists of five sections, one each for guidance, warhead, sustainer, control, and booster functions. The Guidance Section houses the Missile Guidance Unit (MGU) which is initialized by data inputs from the launch platform's Command System immediately prior to launch. Following launch, the MGU integrates acceleration and altitude data to maintain the missile on the programmed flight profile, until the seeker acquires the target, after which the

Above: Harpoon anti-ship missile is fired from a deck-mounted canister.

MGU uses seeker data to enable the missile to home in on the target. The Warhead Section houses a 215lb (98kg) HE charge and a contact fuze, which is armed only once the missile has left the launcher. The Sustainer Section has four fixed fins to provide lift and contains the turbojet engine, air-inlet duct, and a fuel tank for JP-10 fuel. The Control Section consists of four electro-mechanical actuators which receive signals from the Guidance Section and then turn four fins to control the missile's flight. The Booster Section consists of a solid-fuel rocket motor which accelerates ship- or submarine-launched missiles to flight speed, following which it is jettisoned.

The AGM-84E Stand-Off Land Attack Missile (SLAM) (Harpoon Block 1E) is an air-launched weapon created in the 1980s by taking most of the elements of the existing Harpoon, except for the Guidance, Seeker, and Warhead Sections, which were replaced by a Global Positioning System (GPS) receiver, a Walleye optical guidance system, and a Maverick data-link. The original warhead was replaced by a Tomahawk warhead, since this gives better penetration. The resulting SLAM missile can be launched from land- or carrier-based F/A-18 Hornet aircraft and has been successfully used in Operation Desert Storm and in operations in former Yugoslavia.

The SLAM has subsequently been upgraded to AGM-84F Harpoon Block 1F, which is also designated SLAM-ER (Expanded Response). This gives a range of more than 150nm. It has a titanium warhead which considerably increases target penetration capability, while software improvements allow the pilot to retarget the impact point of the missile during the terminal phase of attack. SLAM-ER achieved its first flight in March of 1997 and the process of converting all Navy SLAM missiles to the ER standard has recently been completed.

A yet further enhancement, SLAM-ATA (Automatic Target Acquisition) AGM-84F (Harpoon Block 1G) introduces a reattack capability, which will

improve the missile's ability to strike targets in cluttered spaces, such as urban areas. It will also improve missile targeting capability in poor weather, countermeasure-protected environments, and will better enable offset aimpoint targeting.

As a final variant of this extremely capable and adaptable missile system, the launcher can also be mounted on a truck, while the Command Launch System electronics and a generator are mounted on a second truck. These two vehicles need only to be parked adjacent to each other, connected by cabling and powered up, and a very sophisticated anti-ship missile battery is ready to dominate littoral waters by deterring ships from transiting straits or approaching friendly territory.

Below: Harpoon cruises just above the sea, making it very difficult to detect.

BGM-109 Tomahawk

Type: long-range subsonic cruise missile for attacking land targets.
Manufacturer: Raytheon.
Weight: 2,650lb (1,193kg); 3,200lb (1,440kg) with booster.
Dimensions: length with booster: 20.5ft (6.3 m); length without booster 18.3ft (5.6m); diameter 20.4in (51.8cm); wing span 8.8ft (2.7m).
Guidance: inertial and TERCOM.
Powerplant: Williams International F107-WR-402 cruise turbo-fan engine; solid-fuel booster.
Performance: maximum speed about 550mph (880kmh); range (land attack, conventional warhead) 600nm (690 miles/1,104km).
Warhead: (all conventional) 1,000lb (454kg) Bullpup, or submunitions dispenser with combined effect bomblets, or WDU-36 warhead.

The Tomahawk land-attack cruise missile is an all-weather submarine- or ship-launched system, providing a long-range, highly survivable, unmanned land attack weapon system which has repeatedly demonstrated its accuracy and effectiveness under combat conditions. The basic system is very similar to Harpoon, with a solid-propellant booster accelerating the missile to cruise speed where a small turbofan engine takes over and the booster is jettisoned. Tomahawk is extremely hard to detect by hostile radar, due to its very small radar cross-section and low-altitude flight profile, while infrared detection is also very difficult as a result of careful design combined with the low heat emissions of its turbojet engine.

The system was conceived during the Cold War as the Tomahawk Land Attack Missile (TLAM) to attack fixed, non-hardened targets in known locations, with pinpoint accuracy. The strategic scenario has, however, changed and Tomahawk's primary mission today is for rapid and flexible response to changing scenarios and attacks against unpredicted targets in regional conflicts. During the critical early days of a regional conflict, Tomahawk, in conjunction

Below: Tomahawk is launched from a deck-mounted canister launcher.

Above: Submarine-launched Tomahawk emerges from the depths.

with other land attack systems and tactical aircraft, is used to deny the forward movement of enemy forces, to neutralize his ability to conduct air operations, and to suppress enemy air defenses (SEAD). In addition, Tomahawk is used to attack high value targets such as electrical generating facilities, command centers nodes, and weapons dumps. The missile is treated as a "wooden round" – ie, there is no further inspection between factory gate and launcher.

The models in current use are Blocks II and III, either C (unitary warhead) or D (bomblets) versions. Following the Gulf War, the Navy took steps to improve Tomahawk's operational responsiveness, target penetration, range, and accuracy, the outcome being the Block III system upgrade, which includes jam-resistant Global Positioning System (GPS) receivers, freeing the guidance system from its dependence on terrain features. The new warhead has a more powerful explosive and more responsive fuzing systems. Block III missiles were first used in September 1995 against Bosnia and a year later against Iraq.

Next generation version is Block IV Phase I Tomahawk, with an initial target of 1,253 produced by remanufacturing Tomahawk antiship (TASM) variants, which are no longer required. Tactical Tomahawk is an alternative to Block IV. In this system the missile will take off with up to fifteen potential targets programmed into its system. The tactical commander will then be able to select any one of these while the missile is in flight, to send it to an unpredicted target by giving it a set of GPS coordinates, or even to have it loiter over the battlefield, using the onboard TV camera to assess the situation before finally committing it to an attack. Also under consideration is a Block V version pioneering new production methods using modular design and novel construction technology which will dramatically lower unit costs.

RIM-116 Rolling Air-frame Missile (RAM)

Type: short-range air defense missile.
Manufacturer: Raytheon.
Weight: 162lb (73.5kg).
Dimensions: length 9.2ft (2.8m); diameter 5in (12.7cm).
Guidance: passive IR or RF/IR.
Powerplant: solid-fuel rocket.
Performance: maximum speed Mach 2+; range 6nm (12km).
Warhead: 5lb (2.3kg).

RAM is a joint U.S./German project which provides surface ships with an effective self-defense "fire-and-forget" system to defeat incoming antiship cruise missiles. The 5in (12.7cm) diameter missile utilizes technology from the Sidewinder air-to-air missile for the warhead and rocket motor, and the seeker from the Stinger shoulder-launched air-defense missile as the basis of the guidance system. Cueing is provided by the ship's ESM suite or radar and in the first missile design (Block 0) in-flight guidance was achieved by a passive RF seeker, which detected the incoming target's RF emissions until the IR seeker could take over for the terminal homing phase. Tested in the early 1990s, this proved inadequate and a redesign resulted in the Block I system which, in essence, retained the guidance system of the Block 0 as one option, but added a new "IR all-the-way" alternative. The missile is wingless and rotates as it flies, the spin being imparted by four offset tail fins. Control is by means of two fins situated just behind the nose.

The RAM is stored and launched from a twenty-one-missile Mark 49 launcher, which is being installed in all LHAs, LHDs, and LSDs, while a ten-

Standard Missile: SM-2 to SM-5

Missile	SM-2MR	SM-2ER	SM-2/IV	SM-3 LEAP	SM-4 LASM
Designation	RIM-66	RIM-67	RIM-156	RIM-67	See note*
Length (4.7m)	15.42ft (8.0m)	26.25ft (6.6m)	21.65ft (6.6m)	21.65ft (4.7m)	15.42ft
Diameter Missile	13.39in (34cm)	13.39in (34cm)	13.78in (35cm)	13.78in (35cm)	13.78in (35cm)
Booster	14.57in (37cm)	14.57in (34cm)	20.87in (53cm)	20.87in (53cm)	20.87in (53cm)
Wingspan	3.61ft (1.1m)	5.25ft (1.6m)	5.25ft (1.6m)		5.25ft (1.6m)
Weight	1,554lb (705kg)	2,957lb (1,341kg)	3,200lb (1,451.5kg)	3,310lb (1,501kg)	1,696lb (769kg)

Above: RIM-116 missile leaves the 10-round box launcher.

round launcher is being installed in Ticonderoga-class cruisers from 2001 onwards in place of the Phalanx CIWS. The RAM system will also be widely deployed aboard ships of the German Navy.

Speed	Mach 2.5	Mach 2.5	Mach 2.5	-	Mach 2.5
Range	106 miles (170km)	116 miles (185km)	150 miles (240km)	-	150 miles (240km)
Altitude	12.38 miles (19.8km)	5.63 miles (25km)	20.63 miles (33km)	<62.5 miles (<100km)	-

* No designation for this missile has yet been made public.

The Standard Missile (SM) family has been in frontline service with the U.S. Navy since 1968 and versions of relevance today are as follows. SM-2 (RIM-66C) was developed from the original SM-1, but with an added programmable autopilot; it the basis of the Aegis system. SM-3 Lightweight Exo- Atmospheric Projectile (LEAP) is a modified SM-2 airframe designed to destroy theater ballistic missiles, while the SM-4 Land Attack Standard Missile (LASM) uses a modified airframe to produce a highly effective ship-shore missile, and the SM-5 is a concept study for a missile to intercept cruise missiles over land, which began in Spring 1998. The original model, SM-1, remains in service with the Navy only aboard the few remaining Perry-class frigates.

Internally, the missile is divided into five discrete sections, at the front being the Guidance Section, followed by the Ordnance Section, consisting of a 254lb (115kg) warhead fitted with impact and proximity fuzes. Next comes the Autopilot Section, containing the autopilot and the missile battery, except in the SM-2 Block IVA, where many autopilot functions are transferred to the Guidance Section, and consequently the autopilot section is renamed the Power-control and Telemetry Section. This is followed by the Propulsion Section, containing the dual-thrust rocket motor, and finally the Steering Control Section, which includes the electrical actuation system and tailfins. In the Extended-Range (ER) version, the dual-thrust rocket motor of the MR is replaced by a different sustainer motor, and a full-diameter, cylindrical booster with cropped triangular fins is added.

The steadily evolving members of the SM-2 family are known by their "Block" numbers. Thus, SM-2 Block I was an upgraded version of SM-1 with improvements to the guidance and propulsion systems, achieving IOC in 1979; it was an interim weapon pending introduction of Block II and is no longer operational. Block II was the first major production version, entering service in 1984, and it has since been deployed aboard Ticonderoga-class cruisers, Arleigh Burke-class destroyers, some nuclear-powered cruisers (now retired), and Kidd-class destroyers which are being sold to Taiwan, but without the SM-2 missiles.

The Block III missiles entered service in 1990, replacing Block II weapons in U.S. Navy cruisers and destroyers, and gave an improved capability against low altitude targets. Block IIIA extended the capability to even lower altitudes and also included a new warhead which imparts great velocity to fragments in the direction of the target, while Block IIIB improved the homing capability.

The next development was the Block IV missile (also known as SM-2 Aegis (ER)) which provides yet greater range, improved cross-range and higher altitude performance for Aegis VLS ships, as well as improved performance against low RCS targets and in a complex ECM environment. Development of Block IV was deferred in 1995 to await the outcome of the Block IVA development program, but was then reinstated and it will achieve IOC in 2003.

Block IVA provides the endoatmospheric (ie, below 98,000ft/30,000m) capability for the Theater Ballistic Missile Defense (TBMD) system and will also intercept air targets, even at sea-level. Cruisers *Lake Erie* (CG-70) and *Port Royal* (CG-73) will be the first to receive Block IVA missiles and Theater Ballistic Missile Defense system modifications.

SM-3 (LEAP) meets the Navy's TBMD or "upper tier" exoatmospheric requirement, and is a modified SM-2 carrying a Lightweight Exo-Atmospheric Projectile (LEAP) armed with a kinetic warhead. All Ticonderoga-class cruisers with

Below: Standard missiles on a Mark 26 twin-arm launcher.

Above: Standard missile launched from Mark 41 vertical launch system (VLS).

Mark 41 vertical launch systems (*Bunker Hill* [CG-52] onwards) will be able to carry SM-3. It is basically an SM-2 airframe with an additional third stage (the Advanced Solid Axial Stage [ASAS]) and a new homing vehicle (fourth stage). The ASAS separates at some 187,000ft (57,000m) and continues, still under control from the ship, to about 300,000ft (91,000m) where it ejects the nose-cone to expose the warhead sensor. The warhead then separates and closes with the aim of scoring a direct hit; even a graze hit will ensure the target's destruction.

SM-4 (LASM) (Land-attack Standard Missile) uses surplus Standard SM-2 (MR) Blocks II and III airframes to carry a modified payload section incorporating an inertial guidance system (INS) and a Global Positioning System (GPS) receiver. The missile is launched from the Mark 41 VLS, and initial deployment will be aboard twenty-two Ticonderoga-class cruisers and Arleigh Burke-class Flight IIA destroyers (*Winston Churchill* [DDG-51] onwards.). The blast/fragmentation warhead is delivered with an accuracy of 43ft (13m) and a range of 60 miles (95km). In all physical and technical respects the SM-4 (LASM) is simply another round for the Mark 41 VLS. There are some 2,000 surplus SM-2 airframes available for conversion. The original Navy plan was to convert 800, but this has now been reduced to 500, with an IOC of 2003.

RIM-7 Sea Sparrow/Evolved Sea Sparrow (ESSM)

Type: ship-launched air defense missile.
Manufacturer: Raytheon.
Weight: 500lb (227kg).
Dimensions: length 145in (3.7m); diameter 8in (20.3cm); wing span, open 40in (102cm), folded 25in (64cm).
Guidance: semi-active homing radar.
Powerplant: Hercules Mark-58 solid-propellant rocket motor.
Performance: maximum speed <Mach 3.5 (4,525kmh); range 34nm (55km).
Warhead: 90lb (40.5kg) continuous rod.
Specifications for RIM-7P.

The Sea Sparrow is the most widely used naval surface-to-air missile in the world, with large numbers already produced. In its latest Evolved Sea Sparrow Missile (ESSM) version it will continue in production for many years to come.

Sea Sparrow was originally slant-launched, but during the late 1970s the air threat became so severe that shorter reaction times for close area air defense systems became essential; thus, since 1987 all production missiles have been capable of either slant launch (Mark 29 rail-launcher) or vertical launch (Mark 41/Mark 48 launchers).

The target is detected by the ship's search radar and designated through the combat information center, whose bearing and elevation data are used to cue the directors. Range and angle tracking data are provided through the signal data processor and passed to the firing officer's console. In the case of vertical launchers, similar information is passed to the missile's jet vane controller (JVC) and once pre-launch data and firing commands have been relayed to the missile, it is then launched, whereupon it follows a proportional guidance path

Above: RIM-7 Sea Sparrow is launched from a Mark 29 railed launcher.

directly to the intercept point. Vertically launched missiles rise to a height of about 13ft (4m), which takes approximately 0.7 seconds, and then pitch over to the correct course to intercept the target. The missile does not rise above 200ft (61m) when launched against a low-flying target and is fully tipped over within 250ft (76m) of leaving the launcher. The JVC unit, which is used only for the launch portion of the flight, is jettisoned after approximately two seconds.

There have been many versions of the Sea Sparrow, the oldest still in service being RIM-7M, which has a solid-state onboard computer, with WAU-17 warhead, and autopilot for multiple engagements; some 3,200 rounds were produced, ending in 1989/90. This was followed by the RIM-7P, which has an improved low-altitude guidance mode and enhanced sub-clutter performance against very low-altitude targets; production totaled some 4,000, plus a number of RIM-7M upgraded to -P standard.

In the late 1980s two proposals for a new naval short-range missile system were considered. One collapsed, leaving the Evolved Sea Sparrow Missile (ESSM) (RIM-7PTC) as the only practicable solution. A NATO consortium (plus Australia) is undertaking production which will exceed 3,000 missiles. ESSM is the same length as RIM-7P but the missile has a diameter of 10in (25.4cm) and is somewhat heavier at 560lb (245kg). The front end of the ESSM contains a new radar seeker, while the guidance section is based on that of RIM-7P, but includes a mid-course guidance module. The warhead is identical to that in RIM-7P, but there is a new 10in diameter, 80lb (36kg) booster-sustainer. Vertical-launch missiles will also have a thrust-vector control unit with separable vanes. The missile is tail-controlled and retains all the operational capabilities of RIM-7P but with the additional capability of attacking maneuvering anti-ship missiles. It can be launched either from rail launchers (Mark 29) or from the Mark 41 vertical launcher, with four ESSMs in a "Quadra-Pack" occupying one cell. It can also be launched from the Mark 48 VLS.

Left: Sea Sparrow is the world's most widely used naval anti-air missile.

Mark 45, 5-inch/54-caliber Lightweight Gun

Type: fully automatic, lightweight gun mount.
Date deployed: 1971 (Mark 45).
Caliber: 5 inch (127mm).
Dimensions: barrel length 54 calibers (270in/686cm).
Weight: mount 22.2 tons (20,200kg); projectile 70lb (31.8kg).
Range: horizontal 13nm (23,980m); vertical 32,000ft (14,840m).
Guidance system: radar controlled; elevation -5deg to +65deg.
Type of fire: 16-20 rounds per minute automatic; muzzle velocity 2,651ft/s (808m/s).
Magazine capacity: 475-500 rounds per magazine.
Crew: gun house; handling room 6.

The Mark 45 single-barrel mounting is installed in Ticonderoga-class cruisers and Spruance- and Arleigh Burke-class destroyers to provide accurate naval gunfire against surface targets, air threats (as a back-up to missiles), and shore targets. Development has been completed on an enhanced version, the Mark 45 Gun System Technical Improvement Program (Mark 45 Mod 4). This has a new faceted gunshield with a low radar cross-section and a new 62-caliber barrel, which, in conjunction with a strengthened chamber and trunnion supports and lengthened recoil stroke increases the rate-of-fire to 45rpm. This new weapon is at sea with *Winston S Churchill* (DDG-81) and succeeding Arleigh Burke Flight IIA destroyers; it will definitely be backfitted to Ticonderoga-class cruisers and may also be backfitted to earlier Arleigh Burke-class destroyers. An Extended Range Guided Munition (ERGM) is under development, which will have an accuracy of 11-22yd (10-20m) at its maximum range of 63nm.

The Mark 45 is the largest caliber gun at sea with the

U.S. Navy, but a larger weapon, the 155mm Advanced Gun System (AGS), is currently under development. This will be mounted in the DD-21 destroyer and is intended to provide flexible, sustained, long-range naval surface fire support (NSFS) against targets well inland, as well as at sea. The AGS will be a conventional, single-barrel, low-signature weapon, capable of rapid reaction and fully stabilized training and elevation. The stowage system will accommodate 750 rounds and a full automated ammunition handling system will enable it to fire twelve rounds per minute to a maximum range of 100nm.

Below: Mark 45 5in gun aboard Ticonderoga-class cruiser, USS Lake Champlain (CG-57).

Mark 75 76mm/62 gun

Type: fully-automatic, rapid fire, lightweight gun mount.
Date deployed: 1978 (Oliver Hazard Perry-class).
Caliber: 3 inch (76mm).
Dimensions: barrel length 62 calibers (186in/472cm).
Weight: mount 6.2 tons; projectile 14lb (6.4kg).
Range: horizontal 10nm (18,400m); vertical 39,000ft (11,900m).
Guidance system: radar-controlled.
Type of fire: 80 rounds per minute automatic; muzzle velocity 2,953ft/ (900m/s); training 360deg at 70/s; elevation -15 to +85 at 40/s.
Magazine capacity: 85 rounds.
Crew: gun house 0; handling room 4.

The Mark75 76mm/62 gun is the U.S. Navy version of the Italian OTO Melar (now OTOBreda) 76/62, and is produced under license in the United States b United Defense (formerly Northern Ordnance). Together, these are the mos widely used naval guns in the world and in the U.S. Navy is mounted in th Oliver Hazard Perry-class frigates and in several classes of Coastguard cutters
The gun is fully automatic, controlled by a Mark 92 fire-control system, an the barrel is fitted with a muzzle-brake which reduces recoil by some 3! percent, and a water-cooling system, which enables it to fire at a rate of som 80 rounds per minute. A total of 85 rounds is held on the mount, which enable

Phalanx Mk 15 CIWS (Close-In Weapons System)

Type: fast-reaction, rapid-fire 20mm gun system for defense against antiship missiles.
Date deployed: Block 0 1980 (USS *Coral Sea*); Block 1 1988 (USS *Wisconsin*) Block 1B 1999 (USS *Underwood*).
Gun type/caliber: M-61A1 Gatling; 20mm.
Weight:12,500lb (5,625 kg); later models 13,600lb (6,120 kg).
Range: horizontal 1,625yd (1,490m).
Guidance system: self-contained search-and-track radar with integrated FLIR.
Type of fire: Block 0 3,000 rounds/min automatic; Block 1 onwards 4,500 rounds/min.
Elevation/depression: +80/-20 degrees.
Ammunition: armor-piercing discarding sabot (APDS), depleted uranium sub caliber penetrator. Penetrator changed to tungsten 1988.
Magazine capacity: Block 0 989 rounds; Block 1 onwards 1,550 rounds.

Phalanx was designed in the 1970s to provide a "last-ditch" defense against incoming antiship missiles or aircraft that have penetrated the longer range defensive systems such as surface-to-air missiles. This is achieved by automatically detecting, tracking, and engaging such targets. Phalanx has an advanced search-and-track radar, which is integrated with a stabilized, forward-looking infra-red (FLIR) detector to give a multi-spectra capability. Phalanx is capable of fully autonomous operation, but can also be integrated into existing combat systems to provide additonal sensor and fire-control capability.
In a typical engagement one radar is used to track the target while the

Above: Mark 75 is the U.S. version of the Italian-designed 76mm naval gun.

ong bursts to be fired without pauses for reloading. The only significant
limitation of this otherwise excellent weapon is that it cannot fire some of the
more sophisticated 3in (76mm) rounds which are now available.

*Right: Phalanx fires at 4,500
rounds per minute, and is
totally self-contained.*

second tracks the projecticle
stream and a computer is
constantly issuing directions for
training and elevation to the gun
in order to bring the difference
between the two to zero and
thus destroy the target.

The gun element is a Vulcan
Gatling, originally designed for
use in aircraft, in which a cluster
of six barrels rotates at high
speed, in either continuous fire
or in burst lengths of 60 or 100
rounds. In most engagements
the weapon fires a 20mm sub-
caliber projectile, consisting of a
heavy-metal (tungsten or
depleted uranium) 15mm
penetrator, which is surrounded by a plastic sabot and a light-weight metal
pusher.

The latest Block 1B standard includes improvements to the tracking and
search radars, longer, heavier barrels to reduce wear, a heavier mount to
reduce dispersion, and an infra-red imaging and tracking system. In addition, it
introduces a "man-in-the-loop" facility, making the system more suitable for
use in engagements against small, high-speed surface craft, small terrorist
aircraft, helicopters and surface mines. The Block 1B weapon is also capable of
firing a new Enhanced Lethality Cartridge (ELC) with a heavier penetrator.

Torpedoes

The torpedo is a self-propelled, guided projectile, operating underwater an
designed to detonate either on contact with or in proximity to a target. It can b
launched from submarines, surface ships, helicopters or fixed-wing aircraft.

The Mark 46 12.8in (324mm) lightweight torpedo is in service with U.S
forces in two versions, one of which is for use by cruisers, destroyers, an
frigates, being launched from deck-mounted Mark 32 torpedo tubes. Th
second version is air-launched from fixed- or rotary-winged aircraft, and

Above: Two Mk 46 torpedoes (foreground and right) aboard Kennedy (CV-67).

Above: A pair of Mk 48 ADCAP torpedoes aboard Oklahoma City (SSN-723).

parachute-retarded. The original Mark 46 Mod 1 and Mod 2 torpedoes have been upgraded to Mark 46 Mod 6 NEARTIP (Near Term Improvement Program) with enhanced homing and counter-measures, while Mod 5s have been upgraded to Mod 5A, with improved sonar. A Mod 7, with improved shallow-water capabilities, is under development. The Mark 46 Mod 5 has twin contra-rotating propellers and is 8.5ft (2.6m) long; it weighs 518lb (235kg), of which 98lb (44kg) is the high-explosive warhead. It has a speed in excess of 28kt and a range of some 8,000yd (7,315m). Following launch it follows a straight course for a predetermined distance and then commences a helical search, before employing either active or passive/active acoustic homing for the final run-in.

The Mark 48 Mod 5 ADCAP (Advanced Capability) heavyweight 21in (533mm) torpedo is in service aboard the fleet's Ohio-class SSBNs and Los Angeles-class SSNs, and will also be the principal weapon aboard the Seawolf- and Virginia-classes. Developed from the original Mark 48, the ADCAP version entered service in 1988 and is 19ft (5.8m) long. It weighs 3,695lb (1,663kg), of which the warhead accounts for 650lb (293kg). The torpedo is powered by a

Mines

The sea mine can be used offensively to prevent the enemy from using certain areas or channels, and defensively to stop enemy hostile ships or submarines approaching sea areas vital to U.S. interests, such as harbor entrances. In a future conflict, the great majority of sea mines would be laid by aircraft (S-3, P-3, or B-52H) or by submarines. The U.S. Navy does not operate surface minelayers, apart from one LCU, whose employment would obviously be very limited. There are two types of mines: bottom mines, which lie on the seabed, and the moored mine, which drops an anchor on a cable, thus enabling it to be used at a predetermined depth. The oldest mine in current use is the Mark 56 ASW mine, first deployed in 1966, but since then technological advances have led to the development of the Mark 60 CAPTOR (encapsulated torpedo), various Quickstrike mines, and the Submarine-Launched Mobile Mine.

The Mark 56 is an air-laid, moored mine with a magnetic exploder, intended to attack enemy shipping. It is 9.53ft (2.9m) long, 22.4in (570mm) in diameter, and weighs 2,000lb (909kg), of which 360lb (164kg) is the HBX-3 warhead.

The Mark 60 CAPTOR is the Navy's principal ASW mine and can be laid by either aircraft or submarine. It is a bottom-lying device which lies in wait at depths of up to 984ft (300m) until a target is detected, whereupon it launches an acoustic-homing torpedo. Development was very lengthy, starting in 1961 but with entry into service not achieved until 1979. The weapon is based on a Mark 46 Mod 4 torpedo and the submarine-launched version is 11.0ft (3.35m) long, 21in (533mm) in diameter, and weighs 2,056lb (932kg); the warhead is 96lb (43.5kg) of PXBN-103.

The Mark 67 SLMM Submarine Launched Mobile Mine is unique in its deployment method, being launched from a submarine torpedo tube and then traveling up to 10 miles (16km) under its own power to a predetermined location, where it then becomes a conventional bottom-lying mine. The weapon is based on the Mark 37 19in (485mm) torpedo, which has had its wire-guidance unit removed and a new 516lb (234kg) warhead added, which is activated by either a magnetic/seismic or a pressure/magnetic/ seismic target detection devices (TDD). Maximum depth is 600ft (183m). The Mark 67, which entered service in 1983, is now approaching obsolescence and a new program (Improved SLMM) is now piston engine driving a pump-jet, which gives it a speed greater than 28 knots, with a range in excess of 5nm. It is wire-guided, with passive/active acoustic homing. An upgraded version, Mark 46 Mod 6, is being produced by modifying in-service Mod 5s. This results in quieter running, and also gives improved guidance, control and terminal homing.

The Mark 50 Advanced Lightweight Torpedo (ALWI) is 12.75in (324mm) in diameter and is intended for use against the latest, faster, and deeper-diving submarines. The Mark 50 can be launched from all ASW aircraft, and from torpedo tubes aboard surface combatant ships. The Mark 50 is 9.3ft (2.83m) long and weighs 750lb (340kg), with a 100lb (4,5kg) shaped-charge warhead. It has a speed in excess of 40kt.

The Mark 54 Lightweight Hybrid Torpedo (LHT) program involves the remanufacture of both Mark46 and Mark 50 lightweight torpedoes to an enhanced and common standard, combining the Mark 46's warhead and propulsion system, with the Mark 50's sensors and the Mark 48 ADCAP's speed control system. In addition, it has a new digitized data system and processor. The first models enter service in 2003.

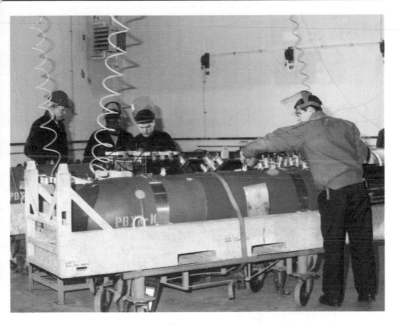

Above: Ordnancemen install firing mechanism in a Mk 64 Quickstrike mine.

under way. This is based on a Mark 48 torpedo, which is used to deploy two bottom-lying mines at different locations.

The Quickstrike series are air-dropped mines adapted from standard aircraft bombs: Mark 62 mine – Mark 82 500lb (227kg) bomb; Mark 63 mine – Mark 83 1,000lb (454kg) bomb; Mark 64 mine – Mark 84 2,000lb (908kg)bomb. They are fitted with the TDD appropriate to their mission: Mark 57 (magnetic/seismic); Mark 58 (magnetic/seismic/pressure); Mark 70 (magnetic/seismic); or Mark 71 (pressure/magnetic/seismic). The Mark 62 uses the same fins as the Snakeye bomb, but all others are fitted with a parachute retarder in order to reduce the impact on hitting the water.

Aegis Weapon System

The most sophisticated command and weapon control system developed by any navy, Aegis is named after the shield used by Zeus, chief of the gods, in Greek mythology. Aegis integrates the management of a naval task group's assets and is designed to react quickly and with sufficient fire-power to destroy fast, intelligent targets in severe ECCM and environmental conditions. The system is based on a federated architecture of four subsystems: multi-function radar; Command and Decision System (CDS); Aegis Display System (ADS); and the Weapons Control System (WCS). There are currently five basic configurations (known as "baselines") and seven versions (designated "modifications" [Mods]), and both hardware and software are being continually upgraded.

The SPY-1 multifunction radar conducts horizon and hemispherical searching, multiple target tracking and multiple target designation, and also provides two-way links with missiles for mid-course guidance, when instructed to do so by the WCS.

Below: SPY-1 antennas can be seen on the forward edge of the bridge.

Above: Standard SM-2 missile climbs away, directed by the Aegis system.

Ticonderoga-class cruisers with Baselines 0-2 have the SPY-1A system, while those with Baseline 3 have the more advanced SPY-1B and Baseline 4 the latest SPY-1B(V). Arleigh Burke-class destroyers up to DDG-86 have the lightweight SPY-1D and from DDG-87 onwards the SPY- 1E.

All versions of SPY-1 have the four instantly recognizable antennae installed in the superstructure, which are angled upwards at approximately 45 degrees to enable them to maintain accurate coordination even when the ship is rolling at angles of ±30 or pitching at ±15. The SPY-1 radar is supplemented by a number of dedicated radars, including the SPS-49 very long-range, air-search radar, whose high average power can help detect low cross-section threats with great precision, even in severe EW environments. The SPS-55 surface search and navigation radar is used to detect small surface targets, for tracking low-flying aircraft and for detecting submarine periscopes.

All sensor inputs are passed to the Command and Decision System (CDS), which provides overall operational direction and co-ordination, such inputs including data not only from onboard sensors, but also from offboard sensors via Link 11 and Link 14 data channels. In addition to inputs from radar and sonar sensors, the CDS also receives electronic warfare inputs, enabling it to assess threats and assign engagement instructions to the WCS.

The Aegis Display System (ADS) enables the ship's commander, his tactical action officer and the task group commander (if embarked) to assess the operational situation and to issue orders both to onboard and

offboard weapon systems and units.

The Weapons Control System (WCS) conducts the engagement of air, surface, and underwater targets, although priority is given to the anti air battle. Virtually all weapons systems aboard these warships have their own fire-control system (for example, Mark 86 Mod 9 for 5in/127mm guns and Mark 116 for underwater warfare) and the Aegis WCS controls them all, as well as providing its own integral fire-control for surface-to-air missile engagements. The Aegis WCS has four operating modes: automatic, automatic special, semi-automatic, and casualty. The automatic special mode ensures that targets which meet predetermined threat criteria will be automatically engaged unless the order is overridden manually. The other modes are self-explanatory, but in all of them the firing is initiated manually.

Below: Ticonderoga-class cruiser, Shiloh (CG-47) launches SM-2 missile.

Tanks and Fighting Vehicles

The cutting edge fighting capability of the U.S. Army and Marine Corps are their fighting vehicles, and pre-eminent among these is the main battle tank. Today, all armored units in both forces use the M1 Abrams, which proved its quality to devastating effect during Desert Storm in 1991. Like all other frontline equipment, the M1 is being constantly upgraded, the latest version being the Army's M1A3, while the Marines use the M1A1 with a deep water fording kit. Although a relatively small number of the older M60A3 remain in reserve stocks, the only active main battle tank is the M1 Abrams, which gives all the tactical and logistic benefits of standardization.

The outstanding M113 armored personnel carrier remains one of the most widely used military vehicles in the world and, despite the advent of the M2/M3 Bradley, the older M113 in its many versions will continue to give service to the U.S. armed forces for many years to come. The M113 is famed for its simplicity and reliability. Many feared that the complexity of the M2 Bradley would have a detrimental effect on its reliability, but as was shown in Desert Storm this is simply not the case, and the M2t is setting new standards for availability. Similarly, the HMMWV, known around the world as the "Humm-Vee," is proving a worthy successor to the Jeep.

While the M1, M2, and HMMWV are in service in vast numbers, some vehicles are bought in much smaller quantities, but still have a valuable place. The amphibious carrier, the AAVPT-7 (formerly the LVPT-7) is the only vehicle in its class in the world, with a long range at sea, the ability to land through surf and then to operate as an armored personnel carrier in the land battle, and all while carrying eighteen Marines. But even this vehicle is old and will soon be replaced by the new Advanced Amphibian Vehicle which has an even more remarkable performance. The Desert Patrol Vehicle (DPV) will be purchased in even smaller numbers, possibly less than a hundred. However, it provides the SEALs, which are a very small organization, with a very specialized scouting and attack capability, particularly in the deserts of the Middle East, where much recent fighting has taken place and which seem set to be the scenes of much more conflict in the future.

It has long been forgotten that the early days of several of these fine vehicles were shrouded in controversy. There were years of debate about the future of the tank, and several false starts with projects that had to be canceled, before the M1 was selected. Similarly, the nature of the vehicle required by the infantry was debated endlessly before the M2 Bradley was chosen. It is in the nature of democracy that there should be such lengthy debates about these matters, with the military, the government, Congress, and the public all wanting to have their say, which is often frustrating to the experts since it inevitably leads to delay and sometimes to confusion. But, despite all that, the products, as exemplified by the M1 and M2, are almost invariably first-class.

Right: M1A1 of 1st Armored Division in Saudi Arabia during Desert Storm.

M1A1/M1A2 Abrams

Type: main battle tank (MBT).
Manufacturer: Chrysler.
Weight: combat 125,890lb (57,154kg).
Ground pressure: 13.65b/in^2 (0.96kg/cm^2).
Dimensions: length (gun forward) 32.3ft (9.8m); length (hull) 25.9ft (7.9m); width 11.9ft (3.7m); height 9.5ft (2.9m).
Powerplant: Textron Lycoming AGT-1500 gas-turbine; 1,500bhp at 30,000rpm
Performance: road speed 41mph (67kmh); range 300 miles (480km); vertical obstacle 3.5ft (1.1m); trench 9.0ft (2.74m); gradient 60 percent.
Armor: classified.
Armament: 1 x M256 Rheinmetall 120mm smoothbore gun; 1 x M240 7.62mm co-axial machine gun; 1 x M2 12.7mm; 1 x M240 7.62mm anti-aircraft machinegun.
Crew: four.
Specifications for M1A2.

The M1 main battle tank (MBT) is named after the late General Creighton W Abrams, onetime Commanding Officer, 37th Armored Battalion, then one of the most successful commanders during the Vietnam War, and later Army Chief of Staff. The M1 forms the central pillar of the military might of the U.S. Army and is also a vital element of the power of the Marine Corps. Its powerful gun and exceptional mobility enable it to provide the mobile firepower for armored units, and it can outfight any MBT in any other army in the world, by day or by night and in any weather. It also provides armored protection for its crew in any combat environment they are likely to encounter on the moderrn battlefield.

Below: M1A2 Abrams showing its exceptionally well-profiled turret.

Above: M1A1/M1A2, powered by a Textron-Lycoming gas-turbine engine.

The M1 has been produced in large numbers for the Army and Marine Corps, and has been sold abroad to Egypt, Kuwait, and Saudi Arabia. It exists in four main versions: M1, M1 (Improved), M1A1, and M1A2. The initial production version was the M1, armed with a 105mm gun, of which 2,674 were built, with the last 300 having better armored protection and being designated M1 (Improved). A major advance was made with M1A1, produced from 1985 through 1993, with the M1's 105mm main gun being replaced by the Rheinmetall 120mm smoothbore gun and numerous other enhancements, including an improved suspension, new turret, increased armor protection, and a nuclear-chemical-biological protection system. A total of 403 M1A1s were also built for the Marine Corps, and these are virtually identical to the Army's M1A1, except that they have a deep water fording kit for use in amphibious landings. The latest M1A2 series includes all of the M1A1 features, plus an independent commander's station incorporating a thermal viewer, new navigation equipment, a digital data-bus, and a radio interface unit which links all M1A2s on the battlefield to give them a common battlefield picture. A total of seventy-seven new M1A2s have been built, but approximately 1,000 of the original M1s are being rebuilt to this latest standard.

The history of the M1 stretches back to the 1960s when, having fielded the M60, the Army began what turned out to be a long search for the next generation of MBT to replace the M48. One avenue that was explored was an international project with the Federal Republic of Germany; known as MBT-70, this turned into a controversial and very expensive fiasco, and eventually had to be canceled. A competition was then run for a replacement, with contracts being awarded in 1973 to Chrysler and General Motors (Detroit Diesel Division) to build prototypes of their designs. After rigorous testing throughout 1976 it was announced that the Chrysler model had won and would enter production, which duly commenced in 1979, with the first batch of production M1s being delivered in February 1980.

The hull and turret of the M1 are constructed with Chobham armor, a material developed in the United Kingdom, which is claimed to provide complete protection against attack from current missiles and tank guns.

The main armament in the M1 is the 105mm gun, which was developed in the United Kingdom and produced under license in the United States. But the main weapon of the M1A1and M1A2 is the M256 120mm smoothbore cannon, which was designed by the Rheinmetall Corporation of Germany and is also being built in the United States. In both cases, the main gun can be aimed and fired while the tank is on the move, with either the commander or the gunner selecting a target, following which the gunner uses the laser rangefinder to take the range and then depresses the firing switch. The computer makes all the necessary calculations and adjustments required to ensure a first-round hit. Secondary armament comprises a coaxial 7.62mm machine gun and two machine guns mounted on the turret roof – a 12.7mm machine gun at the commander's station and a 7.62mm machine gun at the loader's station. Depending on the version, the tank carries either 55 rounds of 105mm or 40 rounds of 120mm, plus 1,000 rounds of 12.7mm and 11,400 rounds of 7.62mm machine gun ammunition.

In the past a major cause of the destruction of tanks has been fire, resulting from either the detonation of the tank's own ammunition or by the ignition of the fuel. Considerable care has been taken in the M1 to prevent this, with the main armament ammunition being stowed in armored boxes, isolated from the firing compartment by sliding armored doors. In addition, the crew compartment is separated from the fuel tanks by armored bulkheads and there is an automatically activated Halon fire extinguishing system. Finally, in the event of penetration by a HEAT projectile. the explosive force is diverted outwards by the top panels of the tank, which blow-off autotmatically once a specific internal pressure is exceeded. On the outside of the turret are two six-barreled M250 smoke grenade launchers, one on each side of the main gun, which can launch greandes to hide the tank from view in an emergency. It is also possiblke to generate a denser smokescreen by injecting fuel into the

engine exhausts.

Nuclear, biological and chemical (NBC) warfare protection is provided by an overpressure clean-air conditioning air system, a radiological warning system, and a chemical agent detector. The crew are individually equipped with protective suits and masks.

The M1 is powered by the Textron Lycoming AGT-1500 gas-turbine, with a fully automatic transmission, equipped with four forward and two reverse gears. The two prime measures of battlefield agility are the power-to-weight ratio, which in the case of the M1 is very high, 27hp/tonne, and acceleration, where the M1 is capable of reaching 20mph (32kmh) from a standing start in six seconds. Prolonged service use has also demonstrated that the AGT-1500 is very reliable, mechanically simple, and particularly easy to service. On the other hand, it is definitely noisy (acoustic signature), emits a very hot exhaust (strong infra-red signature), and is thirsty on fuel, although the logistic support during Desert Storm was so effective that this was not a problem.

Over the past twenty to thirty years, a number of foreign armies have reduced their tank crews from four to three, but the U.S. Army did not follow this trend. The M1 has the traditional crew of four: commander, gunner, loader, and driver. The driver's position is at the center front of the hull, where he sits in a semi-reclined seat, protected by a massive and very well-sloped glacis plate. The other three are in the turret, the commander and gunner on the right, the loader on the left. The commander is equipped with an Independent Thermal Viewer (ITV) which provides stabilized day and night vision with a 360deg view automatic sector scanning, and enables him to cue the gunner's sight without any need for verbal communication. There is also a complete stand-by fire control system, which enables the commander to fire the main gun without reference to the gunner.The commander's position also has six periscopes providing a 360 degree view.

The gunner's station has a visual sight, a thermal-imaging system, and a laser

Below: Main gun on the M1A2 is the M256 Rheinmetal 120mm smoothbore.

range finder, all of which input to the onboard digital fire control computer. The computer also accepts automatically calculated inputs concerning the bend of the tube (measured by the muzzle reference system), wind velocity, and trunnion tilt (the angle between the gun and the "normal" due to the tank being on sloping ground). Either the commander or the gunner manually inputs data on the type of round to be used, temperature, and barometric pressure. The loader has no special fire control equipment.

M1A1(HAP) (= heavy armor package) was produced for tanks destined to fight in Europe, still potentially the most sophisticated armor battleground. In the HAP certain parts of the hull, particularly at the front, are fabricated from a new type of armor, essentially depleted uranium (DU) encased in steel, which has a deinsity some 250 percent greater than normal steel and is intended to counter the latest kinetic energy penetrators. Depleted uranium has very low radioactivity, but results in an increase in the tank's overall weight.

The Marine Corps is developing the M1A1 Firepower Enhancement Program (FEP) which aims to increase the target acquisition and engagement ranges; it will include a second-generation thermal sight and a north finding/target locating capability.

The M1A1D is a program to digitize the M1A1 under the System Enhancement Program (SEP). This involves installing the digital command and control package, as well as replacing some of the remaining analog units, such as the Turret Network Box and Hull Network Box (HNB) with new digital units. When the SEP enters production, the Army will have a total of 627 M1A2s, all of which will eventually be converted to the SEP configuration as M1A2 SEP.

Although fielded in 1980, the M1 remained untested for over ten years until

Saddam Hussein's Iraq invaded Kuwait in August 1990. Doubters expressed concern that the Abrams would fall victim to the sand, long periods of continuous operation, and the lack of peacetime maintenance facilities. The first battle test for the M1 came in Operations Desert Shield/Desert Storm when it faced some 500 modern T-72 tanks, about 1,600 older T-62s, and about 700 1950s-vintage T-54s. U.S. forces fielded 1,848 MBTs during the campaign, of which the majority were M1A1, but some were the M1A1(HA) (= heavy armor) version. Prior to the land advance Allied air power destroyed some 50 percent of the Iraqi tanks, but as soon as the Abrams were unleashed they quickly dealt with the remainder in their sector, destroying large numbers of enemy while incurring only eighteen battle losses, of which nine were permanent and nine were repaired. Not one crewman was lost.

To summarize the latest (mid-2002) position, some 8,934 M1s are in service with the U.S. armed forces and approximately 10,000 world-wide, with the only new-build vehicles being produced in Egypt. The U.S. Army's fleet comprises: M1 – 2,674, all to be converted to M1A2; M1 Improved – 894; M1A1 – 4,796; M1A2 – 77 new-build completed, with M1s being upgraded.

Various improvement programs are under way. AIM XXI (Abrams Integrated Management System for 21st Century) is intended to refurbish M1A1 to "as new" condition. To overcome concern about high fuel consumption a diesel-engined version has been developed, but only for the export market. Other improvements are more detailed and include new tracks, suspensions, and electronics. What is certain is that the M1 series is going to be around in large numbers for many years to come.

Below: M1A/M1A2 performed remarkably well in Operation Desert Storm.

M60A3

Type: main battle tank.
Manufacturer: Chrysler.
Weight: combat 107,900lb (48,987kg).
Ground pressure: 12.37lb/in^2 (0.87kg/cm^2).
Dimensions: length (including main armament) 30.9ft (9.4m); length (hull) 22.8ft (7.0m); width 11.9ft (3.6m); height 10.8ft (3.3m); ground clearance 18in (460mm).
Powerplant: Continental AVDS-1790-2c, 12-cylinder, air-cooled, diesel engine; 750bhp at 2,400rpm.
Performance: road speed 30mph (48kmh); reverse speed 10mph (16kmh); range 300 miles (480km); vertical obstacle 49in (1.2m); trench 8.5ft (2.6m); fording depth 48in (1.2m); gradient 60 percent.
Armor: rolled steel.
Armament: 1 x M68 105mm rifled gun; one M240 7.62mm co-axial machine gun; one M85 0.5in (12.7mm) anti-aircraft machine gun.
Crew: four.

In the 1950s the standard tank of the U.S. Army was the M48 and in 1957 one of these M48s tank was fitted with a new engine for trials purposes, followed by a further three prototypes in 1958. Late in 1958 it was decided to arm the new tank with the British 105mm L7 series gun, which was then built in the United States under the designation M68. In 1959 the first production order for the new tank, now designated the M60 MBT, was placed with Chrysler, and the type entered production at the Detroit Tank Arsenal in late 1959, with the first production tanks being completed the following year. From late 1962, the M60 was replaced in production by the M60A1, which had a number of improvements, the most important being the redesigned hull and turret, which were now of all-cast construction

The driver is seated at the front of the hull with the other three crew members in the turret, commander and gunner on the right and the loader on the left. The Continental 12-cylinder, air-cooled diesel and the transmission are at the rear, the latter having one reverse and two forward ranges. The M60 has torsion-bar suspension and six road wheels, with the idler at the front and the drive sprocket at the rear; there are four track-return rollers.

The M68 105mm gun has an elevation of +20E and a depression of -10E, with a full 360E traverse; both elevation and traverse are powered. An M73 7.62mm machinegun is mounted co-axially with the main armament and there is a 12.7mm M85 machine-gun in the commander's cupola. The latter can be aimed and fired from within the turret, and has an elevation of +60deg and a depression of -15deg. Some 60 rounds of 105mm, 900 rounds of 12.7mm and 5,950 rounds of 7.62mm ammunition are carried. Infra-red driving lights are fitted as standard and infra-red/white light is mounted over the main armament. All M60s have an NBC system. The tank can also be fitted with a dozer blade on the front of the hull. The tank can ford to a depth of 4ft (1.2m) without preparation or 8ft (2.4m) with the aid of a kit. For deep fording operations a schnorkel can be fitted, allowing the M60 to ford to a depth of 13.5ft (4.1m).

A radical departure was made with the M60A2, developed in the mid-

Below: An M60 during training in desert terrain, ideal habitat for an MBT.

1960s, in which a standard M60 hull was mated to a new turret mounting the (then) new 152mm gun/launcher firing either a Shillelagh missile or various types of 152mm, which were fitted with combustible cartridge cases. This program suffered seemingly endless problems and only 526 M60A2s were built before production was terminated. Those tanks that had been deployed to Germany were withdrawn to the United States and some years later the troubled tank was withdrawn from service.

Meanwhile, plans were being made to improve the 105mm gun-armed version. A new fire control system, a laser rangefinder, and a computer substantially enhanced the probability of a first-round hit, later helped even more by the addition of a Tank Thermal Sight. Many of these M60A3s came from new production, but others were upgraded M60A1s. The M60 series was phased out of U.S. frontline service in 1997, although a number remain in the inventory with Reserve and Army National Guard units.

A very large number of M60s will remain in service with foreign armies for many years to come, the largest single current user being the Israeli Army, which has some 1,350 M60s, M60A1s, and M60A3s, which are being constantly upgraded. All have been given more powerful versions of the Teledyne Continental diesel engine, while the locally produced M68 105mm

rifled gun has been fitted with an Israeli-developed thermal sleeve. Israeli M60s have also been fitted with Blazer explosive reactive armor, which consists of specially tailored blocks bolted to the outside of the hull and turret, to give protection against chemical energy warheads. A newer add-on armor, called MAGACH-7, is now being fitted; this is more bulky and substantially changes the appearance of the tank, particularly of the turret. It gives increased protection against both CE and kinetic energy projectiles. A new fire control system called MATADOR is also being installed. There are twenty other known users of the tank.

The M60 served as the primary main battle tank of the U.S. Army and Marine Corps for two decades until replaced by the M1. It was criticized for its considerable height of 10.8ft (3.3m) and a perceived limitation in its cross-country capabilities, but over 15,000 were built by Chrysler and it has performed satisfactorily in all the combats it has participated in. Its last operational service under the U.S. flag was in Operation Desert Shield/Desert Storm when 1st Marine Expeditionary Force fielded 210 M60A1s which played a very active role in the advance into Kuwait City.

Below: Marine Corps M60 at Beirut International Airport in the early 1980s.

M2/M3 Bradley

Type: M2 – Infantry Fighting Vehicle (IFV); M3 – Cavalry Fighting Vehicle (CFV).
Manufacturer: United Defense.
Weight: 50,000lb (22,680kg).
Dimensions: length 21.3ft (6.5m); width 11.8ft (3.6m); height 9.8ft (3.0m).
Powerplant: Cummins VTA-903T, water-cooled, 4-stroke diesel; 506bhp.
Performance: road speed 41mph (66kmh); road range 300 miles (483km); water speed 4.5mph (7.2kmh).
Armor: welded aluminum/spaced laminate armor.
Armament: 1 x 25mm cannon (chain-gun); 1 x 7.62 mm coaxial machine gun; 1 x twin-tube TOW missile launcher.
Crew: M2 – 3 crew, 7 infantry; M2A2 – 3 crew, 6 infantry; M3 – 3 crew, 2 scouts.

Until mid-way through World War II the infantryman traveled on the battlefield, as he always had done, on foot, with longer journeys sometimes made by truck. However, this made him slow-moving compared to the ever-increasing number of tanks, while the truck provided no protection if it came under fire, and had a very limited cross-country capability. So, a new type of vehicle began to appear, known as the armored personnel carrier (APC), which was accurately described as a

"battle taxi" since it was essentially a wheeled or tracked box, which delivered the infantry to a spot from which they could deploy to fight. Such vehicles provided limited protection against shell splinters, and the infantry inside were often unable to see outside and certainly unable to use their weapons. It was then realized that the large numbers of APCs provided ideal weapons platforms, so they were fitted with machine guns for use either against other infantry or in the anti-aircraft role. The next step was to turn such vehicles into fully fledged combat vehicles in their own right, and the U.S. Army's M2 Bradley, known as an Infantry Fighting Vehicle is a very sophisticated vehicle and far removed from the "battle taxi" concept. When the M2 IFV was being developed, it was decided to combine it with the requirement for a new reconnaissance/scouting vehicle for the cavalry, which led to a common vehicle with minor internal differences for the cavalry vehicle. It is designated the M3. A total of 6,724 M2/M3s were produced for the U.S. Army between 1981 and 1994.

The role of the M2 IFV is to move infantry about the battlefield, to provide covering fire to dismounted troops, and to suppress enemy tanks, other fighting

Below: M2 Bradley Infantry Fighting Vehicle (IFV).

vehicles and soft-skinned transport. To achieve this the M2 carries three crew plus six fully equipped infantrymen. The M3 performs scouting missions, fo which it carries three crew plus two scouts.

The M2/M3 vehicle is constructed of welded aluminum armor, reinforced ir critical areas by spaced laminated armor plates, and is divided into three mair areas: driving compartment, turret, and infantry compartment. The vehicle is powered by a Cummins VTA-903T turbo-diesel with a Lockheed Martin HMPT-50C hydromechanical transmission. The reliability of this system has far exceeded initial expectations, with only three vehicles (out of 2,200 deployed) being disabled during Operation Desert Storm. The M2/M3 has excellent cross-country capability and is fully able to keep pace with the M1 Abrams MBT in all types of terrain. The driver is equipped with four periscopes, three facing forward and one to the left. The central periscope can be replaced by an image intensifier for night driving.

All Bradleys are amphibious, being propelled in the water by their tracks, with a maximum speed of 4.5mph (7.2kmh) in still water, but varying up or down according to the current. Early models had a skirt that was erected before entering the water, which took about 30 minutes. Later models are fitted with an inflatable pontoon, which takes about 15 minutes to inflate and is then continuously pressurized during operation.

Main armament is a Boeing (McDonnell Douglas) M242 25mm Bushmaster "chain gun" which has a single barrel with an integrated dual feed mechanism and remote feed selection. A wide range of ammunition is available, but the most likely combination is armor-piercing (AP) and high-explosive (HE); the gunner can change from one to another at the flick of a switch. The standard rate of fire is 200rpm, but this can be increased to 500rpm, if required, and range is some 2,200yd (2,000m) depending on the type of ammunition used. An M240C 7.62 mm machine gun is mounted coaxially to right of the Bushmaster.

Above: The two-man Stinger detachment has dismounted to launch a missile.

A twin-tube Raytheon BGM-71 TOW anti-tank missile launcher is mounted on the left side of the turret. A twin-wire command link is dispensed from the missile in flight. This enables the gunner to control the missile up to impact on the target. Maximum range is 4,155yd (3.8km). Unlike the chain gun, the TOW can be launched and controlled only while the vehicle is stationary. The TOW missile is very accurate and is capable of destroying any armored vehicle in existence. The gunner is provided with an integrated sight which includes a day/thermal sight (x4/x12 magnification) and the image in the gunner's sight can be transferred by optical relay to the commander's sight. The gunner also has periscopes for forward and side observation. The M2/M3 also carries two M257 smoke grenade dischargers, each with four smoke grenades, and can also generate a smoke screen by injecting fuel into the exhausts.

The M3 Cavalry Fighting Vehicle [CFV] is identical to the M2 IFV, except that instead of carrying six infantry in the rear compartment it carries a pair of scouts, for whom there are no external firing ports. It also carries additional radios and ammunition, including TOW Dragon or Javelin missiles.

The next production version was the M2A2/M3A2, which is fitted with additional appliqué steel armor, with provision for explosive reactive armor (ERA), if tactically necessary, to provide increased protection against HEAT (shaped charge) weapons.

The M2A3/M3A3 upgrade program is based on operational experience in the Gulf War; the first vehicles entered service in 2000 and full production started in May 2001, with 926 earlier model M2/M3s due to be upgraded. The M2A3/M3A3 is intended to improve battlefield command and control, and to have enhanced lethality. It will be employed in Combined Arms units alongside the M1A1D and M1A2 SEP tank (see M1 entry).

M113 family of vehicles

Type: armored personnel carrier (APC), plus many vairants.
Manufacturer: United Defense.
Weight: empty 23,880lb (10,832 kg); combat loaded 27,180lb (12,329kg maximum (with strap-on armor) 31,000lb (14,061kg); airdrop 22,128l (10,037kg).
Ground pressure: 8.63lb/in^2 psi (0.60kg/cm^2).
Dimensions: length 15.9ft (4.9m); width 8.8ft (2.7m); height 7.2ft (2.2m ground clearance 1.3ft (0.4m).
Powerplant: Detroit Diesel 6V53T, 5.2 liter; 275hp; 20.2 hp/ton.
Performance: road speed 41mph (66kmh); water speed 3.6mph (5.8kmh); roa range 300 miles (483km); maximum gradient 60 percent; vertical wall 24i (61cm); trench 66in (168cm).
Armor: aluminum.
Armament: 1 x 0.5in (12.7mm) machine gun.
Crew: two plus eleven troops.
Specifications for M113A3 with RISE package (see text).

There had been tracked armored personnel carriers (APC) before the M113, bu when this vehicle entered service in 1960 it brought about a revolution on th battlefield in general and on mobile military operations in particular. These nev vehicles carried a standard infantry squad of eleven men plus a vehicle crew c two, who were transported around the battlefield rapidly and in relative safety and who could exit through the large, bottom-hinged rear door quickly. I addition, the M113 was easy to drive, easy to maintain, and was made c aircraft-quality aluminum armor which meant that its weight was sufficientl low – 23,880lb (10,832 kg) empty – that it could be transported by the C-13(and, if necessary, air-dropped by parachute, and could swim without an lengthy preparation. As a result it was a "winner" from the start and is still i frontline service forty years later, with upgrades and new versions likely to kee

Below: M113, seen here in the Gulf War, will stay in service for many years.

Above: The basic M113, with pintle-mounted 0.5in (12.7mm) machine gun.

it in service for at loast another twenty years.

The majority of vehicles in service are the standard infantry carrying vehicles, but the M113 family of vehicles includes over forty major variants, many of which include minor sub-variants. There are two major designs on which all the others are based; one is the box-shaped, armored infantry carrier, the other the unarmored load carrier, with a cab and a flat, open platform at the rear. Among the major variants based on the armored chassis which have seen service with U.S. forces are: M58 Smoke Generator (Wolf); M106 107mm mortar carrier; M113 armored ambulance; M125 81mm mortar carrier; M577 command-post vehicle; M901 improved TOW missile carrier; M981 fire support team vehicle; M1059 smoke generator (Lynx); M1064 120mm mortar carrier; and M1068 Standard Integrated Command Post System (SICPS) carrier. Others, based on the unarmored chassis, include the M548 cargo carrier, and many no longer in service, such as the M667 Lance missile carrier and M730 Chaparral guided-missilecarrier.

The original model entered service in 1960 and was followed by the first major upgrade, M113A1, in 1964. This replaced the original gasoline engine with a diesel, thus greatly enhancing the safety of both vehicle and crew. All original M113s were backfitted to this standard. The next significan upgrade was the M113A2, which began to be fielded in 1979, and included suspension and cooling enhancements.

The current (2002) standard is the M113A3 RISE, to which all earlier M113s were converted bewtteen 1987 and 2001, and of which some 4,000 are in service. The RISE (Reliability Improvements for Selected Equipment) package includes an upgraded powertrain, consisting of a new 275bhp (turbocharged engine and new transmission, new power brakes and conventional steering controls (as opposed to levers), external fuel tanks, and 200amp alternator with four batteries. Additional A3 improvements include incorporation of spall liners and provisions for mounting external armor. One indication of the result is that whereas M113A2 accelerated from 0-35mph (56kmh) in 69 seconds, the M113A3 can do so in 27 seconds. The effectiveness of this upgrade was shown during Operation Desert Storm, when the M113A3 was able to keep pace with M1 MBTs, whereas the earlier M113A2 proved underpowered.

As with almost every other item of military equipment, the M113 has shown a slow but steady increase in weight: M113 – 23,520lb (10,670kg); M113A1 – 24,594lb (11,160kg); M113A2 – 24,728lb (11,217kg); and M113A3 – 27,000lb (12,250kg). However, it is still well within the capabilities of the C-130 for air transportation, while the increase in engine power and more efficient transmissions ensure that its agility has actually increased.

Despite having beeni in service for forty years the M113 still provides an excellent basis for future developments in the lightweight tracked vehicle field and numerous concepts are known to be under consideration. Many of these future projects are based on a hull which has been lengthened by 2.8ft (0.9m) and equipped with an additional road wheel, to give six on each side, which results in a considerable increase in carrying capacity. The base vehicle of this new lengthened range is the M113A3-Plus Mobile Tactical Vehicle Light (MTVL), developed with private-industry funding from United Defense. One potential application is the M113-Plus Engineer Support Vehcilce (ESV) which is intended to enable the engineer squad carry out offensive and defensive obstacle/counter-obstacle operations, and can also carry the Volcano mine dispenser, the Pathfinder marking system, and tow various engineer trailers.

Above: M113 has carried many weapons; this is a 20mm cannon.

Another project for conversion from surplus assets is the M113 Hazardous Materials Recovery Vehicle (HAZMAT) which would utilize a stretched hull, but with the addition of a light dozer blade and a hydraulic manipulator arm. Yet another potential application of the lengthened chassis is the Infantry Fighting Vehicle Light (IFVL), which has a one-man stabilized turret mounting a stabilized 25mm chaingun and coaxial 7.62mm machine gun. The vehicle is powered by a 400hp 6V53TIA engine driving cross-drive transmission, while exterior fittings enable various types and combinations of of appliqué armor to be fitted, depending on the threat to be countered. The vehicle carries a crew of two or three and a squad of up to ten infantrymen. As with all M113 variants, it is roll-on/roll-off-transportable on a C-130.

A more definite plan is that many of the vehicles in the M113A3 fleet will be fitted with high-speed digital networks and data transfer systems as part of the Army's Modernization Plan. Current plans require these systems to be integrated into the M113A3 fleet by 2006.

Left: M901 Improved TOW vehicle with raised launcher.

AAVP7A1 (formerly LVTP-7A1)

Type: fully tracked amphibious vehicle.
Manufacturer: FMC Corporation, Ordnance Division.
Weight: empty 38,450lb (17,477kg); loaded 50,350lb (22,866kg).
Dimensions: length 26.0ft (7.9m); width 10.8ft (3.3m); height 10.3ft (3.1m); ground clearance 16in (41cm); draft (afloat) 5.7ft (1.7m).
Powerplant: Cummins VT-700 turbo-supercharged diesel; 525bhp; drives tracks on land, waterjets in water.
Performance: road – maximum speed 40mph (64kmh), range 300 miles at 25mph (483km at 40kmh); water – maximum speed 8.4mph (14kmh), range 55 miles at 8mph (89km at 13kmh); power:weight ratio 17hp/ton.
Armor: hull sides 1.2-1.8in (30-45mm); hull roof 1.2in (30mm).
Armament: 1 x 0.5in (12.7mm) machine gun; 1 x 40mm grenade launcher Mk 19.
Crew: three crew plus twenty-one Marines.

This vehicle design started as the experimental LVTPX-12, fifteen of which were tested by the Marine Corps in 1967-70 as potential replacements for the LVTP-5 troop carrier which had been in service since the early 1950s. The trials led to some modifications, following which the design was standardized as the LVTP-7 – but known always as the "Amtrack" to the Marine Corps – with 965 being produced between 1970 and 1974, followed by more in several smaller prduction batches. Over the years more equipment was added and there was a major modernization in the 1980s, but increasing age and yet more equipment resulted in the vehicle not only losing some of its ground clearance and land

Above: AAVP7A1 brings Marines ashore during a NATO exercise in Norway.

mobility, but also becoming an increasing maintenance burden. This led to a major SLEP (Service Life Extension Program) starting in the late 1990s during which 680 vehicles were completely rebuilt and emerged under the designation

LVTP-7A1, although this has since been changed to AAVP-7 (AAV = Assault Amphibious Vehicle). In the upgrade a new engine was fitted, increasing power output from 400 to 525shp, and the suspension was completely replaced using a modified version of that used on the M2 Bradley, increasing ground clearance from 12 to 16in (31 to 41cm). Power-to-weight ratio was also increased from 13hp/ton to 17hp/ton. The rebuild cost just over $400,000 per vehicle, much less than the $2,000,000 cost of a new vehicle, while much improved maintenance will also lower the ownership costs. It is now anticipated that this vehicle will soldier on until replaced by the Advanced Amphibious Vehicle (AAV) in 2014.

The AAVP7A1 is the only truly amphibious vehicle in the U.S. inventory, being able to launch from an amphibious ship well offshore, carry up to twenty-one combat-loaded Marines to the shore, beach through heavy surf, and then assault well inland, acting as an infantry fighting vehicle and providing supporting fire from its on-board weapons. There is a crew of three (commander, gunner, driver) and the twenty-one Marines can be carried in the passenger compartment. There are hatches in the roof which enable the Marines to see out and, if appropriate, to fire their weapons, but they normally exit through the bottom-hinged rear door.

The main armament was originally intended to

Left: AAVP7A1 has been the backbone of USMC amphibious operations for 30 years.

be a turret-mounted 20mm cannon but this was not pursued and production vehicles are fitted with a 360deg turret mounting a 0.50in (12.7mm) M2HB machine gun and a coaxial 40mm grenade launcher. A three-rail mine-clearance rocket launcher can be fitted to any of the personnel carriers.

There are two other variants, the most numerous being the AAVC7 (formerly LVTC-7) Command and Control vehicle, which is fitted with radios, cryptographic equipment, map tables, and other equipment to serve as an amphibious command post. It normally carries twelve, consisting of a vehicle crew of three, plus the unit commander, three staff officers/NCOs, and five radio operators. Loaded weight is 44,111lb (20.050kg) and armament is one 7.62mm machine gun. A total of 108 were built, of which 77 are being upgraded to the AAVC7A1 standard.

The second major variant is the AAVR7 (formerly LVTP-7) amphibious

recovery vehicle, which has a vehicle crew of three plus two mechanics. Specialist recovery equipment comprises a winch with a 30,000lb (13,636kg) pull, and a telescopic boom-type crane with a 6,000lb (2,730kg) capacity A total of 64 were built and all are being upgraded to -A1 standard. A third variant, a proposed engineer vehicle, was tested but was not put into production.

There are two AAV battalions in the Marine Corps, both in the continental United States, with two platoons in Hawaii and a separate company on Okinawa. An AAV platoon operates ten AAVs, there are three platoons in a company and four companies in a battalion. An AAV platoon can lift a an infantry company, an AAV company can lift an infantry battalion, and an AAV battalion can lift an infantry regiment.

Below: Marines charge up the beach; note this AAVP7A1's add-on armor.

M998 Truck – HMMWV

Type: multi-purpose truck.
Manufacturer: AM General.
Weight: 5,200lb (2,359kg).
Dimensions: length 15.0ft (4.6m); width 7.1ft (2.2m); height 6.0ft (1.8m) reducible to 4.5ft (1.4m).
Powerplant: V8, 6.2-litre displacement, fuel injected diesel, liquid-cooled, compression ignition; 150hp at 3,600rpm.
Performance: maximum road speed 55mph (89kmh); road range 350 miles (220km); fording, without preparation 2.5ft (76.2cm), with deep water fording kit 5ft (1.5m); maximum grade 60 percent; side slope 40deg??????.
Armor: none.
Armament: according to role.
Crew: two

The High Mobility Multi-purpose Wheeled Vehicle (HMMWV/"Humm-Vee") is a lightweight, four-wheel drive, air-transportable, air-droppable family of vehicles which include versions for utility/cargo, carrying shelters, weapons carriers, ambulance, TOW launcher carrier, and scout-reconnaissance, to name but a few. There are also many versions purpose-built to meet the needs of Special Operations Forces (SOF). Payload varies according to the body style, ranging from 1,920lb (871kg) on the M997 four-litter ambulance to 5,300lb (2,404kg) on the Expanded Capacity variant, but is generally in the 1.25-ton range.

The HMMWV was produced as the replacement for the M151 series of Jeeps. It is powered by a high-performance diesel engine, and has automatic transmission and four wheel drive. It is produced in several configurations to support weapons systems; command and control systems; field ambulances; and ammunition, troop and general cargo transport. All HMMWVs are designed for use over all types of roads, in all weather conditions, and are extremely effective in the most difficult terrain. The HMMWV's high power-to-weight ratio, four wheeled drive and high ground clearance combine to give it outstanding cross-country mobility.

The M988 Cargo/Troop Carrier Without Winch is the basic item from which all other versions are derived. In many cases there are two vehicles for the same role, differing only because one has a self-recovery winch and the other does not. For example, the "M1038 cargo/troop carrier with winch" is identical to the M988 mentioned above except for the addition of the winch. Both vehicles are used to transport equipment, materials, and/or personnel. In the cargo carrier configuration, the vehicle is capable of transporting a payload, including the two-man crew, of 2,500lb (1,134kg). A troop seat kit is required to convert it into a troop carrier in which configuration it can carry ten people, normally two crew and eight passengers. Alternatively, the vehicle can be configured for a four-man crew. The vehicle can, when fully loaded, climb 60 percent slopes, traverse a side slope of up to 40 percent, and ford hard-bottom water crossings up to 30in (76cm) deep without a water fording kit and up to 60in (152cm) deep with the kit. The M1038's winch is capable of up to 6,000lb (2,720kg) 1:1 ratio line pull capacity and can support payloads from 2,500-4,400lb (1,134-1,996kg) depending on the model. In both cases, the M998A1 and M1038A1 are the models with the latest modifications.

The M1097 is a higher-payload capacity version, capable of transporting a payload (including crew) of 4,575lb (2,075kg) in the cargo role, or a two-man crew and eight passengers in the troop-carrier role. It has a troop seat kit for personnel transport operations, a 200amp umbilical power cable to power shelter equipment, and stowage racks for ammunition and equipment. To accommodate the higher payload capacity, the vehicle has a reinforced frame, crossmembers, lifting shackles, heavy duty rear springs, shock absorbers, reinforced control arms, heavy duty tires, and a transfer case and differential with modified gear ratio.

Below: Marine Corps HMMWV, armed with TOW anti-tank missile launcher.

LAV

Type: light armored vehicle.
Manufacturer: General Motors of Canada.
Weight: empty 24,100lb (10,941kg); combat 28,200lb (12,803kg).
Dimensions: length 21.0ft (6.4m); width (turret facing forward) 8.2ft (2.5m);
height 8.83ft (2.7m).
Powerplant: Detroit Diesel 6V53T.
Performance: road speed maximum 62mph (99kmh); road range 410 miles
655km); maximum trench 81in (206cm).; maximum grade 60 percent
maximum side slope 30 percent; swim speed 6mph (9.6kmh).
Armor: rolled steel.
Armament: 1 x M242 25mm chain gun; 1 x coaxial M240E1 7.62mm machine
gun; 1 x pintle-mounted M240E1 7.62mm machine gun.
Crew: three (driver, gunner, commander) and six troops.
Specifications for LAV-25.

The Light Armored Vehicle originated as a 1981-82 Army-led requiremen
for an amphibious, light, but highly mobile fighting vehicle to be procured fo
the Army and Marine Corps for service in what was then termed the Rapid
Deployment Force (RDF). Four vehicles were tested and the winner was a
development of the Swiss-designed MOWAG Piranha, which was already
in production in Canada for the Canadian armed forces. The Army's origina
requirement was for 2,315 vehicles, but this was reduced first to 680 and
then to zero, following which this became a Marine Corps project. The
Marine Corps procured 401 vehicles of six types, the majority being the
fighting vehicle, the LAV-25, which is armed with a 25mm chain-gun, bu

there are five other versions for specialized tasks.

The LAV-25 is an eight-wheeled, all-terrain, all-weather, fully amphibious vehicle with a full night operating capability. It is powered by a Detroit Diesel 275hp, V-six engine, which drives the two rear axles permanently but can be selected to drive the front two as well to give full eight-wheel drive. In the water the engine drives two propellers, giving a maximum of 6mph (9.6kmh), depending on the current. Steering is by means of four rudders. It can be transported in C-5, C-141, and C-130 fixed-wing aircraft and in CH-53E Super Stallion helicopters. It is fitted with a 15,000lb (6,800kg) front-mounted winch for self-recovery.

Main armament of the LAV-25 is a 25mm Bushmaster chaingun for which 420 rounds are carried. There are also two M240 7.62mm machine guns, one mounted coaxially with the main gun and one which can be mounted on a pintle at the commander's station in the turret, when required.

There are also five specialist types. LAV-C2 (command-and-control) is a command vehicle fitted with extra radios and staff facilities; it has a vehicle crew of two (driver, vehicle commander) plus the battalion commander, two staff officers and two radio operators. The LAV-AT (anti-tank) carries a TOW launcher and sixteen missiles, while the LAV-M (mortar) carries an M252 81mm mortar with 90 rounds. The LAV-R is a recovery vehicle fitted with a boom crane (9,000lb/4,086kg capacity) and a 30,000lb (13,620kg) winch. Finally, there is the general-purpose load carrier, LAV-L (L = logistics) which has a carrying capacity of 5,240lb (2,378.96kg).

Below: In a reversal of roles an LVA-L (logistics) tows an LAV-R (recovery).

Desert Patrol/Light Strike Vehicle

Type: desert patrol vehicle.
Manufacturer: Chenowyth Racing.
Weight: gross 2,700lb (1,225kg).
Dimensions: length 13.4ft (4.1m); height 6.6ft (2.0m); width 7.9ft (2.4m).
Powerplant: VolksWagen gasoline engine; 200hp.
Performance: maximum road speed <60mph (97kmh); acceleration 0-30mph (0 49kmh) in 4sec; range <200 miles (322km); maximum slope 75 percent; maximum side slope 50 percent; ground clearance 16in (41cm); payload 1,500lb (680kg).
Armor: none.
Armament: see text.
Crew: three.

The Desert Patrol Vehicle (DPV), a joint program between the Marine Corps and Special Operations Command (USSOCOM), is a modified version of the off road, three-man, 2 x 4 racing vehicle designed and built by Chenowyth Racing of El Cajon, California. The DPV was designed to provide greater mobility than that of the HMMWV and to operate anywhere a four-wheel drive vehicle can but with greater speed and increased maneuverability. The DPV is air transportable in most fixed-wing transport aircraft – the C-130, for example, can carry three – as well as the MV-22 Osprey, CH-53 Super Stallion, and the MH-47D Chinook.

Advanced Amphibian Assault Vehicle (AAAV)

Type: amphibious assault vehicle.
Manufacturer: General Dynamics.
Weight: empty 62,880lb (28,522kg); combat equipped 74,500lb (33,793kg).
Ground pressure: soft soil 8.9psi; hard surface 24.4 psi.
Dimensions: length (land) 29.5ft (9.0m); height 9.2ft (2.8m); width 14.8ft (4.5m).
Powerplant: MTU MT883 Ra-523, 4-stroke, 12-cylinder, 90deg-vee, water cooled, 850bhp at 2600rpm; two water jets in water-borne mode.
Performance: maximum speed, land 45mph (72kmh), water 25kt; cruising speed, land 20-30mph (32-48kmh), water 20kt; cruising range, land at 25mph (40kmh) 300 miles (480km), water at 20kt, 65nm; power:weight ratio (combat equipped) 22.8hp/ton; trench 8ft (2.44m); vertical wall 3ft (0.91m); maximum forward grade (combat equipped) 60 percent; maximum side slope (combat equipped) 40 percent; ground clearance (combat equipped) 16in (40.6cm).
Armor: protection against 14.5mm AP at 985ft (300m); 155/152mm fragment at 50ft (15m).
Armament: 1 x Bushmaster II 30mm cannon; 1 x coaxial M240 7.62 mm machine gun.
Crew: three (commander, gunner, driver) plus eighteen combat-equipped Marines (285lb person and gear) or 5,000lb (2,270kg) cargo.

Several attempts have been made to develop a replacement for the AAVP7A amphibious tracked carrier, which has been in service since the 1970s, but unt

Right: The DPV; one of the most exciting vehicles in today's U.S. forces.

This high-performance vehicle can perform numerous combat roles including: special operations delivery vehicle, rescue of downed aircrew, command and control vehicle, weapons platform, rear area combat operation vehicle, reconnaissance vehicle, forward observation/liaising team, military police vehicle, artillery forward observer vehicle, and many more.

The vehicle has three weapons stations, which can accommodate any three from: Mk 19 40mm automatic grenade launcher, 0.50in (12.7mm) M2HB machine gun, M60 7.62 machine gun, AT-4 anti-tank missile, low-recoil 30mm cannon, and TOW missile launcher. Hand-held missile launchers such as Dragon and Stinger can also be carried.

The vehicle is currently operated only by SEAL Team Three, which covers the Middle East theater of operations, and normally deploys them in pairs for mutual support. It will in future be operated more widely, the new vehicles being due to enter service in 2004-05; USSOCOM plans to procure forty-four, although this may be increased to fifty.

Right: With its planing board raised and water jets at full power, the AAAV as a water speed of 25 knots.

now they have failed for one reason or another. It is now firm, however, that the new amphibious carrier will be the Advanced Amphibian Assault Vehicle (AAAV) with deliveries starting in about 2010. This project has been declared the Marine Corps' top priority and plans are already in place to procure 1,013 AAAVs at a program cost of $7.6 billion.

The vehicle is required to meet a very ambitious set of requirements, combining high waterborne speed, with the ability to carry eighteen fully equipped Marines ashore from a ship "over-the-horizon" and then once on land to be able to keep pace with the M1 Abrams MBT. In other words, combining everything the M2 Bradley does on land with that of a high-speed motor-boat at sea, plus the ability to come ashore through surf, and all this while carrying twice the number of troops. These criteria are challenging, but carefully thought out. The high speed, for example, is required to minimize the time the AAV spends on the approach to land, when it is at its most vulnerable, while the amphibious shipping is kept out of sight to reduce the danger posed by shore-based enemy aircraft, missiles, and mines.

Land Warfare – Indirect Fire Weapons

The need for indirect firepower was demonstrated yet again during Operation Desert Storm when the many in-theater gun and missile systems played a crucial role in the defeat of the invading Iraqi forces. As a result of that war and many subsequent campaigns there are, today, many exciting developments on the way in artillery, both in upgrading existing equipments and in developing entirely new systems. Most of these developments are in the sphere of conventional maneuver warfare against opponents, some of whom may have very sophisticated land forces, and cover self-propelled systems, mostly tracked.

The Multiple-Launch Rocket System (MLRS), one of the most successful of all current artillery systems, is being constantly upgraded, as is the Army Tactical Missile System (ATACMS) which uses the same launcher. In order to get a lighter version of MLRS into a new conflict area as soon as possible, the High-Mobility Artillery Rocket System (HIMARS) mounts fewer launchers on a on a five-ton truck chassis and is air-transportable in a C-130 aircraft. The well-proven M109 155mm self-propelled howitzer is now being fielded in its M109A6 Paladin version, but any one design can only cope with so many upgrades and there is little more potential remaining in the M109 design. Thus, it will be replaced by the totally new Crusader 155mm system, which comprises a tracked self-propelled howitzer and its resupply vehicles, which may be either tracked or wheeled. The entire system will be fully automated and computerized; it is designed for use on the digital battlefield and will offer substantial improvements in lethality, range, and mobility.

One of the areas in which the Army is carrying out major modernization is in the procurement of weapons to make lighter forces more lethal. An example of such systems is the Lightweight 155mm Howitzer (LW155), a new towed cannon system designed to meet the operational requirements of both the Army and Marine Corps, with current plans calling for procurement of 686. This new weapon will be substantially lighter than the M198 howitzer it replaces and will greatly enhance ship-to-shore mobility, while increasing the survivability and responsiveness of artillery support for ground operations. The howitzer will incorporate an Army-developed digital fire control system with a self-locating capability, further enhancing operational effectiveness. The LW155 is currently in engineering and manufacturing development.

A "legacy" system which has only a few more years in service is the M55 chemical rocket; several hundred thousand are in the stockpile, but all will be destroyed in carefully controlled conditions after December 2004.

These rockets and 155mm gun systems tend to steal the limelight, but it must not be forgotten that there are lighter weapons in use. The M119 105mm is a lightweight weapon which is transportable as an underslung load, and is specifically intended to provide firepower for light forces in regional conflicts. Finally, there are the mortars, which despite their simplicity and lack of sophistication are weapons that are vital to every infantry battalion commander's battle plans.

Right: Indirect fire, as represented by this M198 155mm howitzer, plays a major role in modern land warfare.

Crusader 155mm Artillery System

Type: self-propelled howitzer/logistic resupply system.
Manufacturer: Team Crusader (United Defense).
Weight: empty 79,600lb (36,106kg); combat maximum 100,000lb (45,360kg).
Dimensions: length overall 42.3ft (12.9m); length hull 24.7ft (7.5m);width hull 11.5ft (3.5m).
Powerplant: Honeywell LV100-5 gas-turbine.
Performance: (vehicle) road speed 42mph (67kmhr); cross-country speed 30mph (48kmh); road range 251 miles (404km); maximum gradient 60 percent; maximum side slope 40 percent; vertical obstacle 2.7ft (0.8m); trench 8.1ft (2.5m).
Armament: XM2001 155mm/56 caliber howitzer, 48 projectiles/208 charges; 1 x 0.5in (12.7mm) M2HB machine gun.
Performance: (gun) maximum range 43,700yd (39,960m); minimum range 5,470yd (5,000m); maximum 10-12 rounds for 3-5 minutes; muzzle velocity 3,143ft/s (958m/s); elevation +75/-3; traverse ±20.
Crew: three.
Specifications for XM2001 howitzer; see text for resupply vehicle.

The Crusader must be considered as an integrated system comprising the self-propelled howitzer (SPH) and its resupply vehicle; one cannot be considered in isolation from the other. The artillery element is the XM2001 tracked howitzer, but a decision on which resupply vehicle to adopt has yet to be made, the candidates being the tracked XM2002 Resupply Vehicle (RSV) and the wheeled Resupply Module (RSM). The whole system is currently in full development to replace the M109A6 Paladin, and under present plans the first production vehicles are due in 2006, with the system fully operational by 2008. Early plans called for 800 systems, but this has since been reduced to the current target of 480. By the time the system is in service, the program will have lasted fourteen years and cost some US$11 billion, which indicates that each two-vehicle system will cost in the region of US$23 million.

One reason for the length of the program is the number of changes that have taken place. An early requirement was that the howitzer would use liquid propellant

Below: Crusader system's firing element – XM2001 155mm tracked howitzer.

Above: Interior of the XM2001 howitzer; only three crew are required.

to fire the projectiles, but after two years' work it was clear that such a system would be technically risky and very expensive, and the requirement was dropped. An even more important change took place in 2000, when the Army reduced the weight limit for the XM2001 from 61 tons to 41 tons, requiring a major redesign.

The XM2001 155mm SPH has a totally automated ammunition handling and firing system, enabling the 48 on-board rounds to be fired at rates of up to 10 rounds per minute to ranges in excess of 43,750yd (40km), with the first round of a mission being fired in under 30 seconds. A novel feature is that the digital fire control system can calculate separate firing solutions for each of eight projectiles so that they all hit the target simultaneously.

The vehicle has three main compartments: a three-man cockpit; the fully automated ammunition handling and firing system; and the engine compartment. The howitzer consists of the weapon, the mount, and a laser ignition system. Until now 155mm tubes have always been air-cooled, but the Crusader tube has Integral Midwall Cooling (IMC) which enables the gun to fire at a high rate for a protracted period. The tube and chamber are both chrome-plated to ensure long life. Within the vehicle the transfer of projectiles and charges from their respective magazines to the gun are totally automated and require no human intervention whatsoever. The howitzer vehicle carries 48 rounds and fires up to 10 to 12 rounds per minute. The loader and barrel can handle any 155mm shell and charge in service with the U.S. Army, including high-explosive, white phosphorus, and smoke, DPICM, illumination and SADARM rounds.

The Honeywell LV100-5 gas turbine engine for the Crusader will be the same model as that used in the M1A2/A3 Abrams MBT, as part of the Abrams/Crusader Common Engine Program. The LV100-5 is lighter and smaller than the existing Abrams engine with better acceleration, quieter running, and no visible exhaust. The engine and hydropneumatic suspension give a road speed of up to 42mph (67kmh) and a cross-country speed (depending upon the terrain) of 30mph (48kmh). The sophisticated driving system features drive-by-wire and positional navigation, while the transmission incorporates automatic scheduling of engine speed and transmission ratio for maximum fuel economy.

The SPH will be supplied by a dedicated logistic vehicle, although the choice between the tracked XM2002 Resupply Vehicle (RSV) and the Resupply Module (RSM) mounted on a ten-wheeled truck has yet to be made. The logistic cycle will start at the resupply point where the RSV/RSM will be manually replenished with 100 rounds of ammunition, 100 charges, and diesel fuel, an operation that takes a maximum of 65 minutes. The RSV/RSM then drive to the first howitzer's position where it transfers 48 rounds of ammunition and 48 charges and fuel, but in this case the process is fully automated and takes a maximum of 10 minutes. Once the resupply vehicle reaches the howitzer, it parks in the designated position and extends the 6.6ft (2m) long resupply boom to make the connection, which is designed to accommodate up to 10deg of misalignment, to make allowances for unevenness of the ground. The fuzed projectiles and the charges are transferred alternately to the howitzer to be loaded into their respective magazines, so that, should the resupply operation be interrupted (for example, by hostile action) and the two vehicles are forced to separate, the SPH will have received a balanced load and thus be able to continue fighting. While the transfer is taking place a data link between the two vehicles will enable the RSV/RSM to transfer both logistic data concerning the ammunition and tactical data which it may have received at the resupply point. No member of either crew needs to leave his vehicle while this is taking place, thus maintaining NBC integrity. Once the transfer has been completed the RSV/RSM can then move on to a second howitzer and repeat the process before returning to the resupply point. The RSV is a fully tracked vehicle, with maximum mechanical and component commonality with the SPH; fully loaded, it weighs some 40 tons.

The wheeled version of the logistic support vehicle consists of the fully enclosed XM2003 automated resupply module carried on an M1075 ten-wheeled truck, which together weigh roughly 34 tons. The resupply operation at the SPH

ocation is essentially the same as that of the tracked RSV, using a portable control panel which is operated from within the cab of the M1075 truck, thus ensuring that the crew do not have to leave the cab. With a road speed of 55mph (88kmh) and a cross-country speed (depending on terrain) of 40mph (64kmh) the RSM will considerably speed up the logistic cycle. The fully loaded RSM, plus its prime mover, weigh 34 tons.

There are criticisms of the Crusader system which may force changes before it is fielded later in this decade, the most general being that the program is extremely expensive and that it does not seem to accord with the Army's far-term vision of a lighter, more mobile force. Secondly, despite the weight reduction of the XM2001 to a maximum 41 tons, weight remains a major problem for the Crusader, not least when it is considered that the howitzer and its fully loaded resupply vehicle have a combined weight of some 81 tons. In addition, because the transfer of ammunition from the RSV/RSM and the loading of the gun within the XM2001 are all fully automated, the rate of fire no longer depends upon the physical abilities and organization of the crew. The gun is capable of delivering a devastating volume of fire: a battery of six Crusaders can deliver 15 tons of ammunition in less than 5 minutes. If, however, there is a failure in the automatic loading system there is no manual stand-by system, and, in any case, a three-man crew could not continue to serve and fire a 155mm weapon for very long. A further problem is that the very high rate of fire will place a very high load on the logistic system to maintain the supply of ammunition to the guns.

Below: Crusader comprises weapon (center) and ammunition vehicles.

MLRS/HIMARS

M270 Launch Vehicle
Type: carrier/launcher for MLRS system.
Manufacturer: Lockheed Martin Vought.
Weight: 61,600lb (28.,000kg).
Dimensions: length 22.58ft (7.0m) ; width 9.67ft (3.0m); height 8.5ft (2.6m).
Powerplant: Cummins, VTA-903T, Vee-8; turbo-charged; 506bhp at 2.600rpm
Performance: maximum speed 40mph (64kmh); range 302 miles (483km
gradient 60 percent; step 3.3ft (1m); fording depth (without preparation) 43i
(1.1m).
Armor: none.
Armament: none.
Crew: three (driver, gunner, section chief).

MLRS M26 basic tactical rocket
Type: tactical rocket for use with MLRS.
Manufacturer: Lockheed Martin Vought.
Weight: 600lb (272kg).
Dimensions: length 13ft (4.0m); diameter 8.9in (227mm).
Motor: Atlantic Research solid-fuel rocket motor.
Performance: speed <Mach 1.0; range <18.6 miles (30km).
Warhead: 644 x M42 bomblets.

The Multiple Launch Rocket System (MLRS) entered service in 1983 and since
then has been issued to all active force divisions of the U.S. Army and has also
been sold widely abroad. The system is designed to complement cannon
artillery, its primary mission being to suppress, neutralize or destroy hostile fire
support, mechanized units, armored formations, and air defense targets
Without leaving their cab, the crew can launch 12 rockets (2 pods) within one
minute, which will devastate an area target covering some 550 x 550yd (500 x
500m) at a maximum range of 49,200yd (45,000m). MLRS is designed to ge

Below: MLRS gunner at his weapon control computer – there is a 3-man crew

Above: MLRS showed its devastating firepower during the Gulf War.

nto and out of action and to reload quickly, enabling it to attack time-urgent targets and also to avoid enemy counter-battery fire. Significant numbers of MLRS launchers were fielded by both the U.S. and British Armies in Operation Desert Storm and performed very well. Numerous improvements programs are under way to enhance its already formidable capabilities, including the enhanced range rocket, the improved fire control system, and the improved launcher mechanical systems.

Rockets for the MLRS system are assembled, checked, and then packaged n dual-purpose launch-storage tubes, following which six tubes are loaded into a Launch Pod/Container (LP/C). This LP/C is then used to transport the rounds to the depots, store them for up to fifteen years and finally to transfer them to the frontline where they are loaded into the launch vehicle and fired. Thus, there is no further assembly or inspection following departure from the factory.

The MLRS M26 basic tactical rocket consists of three elements. At the front end is the warhead, which contains 644 M77 dual-purpose submunitions, each of which detonates on impact; they can either penetrate up to 4in (102mm) armor or produce an anti-personnel effect with a lethal radius of some 13ft (4m). The propulsion section houses an Atlantic Research rocket motor, which is ignited by electrical command from the FCS and as the missile travels up the tube it is given initial spin by offset, internally mounted launch rails. When the rocket leaves the tube spring-loaded folded fins snap out and lock in place, and the maintain the spin to stabilize the rocket in flight.

The recently fielded Extended Range Rocket (ER-MLRS) has identical dimensions to the basic M26 rocket, except that the motor is lengthened to extend the burn time and thus the range. This is compensated for by a smaller warhead section with fewer submunitions. There are some other minor improvements, including a modified center core burster, a new warhead fuze, and a self-destruct fuze for the M85 Dual-Purpose Improved Conventional Munition (DPICM) submunitions, which replaces the M77. There is also a low level wind measuring device on the launcher.

The Armored Vehicle Mounted Rocket Launcher (M270) is a stretched version of the M2 Bradley IFV, which mounts a highly automated twin-arm loading and aiming system, together with the FCS which integrates the vehicle and rocket-launching operations. The rockets can be fired individually or in ripples of two to twelve, with accuracy being maintained in all firing modes because the computer re-aims the launcher between rounds. The cab gives the crew NBC protection, and the vehicle can enter a site, prepare for launch, carry out the launch, and then depart without the crew having to leave the cab. This launch platform is also used to carry and launch two Army Tactical Missile System (ATACMS) missiles. The M270 launcher can be transported by C-5 and C-17 aircraft, and on a limited basis by the C-141 after some reconfiguration; cannot be transported by the C-130.

One of the major problems with a high-rate-of-fire rocket system is that of resupply, and MLRS is no exception. Each battery of nine launchers has its own ammunition platoon of eighteen resupply vehicles and trailers, and there are more further back in the logistic system.

The upgraded MLRS M270A1 was fielded in September 2000 and includes the Improved Fire Control System (IFCS), the Improved Mechanical Launch System (IMLS), and the extended range rocket (ER-MLRS). The IFCS is designed to avoid the problem of electronic obsolescence and also includes measures to accommodate new missiles. The ILES speeds up response times by reducing aiming time from 93 seconds to 16 seconds, and cutting reload time by some 38 percent and reload times by 50 percent. The improvements combine to reduce the time in the launch site by 60 percent and to increase

ystem reliability by 45 percent. Operating and support costs are also reduced.

The High Mobility Artillery Rocket System (HIMARS) launches the same ange of munitions as MLRS, but on a wheeled chassis. Lockheed Martin was iven a development contract in 1996 and low-rate initial production will start in 003, with the system attaining in-service status in 2005. The standard MLRS ystem comprises two six-pack rocket pods on a tracked carrier/launcher, but HIMARS carries a single six-pack on an Army Family of Medium Tactical 'ehicles (FMTV), 6x6, all-wheel drive, 5-ton truck. The all-up weight for the HIMARS vehicle is some 24,000lb (10,886kg) compared to more than 44,000lb 19,958kg) for the MLRS M270 launcher. Unlike the M270 MLRS launcher, HIMARS can be carried by the C-130 aircraft, thus enabling the system to be leployed into areas inaccessible to the larger C-141 and C-5 aircraft. The HIMARS vehicle is 23ft (7m) long, 7.9ft (2.4m) wide and 10.5ft (3.2m) high, and las a road speed of 53mph (85kmh) and range of 300 miles (480km).

HIMARS has the same self-loading and autonomous operation features as he MLRS and will incorporate as standard the current upgrades being added to MLRS, such as the Improved Fire Control System (IFCS) and Improved Launcher Mechanical System (ILMS). It is operated by a three-person crew driver, gunner, section chief), although the computerized fire control system FCS) enables it to be operated by two, or in an emergency by a single soldier. The FCS includes video, keyboard control, a gigabyte of program storage, and Global Positioning System, and enables missions to be fired in either automatic or manual mode. HIMARS is capable of launching the complete range of MLRS munitions, and can also carry and launch one Army Tactical Missile System ATACMS) missile instead of the six MLRS rockets.

The MLRS Smart Tactical Rocket (MSTAR) was to have been the next step n the evolution of the MLRS Rocket, using an on-board guidance system to detect and engage stationary or moving targets. However, the project was "zero-funded" in the Army's FY2001 budget and the project is now dormant.

Below: Each MLRS M26 tactical rocket carries 644 M42 bomblets.

MGM-140 Army Tactical Missile System (ATACMS)

Type: corps-level tactical missile.
Manufacturer: Lockheed Martin Vought Systems.
Weight: MGM-140A 3,690lb (1,670kg); MGM-140B 2,910lb (1,320kg); MGM-140C 3,270lb (1,480kg).
Dimensions: length 13.0ft (4.0m); diameter 24in (0.6m); finspan 55in (1.4m).
Powerplant: solid-fueled rocket.
Performance: range MGM-140A 102 miles (165km), MGM-140B 186 miles (300km), MGM-140C 87 miles (140km); ceiling >30 miles (50km).
Platform: M270 MLRS tracked launcher.
Warhead: MGM-140A 1,240lb (560kg); MGM-140B 353lb (160kg); MGM-140C 592lb (268kg).

The history of this missile stretches back into the 1970s, when the Army started work on a successor to MGM-72 Lance, designated the Corps Support Weapon System (CSWS). In 1982 the DoD combined this with the Air Force's Conventional Standoff Weapon (CSW) to form the Joint Tactical Missile System (JTACMS) program, but in 1985 the Air Force pulled out although the program continued under the new name Army Tactical Missile System (ATACMS). The first flight of the prototype XMGM-140A took place in April 1988. Low-rate production started in December 1988 and the system became operational in January 1991 as MGM-140A (ATACMS is also known as M39 in the Army). Design of an improved missile, MGM-140B (ATACMS Block IA) began in 1992. This had GPS in its guidance system, significantly increasing accuracy at long ranges, and the weight of warhead was reduced from 3,690lb (1,670kg) to 2,910lb (1,320kg), thus increasing range from 102 miles (165km) to 186 miles (300km). MGM-140B entered service in 1998.

Meanwhile, following the experiences in the 1991 Gulf War, it was decided to develop another version of ATACMS which would be specifically intended to destroy moving, high-value targets, such as tank formations and and the transporter-erector vehicles (TELs) for surface-to-surface missile systems such as the Iraqi Scud. This led to the MGM-140C Block II ATACMS, which first flew in 1996. Development has been slow and a production contract for MGM-140C was not placed until August 2001. MGM-140C has the same inertial/GPS guidance system as the MGM-140B and carries 13 BAT submunitions in the enlarged warhead section; range is about 87 miles (140km). Once released, the BAT uses passive acoustic sensors in its wingtips for initial target acquisition, and an IIR (Imaging Infrared) sensor for terminal guidance. The BAT is 36in (91cm)

long, 5.5in (14cm) in diameter (wings folded), has a wingspan of 36in (91cm), weighs about 44lb (20kg) and has a tandem shaped-charge warhead. The ATACMS Block IIA would have been an improved version of Block II, carrying six Improved BAT (IBAT) submunitions, but this was zero-funded in the Army's FY2002 program.

A ship-launched ATACMS variant for the U.S. Navy (called NATACMS) is also under development. A modified version of MGM-140B, called Block IA Unitary was flight-tested for the first time in April 2001. In this version, a 500lb (227kg) unitary HE warhead replaces the M74 bomblets. A production decision has not yet been made.

The ATACMS is a JTF/corps commander's asset designed for precise engagements against high priority targets at long ranges. The missile is launched from the same M270 launcher as the Multiple-Launch Rocket System (MLRS).

Below: A trials ATACMs missile is launched on a test range.

M109A6 155mm

Type: self-propelled howitzer.
Manufacturer: Team Paladin (United Defense).
Weight: combat 63,600lb (28,800kg).
Dimensions: length overall (howitzer forward) 32.0ft (9.8m); length, hull 22./6ft (6.9m);width, hull 12.9ft (3.9m).
Powerplant: General Motors 8V71T, 8-cylinder, 2-cycle, V-8, supercharged diesel, 345bhp at 2,300rpm.
Performance: (vehicle) road speed 38mph (61kmh); road range 186 miles (300km); maximum gradient 60 percent; maximum side slope 40 percent; vertical obstacle 1.8ft (0.5m); trench 6.0ft (1.8m).
Armament: M284 155mm/39 caliber howitzer, 39 projectiles; 1 x 0.5in (12.7mm) M2HB machine gun.
Performance: (gun) maximum range, unassisted 24,060yd (22,000m); maximum range, rocket-assisted 32,800yd (30,000m); elevation +75/-3; traverse 360.
Crew: four.

The M109 series of self-propelled 155mm howitzers have been in service since the early 1960s and provide the core artillery capability for the U.S. Army and for many foreign armies as well. The latest version to enter service with the Army is the Paladin M109A6 which is the fourth major upgrade and includes significant enhancements in the areas of responsiveness, terminal effects, range, and survivability, as well as in reliability and ease-of-maintenance. Under current plans only 824 of the M109 fleet will be upgraded to this new standard.

The M109A6 is an armored, full-tracked weapon, mounting the M284 howitzer and carrying thirty-seven complete conventional rounds plus two Copperhead projectiles, and is operated by a crew of four. It has a new, Kevlar-lined turret, which incorporates considerable improvements to the crew compartment, as well as a full-width bustle with armor shielding to improve the protection of the propelling charges. The vehicle can travel at a maximum speed of 38mph (61kmh) with a cruising range of some 186 miles (300km). When on the move it is normal for the barrel to be held in a travel lock, which used to be done manually, but in the M109A6 is done by remote control.

The M109A6 has an Automatic Fire Control System (AFCS) with on-board ballistic computation and automatic weapon pointing, and an integrated inertial navigation system (INS) with embedded GPS processing. This enables a moving M109A6 to receive a fire mission, compute firing data, select and take up a fire position, automatically unlock and point its cannon, and fire the first round – all in under sixty seconds. This "shoot-and-scoot" capability, which is achieved by day or by night, not only significantly improves responsiveness to calls for fire, but also protects the vehicle and crew since they leave the site before the enemy can respond with counterbattery fire.

The M109A6 uses the M284 cannon assembly which has a new tube, combined with structural improvements to the bore evacuator and muzzle brake, as well as improvements to the breech and recoil system to increase component life. The new M203-series charges provide a maximum range of at least 24,060yd (22km), a dramatic increase over the original M109's maximum range of 16,070yd (14.7km). Even this excellent range is increased to 32,800yd (30km) with rocket-assisted projectiles (RAP).

The SPH cannot be considered in isolation from its M992A2 Field Artillery Ammunition Support Vehicle (FAASV); the two comprise a howitzer section and travel together. The FAASV is a tracked vehicle, with the same mobility, survivability, and speed as the SPH, and is fitted with a hydraulically powered conveyor for transferring single rounds to the SPH. In addition to its ammunition-handling equipment, the FAASV features an ammunition storage compartment, a diesel auxiliary power unit (APU) to drive the hydraulic system, and an automatic fire extinguishing system. The FAASV has a crew of five.

Below: M190A6 Paladin, latest in the outstanding M109-series of howitzers.

M119A1 105mm Lightweight Towed Howitzer

Type: light gun for use by light and airborne forces.
Weight: combat 4,520lb (2050.3kg).
Dimensions: length (folded position) 16ft (4.9m); length (tube in firing position) 20.8ft (6.3m); width 5.9ft (1.8m); height (folded position) 4.5ft (1.4m).
Towing vehicle: HMMWV (M1097).
Armament: 105mm caliber; elevation -6deg to +70deg; traverse 11deg; rate-of-fire, maximum 6rpm for 2 min, sustained 3rpm for 30 min.
Performance: range, charge 7 – 12,580yd (11,500m); charge 8 – 15,315yd (14,000m); M913 RAP – 20,785yd (19,000m).
Crew: seven.

This gun was designed and developed in the United Kingdom as the 105mm Light Gun and was available in two forms, differing only in the type of barrel. The L118 fired British separate-loading ammunition, as used in the Abbot self-propelled gun, then in service with the British Army, while the L119 fired the full range of standardized, semi-fixed NATO 105mm ammunition. The Light Gun was a great success with British forces in the Falklands War in 1981, as a result of which the U.S. Army purchased a number for testing to see whether it would meet the operational requirement for an air-portable artillery piece for the new Light Division concept, in which transport by helicopter was a particular requirement. The Light Gun met all requirements with ease and a license was obtained in 1987 for production in the United States as the M119A1.

The task of the M119A1 is to provide direct and indirect fire support for light

infantry forces. It can be moved quickly into and out of position, where it has a low silhouette, and the gun position requires virtually no preparation or digging. The gun fires all current 105mm ammunition and a rocket-propelled projectile (RAP) is under development which will increase the range to approximately 20,780yd (19km).

The lightness of the gun is the result of an ingenious design in which the barrel rotates forward over the trail for towing, using an attachment which clips onto the muzzlebrake. The barrel can be removed and replaced in thirty minutes using one simple tool. New production methods have been used for the gun and trail, combining unprecedented strength with light weight. As a result the gun can be towed by almost any military vehicle, but is most usually seen behind a standard HMMWV. With its crew and basic load of ammunition it is air-transportable by the UH-60 helicopter and two can be carried by the CH-47 Chinook. It can be carried with ease by almost any fixed-wing transport and is air-droppable.

While the original British design met all the U.S. Army's requirements, nevertheless a number of improvements have been made, primarily to improve standardization, maintainability and safety, which resulted in the M119A1.

The M119 replaced the M102 in the U.S. Army and entered service in 1989 with 7th Infantry Division and subsequently (as M119A1) 82nd Airborne Division (1991) and 101st Airborne (Air Assault) Division (1992). Active force fielding was completed in 1995 and more were issued to the Army National Guard in 1996-97. The M119A1 is due to be replaced in about 2008-09.

Below: Artillerymen bring an M119A1 into action at Elmendorf AFB, Alaska.

M198 155mm Towed Howitzer

Type: towed medium howitzer.
Manufacturer: Rock Island Arsenal.
Weight: 15,758lb (7,154kg).
Dimensions: length (towed) 23.2ft (7.1m), (firing) 36.1ft (11.0m); width (towed) 9.1ft (2.8m); height (towed) 9.5ft (2.9m).
Performance: maximum effective range, conventional ammunition 24,500yd (22,400m), rocket-assisted projectile (RAP) 32,820yd (30,000m), Copperhead 17,615yd (16,100m); time into action >6 minutes; rate-of-fire 4rpm maximum, 2rpm sustained.
Armament: bore 155mm (6.21in); elevation -2deg to +72deg; traverse left/right 22.5deg, 360deg with speed traverse.
Crew: ten.

In the late 1960s Rock Island Arsenal started work on a replacement for the M114A2 155mm howitzer, which had been in service since World War II. The new weapon, the M198, offered significant improvements over the M114A2, particularly in range, lethality, reliability, and mobility, and after ten prototypes had been given very thorough trials, which included firing well over 45,000 rounds, it was accepted for production. It entered service in 1982 with a total of 772 built for the U.S. Army and Marine Corps and a large number were also sold to foreign armies.

The M198, in service with the Army, Marine Corps, and Army National Guard, is normally towed by a 6 x 6 five-ton truck or a tracked M548 cargo carrier (version of M113). It can be carried underslung by CH-53 or CH-47 helicopters, although neither of its normal towing vehicles can. The M198 fires all the standard range of 155mm projectiles and also new types, such as the Copperhead and rocket-assisted projectiles.

In the traveling position the barrel is swung forward through 180deg to rest over the trail, which considerably reduces the length for road or air travel. In the firing position the barrel is swung back to its normal position, the trail legs are opened, and the suspension system is raised so that the weapon rests on a non-anchored firing platform. A hydraulic ram cylinder and a 23in (58.4cm) diameter float mounted in the bottom carriage at the on-carriage traverse centerline provides for rapid shift of the carriage to ensure 360deg traverse. There is a hydropneumatic recoil system and a double-baffle muzzle brake. Normal rate of fire is two rounds per minute,

Below: Marine Corps M198 155mm towed howitzer, Skopje, Macedonia.

Above: Marine M198 shows the operation of its muzzle-brake.

but there is a maximum rate of four rounds every minute for three minutes. A thermal warning device is fitted which warns the crew if the barrel is becoming overheated.

Among the recent upgrades is the "HyPAK" (Hydraulic Power-Assist Kit), which provides an electrically powered (24v DC) hydraulic system to raise and lower the M198's wheels when moving into and out of a firing position, as well as during carriage speed shifting. The HyPAK adds approximately 40lb (18kg) to the overall weight but means that a job which previously required two people can now be performed much more quickly by just one. Another upgrade, the RE 198 Recoil Exerciser, is an electrically controlled, hydraulically operated device which prevents recoil cylinder leaks and thus reduces the failure rate in the recoil mechanism.

YMGM-157B Enhanced Fiber-Optic Guided Missile (EFOGM)

Type: non-line-of-sight battlefield guided missile.
Manufacturer: Raytheon Electronic Systems/Systems Electronics Inc.
Weight: missile plus canister 173lb (78.5kg); missile only 113.1lb (51.3kg).
Dimensions: missile length 6.2ft (1.9m); diameter 7.9in (0.2m); span 3.6ft (1.1m).
Powerplant: two-stage, solid propellant rocket motor.
Performance: flyout speed 328ft/sec (100m/sec); range 0.6-9.3 miles (1-15km).
Warhead: shaped-charge.
Guidance: wire-guided (fibre diameter 240 microns).
Platform: HMMWV (modified), 8 missiles.
Crew: two.

Virtually all battlefield "man-in-the-loop" guided missiles are line-of-sight systems; ie, the firer must be able to see the target throughout the engagement, and the missile flies directly from the launcher to the target, subject only to minor variations to bring it back onto the correct track. The YMGM-157B Enhanced Fiber-Optic Guided Missile (EFOGM) takes a different approach, using a fiber-optic cable which not only enables TV pictures to be transmitted from the missile to the firer, but also enables the missile to operate out-of-sight of the firer. This means that the firer can seek targets of opportunity during the missile's flight, that the missile can attack targets out of the firer's view (behind a hill or a building, for example), and that the final target can be precisely determined to achieve maximum accuracy. EFOGM is primarily an anti-armor missile but can also be used in an anti-helicopter role.

Based on the TOW anti-tank missile, the EFOGM has a high resolution infrared video camera in the nose, and a fiber-optic cable dispenser in the tail. This cable relays TV images down to the gunner's station, and control data up to the missile. The Fire Unit is a modified version of the HMMWV, with a crew of two and an eight-missile launcher; it is equipped with a gunner's console and a Battle Command Computer for navigation and mission planning.

Prior to launch the flight-path is programmed into the missile's on-board computer. Once airborne, the missile uses its inertial instruments to navigate itself along the programmed non-ballistic flight-path, which can be up to 9.38 miles (15km) long and with several waypoints. During the flight the gunner pans the missile's seeker to investigate targets of opportunity, thus acting as a discriminating "man-in-the-loop" sensor, who can identify and designate targets, and also assist by refining the missile's aimpoint on vulnerable locations of the target; the automatic tracker locks on to the image of the target. The missile has a shaped-charge and normally attacks targets from above.

Following successful flight tests an initial order for 300 missiles, twelve Fire Units and three Platoon Leader Vehicles has been placed, and the system underwent a two year Extended User Evaluation by XVIII Airborne Corps in 2000-2002.

Left: EFOGM is currently undergoing a two-year trial by XVIII Airborne.

Above: EFOGM uses a modified TOW missile to attack out-of-sight targets.

Mortars

System	M224	M252	M120
Bore	60mm	81mm	120mm
Length, barrel	40in (102cm)	56in (142cm)	69in (175cm)
Weight, combat (total)*	46.5lb (21.1kg)	89lb (40.4kg)	319lb (145kg)
Weight, 1 round HE**	4lb (1.8kg)	15lb (6.8kg)	33lb (15kg)
Range (HE)** maximum minimum	3,817yd (3,490m) 44yd (40m)	6,234yd (5,700m) 88yd (80m)	7,874yd (7,200m) 220yd (200m)
Elevation limits	45-85deg	45-85deg	40-85deg
Rates of fire maximum sustained	30rpm/4min 20rpm	30rpm/2min 8rpm	16rpm/1min 4 rounds/min
Crew	2	3	5

* Includes baseplate and sight unit in all cases, but does not include M1100 two-wheel trailer for M120 120mm mortar.
** Weights and ranges vary between different types of round.

Mortars are known in most armies as the "battalion commander's artillery" since they are the major fire support assets under his direct command. Mortars are capable of rapid, high-angle, plunging fire that is invaluable against dug-in enemy troops and targets behind cover, which cannot be effectively engaged by direct fire from other weapons in an infantry battalion. Thus, mortars provide a very effective means of bringing heavy fire to bear both speedily and accurately, while their light weight and simplicity of operation make them ideal weapons for the infantry.

The U.S. Army has three calibers of mortar currently in service: 60mm, 81mmm and 120mm. The smallest is the M224 60mm Lightweight Mortar, which replaced the older, World War II-vintage M29 after it had been found to be too heavy during the Vietnam War, even when disassembled into its three component parts. The M224 is a smooth-bore, muzzle-loading, high-angle (45-85deg) weapon used for close-support of forward units, and is normally allocated to platoons. It is provided with a bipod, but can also be fired with the mortarman holding the barrel with one hand. The rounds are dropped down the barrel and are either drop-fired (ie, they hit the fixed trigger and are immediately fired) or they rest at the bottom of the barrel until the mortarman activates the trigger. If fired with a bipod, the mortar is aimed using an optical sight, with the elevation and traverse being set by adjusting screws.

The M252 81mm Medium Mortar replaced the M29A1, which had been in service for many years. The muzzle of the smooth-bore barrel is fitted with cooling fins around the base and a conical Blast Attenuator Device (BAD) at

Above: Marines with M224 60mm mortars in Operation Desert Shield.

the muzzle end, which has been found necessary to deflect over-pressures away from the mortar crew. If it is required to be man-packed the M252 is broken down into three major components – tube 35lb (16kg), mount 27lb (12.3kg) and baseplate 29lb (11.6kg) – of which the baseplate, due to its combination of weight and awkward shape, is the most difficult to carry. It should be noted, however, that in addition to the mortar, the ammunition must also be carried, and since each round weighs approximately 15lb (6.8kg) this adds up to a significant burden for the infantrymen involved.

The smoothbore 120mm M120 Heavy Mortar replaced the M30 4.2in (107mm) rifled mortar and is in service in two versions. The M120 is transported disassembled on the purpose-designed, two-wheeled M1100 trailer, which is normally towed by an HMMWV, and then assembled on its baseplate for firing. The components of the M120 are a tube assembly (110lb/50kg); bipod assembly (70lb/32kg); baseplate (136lb/62kg); and trailer (400lb/181kg). The M121 has an identical tube, but is mounted in an M1064 mortar vehicle, a version of the M113 tracked carrier. Both fire identical ammunition, with an average weight of 33lb (15kg) per round. The maximum

range is 7,874yd (7,200m), but as these weapons are sited well within forward battalions' areas this gives them a very significant reach into enemy territory.

Below: An 81mm mortar being used by Marines on exercise at Camp Lejeune.

Land Warfare – Direct Fire Weapons

During Cold War the major land threat was in Europe where the biggest component of the threat – at least during a conventional (non-nuclear) phase – was a mass attack by Soviet tanks. As a result, the U.S. and other NATO countries put great efforts and resources into developing anti-armor weapons. In part, this requirement was met by tanks, since in many respects a tank gun is the best anti-tank weapon. However, tanks are very expensive and could not be not be everywhere, and so there was a consequent need for other types of anti-tank weapon. The battlefield in Europe remained, fortunately, theoretical, but the armor/anti-armor war was fought in the design agencies as first the tank scientists came up with a new armor and then the anti-tank people came up with a new weapon or warhead to defeat it, which led to a new armor, and so on. In part this was met by artillery and increasingly by helicopters armed with anti-tank missiles, but there remained a requirement for the infantry to have its own dedicated anti-tank weapons.

Now that the Cold War is over, there is unlikely to be a massive tank attack in Central Europe. However, the most probable form of warfare will require U.S. land forces to deploy into a distant country, not always by invitation, where there may well be an armored threat during the early days against the forward airfields and entry ports. There is, therefore, a need for anti-tank weapons

systems to be among the earliest elements deployed, which must be capable of killing modern tanks.

Anti-tank defense needs to be layered, with the aim of dealing with the threat from as great a distance as possible. However, it should be noted that the firer's line-of-sight to the target is limited by undulations in the ground, trees, buildings, haze, and smoke, which will often reduce the practical distance at which an engagement can take place to much less than the maximum range of the projectile. During the Cold War, for example, it was calculated that Western Europe's rolling countryside, many trees, and numerous small villages would seldom enable a target to be engaged at more than 2,000yd (1,830m), and often even less.

Among the current range of direct fire weapons available to U.S. forces the TOW is outstanding and it continues to be developed after 30 years' frontline service. One of the most intriguing of the next generation weapons is LOSAT (Line-Of-Sight Anti-Tank) which turns preconceived ideas on their head by firing a kinetic energy projectile as a rocket-propelled missile, whereas it had previously been assumed that this was feasible only from a tank gun.

Below: Tripod-mounted TOW, manned by men of the 13th MEUSOC.

Javelin Anti-tank Missile

Type: manportable anti-tank weapon.
Manufacturer: Raytheon/Lockheed Martin.
Weight: total – 49.5lb (22.3kg); missile – 26.1lb (11.8kg); launch-tube assembly – 9.0lb (4.1kg).
Dimensions: missile – length 42.6in (1.1m), diameter 5.0in (127mm); launch tube assembly – 47.2in (1.2m); diameter 5.6in (142mm).
Powerplant: 2-stage solid-propellant rocket.
Performance: range, maximum 2,734yd (2,500m), minimum 82yd (75m); armor penetration >2.4in (600mm).
Platform: man-portable; disposable launch tube.
Sensors: imaging infra-red (IIR).
Guidance: lock-on before launch, automatic self-guiding.
Warhead: tandem shaped-charge (HEAT); 18.5lb (8.4kg).
Crew: two.

The Javelin is a manportable, fire-and-forget, anti-tank missile employed by dismounted infantry to defeat current and future threat armored combat vehicles. It is in the process of replacing the Dragon system in both the Army and the Marine Corps. It is normally shoulder-launched, but can also be installed on tracked, wheeled or amphibious vehicles.

Pre-launch preparation takes less than thirty seconds, while reloading takes twenty seconds. The missile tube is attached to the Command Launch Unit

(CLU) whereupon the gunner looks through the sight where all he has to do is to place a cursor box over the selected target and then send first a "lock-on-before- launch" command and then a direct/top attack direction to the missile. Once locked-on, the missile is ready to fire; on the launch button being pressed the first stage motor fires propelling the missile out of its tube at a relatively low velocity until it is well away from the firer, at which point the second stage motor fires and accelerates the missile to a speed around Mach 1. This is known as a "soft launch" and enables the missile to be fired from inside buildings or covered positions. If the target is a tank the missile will be set for top attack; following launch the missile climbs to an altitude of about 500ft (150m) before turning over into a dive to attack the tank though its thinnest protection – the roof. Direct attack is selected to engage covered targets, bunkers, buildings, and helicopters, and the missile will reach a height of some 164ft (50m) during its flight.

Unlike the previous generation of anti-tank missiles, Javelin is a fire-and-forget missile which automatically guides itself to the target after launch. Thus the firing team can leave their position as soon as the missile has left the launch tube. Javelin defeats all armor types. Two precision shaped-charges combine to slice through armor. This tandem warhead has repeatedly demonstrated its effectiveness against a variety of the most difficult stationary and moving targets. The tandem warhead is fitted with two shaped-charges: a precursor warhead to initiate explosive reactive armor and a main warhead to penetrate base armor

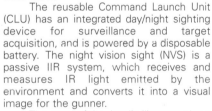

The reusable Command Launch Unit (CLU) has an integrated day/night sighting device for surveillance and target acquisition, and is powered by a disposable battery. The night vision sight (NVS) is a passive IIR system, which receives and measures IR light emitted by the environment and converts it into a visual image for the gunner.

The story of the Javelin illustrates how even a small weapon can take many years to get into service. An Army report in January 1978 made it clear that the Army's current manportable anti-armor weapon, Dragon, suffered from major shortcomings, but it was not until 1986 that a Joint Service Operational Requirements document was approved in 1986 and even then it was amended in 1988. The development contract was placed in 1989 and after building prototypes and many trials a report in 1992 said that Javelin was effective, but required further assessment. This led to a Limited User Test (LUT) which lasted from April to June 1996. Full-rate production was authorized in May 1997, some nineteen years after the weapon was first proposed.

Left: Javelin "fire-and-forget" anti-tank missile guides itself to the target.

Line-Of-Sight Anti-Tank Weapon (LOSAT)

Type: vehicle-mounted hyper-velocity anti-tank weapon.
Manufacturer: Lockheed Martin (formerly Lockheed Martin Vought).
Weight: 177lb (80kg).
Dimensions: length 9.3ft (2.8m); diameter 6.4in (162mm) .
Powerplant: single-stage rocket motor.
Performance: maximum speed 5,000ft/sec (1,524m/s); maximum range >4,375yd (4,000m), minimum range approximately 1,000yd (914m); time of flight to maximum range approximately four seconds.
Platform: HMMWV (four missiles ready to fire).
Sensors/Guidance: see text.
Warhead: high-density, long-rod penetrator.
Crew: five (two vehicles).

During the Cold War the U.S. Army developed a series of anti-tank weapons to counter the Warsaw Pact threat of a massive armored attack against NATO. In general terms, these anti-tank weapons had two types of warhead. First, the solid-shot kinetic energy round depended upon high velocity and great density to penetrate armor; the greater the speed and the denser the material, the more effective it would be, leading to sub-caliber armor-piercing discarding sabot (APDS) rounds, made of metals such as tungsten carbide. Second, the high-explosive anti-tank (HEAT) warhead (also known as "hollow charge") generated a highly focused spray of molten metal which bored its way through the armor. One of the "givens" for some thirty years was that APDS rounds of sufficient density and velocity could be fired only from gun tubes of 105mm caliber or greater, while missiles could be armed only with HEAT warheads. Since the 1980s, however, the U.S. Army has been developing LOSAT which reverses those concepts by using a high density, hyper-velocity penetrator, but as a rocket-powered missile rather than a gun-fired projectile.

LOSAT was conceived in the 1980s for deployment in Central Europe, turret-mounted on a lengthened Bradley IFV chassis. But with the end of the Cold War the requirement changed to providing anti-tank support to an entry force, to prevent hostile tanks overrunning the entry airfield. This requires the weapon to be mounted in a light vehicle transportable in fixed-wing aircraft – C-5 (ten), C-17 (seven), C-141 (three), and C-130J (two) – and moved around as an underslung load beneath the UH-60. It is intended that it will be fielded in the five light divisions currently equipped with TOW and Javelin, with LOSAT deployed in squads of two HMMWVs and a high-mobility trailer, manned by five soldiers. The launch vehicle carries four ready-to-fire missiles, while the second HMMWV tows a trailer carrying eight additional missiles.

The Kinetic Energy Missile (KEM) is 9.3ft (2.8m) long, but with a small diameter (6.4in/162mm) and weighs 177lb (80kg). It has four stabilizer fins. The single-stage rocket motor is about 6.0ft (1.8m) long and weighs 110lb (50kg) – the large size dictated by the need to accelerate the missile to its speed of 5000ft/s (1,524m/sec), which is reached in less than four seconds. The system is claimed to penetrate any known armor, even at high oblique angles of impact.

The fire control system (FCS) is based on the Improved Bradley Acquisition System, using a second-generation, Forward-Looking Infrared (FLIR) sensor and a daylight TV. The FCS enables the gunner/commander to acquire and auto-track two targets simultaneously; once the gunner designates a target the system inside the missile automatically initializes and guides the missile to its target.

Right: LOSAT system comprises four missiles mounted on the widely used 4 x 4 HMMWV ("Humm-V") chassis.

Right: LOSAT missile has a speed of 5,000ft/sec, and defeats armor by kinetic energy, using a long rod penetrator.

Right: A complete LOSAT detachment on the road; it can be carried underslung by a UH-60 helicopter.

Despite its innovative concept, most of the technology involved – kinetic energy, long-rod penetrators and very high acceleration, hyper-velocity rockets motors – is well-established, the one area of uncertainty being the on-board guidance system, which, in view of the missile's exceptional speed, must act/react with great rapidity.

M47 Dragon

Type: man-portable anti-tank guided missile.
Manufacturer: Boeing (McDonnell Douglas).
Weight: 24,4lb (11.1kg),
Dimensions: length 33.5in (85.2cm); body diameter 4.5in (11.4cm); finspan 13in (33cm).
Powerplant: recoilless gas-generator in launch tube; sustainer propulsion by 60 small side thrusters fired in pairs on tracker demand.
Performance: speed about 230mph (370km/h); range, maximum 1,640yd (1,500m), minimum 82yd (75m).
Warhead: high-explosive anti-tank (HEAT); 5.4 lb (2.5kg).
Guidance: semi-automatic, wire.
Crew: two.

Dragon was designed as a medium-range complement to TOW and has been in service since 1971. It is a wire-guided system in which the missile deploys a thin wire as it flies, through which the commands are passed.. The missile has been upgraded several times since it entered service and the latest version is capable of defeating most armored vehicles, as well as fortified bunkers, concrete gun emplacements, and other hard targets.

The missile leaves the factory in a sealed fiberglass tube, which serves as storage, transport, and launcher for the missile; the rear-end of the tube contains the launch charge. The operator has a tracker unit, which comprises a telescopic sight, IR sensor, and electronics box, attached to a bipod. To prepare for the launch, the operator attaches the tube to the tracker unit and then takes aim. When the cross-hairs in the sight are on the target he presses the launch button and then maintains the cross-hairs on the target until impact. A tracking sensor measures the difference between the missile and the line-of-sight and sends commands to the missile via the wire; these commands fire the appropriate side thrusters, instructing it always to reduce the difference to zero. When the missile is launched three curved fins flick open and start the missile

Below: Marine anti-tank team armed with M47 Dragon anti-tank missile.

Above: Dragon at moment of launch, with a clear view of the tripod support.

spinning. On completion of the engagement the launch tube is thrown away and a new one attached to the tracker.

During its long service career the Dragon has been redesigned. The Marines developed a product improved (PI) version, designated Dragon II, which was fielded in 1985; this was, in effect, a new and much improved warhead added to the existing Dragon I missiles. The current version, sometimes known as SuperDragon, was fielded in 1990 and is capable of penetrating 18in (45cm) of armor at a maximum effective range of 1,640yd (1,500m).

Although it was a considerable advance on previous infantry-manned anti-tank missiles, the Dragon's guidance system has been criticized for being inaccurate and requiring excessive control by the gunner, who must maintain an uninterrupted view of the target until impact. The system of side thrusters was also considered over-complicated and was certainly unreliable at first, although this was later overcome; the idea has, however, never been repeated.

There are currently some 7,000 launchers and 33,000 missiles in service with the Army, while the Marine Corps has some 17,000 missiles.

Several attempts have been made to develop a replacement for Dragon, one, designated IMAAWS, being canceled in 1980, and another called Rattler in the early 1990s. Dragont is now being replaced by Javelin but some will remain in limited service or storage for several years to come.

M136 AT-4

Type: light anti-armor rocket-launcher.
Manufacturer: Alliant Techsystems (USA)/FFV Ordnance (Sweden).
Weight: launcher 14.8lb (6.7kg); rocket 4lb (1.8kg).
Dimensions: launcher length 40in (102cm); rocket caliber 3.3in (8.4cm); length 18in (46cm).
Powerplant: one-stage rocket motor.
Performance: muzzle velocity 950ft/s (290m/s); maximum range 2,300yd (2,100m); maximum effective range 330yd (300m); minimum range 11yd (10m); time of flight to 275yd (250m) less than one second.
Warhead: rocket with shaped-charge warhead.
Crew: one.
Specifications apply to M136 AT-4.

The M136 recoilless anti-tank rocket-launcher was designed the AT-4 by FFV Ordnance in Sweden and was selected as the replacement for the U.S. M72 Light Anti-tank Weapon (LAW); it was manufactured by Honeywell in the United States for the U.S. Armed Forces. It is a lightweight, self-contained, reinforced, fiberglass launcher that fires a single rocket against enemy tanks and armored vehicles; the launcher is discarded after use.

The M136 AT-4's rocket projectile is launched from the right shoulder and as soon as it has left the tube six spring-loaded stabilizing fins spring out and lock into position. The projectile is extremely destructive and its 16oz (440gm) shaped-charge warhead (also known as High Explosive Anti-Tank/HEAT) penetrates more than 14in (36cm) of standard armor plate. On impact, the

BGM-71D/E/F TOW 2/2A/2B

Type: anti-tank guided missile weapon system.
Manufacturer: Hughes (prime).
Weight: launch weight TOW 2A 49.9lb (22.7kg); TOW 2B 49.8lb (22.6kg).
Dimensions: length,TOW 2A 45.1in (117.4cm), with probe extended, 55.1in (140cm); TOW 2B 46in (116.8cm); diameter (both) 5.9in (15.2cm); span (both) 13.4in (34cm).
Powerplant: Alliant two-stage solid-propellant rocket motor.
Performance: speed 1,181ft/sec (360m/sec); range 4,090yd (3,750m); time-of-flight to maximum effective range, TOW 2A 20 seconds, TOW 2B 21 seconds.
Guidance: command-to line-of-sight.
Warhead: TOW 2A tandem shaped-charge; TOW 2B two EFP (explosively formed penetrator) warheads.
Crew: (ground launcher) four.

Prime contractor Hughes Aircraft began work in 1965 on a new anti-tank weapon to replace the World War II-era 106mm recoilless rifle, and the resulting TOW (Tube-launched, Optically-tracked, Wire-guided) heavy anti-tank missile entered service just five years later. Since then it has been produced in vast numbers and is in service with over 40 armies around the world. TOW has an exceptional armor penetrating capability at a maximum range of well over 3,280yd (3,000m). It can be launched from ground-mounted tripods, vehicles or helicopters. It is primarily used in anti-tank warfare, although it can also be used against bunkers and other hard targets. It is a command-to-line of sight, wire-guided weapon and will operate in any weather conditions in which the firer can see the target. Well over 500,000 missiles have been built and the system is

Above: M136 anti-armor rocket-launcher was designed and built in Sweden.

nose-cone crumples and the impact sensor activates the piezo-electric fuze element, which, in its turn, activates the electric detonator, thus initiating the main charge. On firing, the copper-lined reverse-cone shape of the front end of the high explosive melts the copper body-liner into a highly focused gas jet that penetrates the armor plate. Inside the tank there is a flash of blinding light followed by spalling as fragments ricochet around the crew compartment, destroying all in their path.

The M136 AI-4 can be employed in limited visibility, provided always that the firer can see sufficiently well to identify the target, ensure that it is hostile, and estimate its range. Normal maximum effective range is about 275yd (250m). Since the weapon was first fielded, a reusable night sight bracket was developed enabling standard night vision equipment to be attached to the tube.

Above: TOW in its dismounted mode, using a tripod.

fitted on countless vehicle mounts, with Airborne TOW in service with some fifteen armies and at least ten different helicopter platforms.

Considerable improvements have been made to the missile since 1970. There are six missiles available for the TOW. launcher, although three of them – Basic TOW, Improved TOW, and TOW 2 – are no longer being produced for U.S. forces (although these versions are still used by forty allied countries).

Basic TOW (BGM-71A) was the original missile, with a diameter of 5in (12.7cm) and a range of 3,280yd (3,000m). Compared to the now-familiar outline of later TOWs, this did not have a nose probe. This first missile was followed by BGM-71A-1 which differed only in having slightly greater range. Next came Improved TOW (ITOW, BGM-71C), delivered from 1982 onwards, which introduced the extended nose probe to achieve greater standoff and thus better penetration by the HEAT warhead. ITOW also had an enhanced motor, increasing range to 4,100yd (3,750m). TOW 2 (BGM-71D) introduced improved propellant in the flight motor, a hardened guidance link, and a thermal beacon, which enabled the gunner to track the missile more easily at night, or in dust or smoke. The TOW 2 missile has a 6in (23.6cm) diameter warhead and retains the extended probe first introduced with ITOW. Over 80,000 TOW 2 (BGM-71D) missiles were delivered before production ended.

TOW 2A (BGM-71E) entered production in the late 1980s in response to the introduction of explosive reactive armor (ERA) by the Soviet Army. The TOW 2A uses two shaped-charge warheads in tandem to defeat this threat, where the first charge penetrates the outer armor layer, enabling the second charge to

blast its way through the inner layer. TOW 2A entered production in 1987 and over 118,000 missiles were delivered. TOW 2B (BGM-71F), which entered production in late 1991, provides additional capability against future armored threats and incorporates new fly-over/shoot-down technology. The missile's trajectory places it slightly above the target, so that its two warheads explode downward attacking the target at its most vulnerable point, the roof. TOW 2B is designed to complement rather than replace TOW 2A and both missiles are operational with the U.S. Army. Over 40,000 missiles have been delivered.

TOW Fire-and-Forget (TOW F&F) is intended to be the next generation heavy antitank missile that will replace the current TOW series missiles. It will not have the wire connection between the missile and firer of all previous versions but tactical employment will remain the same as the current TOW with adjustments made for TOW F&F's unique characteristics. The engineering development contact was placed in late 2000 and, if all proceeds according to plan, it will enter service in 2005-06.

The next generation anti-armor missile is currently known as "Follow-On To TOW" (FOTT) and is intended to provide greater range and increased lethality. It will be launched from current TOW launchers (except for helicopters), will be a fire-and-forget weapon, and will take advantage of the increased range of emerging second generation FLIR target acquisition systems. FOTT will provide improved, long-range anti-armor capability and, with its "fire-and-forget" enhancement, will improve survivability.

Left: TOW mounted on an HMWWV. The latest TOW 2A missile has a tandem warhead which is intended to defeat explosive reactive armor (ERA); some 118,000 rounds were produced. TOW 2B adds a fly-over/shoot-down capability.

Shoulder-launched Multiple-purpose Assault Weapon (SMAW)

Type: portable, anti-armor rocket launcher.
Manufacturer: Talley Defense Systems.
Weight: to carry 16.6lb (7.5kg); ready-to-fire (HEDP) 29.5lb (13.4kg); ready-to-fire (HEAA) 30.5lb (13.9kg).
Dimensions: bore diameter 3.3in (8.3cm); length, to carry 29.9in (75.9cm) ready-to-fire 54in (137.2cm).
Powerplant: rocket motor.
Performance: maximum effective range 574yd (500m).
Warhead: shaped charge.
Crew: two.

SMAW was fielded in 1984 and was formed by combining the Israeli B-300 rocket launcher with a British-designed 9mm spotting rifle. The launcher consists of a fiberglass launch tube with the 9mm spotting rifle built into its right side, and a combination of open battle sights and a mount for optical or night sights. The system can launch two types of 3.3in (8.3cm) diameter rockets. The original weapon was the High Explosive, Dual Purpose (HEDP) rocket, which is intended for use against bunkers, brickwork, and concrete walls, as well as against light armor. The second weapon, which was developed and issued later, is the High Explosive Anti-Armor (HEAA) rocket, which is effective against most current tanks, although not those fitted with spaced or explosive reactive armor (ERA). The rounds for the 9mm spotting rifle are ballistically matched to the rockets and increase the probability of a first-round hit. SMAW was a Marine Corps-designed weapons system and is being replaced by Predator in Marine Corps service.

During the Gulf War the U.S. Army borrowed 150 launchers and 5,000 rockets, and this led to the development by the Army of SMAW-D, which was

Below: SMAW; combined Israeli rocket launcher and British spotting rifle.

416

Above: SMAW is being phased out and is being replaced by Predator (p. 418).

in effect, an adapted version of the Marine Corps' SMAW but with a disposable launcher. This was put into small-scale production (6,000 missiles). SMAW-D fires the same HE warhead as the Marines' SMAW but weighs only 15lb (6.8kg); it can breach earth and timber defenses and masonry walls, and defeat lightly skinned armored vehicles at effective ranges of 16-550yd (15-500m).

The Army then turned to the XM-141 Bunker Defeat Munition (BDM) – see Predator entry.

Predator/MPIM

Type: shoulder-launched anti-armor/anti-personnel weapon.
Manufacturer: Lockheed Martin.
Weight: 20lb (9.1kg).
Dimensions: length 35in (89cm).
Powerplant: two-stage (soft launch) rocket.
Performance: range 19-656yd (17-600m).
Warhead: explosively formed penetrator/follow through fragmentation grenade.
Crew: one.

In the early 1990s the Marine Corps and the Army discovered that they were both developing an individual, shoulder-launched, short-range rocket system. The Marines were working on the Short-Range Anti-Armor Weapon (SRAW), whose primary purpose was as an anti-tank weapon, while the Army was developing the Multi-Purpose Individual Munition (MPIM), which could be used against both tanks and defensive positions, such as bunkers. On examination it transpired that there were many similarities, so it was decided to bring the two programs together to produce a weapon that would deal effectively with hostile armored vehicles, as well as personnel hidden behind walls, or inside earthen or wooden reinforced bunkers. This new joint weapon would then replace LAW, AT-4, and other light shoulder-fired weapons, and would complement, rather than replace, Javelin. The Marine Corps has since named its version "Predator," while the Army has retained the designation MPIM, at least for the time being.

It was decided that the bunker-busting and wall-penetrating requirements could be met by a missile which combined the SRAW propulsion system with the MPIM's warhead, while the anti-armor requirement could be met by the SRAW propulsion system and SRAW warhead. The SRAW launcher was also adopted. In other words, the

Below: Predator is an anti-armor and bunker-busting weapon for the Marines.

Above: Predator/MPIM has two warheads but common rocket/launch system.

solution was the SRAW missile system with two alternative warheads.

Predator is a short-range "fire-and-forget" assault missile, using a "soft" launch technique; ie, on pressing the trigger, a low-thrust rocket propels the missile until it is well clear of the launch tube, whereupon the second, higher-thrust stage kicks in and accelerates the missile towards the target; this both protects the firer and also enables the missile to be launched from within a confined space. Predator has an inertially-guided autopilot, which determines range and lead prior to missile launch, thus increasing accuracy against moving targets. The launcher is fitted with a x2.5 telescopic sight, which is compatible with current and future night vision devices.

In its anti-armor role, the missile has a similar "fly-over, shoot-down" attack profile to that of the TOW-IIB, with the warhead using an explosively formed penetrator which is lethal against all current main battle tanks including those equipped with explosive reactive armor. The complete system weighs some 20lb (9.1kg) and the carrier/launcher is thrown away following launch. This Marine Corps anti-armor version will enter service in 2002-03 and a total of 18,190 are currently on order.

The Army is still working on its BDM version which will employ an Army-developed "double-whammy" warhead, in which an explosively formed penetrator punches a hole through the target, allowing a follow-through anti-personnel fragmentation grenade to enter the enclosure beyond and explode.

Air Defense Systems

The air threat is becoming both very serious and extremely complex, with ground forces (include Army, Marine Corps, and Air Force units) now being faced by a mixture of manned aircraft, tactical ballistic missiles (TMDs) unmanned aerial vehicles (UAVs), and cruise missiles representing a wide variety of differing challenges to the air defense community. As a result air defenses will be based upon the traditional but nevertheless extremely effective concept of defense in depth with, in the Army's case, the Theater High Altitude Area Defense (THAAD) system providing the upper tier and MEADS/Patriot the lower tier, and a number of short-range systems providing local protection.

THAAD can intercept targets both outside and inside the atmosphere, which is of great importance since many shorter-range TBMs reach their apogee within the upper atmosphere. THAAD missiles are updated by their ground-based radar, but also use a specially shielded infrared seeker and a thruster-controlled flight to achieve a hit-to-kill intercept. The latest version of Patriot – PAC-3 – provides the lower tier which, like THAAD, is intended to hit its target directly. This is of particular importance when seeking to destroy incoming TBMs carrying chemical warheads, which tend to be more ruggedly built. PAC-3 is considerably smaller than earlier Patriot missiles, enabling four missiles to be housed in a tube previously occupied by one, and thus

quadrupling a battery's fire power without increasing the airlift requirement.

The contribution made by the Marine Corps' Hawk is of vital importance in expeditionary warfare. This is an excellent example of how, by judicious updating, a system can be kept in the frontline over a period of several decades. Similarly, the Stinger missile, which started as a man-portable, shoulder-launched system has not only been kept up-to-date but has found many applications as a vehicle-based system (Avenger, Bradley-Linebacker, and LAV-AD), but has also now found applications on helicopters, giving them a weapon to use against other helicopters.

Air defense weapons must not be considered on their own, but as part of a system in which an overarching air defense architecture gives all sensors and weapons systems a place and a role. Thus, THAAD, for example, is not a substitute for Patriot but the two systems provide each other with mutual support, with THAAD covering the upper-tier exoatmospheric and very-high-altitude endoatmospheric threats and fast, agile PAC-3 destroying leakers in the endgame. Similarly, the Marines have developed their own system in which ships offshore would provide the most distant defense, followed by Hawk then CLAWS and then the close-in systems such as Avenger and LAV-AD, and, finally, MANPAD Stinger.

Below: Light and mobile, Avenger mounts eight Stinger missiles.

Avenger Air Defense System

Type: forward area, combined missile/machine gun air defense system.
Manufacturer: Boeing.
Weight: under 8,600lb (3,901kg).
Dimensions: length 16.3ft (4.9m); height 8.7ft (2.6m); width 7.2ft (2.2m).
Powerplant: V-8 6.2 liter air-cooled diesel.
Performance: maximum speed 60mph (97kmh); range 300 miles (483km).
Armament: missiles, eight Stingers in two launch pods, reload, eight missiles in less than three minutes; one 0.50 caliber M3P machinegun (200 rounds).
Platform: HMMWV 4 x 4 vehicle.
Turret: combat weight under 2,600lb (1,180kg); dimensions, length 7.0ft (2.1m); height 5.8ft (1.8m), width 7.1ft (2.2m); traverse 360deg; elevation -10deg to +69deg.
Crew: two (driver and gunner).

The Avenger missile/gun system consists of two missile pods, each containing four Stingers, and a single heavy machine gun. These weapons are mounted on a gyro-stabilized turret and carried by a High Mobility Multipurpose Wheeled Vehicle (HMMWV). The turret can be operated in a stand-alone configuration or mounted on any other suitable military vehicle.

Boeing developed Avenger in the early 1980s to meet an urgent Army requirement for a lightweight, shoot-on-the-move, air defense system, based on the widely used Stinger missile, a HMMWV prime mover, and as many off-the-shelf components as possible. One example among many of the latter is that the electric-drive for the turret is the same as that used on the Bradley Fighting Vehicle. Avenger is easily transportable; one C-130 can carry three Avengers and their crews, a C-141 can carry six complete detachments, and the CH-47 and the CH-53 helicopters can each carry two complete units.

The missiles are mounted in two pods, one each side of the turret, which can be elevated from -10deg to +69deg; the eight missiles can be reloaded in under four minutes (see Stinger entry for missile details). In order to cover the area inside the missile's minimum range (the "dead" zone), Avenger is also armed with a Fabrique Nationale (FN) 0.50in (12.7mm) M3P automatic machine gun, for which 200 rounds of ammunition are carried. The gun is recoil-operated, link-belt-fed, and air-cooled, and can, of course, also engage ground targets if necessary.

The fire control system is highly automated, including automatic insertion of lead angle and super elevation at missile launch. Targets are acquired using either the head-up optical sight or the FLIR (Forward Looking Infrared), which is fitted to the left launch beam and is boresighted to the aiming point of the missile pod. The FLIR has three fields of view – wide, narrow, and a rain mode. Range is provided by an eyesafe laser rangefinder. An automatic video tracker locks on to the target and provides a tracking signal to the fire-control computer for control of the turret in elevation and azimuth. An IFF (Identification Friend-or-Foe) system is also fitted. A Remote Control Unit, displaying the same data as that available to the gunner, enables the crew to conduct engagements from remote positions up to 55yd (50m) from the vehicle.

An upgrade kit has been developed to permit the existing link between the FAAD (Forward Area Air Defense) command-and-control system to slew the Avenger turret automatically, thus placing the target in the gunner's field-of-view and giving the Stinger a Beyond Visual Range Engagement capability. Known as "Slew-to-Cue," the upgrade will include a new fire-

Above: Avenger was created from a variety of in-service components.

control computer, land navigation system, and hand-held terminal unit, together with an upgraded remote control unit. Installation of the upgrade kits will be completed in 2003.

Avenger is in service with U.S. Army, Marine Corps, and Army National Guard (and also with Egypt and Taiwan). The Avenger was deployed to the Middle East in 1991 to support Coalition troops during Operation Desert Storm.

M6 Bradley-Linebacker

Type: short-range air defense system.
Manufacturer: Boeing.
Weight: 65,917lb (29,900kg).
Dimensions: length 21.3ft (6.5m); width 11.8ft (3.6m); height 8.5ft (2.6m).
Powerplant: Cummins VTA-903T turbo-charged diesel; 600bhp.
Performance: maximum speed, road 37mph (60kmh), water 4mph (6.5kmh); road range 280 miles (450km).
Armament: 4 x FIM-92C Stinger missiles (plus 6); 1 x 25 mm M242 Bushmaster gun; 1 x 7.62 mm M240C machine gun.
Platform: M2 Bradley IFV.
Crew: 5.

Bradley-Linebacker is the tracked, armored version of the Avenger short-range air defense (SHORAD) system (see previous entry), armed with four Stinger missile launchers and a Bushmaster 25mm gun. Boeing was awarded a U.S. Army contract in 1995 to integrate the Stinger missile system on the Bradley

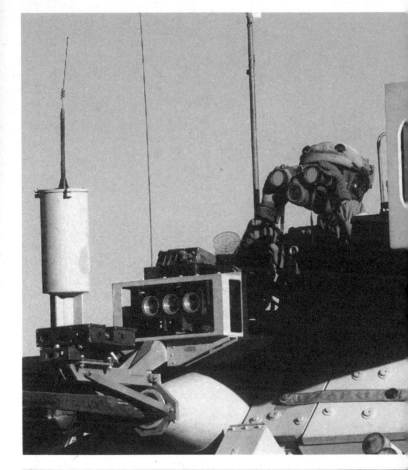

Infantry Fighting Vehicle. Designated Bradley-Linebacker, the system provides short-range air defense at divisional level by engaging fixed-wing aircraft, helicopters, cruise missiles, and unmanned aerial vehicles (UAVs) within the Stinger's range envelope, by day or by night, under all weather conditions, and while on the move. Bradley-Linebacker uses the same system hardware and software as the Avenger system.

Bradley-Linebacker uses the M2A2 Bradley, with an armored Standard Vehicle Mounted Launcher (SVML) on the left side of the standard IFV turret, carrying four ready-to-fire Stinger missiles; a further six missiles are carried inside the vehicle (see Stinger entry for missile details). The Linebacker vehicle also mounts the same 25mm Boeing M242 Bushmaster gun that is standard on the Bradley. There is also a coaxially mounted 7.62 mm M240C machine gun and on each side of the gun turret there is an M257 smoke grenade launcher with four smoke grenades.

The Bradley-Linebacker is fitted with the Avenger "Slew-to-Cue" upgrade (see Avenger entry) and this, coupled with the digital compass and gyro-stabilized turret, aligns the launcher with a designated target, thus enabling targets to be acquired while on the move. This shoot-on-the-move capability has been demonstrated at a speed of 25mph (40kmh). Target classification and location are displayed to the gunner in the Integrated Sight Unit, which also displays missile status and seeker positional information for positive targeting confirmation before launch. The system includes optical, TV, and thermal imaging channels. The Linebacker vehicle is integrated into the SHORAD Command and Control Network by the use of a handheld terminal unit.

The M2A2 is fitted with appliqué steel armor but can also have add-on explosive-reactive armor (ERA) if required. It is air-transportable by C-141, C-5, and C-17 aircraft. The U.S. Army has taken delivery of 99 Linebacker units, which are fielded with the Third Infantry Division at Fort Stewart, Georgia.

Left: Bradley-Linebacker consists of a lethal combination of four Stinger missiles and a Bushmaster 25mm chain-gun, mounted on an M6 Bradley chassis.

FIM-92A Stinger Weapons System

Type: close-in air defense, two-stage missile system.
Manufacturer: Hughes (prime); Raytheon (missile).
Weight: system 34.5lb (15.7kg); missile 22lb (10.0kg); warhead 2.2lb (1.0kg).
Dimensions: length 5.0ft (1.5m); diameter 3.0in (7.6cm); wingspan 3.6in (9.1cm).
Powerplant: Atlantic Research Mk 27 dual-thrust, solid-fuel rocket motor.
Performance: speed 2,300ft/sec (700m/sec); maximum effective altitude FIM-92A 11,480ft (3,500m), FIM-92B/C 12,470ft (3,800m); maximum effective range FIM-92A 4,375yd+ (4,000m+), FIM-92B/C 5,250yd (4,800m); minimum effective range 220yd (200m).
Guidance: FIM-92A passive IR homing; FIM-92B/C passive IR/UV homing.
Warhead: 2.2lb (1.0kg) HE blast smooth-case fragmentation with time-delay contact fuze.
Crew: two.

The FIM-43A Redeye entered service in 1964 to become the world's first manportable air defense missile, but development of a more flexible replacement began in the mid-1960s. Although the new missile, FIM-92A Stinger, suffered from a long and troubled development period, once its problems were resolved it settled down to become an extremely effective weapon which will remain in frontline service to the 2020s and beyond.

Stinger is designed to attack low-altitude jet- and propeller-driven aircraft, and helicopters, and is a "fire-and-forget" weapon, based on a passive infrared seeker, a proportional navigation system, all-aspect engagement capability, and IFF (Identification-Friend-or-Foe). Recent upgrades have improved its range and maneuverability, and enhanced its resistance to countermeasures. In addition, what started as a Man Portable Air Defense System (MANPADS) is now fielded aboard a number of platforms, including the Bradley IFV (Bradley-Linebacker, HMMWV (Avenger), Light Armored vehicle (LAV), and various helicopters, and is in service with the U.S. Navy, Marine Corps, Army, and Air Force, and with many foreign armed forces.

In the MANPADS version the firer has a grip-stock which contains the electronics, sight, and trigger assembly, and all that is required to prepare for launch is to attach a missile tube. The missile is tested and loaded into this tube in the factory and no further testing or maintenance is required. Prior to launch a reusable launch unit is attached to the round; once the missile has been launched the tube is discarded.

Of the 15,669 FIM-92A Basic Stingers produced, most of those remaining in service are with foreign forces. FIM-92B Singer-POST (= Passive Optical Seeker Technique) had a a microprocessor-controlled homing head, using dual infrared (IR) and ultraviolet (UV) image-scanning guidance to enhance target detection capabilities; some 600 were produced in 1983-87. FIM-92C Stinger-RMP

(Reprogrammable Micro-Processor) is intended to correct known operational deficiencies and exists in Block I and Block II versions. Stinger-RMP Block I has software and hardware changes, including a new roll frequency sensor, a new lithium battery, improved computer processor and memory, and a ring-laser gyro which eliminates the need to super elevate prior to firing. The Army will acquire some 10,000 Stinger-RMP Block I missiles, which will remain in the inventory until at least 2014. FIM-92D Stinger-RMP Block II, with yet further enhancements, was under development when it was "zero-funded" in the Army's FY 2001 budget request and is, therefore, effectively dead. Air-to Air Stinger (ATAS) is an adaptation of the manportable Stinger RMP for use in helicopters, and includes a full night capability to give helicopters an anti-helicopter capability.

Stinger is known to have destroyed at least 270 fixed-wing aircraft and helicopters, including one Argentine Pucara shot down by British forces in the 1982 Falklands War and one Indian aircraft in the 1999 Kashmir conflict. By far the largest number of successes were achieved by the Mujahideen in the Afghan war when they were supplied with Basic Stinger; despite minimal training, they achieved an 80 percent success rate against Soviet aircraft and, in particular, helicopters. Stinger systems were widely deployed during the 1991 Gulf War, but there were no known engagements, principally because knowledge of their very presence was sufficient to force the Iraqis to keep their helicopters well out of range.

Below: Stinger man-portable, fire-and-forget, anti-aircraft weapon.

Light Armored Vehicle-Air Defense (LAV-AD)

Type: mobile, forward-area, air defense system.
Manufacturer: Lockheed Martin (General Dynamics).
Weight: empty 24,100lb (10,941kg); combat 29,300lb (13,319kg).
Dimensions: length 252in (640cm); width (turret facing forward) 98.4in (250cm);
height 106.0in (270cm).
Powerplant: Detroit Diesel 6V53T; 275bhp.
Performance: road speed maximum 62mph (99kmh); road range 410 miles (660km); maximum trench 6.8ft (2.1m); maximum grade 60 percent; maximum side slope 30 percent.; swim speed 6mph (9.6kmh).
Armor: rolled steel.
Turret: Traverse 360deg; elevation -8deg to +60deg.
Armament: 8 x Stinger missiles (plus 8); 1 x GAU-121U 25mm Gatling gun.
Crew: three (driver, gunner, commander).

The LAV-AD is in service with the U.S. Marine Corps and is essentially a combination of a modified LAV-25 chassis with a hybrid air defense system, comprising the very successful Stinger missile system and a 25mm Gatling gun. Its mission is to provide low-altitude air defense against fixed-wing aircraft, helicopters, and UAVs, using either its missiles or the gun, and the latter can also be used against ground targets. The vehicles were produced by General Dynamics; delivery of seventeen systems began in 1997 and was completed in 1999.

The turret, known as Blazer, has a forward-looking infrared (FLIR) targeting sight and a laser rangefinder; it is generally similar in its capabilities to the Avenger turret, but is somewhat smaller. The electrically driven turret can be controlled by either the commander or the gunner, has 360deg traverse and elevation limits of -8deg to +60deg, and is fully stabilized for firing on the move at speeds up to 30mph (48kmh). The turret carries two Stinger missile pods, each containing four missiles, which can be fired in rapid succession. The LAV-AD is fully amphibious, and the crew consists of a commander, gunner, and driver.

LAV-AD has a fully automatic digital fire control system, which is set up with firing sequences for both missiles and gun and can be pre-programmed with forty-four on-board air defence engagements. The sensor suite comprises a second-generation, dual field-of-view thermal sight, a daylight TV, and an eye-safe carbon-dioxide laser rangefinder. The thermal imager has a 240 x 4 scanning array and there is high-resolution video output for detailed remote viewing. The sighting system has a two-axis, stabilized, digital line-of-sight director for fire-on-the-move capability.

The LAV-AD is air transportable in the C-130 (one), C-5 (five), and C-141 (two). One can also be carried by the Marines' CH-53E helicopter. The current concept of employment is for the LAV-AD to provide local air defense for the Marines' light armored reconnaissance battalion, operating well forward of the fire support coordination line.

Above: LAV-AD mounts eight Stinger plus 25mm cannon on an LAV chassis.

MIM-23 Hawk Missile System

Type: mobile tactical ballistic missile defense system.
Manufacturer: Raytheon.
Weight: 1,400lb (635kg).
Dimensions: length 12.5ft (3.8m); diameter 13.5in (3.8cm)
Powerplant: Aerojet solid-fuel rocket motor.
Performance: speed greater than Mach 2; range approximately 20nm (23.5 miles/37.75km); ceiling in excess of 40,000ft (12,190m).
Guidance: radar-directed semi-active homing.
Warhead: 300lb (136kg) HE.

Hawk (Homing All-the-Way Killer) is another system, designed in the 1950/60s, which has remained in service ever since, being upgraded at intervals to restore its capabilities against the latest threats. Hawk development began in 1953 with service entry in August 1960 as the MIM-23A, although at the time it was a cumbersome system, with each battery consisting of a pulse acquisition radar, a CW illuminating radar, a range-only radar, two illuminator radars, battery control center, six three-missile launchers, and a tracked loader. This was followed by MIM-63B Improved Hawk, fielded in 1970, and the system has continued to evolve ever since, with today's Marine Corps Hawks being part of an effective tactical ballistic missile defense system in an upgrading completed in 1998.

The missile has a cylindrical body 12.5ft (3.8m) long and 13.5in (3.8cm) in diameter, with four long chord, clipped delta wings, which extend from mid-body to the slightly tapered tail. The Marines normally deploy a complete Light Anti-Aircraft Battalion equipped with Hawk to provide an area air defense system, each battalion

being made up of a number of batteries. Each battery has an HQ with an MPQ-50 pulse/acquisition radar, an MPQ-48 Continuous Wave Acquisition Radar , and a battery control post, with the missiles being dispersed into two firing platoons, each with an MPQ-46 tracking/illuminating engagement radar, an IFF interrogator set, a command post, and three mobile launchers, each with three missiles.

The Hawk battalion forms part of the Marine Air Command & Control System, whose primary air surveillance radar is the TPS-59, which has been modified to detect theater ballistic missiles (TBM) at ranges up to 400nm (460 miles/740km) and at altitudes up to 500,000ft (152,500m). The Hawk battery is linked via the Air Defense Communications Platform (an entirely new addition to the Hawk system) to both these upgraded TPS-59s and to other theater sensors through the Joint Tactical Information Distribution System (JTIDS). These links enable the air defense commander to cue Hawk with other missile defense systems and integrate the Hawk into the theater missile defense architecture. The missile's fuze and warhead were also improved to increase lethality, while improvements to the launcher made the Hawk more mobile and better able to interface with the missiles. In 1996, a single Marine battery equipped with upgraded Hawk intercepted and destroyed a Lance short-range theater ballistic missile and two air breathing drones simultaneously in an operational test at White Sands Missile Range, NM.

Below: Although the system is over 40 years old, Hawk still provides air defense for the Marine Corps and has shown itself capable of intercepting incoming Lance theater ballistic missiles.

MIM-104 Patriot

Type: single-stage, low-to-high-altitude missile system.
Manufacturer: Raytheon.
Weight: 1,984lb (900kg).
Dimensions: length 17.0ft (5.2m); diameter 16in (41cm); finspan 36.2in (92cm).
Powerplant: single-stage solid-propellant rocket motor.
Performance: maximum speed Mach 5; range 43.5-99 miles (70-160km); minimum range 1.9 miles (3km); maximum altitude 75,500ft (23,000m); time of flight 9-210 seconds.
Warhead: HE blast with proximity fuze; 200lb (91kg).
Guidance: command guidance with TVM (track-via-missile) and semi-active homing.
Platform: four-round mobile trainable semi-trailer
Specifications for Patriot PAC-2 missile.

Patriot was developed as a successor to Nike-Hercules and the Army's Hawk, and had a lengthy gestation period, with the operational requirement being finalised in 1961, but development not being completed until 1982. The main reason for the long delay (and cost escalation) was the complexity of the system, particularly of the track-via-missile (TVM) radar guidance, but once the problems had been overcome Patriot proved to be a great success. Conceived for use against aircraft, in the late 1970s it was decided to add an anti-tactical ballistic missile (TBM) capability, which led to the Patriot Advanced Capability-One (PAC-1) system, first flown in 1986. This included software enhancements to enable the phased array radar to view angles from 45deg up to nearly 90deg.

Below. Patriot battery command post with MPQ-432 phased array radar.

Right: MIM-104 Patriot has a highly sophisticated guidance system.

This was quickly followed by PAC-2, in which the missile had an improved warhead and fuze, while the radar was again enhanced, this time to enable it to detect smaller targets. PAC-2 began flight tests in 1987 and was in service in time to be deployed in Desert Storm in 1991, where it showed its ability to destroy Scuds. PAC-2 Configuration 1 was deployed in 1993 and included the Guidance Enhancement Missile – PAC-2(GEM) – and improvements in the system's battle management, command, control, communications and intelligence (BMC^{3}I), all primarily intended to accelerate the handling process and expedite missile launch. PAC-2 Configuration 2 was fielded in 1998. This involved yet further improvements to the radar, communications, and other systems. Work is now in hand on PAC-3 Configuration 3, involving the new PAC-3 missile which is a smaller and much more effective interceptor. In conjunction with an enhanced radar and other improvements it results in a major advance in the system as a whole.

A Patriot firing battery equipment includes the radar set, engagement control station (ECS), and up to sixteen launching stations., which are supported by the usual sections providing power, communications, maintenance, and administration. During air defense operations the ECS is the operations control center of the battery and is the only element to be manned. The ECS contains the weapons control computer (WCC), man/machine interface, and various data and communication terminals. The M901 Launching Station transports, points and launches four missiles and is entirely remotely operated, via either a VHF radio or fiber optic data link from the ECS. The launchers can be up to 1,100yd (1,001m) from the ECS. The MPQ-53 phased-array radar has an electronically controlled beam and illuminates each area of the sky in turn at an extremely rapid rate. It carries out search, target detection, tracking and identification, missile tracking and guidance, and electronic counter-countermeasures (ECCM) functions. It has a range of up to 62 miles (100km), can track up to 100 targets and can provide missile guidance data for up to nine missiles.

The Patriot missile is equipped with a track-via-missile (TVM) guidance system. Mid-course correction commands are transmitted to the guidance system from the ECC. The target acquisition system in the missile acquires the target in the terminal phase of flight and transmits the data using the TVM downlink via the ground radar to the ECC for final course correction calculations., which are then transmitted to the missile. The high explosive 198lb (90kg) warhead is situated behind the terminal guidance section.

Patriot Anti-Cruise Missile (PACM) is a further development, designed to counter threats from cruise missiles. In essence, it is a PAC-2 missile with a dual mode seeker, adding an active radar seeker to the existing TVM guidance. The first flight test was carried out in July 1999.

Medium Extended Air Defense System (MEADS)

Type: single-stage, short-range, low- to high-altitude missile system.
Manufacturer: MEADS International (Lockheed Martin, USA/ Daimler-Chrysler, Germany/Alenia Marconi, Italy).
Weight: 688lb (312kg).
Dimensions: length 17.1ft (5.2m); diameter 9.8in (25cm); wingspan 19.7in (50cm).
Powerplant: Atlantic Research single-stage solid-propellant rocket motor with special attitude-control mechanism for in-flight maneuvering.
Performance: maximum speed Mach 5; maximum range 9.3 miles (15km).
Guidance: inertial with Ka-band active terminal homing.
Warhead: hit-to-kill plus lethality-enhancing 161lb (73kg) proximity fuzed HE blast/fragmentation warhead.
Platform: eight-round mobile trainable semi-trailer
Specifications for Patriot PAC-3 missile.

The Medium Extended Air Defense System (MEADS) is a tri-national cooperative effort between the United States, Germany, and Italy, who all have an operational requirement for a corps-level, mobile air defense missile system capable of countering short-range ballistic missiles and turbojet/turboprop-powered air vehicles, including cruise missiles. MEADS, which was originally known as "Corps SAM," will replace Hawk, and at least some of the current

Below: In MEADS test, Patriot missile successfully destroys an incoming rocket.

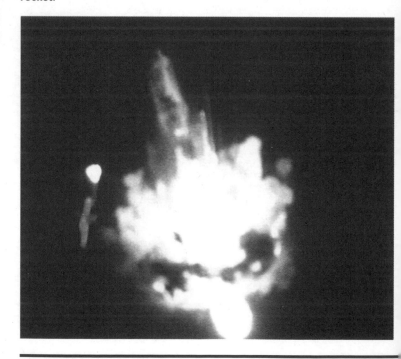

Right: This artist's impression shows a MEADS battery deployed as part of a corps-wide air defense system.

Patriot units, in U.S. service. The project is being managed by the Ballistic Missile Defense Organization (BMDO) in the USA, with overall international cooperation the responsibility of the NATO Medium Extended Air Defense System Management Organization (NAMEADSMO). The international company set up to run the program as the prime contractor is MEADS International. The program is very large in scale, with projected U.S. orders worth about $10 billion and the European potential at least a further $20 billion, if not more.

MEADS is a mobile surface-to-air missile (SAM) system, which is also required to be air-transportable in both C-130 and the slightly smaller twin-engined C-160 Transall (is the standard transport aircraft in the German *Luftwaffe*). Its multi-canister launcher is mounted on a wheeled vehicle, one of many advantages of this being that the missiles will be air-transported on the launcher, which is thus able to drive straight off the aircraft and deploy into its battle position without delay. The many missile launchers will be deployed around the corps area, well separated from the radars, the command elements, and each other, but with the entire system joined by a multi-path communications network. This will enable various sensors to make inputs to the system, reduce the risk of detection of the launchers, and enable command-and-control to be exercised from a variety of locations. MEADS will use a new truck-mounted surveillance radar and a new X-band multi-function, fire-control radar, both with a full 360deg capability. They will also use a common design for the digital receiver and signal/data processor, allowing for validation using a single prototype.

The missile element of the MEADS is the PAC-3 (Patriot Advanced Capability) hit-to-kill missile, which is already under development for the Patriot system, and which has a guidance system that is extremely difficult to jam even by advanced co-operative mode jamming. The missile combines standard aerodynamic control surfaces with multiple single-shot thrusters to achieve the very agile high-g maneuvers required for precise hit-to-kill control.

The missile has a solid-propellant rocket motor and uses an inertial guidance unit to arrive at the target area, where the missile acquires and tracks the target with its forward-looking gimbaled active millimeter-band seeker. Target destruction is achieved through the kinetic energy released by hitting the target head-on, but the missile also carries a lethality-enhancing, high-explosive warhead for use against more robust air-breathing targets, such as cruise missiles.

Under current plans the system is due to enter service in 2005, although whether this will be achieved remains to be seen. Meanwhile, the Department of Defense intends to defer equipping three Patriot battalions with PAC-3, pending a decision on development and deployment of MEADS.

Theater High-Altitude Area Defense [THAAD]

Type: upper-tier anti-ballistic missile defense system.
Weight: classified.
Dimensions: kill vehicle length 7.6ft (2,3m), maximum diameter14.5in (37cm); booster (including interstage) 12.6ft (3.8m) diameter 13.4in (34cm); overall length 20.3ft (6.2m).
Powerplant: single-stage solid propellant booster, with TVC.
Performance: classified.
Warhead: kill vehicle destroys target by kinetic energy.
Platform: Palletized Load System (PLS) truck.
Specifications for User Operational Evaluation System (UOES) round.

The Theater High-Altitude Area Defense [THAAD] system is the most mature of the proposed upper-tier systems and its main role is to provide area coverage to deal with longer-range theater ballistic missile (TBM) threats in exoatmospheric and very high emdoatmoshperic interceptions. Even if some TBMs penetrate the screen it provides THAAD will have substantially reduced the number to be dealt with by the lower-tier/shorter-range systems. THAAD will also have a capability to protect population areas. (It should be noted that this description is based on the system as proposed in early 2002; it may well change by the time it enters service.)

The THAAD missile comprises a booster and the kill vehicle. The cylindrical booster is 12.6ft (3.8m) long and 13.4in (34cm) in diameter, and houses a single-stage, solid-propellant rocket motor which uses Thrust Vector Control (TVC) for steering. The booster does not have fins, using, instead, a segmented skirt which deploys shortly after launch to provide aerodynamic stability. The booster is connected to the kill vehicle by a short interstage (collar) which houses the small explosive device necessary to separate the booster and kill vehicle.

The kill vehicle is the part of the missile that actually intercepts the incoming TBM and is shaped like an elongated cone 7.6ft (2.3m) long, with a diameter at its base of 14.5in (37cm). At the front of the kill vehicle is a forecone, which is covered by a two-piece aerodynamic shroud whose purposes are to protect the seeker window from overheating and to reduce drag. The kill vehicle has no power of its own, relying instead on the velocity generated by the booster to complete its flight with sufficient kinetic energy to hit and destroy the target. In the forecone is an infrared seeker with an uncooled sapphire window. Steering is achieved by the Divert and Attitude Control System (DACS) which operates using four small thrusters at the mid-point and a number of smaller thrusters around the base of the vehicle.

Following factory testing, THAAD missiles are installed and sealed in hermetically sealed graphite-epoxy canisters which serve three purposes: as storage containers, to provide protection during transportation, and launch tubes. A number of missile containers are installed on the launcher, which is based on the U.S. Army Palletized Load System (PLS) truck which provides commonality with the existing Army inventory and increases reload flexibility in the field. The missiles are launched directly from the canister. THAAD launchers are transportable in C-5, C-17, and C-141 aircraft.

The command-control-communications-and -information (C^3I) elements of a THAAD battery are transported in specially designed shelters mounted on HMMWV chassis. There are two configurations, the first being the Tactical Operations Station (TOS) whose functions are to provide planning, analysis, and

Above: THAAD is a high-altitude system with wide area coverage.

logistic support, and conduct surveillance and battle management. The Launcher Control Station (LCS) provides communication links for the TOS and also functions as a communications relay to provide links to remote launchers. A number of TOS and LCS together form a Tactical Station Group (TSG) and there are several TSGs in each battery to provide tactical redundancy. Finally, there is the X-band phased-array radar, which acquires the incoming targets and then tracks them, while also providing information to identify and classify them. It also tracks the THAAD interceptor and provides a kill assessment at the end of the engagement.

A THAAD battalion with four fire units and 288 missiles will require 40 C-5 sorties, or 94 C-141 sorties.

Small Arms

Small arms are of vital concern to virtually every man and woman in all the United States armed services, since such weapons provide the ultimate means of self-protection. More importantly, however, they are the means by which the ground combat troops in the Army, Marine Corps, and Special Operations units project this nation's offensive power. The main purpose is to provide a succession of layers with medium and heavy machine guns reaching the farthest, followed by light machine guns and rifles, and, closest of all, submachine guns, pistols, and shotguns.

As in other areas covered in this book, the U.S. armed forces are very well equipped with a mixture of elderly but good weapons that have been in service for some years and new equipment which has introduced new technologies and concepts. Small arms is an area where the United States has not been reluctant to place orders abroad, if that has proven necessary to obtain the best, although in most cases the contracts state that production must be moved to the United States after two years or so.

Over the past century developments in small arms have been incremental, but the next generation of weapons are likely to introduce some radical changes with dramatic increases in range, lethality, and the means of attack. The potential replacement for both the M2HB 0.5in Machinegun and the Mk 19 grenade machine gun, for example, is a project currently known as the Objective Crew Served Weapon (OCSW). This will combine the firepower of air-bursting munitions with an opto-electronic fire-control system to provide an extremely accurate system with greatly enhanced lethality. The weapon itself will be ultra-light, enabling it to be

operated and carried by a two-man crew, and will be capable of either incapacitating or suppressing enemy soldiers up to 2,200yd (2,000m) distant and damaging lightly armored vehicles, water craft, and helicopters up to about 1,100yd (1000m).

The second major program is the Objective Individual Combat Weapon (OICW), which will be the individual soldier's personal weapon, capable of firing both 5.56mm kinetic energy projectiles and an air-bursting 20mm fragmentation munition. It will be designed to enable soldiers to attack targets at greater ranges, and also, by use of the top-attack munition, to attack them when they are behind cover. Of necessity, it will have to be light and easy to handle, the requirement stating that it must be less than 33in (84cm) long and weigh under 12lb (5.4kg). This will be achieved by taking advantage of the latest advances in integrated fire control, using new high strength/light weight materials, and enhancing terminal effects by use of miniature fuzes and improved explosives. The fire control system will use a laser rangefinder to pinpoint the precise target range at which the HE round is required to burst and then pass this information to the 20mm ammunition fuzing system. The sighting system will provide full 24-hour capability by employing uncooled IR sensor technology for night vision. The weapon will be required to fire 20mm projectiles at a rate of 20rpm to a range of 1,100yd (1,000m) and 5.56mm bullets to at least the same range as M16A2. It is intended that OICW will replace the M16 rifle, M203 grenade launcher and M4 carbine, and that fielding will commence in 2005.

Below: Sniper team undergoing marksmanship training in embassy protection.

M2HB 0.5in (12.7mm) heavy machine gun

Type: heavy machine gun.
Manufacturer: Saco Defense.*
Operation: recoil.
Caliber: 0.50in (12.7mm).
Weight: gun 84lb (38kg); M3 tripod 44lb (19.9kg); total 128lb (58kg).
Dimensions: length overall 61.4in (156cm); length barrel 45.0in (1,143mm).
Range: maximum 7,437yd (6,800m) maximum effective (with tripod) 2,200yd (2,0000m).
Cyclic rate of fire: 500-550 rounds per minute.
Muzzle velocity: 2,930ft/sec (894m/sec).
Rifling: 8 grooves; right-hand.
* Numerous manufacturers have produced earlier versions.

The M2 is employed to provide automatic suppressive fire in both offense and defense, and is used against personnel, soft-skinned and lightly armored vehicles, low and slow flying aircraft (particularly helicopters), and small boats. John Browning's automatic, belt-fed, recoil operated, air-cooled, crew-operated M2 machine gun first appeared in 1933. It was intended principally for use on multiple anti-aircraft mounts, but there was a second version for use as a tank turret gun and a third for use on a ground mount. The latter is crew-transportable, although with a weapon weight of 84lb (38kg) and a further 44lb (19.9kg) for the tripod, that can only be for short distances.

The M2 has spade grips and a leaf-type rear sight. Ammunition is fed into the weapon by a disintegrating metallic link-belt and by minor adjustments to the gun can be fed from left or right. The weapon works on the usual Browning system of short recoil. When the cartridge is fired the barrel and breechblock, securely locked together, recoil for just under an inch when the barrel is stopped by means of an oil buffer. At this stage the pressure has dropped sufficiently for the breechblock to unlock and continue to the rear under the initial impetus given to it by the barrel, extracting and ejecting the empty case and extracting the next live round from the belt. Once the rearward action has stopped, the compressed return spring takes over to drive the working parts sharply forward, chambering the round, locking the breechblock, and firing the cartridge. After this the cycle recommences and continues for as long as the trigger is pressed and there are rounds in the belt. Most guns will fire only automatic, but those intended for ground use are equipped with bolt latches to enable single rounds to be fired if necessary.

When it first appeared the weapon functioned well enough mechanically, but showed an unfortunate tendency to overheat, so that after firing some 70-80 rounds in a continuous burst the firer had to take a considerable pause to allow the barrel to cool. Operationally, this was totally unacceptable so a new

Below: In service since 1933, the M2HB remains one of the best heavy MGs.

heavy barrel version, the M2HB was adopted, as a result of which the problem was completely solved. The M2HB was used by the United States and many other countries in the course of World War II and has continued in wide-scale use up to the present time.

In U.S. service the gun is used either on the M3 tripod mount for ground use, on the M63 anti-aircraft mount for air defense, or various types of ship-board mounting for naval use. There are also a fixed mount and a soft mount for use in a wide variety of vehicles.

The M2HB uses a wide variety of ammunition and new types continue to be developed. One of the most recent is the M903 SLAP which was developed by the U.S. Marines in the 1980s and happened to be ready for use in the Gulf War in 1991. This is, in effect, a miniature version of the armor-piercing discarding sabot (APDS) round used in tank guns, and uses a 0.30in penetrator

Above: Studio shot of tripod-mounted 0.50in (12.7mm) M2HB (heavy barrel).

made of tungsten as the penetrator, which is held in place in the barrel by a 0.50in (12.7mm) sabot, which disntegrates as it leaves the muzzle. The result is a round which requires no modification to the weapon, provided that the barrel has a stellite lining. The round is very fast, with a muzzle velocity of 3,98ft/sec (1,215m/sec) compared to 2,930ft/sec (894m/sec) for a normal round, and it has a significantly flatter trajectory which results in increased accuracy. There is also a M962 SLAP-T (tracer) round to take advantage of this capability. The SLAP round is capable of penetrating two-to-three times the thickness of armor compared to other 0.50in rounds. The maximum effective range of the SLAP round against 0.75in (20mm) "High Hard Armor" (HHA) is 1,640yd (1,500m).

Mk 19 Mod 3 40mm grenade machine gun

Type: automatic grenade launcher.
Manufacturer: Saco Defense Industries.
Operation: blowback.
Caliber: 40mm.
Weight: gun 72.5lb (32.9kg); cradle 21.0lb (9.5kg); tripod 44.0lb (20.0kg); total 137.5lb (62.4kg).
Dimensions: 43.1in (109.5cm).
Range: maximum 2,400yd (2,200m); maximum effective 1,750yd (1,600m).
Rates of fire: cyclic 325-375rpm; rapid 60rpm; sustained 40rpm.
Muzzle velocity: 790ft/sec (240.79 m/s).

Grenades have long been valuable weapons in the infantryman's close-quarter armory, providing significant explosive effects at ranges outside that of hand-to-hand combat, and with much more rapid response than mortars or artillery. They originated as hand-thrown weapons, but during World War II devices were developed which could be attached to the muzzle of a rifle; these had greater range than hand-thrown weapons, but the rate-of-fire was slow. In the early 1960s the Mark 18 rapid-fire grenade launcher was developed, which was hand-cranked and fired 40mm grenades held in a continuous cloth belt. These

were used in some numbers during the Vietnam War, especially by the Navy's riverine patrol units. It was the latter requirement that led the Navy to develop a fully automatic grenade launcher, the Mk 19 Mod 0, which appeared in 1966, but this proved both unsafe and unreliable and although many of the problems were solved with the Mk 19 Mod 1 which appeared in 1972, the weapon did not reach maturity (as the Mk 19 Mk 3) until 1983, when it was also adopted by the Army.

Today's Mk 19 Mod 3 is an air-cooled, blowback-operated weapon, using various types of 40mm grenade. These are fed to the weapon in a disintegrating metal-link belt. The weapon can be ground-mounted on a tripod, ship-mounted on a variety of naval mounts, or mounted in a vehicle turret (eg, LVTP-7A1). There are currently three types of operational ammunition: M383 high-explosive (HE) grenade, and the M430I and M430A1 high-explosive dual-purpose (HEDP) grenades. In addition, there are also the M385I/M918 training rounds and M922/M922A1 dummy rounds. The M430I HEDP 40mm grenade will pierce armor up to 2in (5.1cm) thick, and will produce fragments to kill personnel within 16ft (5m) and wound personnel within 50ft (15m) of the point of impact.

Below: Mk 19 Mod 3 launches 40mm grenades at 40rpm, sustained.

M60 7.62mm machine gun

Type: general-purpose machine gun.
Operation: gas.
Caliber: 7.62mm (.308in).
Weight: 18.8lb (8.5kg).
Dimensions: length 42.4in (108cm); barrel 25.5in (65cm).
Range: maximum 4,050yd (3,725m); maximum effective 3609.1 feet (1,100m).
Rates of fire: cyclic 550-600rpm; rapid 100rpm*; sustained 100rpm*.
Muzzle velocity: : 2,800ft/sec (853m/sec).
Rifling: 4 grooves; right-hand.
* Barrel changes required approximately every 100 rounds.

The U.S. Army based the design of its first post-war general-purpose machine gun (GPMG) on the best features of the German MG42 and its assault rifle version, the FG42. The resulting M60 entered service in 1950 and relies largely on metal stampings, rubber, and plastics. In a major innovation, it used the then newly agreed NATO standard 7.62mm round. It is gas-operated with fixed headspace and timing which permits rapid changing of barrels, which must be done regularly to prevent overheating. There is a built-in folding bipod, fitted with cooling fins, and the weapon can also be mounted on a tripod for use in the sustained fire role.

The latest version is the M60E3, which is lighter than the original M60 and has a number of differences, virtually all of them intended to save weight, including a simplified gas system, which does not require safety-wire to prevent loosening. But the new lightweight barrel is not safe for use

Above: LMG team armed with M60 (front) and M16 rifle (rear).

in overhead fire and is not capable of sustaining a rapid rate of fire of 200 rounds per minute without catastrophic failure. Although the main purpose in the M60E3 is to assist the gunner by reducing the load he has to carry, the outcome is a weapon with some firing limitations and a loss of reliability that severely limits its use. This gun will be replaced by the M240G.

There are three main rounds for combat use – M61 armor-piercing, M62 tracer and M80 ball – with the preferred combat mix being four M80s followed by one M62, which enables the gunner to observe the fall-of-shot and quickly bring his fire onto the target. M61 rounds are used against lightly armored targets and M80 against lighter targets and personnel. As usual there are also rounds for training on the weapon (M63 dummy) and for field exercises (M82 blank), which can be used only if a blank-firing attachment is installed over the muzzle.

The M60 has been widely used on helicopters. The M60C is an electrically controlled version, which was used on the OH-13 Sioux and the OH-23 Raven light scout helicopters, and on the UH-1B "Huey." The M60D model was mounted on a pintle in the cabin doorway on helicopters such as the UH-1, H-2, H-3, CH-47, and UH-60 aircraft.

Left: M60 team on exercise; note blank firing attachment.

M240G medium machine gun

Type: medium machine gun.
Manufacturer: Fabrique Nationale.
Operation: gas.
Caliber: 7.62mm (.308in).
Weight: 24.2lb (11kg).
Dimensions: length overall 48.0in (122cm); length barrel 24.7in (63cm).
Range: maximum 4,100yd (3,700m); maxiumum effective (with tripod) 1,940yd (1,800m).
Rifling: 4 grooves; right-hand.
Muzzle velocity: 2,800ft/sec (854m/sec).
Rates of fire: cyclic 650-950rpm; rapid 200rpm; sustained 100rpm.

The M240 was originally a ground-operated machine gun, developed by Belgian arms company Fabrique Nationale (FN) and known by them as the as the MAG (Mitrailleuse d'Appui Générale = general-purpose machine gun) . It was then selected in 1976 by the U.S. Army for use in armored vehicles and produced under license as the M240. It is now widely used by the U.S. armed forces in its M240, M240C and M240E1 versions as the coaxial, remotely operated MG in a turret, and as a pintle-mounted MG with spade grips. In these forms it is used in numerous vehicles, including the M1 Abrams tank, M2/M3 Bradley

Right: The Belgian-designed M240 machine gun is widely used in U.S. forces. It is used in armored vehicles in both coaxial and pintle-mounts (as here), in helicopters and as a ground-mounted GPMG.

Infantry/Cavalry Fighting Vehicles, and Marine Corps LAVs (light armored vehicles). It was designed around the NATO standard 7.62 x 51mm cartridge. It is also used as the M240D in helicopters.

After extensive operational and technical tests, the M240 was subsequently selected in 1995 as the ground replacement for the M60; this required a bipod to be fitted and a tripod to be developed. In this form it was selected first by the Marine Corps and subsequently by the Army. The M240 shares many similarities with the M60, but has far superior reliability and maintainability. The major changes for the ground role are the addition of a flash suppressor, front sight, carrying handle for the barrel, buttstock, infantry length pistol grip, bipod, and rear sight assembly.

The M240D 7.62mm machine gun is the aircraft version, which is normally mounted on a pintle in the aircraft but can also be dismounted for ground use in an emergency. As configured for aircraft use, the gun is fitted with front and rear sights, spade grip, and rear face trigger. In this form it weighs 25.6lb. and is 42.3 inches long.

When dismounted, a buttstock assembly, buffer assembly, bipod, and a conventional trigger are fitted and it weighs 26.2lb. and is 49.0inches long. In both versions the barrel assembly includes a three-position gas plug, with positions for firing at 750, 850 or 950 rounds per minute.

Squad Automatic Weapon (SAW), M249 light machine gun

Type: bipod-mounted combat machine gun.
Manufacturer: Fabrique Nationale Manufacturing, Inc.
Operation: gas.
Caliber: 5.56mm (.233 inches).
Weight: with bipod and tools 15.2lb (6.9kg); 200-round box magazine 6.9lb (3.2kg); 30-round magazine 1.1lb (0.5kg).
Dimensions: length overall 40.9in (104cm); length barrel 20.6in (52.3cm).
Range: maximum 3,940yd (3,600m); maximum effective (against area target) 1,100yd (1,000m).

Rifling: 6 grooves; right-hand.
Muzzle velocity: 3,000ft/sec (915m/sec).
Rates of fire: cyclic 725rpm; sustained 85rpm.

The M249 SAW is used to engage dismounted infantry, crew-served weapons, antitank guided-missile teams and thin-skinned vehicles. Fielded in the mid-1980s, the SAW filled the void created by the retirement of the Browning Automatic Rifle (BAR) during the 1950s because interim automatic weapons (M14 Series/M16A1 Rifles) had failed as viable "base of fire" weapons. The weapon was developed from the Belgian Fabrique Nationale (FN) "Minimi" specifically to meet the requirements of the U.S. Army and Marine Corps. Original orders were met from the FN factory but a production line was subsequently established in the USA.

The U.S. Army's concept for a Squad Automatic Weapon was formulated in the 1960s when a requirement was established for a weapon under the squad commander's control, which would have greater range than the M16 Armalite but would be lighter and easier to handle than the 7.62mm M60 LMG.

Below: SAW 5.56mm LMG with its 200-round box magazine.

The weapon selected to meet this requirement was the Minimi but with certain minor changes to meet U.S. military specifications and to suit U.S. manufacturing processes, the main external differences being in the shape of the butt and the handguard. The M249 is very smooth in operation and displays an exceptional degree of reliability. Fully combat ready, with a magazine of 200 rounds, bipod, sling, and cleaning kit, the M249 weighs 22lb (9.97kg), which is still 1lb (0.4kg) less than an empty M60! It is normally fired using the built-in bipod, but a tripod is also available.

The M249 SAW is a lightweight, gas-operated, air-cooled magazine or belt-fed (disintegrating metallic link), individually portable machine gun capable of delivering a large volume of effective fire. It is fired from the open-bolt position. The gunner will normally fire at 750 rounds per minute, but this can be increased to 1,000rpm on the squad leader's authority if circumstances require it. The weapon provides accurate fire approaching that of the rifle yet gives the heavy volume of fire common to a machine gun. The M249 replaces the two automatic M16A1 rifles in the rifle squad on a one-for-one basis in all infantry type units and in other units requiring high firepower.

There are six types of ammunition available for the M249 SAW, of which two are combat rounds: M855 ball (light materiel targets, personnel); M856

tracer (observation of fire, incendiary effects, signaling). The usual combination of these (four M855 followed by a single M856), enables the gunner to use the tracer-on-target (TOT) method of adjusting fire to achieve target kill. Other rounds are used for training. M193 ball and M196 tracer are for range work; M199 (inert round for weapon training); and M200 blank (which can be used only if a blank-firing attachment is fitted to the weapon).

The live rounds can be fed to the gun in two ways, the most usual being by a 200-round disintegrating belt, but it can also fire ammunition from a standard M16 magazine, which is inserted into a well in the bottom of the gun. When employed in the sustained fire role, the M249 is mounted on a tripod, to increase its stability, to make minute adjustments in the aim, and to enable it to fire bursts of more than three rounds without wandering off the target.

The FN company also markets a "Para" model with a sliding stock and shorter barrel; it is a little lighter than the standard weapon but is shorter and easier to handle in confined spaces. This is the basis for the U.S. Army's Short Squad Automatic Weapon (SSAW), currently under development, in which the SAW is shortened by more than 10in (25cm). This developmental effort is intended to produce a weapon that is easier to maneuver when fighting in the urban environment and also to give improved airborne/air assault jump capability.

Left: SAW delivers a large volume of fire – 725rpm cyclic; 75rpm sustained.

5.56mm Colt Commando

Type: automatic carbine.
Manufacturer: Colt.
Operation: semi/full auto, gas-operated, locking-bolt.
Caliber: 5.56mm (.223 Remington).
Weight: gun empty 5.4lb (2.4kg); loaded 7.1lb (3.2kg).
Dimensions: length gun, stock extended 29.9in (76cm); length gun, stock compressed 26.8in (68cm); length barrel 11.5in (29cm).
Range: maximum effective 300yd (274m).
Rifling: 6 grooves; right-hand.
Muzzle velocity: 3,050ft/sec (924m/sec).
Magazine: 20- or 30-round box.
Rates of fire: cyclic 700-1,000rpm.

The Colt Commando is one of those weapons which do not fit neatly into any one particular category and is variously described as an assault rifle or carbine or sub machine gun, but in this book it is being treated as a sub machine gun. The weapon is, in fact, a shorter and handier version of the M16 and was intended for use in the Vietnam War as a close-quarter survival weapon that was the same size and weight as a sub machine gun, but with the hitting power and range of a rifle. Mechanically, it was identical to the M16 but with a much shorter barrel, which reduced the muzzle velocity slightly and reduced its accuracy at longer ranges. The short barrel also caused considerable muzzle flash which had to be overcome by a 4in (100mm) flash suppressor, which could be unscrewed, if necessary.

The Colt Commando had a telescopic butt which could be extended when it was necessary to fire the weapon from the shoulder. It featured selective fire and a holding-open device, and was actuated by the same direct gas action as the M16. In spite of the limitations on range, the weapon proved useful in Southeast Asia and, although it had been designed as a survival weapon, it fitted the sub machine gun role so well that it was later issued to the U.S. Special Forces and was also used in small numbers by the British SAS. It was also bought in large numbers by Israel, primarily for issue to civilian guard units.

Above: Army Special Operations troops armed with 5.56mm Colt Commando.

Below left: Commando at the ready, a soldier crosses a deep swamp.

Below: Commando-armed soldier of 10th Special Forces Group (Airborne).

MP5-N Heckler and Koch 9mm submachine gun

Type: Special Operations Forces close-quarter battle sub machine gun.
Manufacturer: Heckler and Koch.
Operation: delayed blowback.
Caliber: 9mm (0.355 inches).
Weight: gun, empty 5.6lb (2.6kg); gun, with 30-round magazine 7.4lb (3.4kg).
Dimensions: length gun, stock extended 26in (66cm); length gun, stock folded 19.3in (49cm); length barrel 8.9in (23cm).
Range: maximum effective 328ft (100m).
Rifling: 6 grooves; right-hand.
Muzzle velocity: 1,312ft/sec (400m/sec).
Magazine: 15- or 30-round box.
Rates of fire: cyclic 800rpm.
Specifications are for MP5-N.

The Heckler and Koch MP5 is used by large numbers of the world's elite forces and it is probably no exaggeration to say that its basic combination of small size, low weight, accuracy, lethality, and excellent reliability make it the world's leading close quarter battle (CQB) weapon. In the U.S. armed forces it is fielded, among others, by Marine Corps Force Reconnaissance Companies and Marine Security Force Battalions, and by numerous civilian agencies,

including the FBI's Hostage Rescue Team. In foreign countries it is the "weapon of choice" for such prestigious units as the German GFSG-9, the British SAS and London's Metropolitan Police.   The MP5 uses the same roller-delayed blowback operating principle as the Heckler & Koch's (H&K) G3 rifle to fire from a closed and locked bolt in both automatic and semi-automatic modes. It features good handling qualities coupled with interchangeability of most parts with other weapons in the H&K range. The MP5 can fire semi-automatic, fully automatic or in three, four or five round bursts. In the latter mode the effect is achieved by a small ratchet counting mechanism which interacts with the sear. Each time the bolt cycles to the rear the ratchet advances one notch until the third, fourth or fifth cycle allows re-engagement of the sear. Firing also ceases the instant the trigger is released, regardless of how many rounds have been fired in the current burst. The actual number of rounds in each burst is pre-set in the factory, and cannot be altered by the firer.

The MP5 uses metal stampings and welded sub-group parts. The receiver is constructed of stamped sheet steel in nineteen operations (several combined) and is attached to the polygonal rifled barrel by a trunnion which is

Below: The German MP5 is used by U.S. Special Operations Forces.

spot-welded to the receiver and pinned to the barrel. The trigger-housing, butt-stock, and fore-end are fabricated from high-impact plastic. There are a variety of specialized versions. MP5K has a shorter barrel with a vertical foregrip underneath, and the butt is replaced by a simple cap. MP5SD is a series of silenced weapons: MP5SD1 has no stock; MP5SD2 has a fixed stock; and MP5SD3 has a retractable stock.

MP-5N Heckler and Koch 9mm submachine gun

The MP5-N, as fielded by the U.S. Marine Corps, has a retractable butt stock, a removable suppressor, and and illuminating flashlight integral to the forward handguard, which is operated by a pressure-switch custom-fitted to the pistol grip.

Below: SEALs demonstrate their skills; all are armed with MP5s.

M16A2 5.56mm
Semi-automatic Rifle, & variants

Type: infantry weapon.
Manufacturer: Colt Manufacturing, Fabrique Nationale.
Operation: gas, semi-automatic.
Caliber: 5.56mm (.233 inches).
Weight: empty 6.4lb (2.9kg); with 30-round magazine 8.8lb (4.0kg).
Dimensions: length overall 39.6in (100.7cm); barrel 20.0in (51cm).
Range: maximum (3,600m); maximum effective, area target 875yd (800m); maximum effective, point target 602yd (550m).
Rifling: 4 grooves; right-hand.
Muzzle velocity: 3,110ft/sec (948m/sec).
Magazine: 30-round box.
Rates of fire: cyclic 800rpm; sustained 12-15rpm; semi-automatic 45rpm; burst 90rpm.
Specifications for M16A2

The forerunner of this brilliant weapon was the 7.62mm AR-10, designed by Eugene Stoner, which first went into production in 1957. It was a very advanced weapon employing plastic and aluminum wherever possible, in contrast to the traditional wood, but the overall design proved too light to fire the powerful NATO cartridge for which it was designed. It was manufactured in small quantities between 1957 and 1962 and purchased by the armies of Burma, Nicaragua, Portugal and the Sudan. With its shortcomings in mind, a new design was produced, which first appeared in 1957; with the company designation AR-15, it was designed around the 5.56mm high velocity round, and was put into production by the Colt company from July 1959 onwards.

This new weapon soon became popular, in particular as a jungle rifle, not

Below: Marine ForceRecon troops armed with 5.56mm M16A2 rifles.

Above: M16A2-armed rapidly moving Army patrol.

least because it was light and easy to handle by small men, and quickly found markets in various countries in the Far East. When U.S. troops first became involved in Vietnam they were armed with the M14, firing the 7.62mm standard NATO round, which quickly proved itself to be most unsuitable, and the AR-15 was soon adopted, under the official designation, as the M16.

Stoner's mechanism has no piston, the gases simply passing through a tube and striking directly on to the bolt; this is simple and efficient, but means that the weapon needs careful and regular cleaning to clear it of fouling. It had been intended that the M16 should have the same effective range as the M14 it had replaced, but it proved most effective at ranges of 215yd (200m) or less, although this was quite adequate for the jungles of Southeast Asia. When first issued to troops, the M16 encountered a number of widely publicized problems, many of them due to stoppages arising from a lack of care and cleaning. But better training, preventive maintenance, and several design changes resulted in the weapon which quickly became the world standard, with some 3,690,000 having been manufactured.

M16A2

The M16A2 is a product-improved version of the M16A1, with many enhancements which result in an even better weapon. The most important of the changes are intended to improve accuracy and controllability. One of the most important of these is a heavier, stiffer barrel with a 1-in-7 twist, enabling it to fire the standard NATO M855 (SS-109) 5.56mm ammunition, which increases effective range and penetration (M16A2 also fires the older M193 ammunition). A burst-control device is fitted so that when in automatic mode only three rounds will be fired at a time, thus both increasing accuracy and reducing ammunition expenditure. In addition, a compensator situated on top of the muzzle reduces muzzle climb, improving the firer's control – and thus accuracy – in both burst and rapid semi-automatic fire. Finally, concerning accuracy, there is an improved rear sight with easy adjustments for range and wind. Other changes include a modified upper receiver which deflects ejected cartridge cases in order to protect left-handed firers, redesigned handguard to give a better grip, and new and stronger buttstock and pistol grip, while the trigger guard can be removed to enable the weapon to be

fired when the firer is wearing mittens. The M16A2 can fire 40mm grenades when equipped with the M203 Grenade Launcher (see below).

M213
When infantry fighting vehicles were being developed it was thought that the best way for infantry to fight from inside would be to stick their rifles through open ports in the side walls of the vehicle. However, the U.S. Army decided that it was preferable to produce a special version of the M16 rifle which is semi- permanently installed in a special port. The working parts of the weapon are the same as those in the M16, but the fore-end of the receiver attaches to the firing port and, since the

Below: Marines armed with M16 and M60 in Operation Restore Hope in 1993.

Above: M16 carbines: 14.5in barrel Model 723 (top), and 11.5in Model 733.

requirement is for volume of fire rather than accuracy, there is no foresight on the muzzle. Usually, the infantrymen will leave the M213 in its port and debus carrying his usual M16A2, but the M213 does have a retractable wire butt, so that it can be removed and used in dismounted fighting, if necessary. The M213 weighs 8.8lb (3.9kg) and is fitted with a 30-round box magazine.

M4/M4A1

The M4 5.56mm carbine is a shortened variant of the M16A2 rifle, with a collapsible stock. It has 80 percent commonality with the M16A2 rifle, which is replacing all M3 .45 caliber submachine guns and selected M9 pistols and M16 rifle series. There is also the M4A1, which differs from the M4 in having a fully automatic firing mode, a detachable carrying handle and a flat top rail for mounting day/night sights. All versions of the M4/M4A1 fire the same

Above: Marine with standard issue 5.56mm M16A2 rifle and box magazine.

Above: M203 grenade launcher fixes below the barrel; note special sight.

ammunition as the M16A2 and mount all the same accessories including the M203 40mm grenade launcher (see below). The M4A1 is being issued to SoF, Rangers, and SoF aviation units.

M203 40mm Grenade Launcher
The compact, single-shot M203 Grenade Launcher is custom-built for attachment to the M16A2 5.56mm rifle and M4 carbine. This breech-loading device attaches beneath the forward end of the M16/M4 and is designed to launch a number of different types of 40mm grenade. The launcher weighs 3lb (1.4kg) and has a maximum effective range of 382yd (350m) against an area target and 164yd (150m) against a point target, and a minimum safe range in combat of 33yd (31m).

M82A/A2 Barrett "Light Fifty"

Type: Anti-materiel sniper rifle.
Manufacturer: Barrett Firearms Manufacturing, Inc.
Operation: recoil-operated.
Caliber: 12.7 x 99mm BMG (.50 caliber).
Weight: unloaded 32.5lb (14.8kg); loaded 44lb (13.4kg).
Dimensions: length overall 57in (145cm); barrel length 29in (73.7cm).
Range: maximum effective (equipment-sized targets) 1,970yd (1,800m); maximum range 8,10-0yd (7,400m).
Rifling: 8 grooves; right-hand.
Muzzle velocity: 2,930ft/sec (893m/sec) (M2 armor piercing ammunition).
Magazine: 10-round box.

Introduced in 1983, the M82A1 Barrett "Light Fifty" fires the 12.7 x 99mm BMG (0.50in Browning Machine Gun) round and is intended to be a high-power, long-range, and extremely accurate weapon for use against equipment targets, such as light armored vehicles and trucks. It is not intended for use as a traditional "sniper rifle" against personnel and is regarded as complementary to and not a replacement for the M40A1 7.62mm sniper rifle, although it can obviously be used in that role if required.

The "Light Fifty" operates on the short-recoil principle, with a substantial amount of energy being imparted by the cartridge to the bolt-face, whereupon both barrel and bolt-carrier start to travel to the rear. Once the bolt-carrier disengages from the barrel, the latter is moved forward again by a spring, while the bolt-carrier continues, extracting and ejecting the spent cartridge case and then loading a new round. Maximum effective range is 1,800m (1,970yd).

The weapon is neither small nor light, being 57in (145cm) long and weighing 32.5lb (14.8kg). It is normally packed in a custom-made, watertight, airtight carrying-case, which also contains all the usual accessories including cleaning equipment. There is also a backpack for cross-country transportation and a bandolier for extra magazines. The rifle is normally used with the Unertl ten-power scope, which is matched to the trajectory of the ammunition. The rifle itself has a carrying handle, metallic sights, and 10-round box magazine; it also has a built-in folding bipod, but can also use the standard U.S. Army M60 tripod. A variety of ammunition is available, the main round having a tungsten core and an incendiary load, which is capable of penetrating up to 2.8in (7cm) of armor and igniting any diesel fuel. The weapon is fitted with a large and

Above: Sniper team with Barrett M82A1A 0.50in (12.7mm) rifle.

efficient muzzle-brake, which reduces recoil by some 65 percent, although this tends to kick up dust or snow when fired, which not only interferes with the firer's view but can also give away his position to the enemy. The M82A1A is normally operated by a crew of two, with one man firing and the other acting as spotted using binoculars.

The next version, the M82A2, which was introduced in 1992, involved some major redesign. Although the basic mechanism remained unchanged, the major components were moved around to change the weapon into a bullpup configuration. This involved placing the shoulder rest beneath the butt, immediately behind the magazine housing, allowing the rear end of the receiver to pass over the firer's shoulder in a manner similar to a recoilless rocket launcher. The pistol grip/trigger group was moved forward of the magazine housing, while a reversed pistol grip served as the forward hand grip. There was no built-in bipod, as in the M82A1, and the weapon could be fired without one. The overall result was a slightly smaller, lighter, and simpler version of the M82A1: length, 55.5in (1,410mm); weight 29lb (12,2kg).

Below: The Barrett "Light Fifty" M82A2 is a most impressive weapon, combining great hitting power with long range and high accuracy.

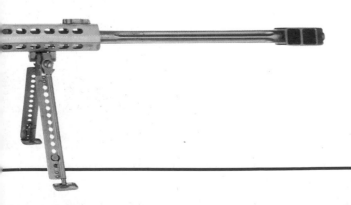

M24 Sniper Weapon System

Type: sniper rifle.
Manufacturer: Remington.
Operation: bolt action.
Caliber: 7.62x51mm NATO (.308 Winchester).
Weight: empty 8.7lb (4.0kg); with loaded magazine 12.1lb (5.5kg).
Dimensions: length 43in (109cm); barrel 24in (61cm).
Range: maximum effective 875yd (800m).
Rifling: 5 grooves; right-hand.
Magazine: 5/10 round, detachable internal magazine.
Muzzle velocity: 2,800ft/sec (853m/sec).

The M14 7.762mm semi-automatic rifle was introduced into U.S. Army service in the 1950s together with an associated sniper version, the M21, which was made more accurate and fitted with a Leatherwood telescopic sight, but otherwise little altered (and was still semi-automatic). Some 1,435 M14s were converted and fielded in time to see service in the Vietnam War, but by the mid-1980s these M21s were in a somewhat worn-out condition. In addition, as the prospect of a war in Western Europe receded, so did the possibility of campaigns in desert or barren countryside increase, where ranges, even for infantry work, would be much longer. As a result, the Army ran a competition for an up-to-date replacement sniper rifle, the operational requirement stating that the new weapon must have an effective range of some 1,100yd (1,000m), a stainless steel barrel, and a Kevlar-graphite stock. In a significant reversion, it was to be bolt-operated. The various competitors were whittled down to two – Steyr of Austria with their SSG rifle and Remington with the Model 700BDL – and, after final shoot-off, the latter was selected.

This weapon was then standardized in 1987 as the Model 24 Sniper Weapons System (M24 SWS) chambered for the 7.62 x 51mm NATO (.308 Winchester) round. This has recently been upgraded to AT1-M24 Tactical Rifle standard, which is an all-round improvement over the original M24. All components in the sniper weapon are carefully machined to ensure smooth, reliable operation, even in the most severe operating conditions.

With the Leupold Ultra M3A 10x42 telescopic sight the M24 has a maximum effective range of some 875yd (800m), but also has detachable emergency iron sights. The M24 has a stainless steel barrel with 5-groove rifling, making one turn in 11.25in (286mm) in a right-rand twist; barrel life is estimated at about 10,000 rounds. The stock is made of Kevlar/graphite/ fiberglass composite, with aluminum bedding-blocks, and both stock length and butt-plate are adjustable to suit the firer. The bipod is removable and a suppressor can be fitted, if required.

Below: Rifle with the large 'scope is the M24 Sniper Weapon System.

M40A1 7.62mm Sniper Rifle

Type: sniper rifle.
Manufacturer: Marine Corps Marksmanship Training Unit, Quantico, Virginia.
Operation: bolt-action; rotating bolt with two lugs.
Caliber: 7.62 x 51mm NATO (.308 Winchester).
Weight: weight, bare weapon 9lb (4.1kg); weight, including scope 14.5lb (6.6kg).
Dimensions: length overall 44in (111.7cm); length, barrel 24in (61cm).
Range: maximum effective 1,000yd (914m).
Muzzle velocity: 2,550ft/sec (777m/sec).
Magazine: 5-round detachable box.

During the Vietnam War the Marine Corps decided to adopt a new sniper rifle and in April 1966 Remington suggested using a specially built version of its very successful Model 700, a highly successful weapon which traced its ancestry back to the British P14/U.S. M1917 rifle of World War I vintage. Designated the Model 40XB by Remington, it was adopted by the Marines as the M40 and some 995 were built by Remington for the Corps. They proved very successful and in the mid-1970s the Marines decided to upgrade them, using the same Remington 700BDL action, but with different stocks and scopes. and this modified weapon, the M40A1, entered service in the late- 1970s. Each weapon is individually built by trained and qualified armorers at the Marine Corps Marksmanship Training Unit, Quantico, Virginia, and must pass the most stringent tests before being released for service.

The M40A1 fires the standard 7.62 x 51mm NATO round (0.308 Winchester) and is fitted with a commercially available, competition-grade, heavy barrel, a special fiberglass stock and butt pad, a modified Winchester floorplate and trigger guard,

Service 12-gauge Repeater Shotguns

Various models of shotgun have been used by the U.S. military for over a hundred years, virtually all of them 12-gauge. The term "gauge" is the traditional measurement used to describe the internal bore size of a shotgun and is the number of lead balls of the diameter of the shotgun bore which would together weigh 1lb (0.45kg). In this case, the diameter of the bore of a 12-gauge shotgun is 0.729 inches (1.85cm) and 12 lead balls of this diameter weigh 1lb (0.45kg). The military shotguns are manually operated by pump action, with a six- or seven-round tubular magazine and a modified choke barrel. Most are equipped with a bayonet stud and sling swivels and have a standard length military stock. In most, barrels and stocks of different lengths are available.

Although normally used as sporting weapons on the civilian market, these shotguns

Right: Marine Corps students practice firing the Remington 870 shotgun.

Above: Marine Corps airborne sniper with M40A1 7.62mm sniper rifle.

and a specially modified, light-pressure trigger. The weapon uses match-grade ammunition and is equipped with a special Unertl x 10 sniper scope and with this scope, but without ammunition, it weighs approximately 14.5lb (6.6kg). It has a built-in five round magazine.

The Remington Model 700 not only provides the basis of the Marines' M40A1, but is used in the Army's M24 Sniper Weapon System (qv) as well being used as a sniper rifle by many police forces across the United States.

have a military application in situations which require a weapon with maximum stopping power at a limited range. Such uses include jungle ambushes, house clearing in urban operations, clearing boarders in attack on ships, guard duty, prisoner supervision, local security and riot control. A neat summary of their use is that they are "re-loadable Claymore mines." The effective range of these weapons depends upon the circumstances in which they are used and the skill of the firer, but is unlikely to be greater than 50yd (46m).

The current inventory consists of three main models of 12-gauge weapons: Mossberg 590, Remington 870, and Winchester 1300. In order to bring some order into this situation a requirement for a Joint Service Combat Shotgun has been issued.

Mossberg 500 ATP

Dimensions: length gun 40.3in (100cm); length barrel 20.3in (31cm).
Weight: gun 6.7lb (3.1kg).
Feed: 8-round tubular magazine .

There are two main types of Mossberg in use, one with a six-shot and the other with an eight-shot magazine, the latter being the more generally used by military forces. The shotgun is designed for maximum reliability and has an aluminium receiver for good balance and light weight. The cylinder-bored barrel is proof-tested to full Magnum loads, provides optimum dispersion patterns and permits firing of a variety of ammunition. The shotgun has two extractors and the slide mechanism has twin guide bars which help prevent twisting or jamming during rapid operation. A later modification was the creation of a muzzle brake by cutting slots in the upper surface, thus allowing gas to escape upwards and exerting a downward force which prevented the muzzle from lifting during firing. The ATP-8 version has no butt-stock, and a pistol grip is added, resulting in an extremely compact weapon, which can be stowed more easily inside a vehicle.

Remington 870

Dimensions: length of gun varies with model; barrel length 14in (355mm) or
18in (457mm).
Weight: (gun) 6.6-7.7lb (3-3.5kg).
Feed: 7/8-round tubular magazine.

The Model 870 pump-action, all-purpose shotgun was introduced by Remington in 1950, and since then it has become a very popular weapon. In 1966 the Marine Corps purchased some thousands of the Remington 870 Mk.1 shotgun (as well as Mossberg 590s and Winchester 1200s). Technically, the Remington 870 is a pump-action shotgun

Right: Sailors aboard USS Dwight D Eisenhower armed with Mossberg 500s.

with dual action bars and a tilting breechblock, which locks directly into the barrel extension. The barrel can be changed in minutes and there are two lengths: 14in (35.6cm) and 18in (45.7cm). The Remington 870 is also widely used by police forces and security guards, for whom versions are available with fixed or folding butt-stocks and pistol grips. Police Remingtons are also usually capable of firing buckshot, slugs and special-purpose munitions, such as tear gas grenades and non-lethal rubber rounds.

Winchester 1300 Marines
Dimensions: length overall 41.8in (106cm); barrel length 18in (46cm).
Weight: (gun) 6.7lb (3.1kg).
Feed: 6/7-round tubular magazine.
The Winchester 1300 is a manually operated (pump), repeating shotgun, with a seven-round tubular magazine, a modified choke barrel, ghost ring sights, a bayonet attachment, sling swivels, and a standard length military stock with phenolic plastic buttplate. Some models have wooden and/or folding stocks.

M9 (Model 92SB/92F) 9mm pistol

Type: semi-automatic pistol/personal defense weapon.
Manufacturer: Beretta, Italy, and Beretta USA.
Operation: Walther, locked-wedge.
Caliber: 9mm (approximately .355 inches).
Weight: 32.0oz (1.0kg).
Dimensions: length gun 8.5in (21.7cm); barrel 4.9in (12.5cm); width 1.5in (3.8cm); height 5.5in (14cm).
Range: maximum effective 153ft (50m).
Rifling: 6 grooves, right-hand.
Magazine: box; 15 rounds.
Muzzle velocity: ca 1,100ft/sec (335m/sec).

The 9mm pistol was the outcome of a direction from Congress for a non-developmental program to standardize all United States forces with one pistol which should also comply with the relevant NATO standards. This involved the replacement of a variety of handguns including the venerable, but greatly respected and liked Colt M1911A1 .45-caliber pistol, which had served the U.S. armed forces for some eighty years, as well as a number of .38 caliber revolvers. The U.S. Army was designated the lead service and duly ran a competition for what was to be an "off-the-shelf" buy. Beretta modified their Model 92 to meet the new requirement. The resulting weapon, the Beretta 92SB, was the clear winner and, following some further changes to meet U.S. Army requirements, the new weapon entered service as the Pistol M9 in 1985; initial orders were for some 500,000 weapons, but with the contract stipulating that production must be transferred from Italy to the United States after two years.

The M9 pistol fires the standard NATO 9mm round and is entirely coated in a Teflon-derived material. The barrel is chrome-plated, while its action uses the locked-wedge design pioneered in the Walther P-38. The weapon is loaded in the orthodox manner by inserting the charged magazine into the butt, following which the slide grip is used to pull the action to the rear, cocking the hammer, and then released to chamber a round. On firing, gas pressure drives the barrel and slide to the rear, locked together by a wedge, but, having traveled some 0.3in (8mm), the locking wedge pivots downwards, disengaging from the slide;

Joint Service Combat Shotgun
Dimensions: length overall <41.8in (106.1cm).
Weight: (gun) 6-8.5lb (2.7-3.9kg).
Feed: 6-round (minimum) tubular magazine.

The Joint Service Combat Shotgun (JSCS) is intended to replace the large numbers of different models of pump-action weapons that are currently in service with all the U.S. armed forces. Its main use will be in Special Operations missions and in the same range of other duties as the present shotguns. The JSCS will be a 12-gauge, semi-automatic weapon with a standard magazine with a minimum capacity of six 2.75in (70mm) cartridges, but will also be capable of firing 12 gauge 3.0in (76mm) Magnum ammunition as well as the standard 2.75in (70mm) ammunition without adjustment to the operating system. It will be constructed of lightweight polymer materials and corrosion-resistant metal components. To enhance mission performance and provide increased operator flexibility, a variety of stocks in various configurations and barrels of various lengths will be available.

Above: The standard sidearm is the M9, a U.S. version of the Beretta 92SB.

the barrel immediately stops but the slide continues rearwards to complete the reloading cycle. Unlike many automatic pistols, these Beretta are of an open slide design; ie, the greater part of the barrel is exposed and not covered by the slide. It has several safety features to help prevent accidental discharge, can be fired in either single- or double-action modes, and can be unloaded while the safety is in the "on" position without having to activate the trigger.

The changes required by the U.S. Army were virtually all concerned with the grip and included an enlarged trigger guard to enable the firer to use a two-handed grip, an extension to the base of the magazine, and a slight curve to the foot of the front edge of the butt. The Beretta M9/92F is now the standard pistol in the U.S., Italian and many other armed forces and para-military forces such as the French *Gendarmerie Nationale*.

MEU(SOC) Pistol

Type: modified .45 caliber pistol.
Manufacturer: specially trained armorers at MCB, Quantico, Virginia.
Operation: semi-automatic.
Caliber: .45 ACP.
Weight: magazine empty 2.5lb (1.1kg); magazine loaded 3.0lb (1.4kg).
Dimensions: length, pistol 8.6in (21.9cm); length, barrel 5.0in (12.8cm).
Range: maximum effective 55yd (50m) (for specially trained user).
Rifling: 6 grooves; left-hand.
Magazine: box, 7 rounds.
Muzzle velocity: 830ft/sec (252m/sec).

The M1911A1 was the principal handgun used by the U.S. military for many decades and the great majority are in the process of being replaced by the Beretta M9 9mm pistol. However, a number of M1911A1s will undoubtedly remain in service for some years to come, including the Marine Corps' MEU(SOC) pistol.

The original M1911A1 semi-automatic pistol was a recoil-operated, magazine-fed semi-automatic weapon, firing a single round each time the trigger was squeezed, which is referred to as "single action only." In this mechanism, the thumb safety may only be activated once the pistol is cocked, whereupon the hammer remains in the fully cocked position until the safety has been deactivated. (This differs from more up-to-date "double action" pistol

designs, which allow the hammer to move forward to an uncocked position when the thumb safety is activated.) The M1911A1 was much liked by users, who set particular store by its reliability and lethality, but its "single action" mechanism required them to be thoroughly familiar with it, especially when carrying it in the "ready-to-fire" mode. As a result, orders were often given for M1911A1s to be carried without a round in the chamber, but even so unintentional discharges were frequent occurrences.

The MEU(SOC) pistol was the outcome of a requirement for a "backup weapon" for Marines armed with the 9mm MP5-N Close Quarters Battle weapon and, as the new M9 9mm was judged unsuitable, selected M1911A1s have been modified for this role. The M1911A1 was chosen because of its inherent reliability and lethality, as well as its availability, while the modifications make the M1911A1 design more "user friendly" by resolving its shortcomings. The modifications included in the MEU(SOC) pistol include: a high quality barrel; more precise trigger; rubber coated grips; rounded hammer spur; new, easier to use combat sights; and an extra-wide grip safety, suitable for both right- and left-handed firers, which gives not only greater comfort and controllability, but also assists the firer in making a quick, follow-up, second shot). In addition, the old magazines are replaced by a new type, made of stainless steel and with rounded plastic follower and extended floor plate. Some 500 M1911A1s were converted, each being hand-built by specially trained armorers at the Rifle Team Equipment (RTE) shop, Quantico, Virginia.

Above: The famous M1911A1, still in service as the MEU(SOC) pistol.

Heckler & Koch 0.45in Mk 23 Mod 0 (SOCOM) Pistol

Type: offensive automatic handgun.
Manufacturer: Heckler & Koch.
Operation: modified Browning system.
Caliber: 0.45in ACP.
Weight: with empty magazine 36.8oz (1,043g); with 12 rounds M1911 ball 51.5oz (1,461g).
Dimensions: length gun 9.7in (245mm); barrel 5.9in (150mm); length with suppressor 16.7in (424mm).
Rifling: polygonal; right-hand.
Magazine: 12-round box.
Muzzle velocity: 850ft/sec (260m/sec).
Range: maximum effective 54.7yd (50.0m); maximum range (M1911 ball) 1,467yd (1,340m).
Specifications are for weapon without suppressor.

In 1990 U.S. Special Operations Command (SOCOM) issued operational requirement for a new Offensive Handgun Weapon System (OHWS) consisting of three elements: a handgun; a laser-aiming module (LAM); and a sound/flash suppressor. A significant feature of this requirement was that, unlike other handguns which are regarded as being solely for personal defense, the new weapon was to be "offensive" in purpose. A number of very demanding criteria were announced publicly and any arms company in the world was allowed to enter, although, in the event, just two did so: Colt, with a Knight's suppressor; and Heckler & Koch with one of thecompany's own suppressors.

Each company produced thirty Phase I prototypes, the eventual winners being the Heckler & Koch pistol, but with the Knight's suppressor, even though it was most unusual for a component from a losing entry to be selected. The LAM was made by Insight Technology of Londonderry, New Hampshire. The pistol was a development of the H&K 0.45in version of the USP, but with a longer slide, a slight extension of the barrel for the screw attachment for the suppressor, and mountings for the LAM. It was accepted for service as the "Pistol, Caliber .45, Mark 23 Mod 0" (but is usually known, simply, as the "SOCOM Pistol"). Deliveries started in May 1996.

The LAM is attached to the underside of the pistol ahead of the trigger guard and projects a red spot onto the target, enabling the weapon to be sighted with great accuracy. The Knight's suppressor is some 7.5in (19cm) long and weighs just under 1lb (0.45kg). It and screws on to the muzzle and provides a substantial reduction in both flash and noise, the latter being aided by the fact that the bullet is

Left: Heckler & Koch 0.45in Mk 23 Mod 0 automatic – popularly known as the "SOCOM pistol" – with the Knight's suppressor attached.

Above: Fully equipped Special Forces trooper with the 0.45in SOCOM pistol.

just sub-sonic, thus avoiding the characteristic "crack" of a supersonic bullet.

The pistol underwent some of the most stringent tests ever required of a new handgun. To meet the reliability criteria, for example, the weapon was required to demonstrate a minimum of 2,000 "mean rounds between stoppages" (MRBS) using both M1911 ball and +P ammunition. In fact, all pistols exceeded the requirement by a very handsome margin, the overall average being approximately 6,000 MRBS.

The service life criterion is that the pistol must fire 30,000 rounds before depot-level maintenance, following which it must fire a further 30,000 rounds. Thus, in another test three weapons were given accuracy tests after firing the stipulated 30,000 rounds, but before being services, and all met the accuracy requirement for new weapons. Among the environmental tests the weapon was required to be fired at +140°F (60°C) and -25°F (-4°C), and also after being submerged at a depth of 66ft (20m) for two hours in sea water. It was also tested in surf, salt-fog, sand-dust, mud, icing, and was fired when unlubricated and fouled.

Above: SOCOM pistol fitted with the Laser-Aiming Module (LAM).